CANADIAN BUSINESS AND SOCIETY

UNDERSTANDING SOCIAL AND ETHICAL CHALLENGES

Robert W. Sexty

Memorial University of Newfoundland

Prentice Hall Canada Inc.
Scarborough, Ontario

Canadian Cataloguing in Publication Data

Sexty, Robert W. (Robert William), 1942– .
    Canadian business and society

ISBN 0-13-340811-6

1. Business enterprises - Canada. 2. Business ethics.
3. Social responsibility of business – Canada.
I. Title.

HF5349.C2S4 1995 658'.00971 C94-932214-8

© 1995 Prentice-Hall Canada Inc., Scarborough, Ontario

Prentice-Hall, Inc., Englewood Cliffs, New Jersey
Prentice-Hall International (UK) Limited, London
Prentice-Hall of Australia, Pty. Limited, Sydney
Prentice-Hall Hispanoamericana, S.A., Mexico City
Prentice-Hall of India Private Limited, New Delhi
Prentice-Hall of Japan, Inc., Tokyo
Simon & Schuster Asia Private Limited, Singapore
Editora Prentice-Hall do Brasil, Ltda., Rio de Janeiro

ISBN 0-13-340811-6

Acquisitions Editor: Jacqueline Wood
Production Editor: Kelly Dickson
Copy Editor: Kimwun Perehinec
Production Coordinator: Anna Orodi
Page Layout: Jaytype Inc.
Cover and Interior Design: Olena Serbyn

1 2 3 4 5 RRD 99 98 97 96 95

Printed and bound in the USA.

Every reasonable effort has been made to obtain permissions for all articles and data used
in this edition. If errors or omissions have occurred, they will be corrected in future
editions provided written notification has been received by the publisher.

Readers wishing additional information on data provided through the cooperation of
Statistics Canada may obtain copies of related publications by mail from: Publications
Sales, Statistics Canada, Ottawa, Ontario, K1A 0T6; by calling: (613) 951-7277 or
toll-free 800-267-6677. Readers may also facsimile their order by dialing (613) 951-1584.

This book is printed on recycled paper.

TABLE OF CONTENTS

PREFACE

This book provides a broad overview of the Canadian business system and its interrelationships with society, enabling readers to analyze the challenges confronting business in a context, rather than as current events.

Four parts and 21 chapters make up the book. Part I provides a background to business including an outline of the stakeholders involved, a concept utilized throughout the book. Part II examines corporate social responsibility, responsiveness and performance from a theoretical perspective by reviewing some of the literature on business' role in society. Part III investigates challenges confronting business. The chapters are organized around main stakeholder groups, for example, Chapter 12, "Reforming Corporate Governance" relates to owners, directors, and managers, and Chapter 17, "Consumers and Their Sovereignty," to consumers. Part IV integrates the consideration of social issues with the main planning approach in corporations, strategic management, and discusses coping with future changes in the environment.

The intention is to provide a general treatment of business and society, or social issues in management, rather than portraying everything as involving "ethics", or overemphazing one, for example, government. The contents of this book have been drawn from many disciplines and the work of many researchers and authors. I am impressed with the wealth of material available in Canadian business, and it is difficult to limit the items that should be incorporated into a book of this type.

This book has been many years in development. I have focussed on Canadian materials, but I have also incorporated research findings from elsewhere. The selection of this material was a challenge, and theories, frameworks, and models were chosen that would aid readers in interpreting the relationships between business and society.

There has been considerable fine tuning of the book's contents in the past to get the manuscript to this stage. No doubt there will be more changes in the future and I welcome your comments and suggestions. I am grateful that several years of students at Memorial University have been exposed to this material through its development. Their reactions to materials have assisted me in conceptualizing the framework for the book, and provided me with numerous ideas. My thanks also go to the reviewers of this textbook: Barbara Austin, Brock University; and Nelson Phillips, McGill University.

During the development of this book, I have gained many insights into the Canadian business system. I now hope that these insights will be passed on to readers and that this results in a better understanding of business in Canadian Society.

Robert W. Sexty
Faculty of Business Administration
Memorial University of Newfoundland
1995

PART I

BACKGROUND ON THE CANADIAN BUSINESS SYSTEM

Chapter

It's a challenge to provide background on the Canadian business system, but a basic level of knowledge is necessary to prepare readers for the challenges of understanding how and why business enterprises and their owners-managers behave the way they do. In other words, the materials in this part of the book will prepare readers for Part II, Corporate Social Responsibility, Responsiveness, and Performance, and Part III, Challenges in the Business Stakeholder Environment.

The contents of this part are designed for particular reasons. Chapter 1 is a general discussion of the business system and its main institution, the corporation, along with some specifics about Canada's business system. A key to understanding the interrelationships between business and society is to identify all those individuals or groups influenced by business enterprises, and all those individuals or groups that influence a given business enterprise. For this reason, Chapter 2 identifies and describes stakeholders in the business enterprise system; these stakeholders are referred to throughout the book.

It is important to appreciate the fundamental concepts or theories upon which Canadian capitalism is based. These fundamentals are derived from other disciplines, in particular economics, and are discussed in Chapter 3 from two perspectives: first, as they exist in theory, and second, as they are operationalized in practice. The contrast is shown deliberately, so that readers will not use terms loosely or out of context, and will recognize that the fundamentals are quite complex.

In Chapter 4, the discussion shifts to an attempt to explain views held in Canada about the role of business in society. Six ideological perspectives are presented to illustrate the diversity of ways the Canadian business system operates or has operated. No definite answer emerges: business has manifested itself in various forms over the years, resulting in no clear ideology. It is important to recognize the difficulty in explaining what business is!

Three groups are key to the conduct of business: owners, directors, and managers. Chapter 5 outlines patterns of ownership along with the traditional role of a freedom of choice to workers, consumers, and entrepreneurs. High productivity and a high standard of living have resulted.

However, there have been defects in the system. Business provided appalling working conditions for labour in the 19th century. Monopolistic behaviour has been evident in the operation of some business enterprises as witnessed by price fixing, stock manipulation, misleading advertising, pollution, and regional disparity. The business enterprise is blamed by some for failing to solve many social problems, for example, inadequate housing, and workplace discrimination against women and minorities.

Many factors have interfered with the operation of the business enterprise system, creating less-than-ideal results. Consumers lack complete information to make optimum decisions, capital requirements to enter some businesses are extremely high, advertising and sales promotion practices exert powerful influences over the market, and government actions interfere with business.

The result is a business enterprise system that has changed over time, and today is quite different from 50 to 75 years ago. It is important to understand the fundamentals on which the system is based, and how the system has changed to accommodate the demands of society. The following is a brief historical overview of business activities in Canada during the past 500 years.

OVERVIEW OF CANADIAN BUSINESS HISTORY

The following is a brief overview of the history of business in Canada. This history covers about 500 years, a large geographic area, and diverse commercial activities. Thus, it is difficult to adequately cover the topic in this short overview. Many materials document this history and two comprehensive books have been published recently: Bliss' *Northern Enterprise: Five Centuries of Canadian Business* (1987), and Taylor and Baskerville's *A Concise History of Business in Canada* (1994). These books are long, 640 and 491 pages respectively, and in addition to outlining commercial activity and major events, provide interpretations of them. Readers interested in business history should review these publications, which in turn provide extensive references to other materials.

Chronological Review of Business History

The first evidence of commercial activity in what is now Canada was probably the fishery off the east coast. European involvement in this fishery later resulted in the establishment of communities in Atlantic Canada. From about 1530, the fur trade was established — starting in the east and eventually spreading across Canada — and remained a major industry for about 300 years. The North West Company and the Hudson's Bay Company were two well known corporations involved in the fur industry.

In the 1600's, colonial businesses were established to provide goods and services to the French colonies. After the 1759 defeat of the French at Quebec, merchants including many Scottish, English, and Jewish entrepreneurs arrived. Fishery and fur industries were still the leading commercial activities among these merchants.

A transition in commercial activity emerged in the late 1700's and in the first half of the 1800's. Wood products became a major industry, resulting in the establishment of numerous shipyards, especially in Atlantic Canada. Financial service enterprises started to appear, for example, the Bank of Montreal was established in 1817. Commercial activity flourished in Atlantic Canada, particularly around Halifax, Saint John, and St. John's.

Transportation modes evolved at the end of this period. Considerable railway building occurred from the 1840's onward. Canals were further developed and the steam powered boat arrived about mid-century. Government involvement was intensive in the building of transportation networks including the Canadian Pacific Railway, completed in 1885.

The West developed, partly as a result of improved transportation systems, as Canada expanded westward in the later part of the 1800's and the early 1900's. Meanwhile, some industrialization occurred in Central Canada from the 1850's onward. A manufacturing sector grew, including such products as alcohol, paper, furniture, shoes, iron and steel, farm equipment, and sugar. These infant industries felt threatened by foreign competition and sought tariff protection that lead to the National Policy — a public policy that endured for over 100 years. The latter half of the 1850's also saw the establishment of major financial services, with large banks forming along with the rise of savings and loans, insurance, and stockbrokers.

The period beginning around the turn of the century also saw expansion in electric utilities, a boom in wheat production, growth of the mining industry, and the development of a textile industry. Steel production grew as did the output of the forestry sector with pulp and paper mills being established. The retailing and wholesale sectors grew to supply the growing population. The Hudson's Bay Company transformed itself from a fur trading company to a major retailer, and the retailing sector grew with names such as Eaton, Simpson, Woodward, Ogilvy and Dupuis.

Railways continued to expand in the 1900's, usually with government assistance, and eventually the Canadian National Railway was formed by the government from failed railway companies. Branch plants of American companies were established in Canada to get around tariffs. Industrial output grew during World War I and created a more industrialized economy. But, the economy experienced a downturn as European demand for Canadian goods declined. Western farmers resented being captive to the industrial East (Ontario). In 1919, the Winnipeg General Strike occurred as a protest against the economic system.

Even tougher economic times were experienced in the 1930's, and the economy didn't turn around significantly until World War II. Government owned corporations increased their industrial and military output to support the war effort. The bankruptcies of the 1930's were replaced by the post-war period of prosperity. In 1947, a major petroleum deposit was discovered in Alberta, which resulted in the establishment of a major industry and the construction of pipelines to the west, south, and east. The atomic energy industry also grew.

During the 1960's, the banks grew larger in size, the automobile industry prospered, and the computer industry emerged. Multi-national corporations formed, including some based in Canada. This was also a period of economic nationalism as Canadians expressed concern over foreign ownership, particularly over the American influence in the economy.

In the early 1980's, a recession slowed economic activity. Major corporate failures occurred, including those of Massey, Dome, Canadair, and several trust companies. The latter half of the decade saw considerable takeover and merger activity as corporations and their managers followed acquisition strategies. The entrepreneurial spirit was revived with the establishment of new enterprises, a phenomenon that continued into the 1990's.

Government involvement in the economy peaked in about 1980 and declined after 1984. Governments began to privatize many of the Crown corporations acquired during and after World War II, and deregulation of business began. During the late 1980's and early 1990's, many major corporations failed due to poor growth strategies involving the acquisition of heavy debt. Another serious downturn in the economy plus increased competition also contributed to failures. Trade agreements reduced tariff and non-tariff barriers, particularly within North America. Corporations began to reverse the expansionist strategies of the 1980's, downsizing and consolidating business activities back to their core business.

This overview identifies the nature of business activity over five centuries and the ups and downs of the economy. The following section considers another approach to viewing Canadian business history through books about business and businesspersons.

Corporate Histories, Biographies, Autobiographies, and Misadventures

Business history has been recorded in hundreds of corporate histories, biographies and autobiographies, and accounts of business misadventures. Corporate histories or stories usually cover the life of a corporation, or some period of its life. According to one author, "business histories are seldom read, unless you have an endless appetite for bland food" (Hubben, 1986: 80). Despite this, they do get written to glorify a family enterprise; to tell a good tale or story; to satisfy curiosity about the past by providing a record of facts and a chronology of events; to celebrate some anniversary or milestone; and to enhance a company's public relations efforts. Corporate histories are usually initiated in one of three ways: by an outsider who approaches the organization with the idea, by the company itself, when it commissions someone to prepare the history, or by an executive or former executive who has a personal interest in the organization. Hundreds of corporate histories have been written. Examples are *Bread Men: How the Westons Built an International Empire* (Davies, 1987),*The Chocolate Ganongs of St. Stephen* (Folster, 1990), and *Quick to the Frontier: Canada's Royal Bank* (McDowall, 1993).

A business biography is the history of a prominent businessperson's life. An author selects a subject, or a businessperson may commission a writer to prepare the biography. There are various reasons and motives for writing biographies. Thus readers should assess biographies by determining why the subject was selected by the author, ascertaining the appropriateness of the form utilized to describe the life, evaluating the sources of information drawn upon, ascertaining the appropriateness of the interpretation given this information, and evaluating the biographer's qualifications. Many business biographies have been written in recent years, including those of Frank Sobey (Bruce, 1985), Samuel Bronfman (Marrus, 1991), and K.C. Irving (DeMont, 1991).

An autobiography is defined as a retrospective prose narrative written by a real person concerning his or her own existence, where the focus is his or her individual life, in particular the story of the personality (Lejeune, 1989: 4). Readers must ascertain the biases, omissions, and distortions of the writer when evaluating autobiographies. Recent autobiographies of Canadian businesspersons include *Bata: Shoemaker to the World* (Bata, 1990), *The Max Ward Story: A Bush Pilot in the Bureaucratic Jungle* (Ward, 1991), and *Sigfusson's Roads* (Sigfusson, 1992).

A corporate misadventures category was necessary because many recently published books do not fall into the history, biography or autobiography categories. In misadventures, usually an event or incident is described and not the full history of the corporation although background on the business or entrepreneur may be provided. The books are not biographies: the life story of an individual is not given in any detail. Autobiographies are not written around a particular event or misfortune in a businessperson's career. Misadventures focus on some corporate or entrepreneurial misfortune, mishap, or tragedy and cover a relatively brief time period, usually the events over five years or less. Examples of recent books describing Canadian corporate misadventures are *Steinberg: The Breakup of a Family Empire* (Gibbon and Hadekel, 1990) and *Public Screening: The Battle for Cineplex Odeon* (Hubbard, 1990).

Thus business histories, biographies and autobiographies of businesspersons, and accounts of corporate misadventures record business history in Canada.

Along with comprehensive overviews, these books provide a historical background for the Canadian business system of today. Now that a background has been provided on the business system, the following section identifies some of the important dimensions of today's business environment.

DIMENSIONS IMPORTANT TO UNDERSTANDING CANADIAN BUSINESS

There are some aspects, or dimensions, of the Canadian business environment that, although not unique, should be kept in mind when attempting to understand the interrelationships between business and society.

Diversity of Business Interests

It should be remembered that Canadian business is not a monolith reacting in a uniform manner to society's demands or government's involvement. The fact that business enterprises are of differing sizes suggests that what is appropriate for large enterprises may be detrimental to smaller ones. Enterprises in some industries may seek government protection through tariffs, while enterprises in other industries may be advocates of free trade. Enterprises in different regions react differently to government involvement. Business enterprises in a slower growth region such as the Atlantic Provinces may be more receptive to government involvement than elsewhere. Some industries are very competitive, for example, the fast food business, while others are natural monopolies, for example, electricity utilities.

Foreign Investment

Foreign ownership has historically been an issue in the Canadian business system, and there has been substantial discussion of the pros and cons of foreign investment in Canada. Nationalism resulted in restrictions on the extent and form of foreign business, but in the past ten years these restrictions have been reduced. The objective of controlling foreign investment has been to encourage foreign business to behave as "good corporate citizens," rather than to drive out foreign investment. Attempts have been made to encourage reinvestment of profits in Canada and to act in a manner consistent with Canadian interests.

Provincialism/Regionalism

Provincialism is also an evident dimension of the Canadian business environment. Despite being part of one country, the provinces have erected barriers to

trade and to the mobility of workers between provinces. The provinces sometimes clash over policies, for example, freer trade may be supported in Western
and Atlantic Canada while being opposed in Ontario, and Alberta may favour
higher energy prices than some other provinces. The consequences of nationalism and provincialism are something that business enterprises have to cope
with. In 1994, the federal and provincial governments reached an agreement to
begin the removal of some international trade barriers.

Resource Based Economy

The Canadian economy is substantially resource based. Agriculture, energy production, mining, forestry, and fishing contribute a large portion of business activity. For example, forestry dominates the British Columbian economy, petroleum
Alberta's, agriculture Saskatchewan's, and fisheries Newfoundland's. The manufacturing sector is small compared to that of some other countries, such as Germany,
the United Kingdom, or the United States, and is concentrated in Ontario and
Quebec. Natural resources, in one form or another, are the bulk of Canada's
exports. As a result, natural resource industries tend to be price takers and are vulnerable to fluctuations in the world supply and demand for commodities.

Because of the resource based nature of the economy, Canada is characterized
by hundreds of single-industry towns. These communities rely on a single industry
for their livelihood and are very vulnerable to changes in the world markets for the
commodities produced, or to the fortunes and misfortunes of the business enterprises operating the local plant, mine, or mill. Refer to Exhibit 1-1 for a definition
and examples of single-industry towns. Another consequence of the dominance of
resources is the existence of megaprojects, which have played a major role in the
economy and involve business enterprises. Examples of megaprojects are the large
scale construction and development undertakings such as hydro generation sites
(like those in Northern Manitoba and Quebec), pipelines (like the Vancouver Island
pipeline), energy developments (such as those off Newfoundland and in Alberta),
and transportation infrastructures (like the causeway to P.E.I.).

Small Domestic Market

The Canadian domestic market is a relatively small one, especially compared to
the United States which is about ten times larger. About 70 percent of the population lives within 175 kilometres of the U.S.-Canadian border with the remainder scattered throughout a large, sparsely inhabited area. Surviving in this
market is difficult, as it is spread over great distances, requiring expensive transportation facilities. The small size of the domestic market does not present much
difficulty for resource based industries as they sell to world markets. However,
for manufacturing industries and some service industries, the domestic market is

Business Corporations Act. Each province has a corporation or companies act governing enterprises operating within provincial boundaries.

A distinction is made between corporations that are closely held by a few individuals, usually less than 50, and those that are widely held, possibly by tens of thousands of people. A private corporation is usually defined as one that has less than 50 shareholders and restricts the sale of its shares or debentures to the general public. In general, private companies are governed by the same law as public companies, but because of their exclusive nature and because the general investing public is not involved, the governing companies acts grant certain concessions that are not permitted to public companies. For example, loans are usually permitted to directors and shareholders to enable them to purchase the shares of a deceased or bankrupt shareholder; a private company is not normally required to file a prospectus; and the requirements of and penalties on directors of public companies in the matter of personal speculation in the shares of the company do not usually apply to private companies.

The distinction between private and public companies was introduced so that small businesses could carry on business in a corporate form without having to comply to all the regulatory requirements of a public, widely-held company. This approach reduces the expense of completing procedures designed to protect the diverse interests in public companies. Public companies must comply with stricter regulations for filing financial reports and follow certain audit procedures and specified restrictions on directors. The principal reason for these limitations is to protect the public investing in the company.

This distinction between "private" versus "public" companies is important to make as it is one element to be considered in discussion of the corporation's role in society and how accountable it is. In addition, as discussed in the next section, there are two theories that help to explain the origin and functioning of an incorporated business: "concession" and "freedom of association."

The Basis for Incorporation

The privilege of incorporation was traditionally viewed as a concession granted by the sovereign. The first corporations were granted by British sovereigns to nobility, allowing them to explore, colonize, or commercially exploit some geographical area. It is often suggested that the Hudson's Bay Company, with charter granted in 1617, was one of the first corporations formed in this manner. The "concession" doctrine held that incorporation was conferred by public act and could not be generated merely by private agreements among several persons to associate together for business purposes. The concession was not followed to the letter, especially as monarchies lost their power to legislatures. There were obvious dangers to individual or group freedoms in the concession approach as the sovereign, and then the state, had the authority to grant the privilege of existence to a corporation. An alternative doctrine of incorporation evolved.

The second doctrine of incorporation is based on the right to "freedom of association." The association of individuals coming together for some purpose is fundamental to forming a corporation. The argument is that it takes more than a formal agreement among incorporators, between the state and the corporation, and between state and the stockholders to create and maintain a corporation. The entity, a "going concern," is given life by real people and exhibits collective behaviour unique to it and governed by rules of its own making. Thus, the corporation can be thought of as a "state within a state" and is the most highly developed and useful means of voluntary cooperation as it provides an easy way for people to join and leave. Therefore, incorporation is a right, not a privilege as it is in the "concession" doctrine.

These two doctrines, and others, underlie the statutes that determine who may and how to incorporate a business activity. Each of the doctrines reflect a different conception of the role government should play in this area. With the freedom of association doctrine, the privilege of incorporation is freely available with a minimum of special conditions and limitations being imposed by government. Legislative safeguards have been interposed at critical junctures where experience has indicated that difficulties may arise. These safeguards exist to protect investors and creditors, and to create and preserve the atmosphere of public confidence necessary for the legitimacy of the business system. In this century, social responsibility has imposed obligations on the modern corporation to function for the benefit of the general public in addition to the benefit of investors, creditors, employees and customers.

The modern corporation is a hybrid that cannot be completely explained by one doctrine or the other. It is neither the state-created entity of the concession doctrine, nor the free association of owners, but a complex social institution. Whether the corporation sees itself to exist according to the concession or the freedom of association doctrine determines how the corporation perceives its responsibility and accountability to society.

THE COMPLEXITY OF BUSINESS AND SOCIETY

Canadian business and society is a fascinating topic. It involves studying the history and background of the Canadian business enterprise system in addition to examining the contemporary issues confronting business. There are many factors in this system, and various institutions in society play differing roles in this system. It is very important to obtain all the viewpoints that contribute, or should contribute, to what business's role will be in society. The Canadian society is a pluralistic one with many groups that interact. Such groups include governments, labour unions, minority groups, environmentalists, consumers, the communications media, business organizations, and a variety of interest groups. All have an important role to play, and all, in some way, influence business decision-making. This book emphasizes several things about the Canadian business system with certain goals in mind, in particular:

1) to increase awareness of the system by describing Canadian capitalism, business ideology, the stakeholders involved, and society's attitudes towards business;

2) to identify business's response to its role in society by examining who owns and runs business enterprises, how business has incorporated social responsibility and ethics into its operations, and how business manages its role;

3) to learn how business enterprises have responded to many challenges in their environment;

4) to address the above from the perspective of the manager and/or owner of an enterprise to emphasize the dynamic nature of the environment in which they manage.

This study of business does not focus upon what is right or wrong. Few things about business are so clearcut that one can establish what is correct and what is wrong beyond any doubt. Instead, emphasis is on the appropriate analysis of problems and issues using information from a variety of sources, including the conflicting and maybe erroneous perceptions of various parties as to the motives, strategies, and tactics of others. Since we are dealing with so many groups, perceptions of business vary from the very negative attitude towards business held by some political parties and public interest groups to the very positive attitudes held by business oriented-groups.

The issues that arise as a result of these differing perceptions and points of view are not easily solved. Solutions are not always straight-forward or simple and tend to be less than optimum for all involved. Tradeoffs are involved, and what is an appropriate solution for one group is not as appropriate for another. An optimum solution is still sought, but it is certainly realized that each group in society will not benefit to the maximum.

An appreciation of the dynamic nature and scope of the subject material covered in the business and society area of study is illustrated in Exhibit 1-2. This exhibit contains a list of questions that are designed to probe into some of the issues relating to the business enterprise system as it operates in Canada today. Any one of these questions could be the topic of a very good essay.

Exhibit 1-2

Some Questions About Business and Society

- Do corporations have inherent rights, or only government privileges?
- Are large corporations inefficient?
- Do corporations earn excessive profits?
- Are corporate profits a "pot of gold" that can eliminate social ills?
- Can corporations collude to achieve higher profits?
- Is corporate executive compensation excessive?
- Are administered prices socially undesirable?
- Do corporations set prices arbitrarily high?
- Does corporate advertising raise prices?
- Are corporate pricing policies a primary cause of inflation?
- Is industrial concentration a concern for society?
- Do corporations suppress technical innovation?
- Does monopoly power cause extensive welfare losses?
- Are managers an elite clique with too much power?
- Should management's control of the corporation be weakened and that of the share-holder strengthened?
- Should corporate managers' liability for third-party injuries be expanded?
- Are shareholders' remedies for the improper acts of corporate officials sufficient?
- Is corporate ownership divorced from control?
- Should corporations assume more social responsibilities?
- Does the corporation discourage individual responsibility?
- Does the corporation operate without the consent of affected citizens?
- Should corporations ignore social goals?
- Are corporations undemocratic, private mini-governments?
- Do multinational corporations escape accountability?
- Do corporations violate employees' civil rights?
- Is an employee bill of rights needed?
- Are corporations indifferent to worker–job alienation?
- Do corporations discriminate against minorities and women?
- Do investors need more information?
- Should line-of-business reporting be expanded?
- What kind of controls on insider trading do we need?
- How important is predatory pricing?
- Can corporations limit entry to their industry?
- Should all mergers be government approved?
- Does the large corporation's access to capital markets discourage entry?
- Does limited liability subsidize corporations at the expense of society?
- Is corporation product advertising a barrier to entry?
- Is planned obsolescence a serious problem?
- Does advertising persuade consumers to buy things they do not need?
- Do corporations overwhelm consumers and voters?
- Should Canadian industry be deconcentrated?
- Should the Competition Bureau be strengthened and enlarged?
- Does competition policy increase economic welfare?

SUMMARY

This chapter provides background on business and society in the Canadian context. The understanding of today's issues and challenges is enhanced by even a brief introduction to the terminology used when referring to the Canadian business system. The phrase "business enterprise system" is used in this book to include all forms of business activity, not only that of corporations.

Canadian business activity started almost 500 years ago. The types of commercial activity have changed over the centuries and there have been periods of economic growth followed by periods of economic recession and even depression. The attitudes of Canadians toward business are influenced somewhat by history. It is important to be aware of the major role government has always played in Canadian business.

The historical review provides the background for identifying the important dimensions of the present-day business system. Canadian business is not a monolith but instead represents a diversity of interests. Among the dimensions that are important are the use of foreign capital; the existence of provincial and regional attitudes; the resource-based nature of the economy; the relatively small size of the domestic market; the importance of trade to the economy; the presence of big corporations along with the growth of small enterprises; and the rise of French-Canadian business. There is no status quo in the system which makes the study of the relationships between business and society more challenging.

Business activity is mainly carried out by the institution of the corporation. How society views the corporation influences how accountable to society enterprises are for their activities.

The conclusion from this overview is that the relationships between business and society are complex. This book examines and explains many of these relationships. The following chapters supply additional background on the Canadian business system by explaining the stakeholder concept, outlining the fundamentals of Canadian capitalism, suggesting ways of looking at business ideology, identifying the principal decision makers, and discussing society's attitudes toward business.

REFERENCES

Bata, Thomas J. with Sonja Sinclair. (1990). *Bata: Shoemaker to the World*. Toronto: Stoddart Publishing.

Bliss, Michael. (1987). *Northern Enterprise: Five Centuries of Canadian Business*. Toronto: McClelland and Stewart.

Bruce, Harry. (1985). *Frank Sobey: The Man and the Empire*. Toronto: MacMillan.

Davies, Charles. (1987). *Bread Man: How the Westons Built an International Empire*. Toronto: Key Porter Books.

DeMont, John. (1991). *Citizens Irving: K.C. Irving and His Legacy.* Toronto: Doubleday.

Folster, David. (1990). *The Chocolate Ganongs of St. Stephen.* Toronto: MacMillan.

Gibbon, Ann and Peter Hadekel. (1990). *Steinberg: The Breakup of a Family Empire.* Toronto: MacMillan.

Hubbard, Jaimie. (1990). *Public Screening: The Battle for Cineplex Odeon.* Toronto: Lester & Orpen Dennys.

Hubben, H. (1986, May). Getting the real story. *Across the Board.*

Lejeune, Philippe. (1989). *An Autobiography.* Minneapolis, MN: Univeristy of Minnesota Press.

Lucas, Rex. (1971). *Minetown, Milltown, Railtown: Life in Canadian Communities of Single Industry.* Toronto: University of Toronto Press.

Marrus, Michael R. (1991). *Mr. Sam: The Life and Times of Samuel Bronfman.* Toronto: Viking.

McDowall, Duncan. (1993). *Quick to the Frontier: Canada's Royal Bank.* Toronto: McClelland and Stewart.

Sigfusson, Svein. (1992). *Sigfusson's Roads.* Winnipeg: Watson & Dwyer Publishing.

Single-Industry Communities. (No Date). Ottawa: Department of Regional Economic Expansion (DREE), Occasional Paper.

Taylor, Graham D. and Peter A. Baskerville. (1994). *A Concise History of Business in Canada.* Toronto: Oxford University Press.

Ward, Max. (1991). *The Max Ward Story: A Bush Pilot in the Bureaucratic Jungle.* Toronto: McClelland and Stewart.

STAKEHOLDERS IN THE BUSINESS ENTERPRISE SYSTEM

INTRODUCTION

The business enterprise system impacts the lives of all citizens. In Canada, and in other democracies with private enterprise systems, business operates in a pluralistic social system where a variety of groups use power or influence to represent the interests of particular groups of citizens. The business corporation is one of many institutions in a pluralistic society, but its influence is widespread.

It is important for persons involved in the business system to understand what a pluralistic social system is as it defines the framework and environment in which business must operate and grow. If this concept is not understood by those involved in business, business will not become a responsive social institution in tune, so to speak, with other institutions in society.

An understanding of pluralism is obtained by comparing it to two extreme doctrines, monism and anarchy. Monism describes a social system in which human affairs are operated by one absolute social institution that provides for all needs. A monolithic institution with centralized power determines what society needs. In the case of business, power over the market would be concentrated in a huge business organization. There is some fear that the existence of big business corporations could lead to this type of social system.

At the other extreme is anarchy, which describes an unorganized system in which everyone does his or her own thing without regard for the interests of others. In most societies, a business system operating in this manner would be as unacceptable as monism. In between these two extremes is pluralism.

Pluralism decentralizes power in society by dispersing it among a variety of institutions. No one institution is completely independent of others, but each institution does possess some autonomy to pursue its own interests. With power diffused in this way, society is somewhat protected from the dominance of one group or one institution.

If business functions in a pluralistic society, the various players, or interest groups, must be identified. In this book, these players are referred to as stakeholders.

DEFINING "STAKEHOLDER"

A stakeholder is an individual, or group, who has some share or interest in the functioning of the business system, and in particular, of the corporation. A leading researcher on the stakeholder concept, R. Edward Freeman, defines a stakeholder as "any group or individual who can affect, or is affected by, the achievement of a corporation's purpose" (1984: vi, 53). Freeman provides an excellent summary of the history of the concept (1984, 31–43). Stakeholders may also be referred to as claimants, influencers, publics, or constituencies. Although all these terms have their merits, the term "stakeholder" is preferable as it provides the most general identification of the parties to which business is responsible or accountable.

It is important for managers to identify the complete array of stakeholders for two reasons: (1) to obtain resources, business has to come to terms with the groups that control scarce resources, and (2) the support of other groups is required to maintain the legitimacy of business as an institution in society. Freeman argues that the use of the word "stakeholder" and the stakeholder concept is important for the following reason:

> By using "stakeholder," managers and theorists alike will come to see these groups as having a "stake." "Stakeholder" connotes "legitimacy," and while managers may not think that certain groups are "legitimate" in the sense that their demands on the firm are inappropriate, they had better give "legitimacy" to these groups in terms of their ability to affect the direction of the firm. Hence, "legitimacy" can be understood in a managerial sense implying that it is "legitimate to spend time and resources" on stakeholders, regardless of the appropriateness of their demand. (1984: 45)

Freeman points out that managers must seek out stakeholders and argues that if "you want to manage effectively, then you must take your stakeholder into account in a systematic fashion" (1984: 48). Furthermore, the corporation should undertake on its own to identify and to satisfy key stakeholders before a solution is imposed, often by government or the courts. It is important that corporations develop managers with the expertise to deal with stakeholders.

All stakeholders have expectations, such as reasonably priced and good quality products, adequate wage levels, good working conditions, and a clean, safe environment. Business must understand the preferences and expectations of the various stakeholder groups. Managers cannot only look inward to the needs of owners but, in order to be successful, must behave in a manner compatible with the beliefs and values of their stakeholders. The complexity of business is often due to changing relationships between a corporation and its stakeholders. It should be remembered that the relationships are two-way. Corporations must recognize how various stakeholders can affect them. A corporation's strategy formulation must consider all stakeholders, to some degree, to satisfy stakeholder expectations, if the corporation's policies or strategies are to be accepted.

IDENTIFYING STAKEHOLDERS

The following is a listing of a corporation's stakeholders. This list is not intended to be in any particular order of importance.

Shareholders

Shareholders are the owners of the corporation, those individuals or groups who have invested in the form of equity, or shares. Shareholders can number in the hundreds of thousands for large corporations, or be a single individual in the case of an unincorporated business. Large institutions, such as trust or pension funds, may hold shares in corporations, as may a government. A corporation may be a shareholder in one or several other corporations. The influence shareholders have on business varies. One generalization is based on the number of shareholders: where there are thousands of investors, each holding a small number of shares, the individual shareholder's influence is usually minimal. But, where ownership is concentrated in the hands of a few shareholders, they usually exert significant influence over the corporation. Exceptions to this generalization are mutual and pension funds, who usually do not exercise their influence despite substantial holdings. Chapter 5 outlines the ownership of Canadian business.

Directors

Directors are elected by shareholders to represent their interests. They may number from two to fifty or more, and comprise a Board that meets to decide on issues confronting the corporation. Directors can be from "inside" or from outside the corporation, in which case they are usually executives, managers, or owners of other corporations. The purpose of a Board of Directors is to monitor and review the corporation's operation and performance, and hire and fire the top executives. In theory, the ultimate responsibility for the corporation rests with the Directors, but in reality, their influence varies. If the Board is comprised mainly of insiders, that is, management, its influence on the corporation is substantial. Often Boards comprised of outsiders are mainly token bodies that rubber stamp management's decisions. However, the Board of Directors has the potential to be a very powerful body. The Board plays a big role in the governance of the corporation which is described in Chapter 5. The reform of corporate governance is examined in Chapter 12.

It should be noted that small, unincorporated business enterprises do not have directors. In these enterprises, the owners are also the operators and/or managers and no Board of Directors exists. However, even small enterprises can be incorporated and the owner/manager often is the principal shareholder and serves on the small Board of Directors, which operates on an informal basis.

Employees

Employees are individuals who work for the corporation and are categorized in several different ways. Managers are employees involved in supervising tasks at low, middle, and top levels in the corporation. Workers may be thought of as blue- versus white-collar. Blue-collar workers are involved in manufacturing, production, or servicing tasks, while white-collar workers are office employees. A corporation employs several professional groups, such as engineers, lawyers, and accountants. Employees may be hired on a part-time or full-time basis, with part-time employment becoming more prevalent recently. Labour unions often represent some employees, especially blue-collar workers. Retired employees, either managers or workers, have a stake in the corporation where company pension plans exist. Recently, more attention has been focused on the employment of disadvantaged groups, including women, minorities, and persons with exceptionalities. Employees are considered to be one of the most obvious and, perhaps, the most important stakeholders. They have considerable influence for the simple reason that they are critical for the operation of the corporation. The challenges associated with managing employees are explored in Chapter 15.

Customers or Consumers

A corporation's customers may be members of the public, usually referred to as consumers; other corporations, referred to as industrial customers; or governments or government agencies. Customers are the source of revenue for the corporation and should be treated carefully. However, where a corporation is a monopoly, or where there is a lack of competition in the market, customers can be taken for granted. It is argued that the needs of individual consumers are ignored by large corporations who, through persuasive promotional practices, manipulate consumers. Instead of consumers influencing production decisions, producers influence or determine what consumers will purchase. The role of consumers in the business system is discussed further in Chapter 17.

Lenders and Creditors

There are different types of individuals or groups who lend the corporation money. Some lend for long terms by purchasing bonds or debentures while others advance funds for short periods, as with trade creditors. The lenders may be individuals or other corporations, usually financial intermediaries who exist to lend money. This stakeholder has substantial influence: if the lender is not paid as agreed upon in the contract, the corporation's assets can often be seized. Mortgagees, lenders, and creditors have a prior claim on the assets of a corporation if it ceases operations or goes bankrupt.

Suppliers

Suppliers are usually other corporations who provide raw materials, component parts, or finished materials that are used in the manufacture or provision of the corporation's goods and services. The influence of suppliers varies. If a supplier is the only source of a particular material or component, then more of the corporation's attention must be devoted to this supplier. If the material component is available from several suppliers, the corporation has alternative sources and is not dependent upon a sole source. Sometimes, a corporation may, for a variety of reasons, own its supplier.

Service Professionals

These are individuals who are not employees of the corporation but provide services on a fee-for-service basis. Included in this type of stakeholder are lawyers, accountants, engineers and management consultants. Their influence is in the form of the advice they provide the corporation. It is in their own interest to see that the advice is reliable as they are then more likely to be rehired. Corporations rely on service professionals as it is often too expensive to employ such expertise on a permanent basis.

Dealers, Distributors, and Franchisees

In some types of business, many other corporations distribute a firm's product to customers. A good example is the automobile industry where hundreds of dealers form a distribution system. Wholesalers are also this type of stakeholder. Some corporations allow others to sell their product or service through a franchising system. The arrangement under which distributors or franchisees operate varies, but can be very complex, especially in the case of franchising. The extent and complexity of these arrangements determine the influence a corporation has over the distributors or franchisees. But this influence is not one-sided, as the corporation depends on these types of businesses to get its products to the customers. If the corporation in question is a dealer, distributor, or franchise, the operations of the business will be impacted substantially by the agreement under which it operates.

Business Organizations

Corporations join together to form hundreds of organizations to represent their interests. An example of such an organization representing large business corporations is the Business Council on National Issues, a group compromising the executives of Canada's largest 150 corporations. Chambers of Commerce or Boards of Trade exist in thousands of communities, and a national coordinating organization operates as the Canadian Chamber of Commerce. There are organizations representing small businesses, including the Canadian Federation of Independent Business. Trade associations represent corporations operating within particular industries, for example, the Canadian Pulp and Paper Association or the Canadian Manufacturers' Association. Business also forms self-regulating agencies such as the Advertising Standards Council, which monitors advertising practices. In some areas, or industries, corporations are represented by employer associations usually dealing with industrial relations matters.

The impact of these types of organizations varies, but by uniting to speak as one they are bound to have more influence than by acting individually. Often it is difficult to obtain consensus within these groups as not all businesspersons think the same. The effectiveness of voluntary, self-regulating agencies has been questioned. The impact of business organizations is examined in Chapter 13, particularly in the discussion of "Lobbying."

Competitors

Competitors are those firms selling the same products. However, competitors should be viewed more broadly. For example, firms producing substitute products should be identified and monitored. Not only should existing competitors be considered, but potential future competitors should be identified. With rapid technological advances, new products and services are constantly being researched and developed. Competitors should not be restricted to those from the domestic environment: those from foreign countries should also be considered. In Chapter 16, the influence of competitors is examined in more detail.

Joint-Venture Participants

Joint-venture participants are partners cooperating in a particular enterprise or project. Usually written agreements outline the relationships between the corporation and its partners. Several other terms are also used to describe this cooperation, including alliances, consortia, networks, and partnerships. The word "strategic" is often used in conjunction with these terms, for example, strategic alliances, cooperative strategies, and strategic partnerships.

Interest Groups

Interest groups are numerous, but their impact on the corporation varies. Examples of groups that are having considerable impact on the corporation presently are environmental, women's, and neighbourhood (community) groups. The approaches to responding to and managing interest groups are discussed in Chapter 19.

Society at Large

This stakeholder group represents the general public, that is, the views of society generally. The views of this stakeholder are a problem for corporations to determine, making it difficult to ascertain this group's impact. Communities in which businesses are located fall into this category — the views of communities are often made explicit to the corporation.

Educational Institutions

Schools, colleges, and universities educate not only employees but the general public. Business relies on these institutions to provide it with educated and skilled employees. These institutions also educate the public about economic systems and the role of business in society. Universities, in particular, are relied upon to perform basic research that is often applied to industrial situations. Educational institutions, although mainly government funded, are now seeking financial and other support from business.

Religious Groups

Churches often speak out on issues related to business. Business persons are individually influenced by the values and beliefs upheld by religious groups.

Charities

Charitable organizations expect business to support them financially. Business enterprises' support of charities is discussed in Chapter 14.

Service, Fraternal, Cultural, and Ethnic Associations

Employees of business corporations join numerous service/fraternal/cultural/ethnic associations such as Rotary and Lions Clubs, Parents for French, and the Association of Ukrainian Businessmen. These memberships often involve the donation of employee time and efforts, and association with such organizations is often viewed as a source of business contacts.

Figure 2-1 Bank of Montreal Stakeholder Map

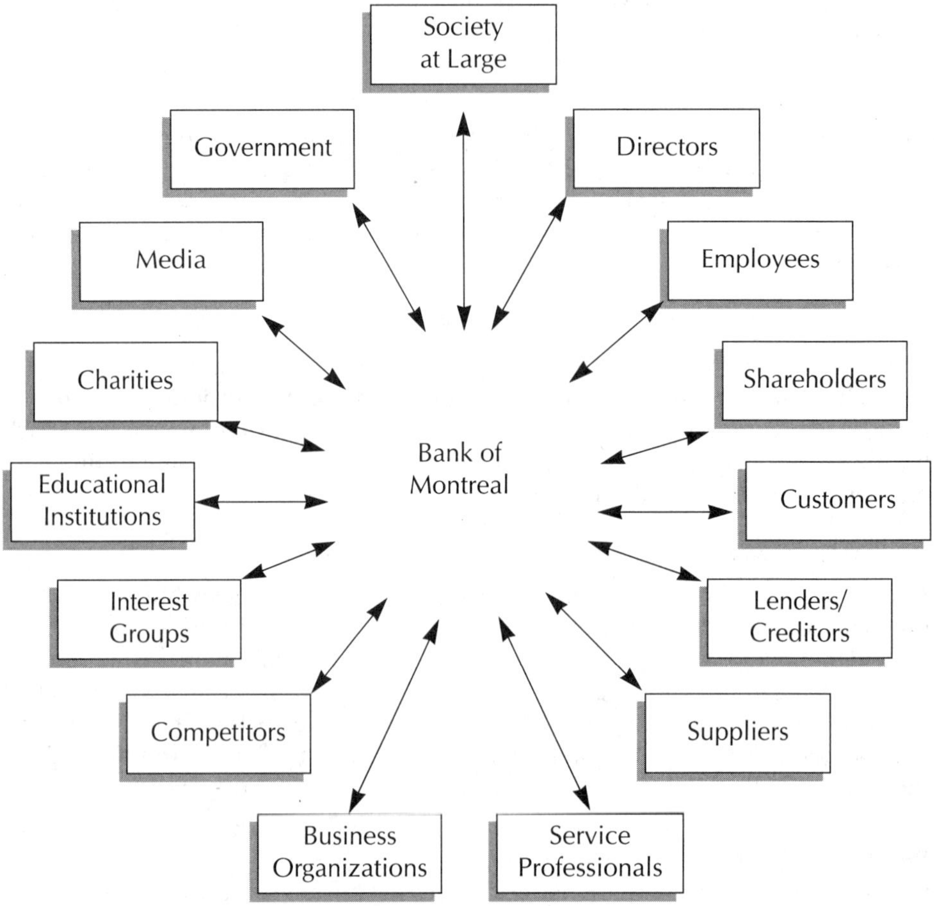

Directors—About 30, regional representation, mostly businesspersons
Employees—Mainly white-collar, non-unionized; about 32 000
Shareholders—Widely held
Customers—Consumer and business accounts
Lenders/Creditors—$1.7 billion in long-term debt
Suppliers—Many, but mostly office materials and equipment. Renter of real estate
Service Professionals—Operations rely upon lawyers and accountants
Business Organizations—Institute of Canadian Bankers
Competitors—Five other major banks and several small ones
  (including some foreign owned), trust companies, and credit unions.
Interest Groups—Consumers' Association of Canada
Educational Institutions—Donates to institutions; major employer
  of graduates
Charities—Support provided
Media—Public Relations Department
Government—Regulated by Bank Act and other legislation
Society at Large—Bank branches (1200) in most communities

Note: The following stakeholders are not shown as they have little or no stake: dealers, distributors, and franchisees; religious groups; service, fraternal, cultural, ethnic associations; and joint-venture participants.

provide support and information to more effectively sell and service their products. An important interdependency exists between the corporation and these stakeholders.

- *Joint-Venture Participants.* This stakeholder is really a partner with the corporation and expects to receive fair treatment according to the contractual arrangement made and the norms of business conduct. This stakeholder has also become more important recently as corporations engage in a greater number of these arrangements.

- *Religious Groups.* Religious groups are often concerned about the conduct of corporations, and expect a responsive hearing of their concerns. Overall, they expect to influence the morality of business conduct.

- *Service, Fraternal, Cultural and Ethnic Associations.* This type of stakeholder expects to receive financial support and to obtain members from the business community.

The relationships between the corporation and its stakeholders is dynamic, often changing, as is illustrated throughout this book.

THE MANAGER: A SPECIAL STAKEHOLDER

The managers of Canadian business enterprises are also stakeholders, of course: they can be employees, and may be shareholders as well. The uniqueness of managers is that they are in charge of enterprises, that is, they are very influential in dealing with other stakeholders.

Managers are responsible for carefully identifying and analyzing the stakeholders influencing the enterprise, and the stakeholders influenced by the enterprise. They are also responsible for responding to stakeholders. This managerial responsibility might be outlined as follows:

- Identify stakeholders influenced by, or having an influence on, the corporation.

- Understand how the corporation presently views the stakeholders.

- Examine how each stakeholder will or might influence the corporation.

- Assess opportunities or threats, and the magnitude of the influence on or of the stakeholder.

- Rank stakeholders by influence.

- Prepare programs or policies detailing how to deal or cope with stakeholders.

The manager-stakeholder is discussed throughout the book. Specific techniques for analyzing stakeholder influence are discussed in Chapter 9, Issues and Stakeholder Management.

SUMMARY

This chapter defines and identifies the stakeholders in the business enterprise system. A stakeholder is an individual, or group, that has some share, interest, or "stake" in the business system and the activities of corporations. Nineteen stakeholders are listed and described, but several things should be remembered about this list.

First, it is not necessarily complete. The list includes the most commonly acknowledged stakeholders and is comprised of generic or general labels. The stakeholder names or participants have to be customized for each corporation.

Second, although some stakeholders — for example, employees, shareholders, and customers — are important to all corporations, the importance of other stakeholders will vary by corporation and over time. Because of this variability, the list is not categorized in any way so the reader is less likely to predetermine the influence of particular stakeholders.

Third, each stakeholder has different goals and expectations of the corporation. Sometimes conflict exists among stakeholders and/or the interests of stakeholders. Overseeing the various stakeholder interests is an important aspect of the modern manager's job. Stakeholders, and their influence, are referred to constantly throughout the book, as is the influence managers have over stakeholders.

The next chapter provides background on the Canadian business enterprise system by discussing the fundamental theories and concepts upon which it is based.

REFERENCES

Facing Realities. (1981). Brussels: European Institute for Advanced Studies in Management.

Frederick, William C., Keith Davis, and James E. Post. (1988). *Business and Society: Corporate Strategy, Public Policy, Ethics.* New York: McGraw-Hill.

Freeman, R. Edward. (1984). *Strategic Management: A Stakeholder Approach.* Boston: Pitman.

Mintzberg, Henry. (1983). *Power In and Around Organizations.* Englewood Cliffs, N.J.: Prentice-Hall, Inc.

Many changes have occurred in the Canadian economy. Government is much bigger because of the 1930's Depression and World War II. Out of necessity, both events resulted in greater government involvement to improve economic conditions and to defend the country against an aggressor, respectively. Interest groups have formed and placed demands on government. Such groups represent consumers, farmers, and environmentalists, but they also represent the different constituencies that make up the business system itself.

There has been a trend to bigness in business, and this may have lessened competition. Employees are frequently represented by larger and highly organized unions. Society seems to be more organizational in nature, with less emphasis on individualism. The free market has been replaced by a system that is also capable of taking into consideration social concerns.

Economic and social problems associated with growth have encouraged government action. Pollution, energy shortages, and inflation are major challenges that the business system itself has not been able to cope with adequately. Insufficient housing and high unemployment have also placed pressures on the system. Lastly, it might be argued that individuals' values are changing along with their expectations of how life should be.

Canada does not have a pure enterprise system, but instead a complex, "patched" up one. This patched system is the best that can be expected given human limitations, that is, no system can be perfect if it is to operate democratically. Moreover, the system is an integrated and complex one, making the separation of fundamental elements difficult. Government involvement has increased as the underlying assumptions of capitalism have become less valid in practice. Some would argue that laissez-faire capitalism was a myth in the first place and never really operational.

Canadians, including businesspersons, tend to use the word "capitalism" in different contexts, increasing the confusion over the word's meaning. Some examples are

- *Democratic Capitalism*   A term used when shareholders vote to change Board members and/or management. It is "democratic" in the sense that a voting procedure is involved and the majority's wishes prevail.

- *People's Capitalism*   This term has been used to reflect the participation of a variety of stakeholders.

(1) When governments in Canada and Great Britain sold their government owned enterprises, they arranged for sales of shares to the society at large. A variety of techniques were used: giving away a token number of shares to every citizen (as done by the B.C. Government when it sold the British Columbia Resources Investment Corporation); selling shares to residents at a very attractive price; allowing residents to pay for shares through instalments (as done in the privatization of Nova Scotia Power);

and limiting the number of shares any one person could own. All these techniques encouraged wide ownership of shares through society, thus referred to as "people's capitalism."

(2) In the past twenty years, Canadians have been investing in business through the purchase of equity mutual funds and contributions to pension plans. As a result, a large number of Canadians now own, even if indirectly, shares in business enterprises. Individual Canadians still invest directly through transactions in stock exchanges, but an even greater number invest through mutual and pension funds.

(3) Employee stock purchase plans have existed for some time, but they became more popular in the 1980's. In some corporations, hundreds and thousands of employees become shareholders. A variation of this practice occurs when an employee buys out a plant or company when the owners decide to close for some reason.

In Chapter 1, capitalism is defined as an economic system that allows for private ownership of the means of production (land, labour, and capital), and assumes that economic decision making is in the hands of individuals or enterprises who make decisions expecting to earn a profit. Canadian capitalism satisfies this definition to some degree, but not all means of production are privately owned, not all economic decision making is in the hands of individuals, and many economic decisions are made where profit is not the motive.

SUMMARY

Eight fundamental elements of Canadian capitalism were identified: the right of private property, individualism and economic freedom, equality of opportunity, competition, profits, the work ethic, consumer sovereignty, and the role of government. The elements represent values that must be held to some extent by a society in order for capitalism to operate effectively as an economic system.

The elements were described in two contexts: from a theoretical perspective that describes them as they exist in a perfect capitalistic system; and from a practical one that more closely describes their existence in the Canadian business enterprise system. These elements were used to define or describe Canadian capitalism, but such a description is not easy. The next chapter, on business ideologies, examines another approach to coming to grips with capitalism in the Canadian setting.

The Socialist "Waffle Resolution"

The "Waffle Resolution" presented at the 1969 New Democratic Party Conference describes the essential aspects of a socialist ideology, a view of the more left-leaning members of the party. The resolution was defeated: the NDP position has always been less radical than stated in this resolution. The resolution is dominated by references to economic nationalism. The writers of the resolution were concerned with foreign ownership, and argued that it is difficult to redistribute economic power in Canada if the economy is owned and controlled by foreigners. Economic independence was required for a socialist state to operate in Canada, and it was doubted that the capitalists controlling the economy had the means to struggle for this independence from foreign control.

Socialist Literature

There are many expressions of the socialist view in Canada. There is an enormous literature explaining and advocating this view (for example, Adler-Karlsson, 1970; Avakumovic, 1978; Clement, 1983; Cunningham, 1978; *Essays on the Left*, 1971; Godfrey, 1970; Hutcheson, 1973; Laxer, 1973; League for Social Reconstruction, 1935/1975; Lewis, 1972; McEwen, 1974; Penner, 1977; Rankin, 1975; Riddell and Young, 1977; Teeple, 1972). Also, such periodicals as *Dimension* and *The Last Post* expound upon socialist approaches. The view presented focuses on such topics as class struggles, the relationship between capital and labour, the exploitation of labour, and capitalism's pursuit of profits. The position taken is that capital dominates labour by using technology and the organization of work. Management, representing capital, has greater control, and management — along with owners of capital — forms elites to dominate society in general and business in particular.

The Monopoly Mentality

The monopoly mentality represents the tendency in the Canadian setting to advocate either government- or privately-owned monopoly or near monopoly business enterprises. This thinking had very early beginnings in 1670 when the Hudson's Bay Company was incorporated as a joint-stock company with exclusive trading rights in the territory traversed by the rivers flowing into Hudson bay. The North West Company was formed in the 1770's by Montreal fur traders to reduce competition among themselves and to resist the advances of the Hudson's Bay Company.

This ideological view ignores the argument that competition is a fundamental element in the business system. Hardin, in his book *A Nation Unaware: The Canadian Economic Culture* (1974), argues that Canadians have been influenced by the American dream ideology based on an individualistic society of the economic person. Thus, Canadians think that their economy should be operating under the assumptions of an "American-ideology-in-Canada," instead of an ideology more appropriate for Canadian circumstances. Hardin feels that the borrowed American ideology distorts and screens out Canadian circumstances. Hardin claims that Canadians mistakenly advocate competition when, in key sectors, monopoly has meant efficiency and market competition has meant "pernicious" waste. According to Hardin, "monopoly is the economic model. Monopoly suits us [Canadians], and always has" (p. 174), and monopoly has a dynamic influence beyond that of competition. In Canada, monopoly is coming into its own as a creative entrepreneurial form.

According to Hardin, most Canadians view Crown corporations (that is, public enterprises) as "stodgy and unadventuresome" and view capitalist entrepreneurs as "vigorous and dynamic." He questions the superiority of private enterprise over public enterprise using examples from Canadian National Railways, Ontario Hydro, and Polymer Corporation, all of which he claims are more innovative than most private enterprises.

Hardin claims that Canadians have overlooked the possibilities of a "monopoly culture." The appropriate public enterprise model would be the monopoly, where entrepreneurship would be freed "from the straitjacket" of market and oligopoly competition. The monopoly public enterprise model would be especially appropriate to an entrepreneurship effort in a nongrowth environment. The monopoly public enterprise would not have to keep on increasing sales and "intensifying propaganda" in order to maintain a market or oligopoly share. Monopoly public enterprises, according to Hardin, are suitable for matching capacity to demand without diminishing service.

While Hardin advocates public ownership of monopoly corporations, businesspersons often argue that monopolies are necessary for Canadian business to compete on a global basis because some Canadian markets are too small to support competition amongst corporations, or that natural monopolies exist. Exhibit 4-2 illustrates the justification for monopoly positions in the airline and telephone industries that have been used recently. Even in its privatization initiatives, the federal government maintained the monopoly of Teleglobe Inc., which transmits all overseas calls from Canada. In 1992, the government justified a five year extension of the monopoly because competition would fragment Canada's small telecommunications market and prevent it from operating effectively on a global scale. Sometimes governments endorse the monopoly mentality, often on the urging of businesspersons, and continue to regulate some industries despite changes in market conditions and technological advances. An example formerly existed in the long-distance market and still exists in the cable television industry. Governments prevent foreign competition and impose ownership limits on non-Canadians. Both these policies assist in preserving monopoly.

Exhibit 4-2

Examples of the Monopoly Mentality Ideology

Solving the Effects of Deregulation

Peter C. Newman, in a *Macleans'* "Business Watch" column, discusses the possibility of Air Canada and Canadian Airlines merging. He quotes Hershel Hardin as stating that the only solution to the problems created by the deregulation of the airline industry may be "to buy up Air Canada and PWA, merge them, and create a single, publicly owned transcontinental carrier." Newman concludes that Hardin may be right and goes on to state: "The advantage of a monopoly (if its rate structures are tightly controlled) is that it allows for the optimum use of aircraft capacities and maximizes the economies of scale." Hardin's views on monopoly have received some attention!

Monopolists Collide

The following is from an editorial in the *Financial Times of Canada*:

> Karl Marx, the arch-enemy of "monopoly capitalism," would be tickled pink by the insults traded recently by Ted Rogers of Rogers Communications Inc. and Raymond Cyr of BCE Inc. Rogers drew first blood: he criticized BCE's telecommunications monopoly. ("Monopolists never change. They become greater monopolists.") And he argued the case for competition in the long-distance telephone market. (Unitel Communications, in which Rogers is a minority shareholder, has an application pending before the Canadian Radio-television and Telecommunications Commission.)
>
> A few days later, Cyr pounced on the irony of such a view coming from "the largest monopolist in cable TV. That's as if, somehow, cable monopolies are all right but a telephone monopoly is not." On the subject of monopolists, does it take one to know one? And will Ted Rogers still favor competition if and when BCE wants to enter the cable TV market? (1992, p. 22)

Extending the Monopoly on Overseas Calls

Federal Communications Minister Perrin Beatty justifies the extension of Teleglobe's monopoly as follows:

> [Extending the monopoly] is essential for Canadian sovereignty and to enable Canadian players to compete internationally.

Although government policies have endorsed the monopoly mentality, another agency, the Competition Bureau, attempts to review mergers that severely reduce competition. Competition policy in the past was ineffectual in preventing mergers and takeovers, but a new Competition Act passed in 1986 is having some impact on preserving competition by questioning mergers and reviewing anti-competitive situations or practices such as refusal to deal, exclusive dealing, tied selling, market restriction, abuse of dominant position, delivered pricing, and specialization agreements. The influence of this agency is outlined in its *Annual Report* (Director of Investigation and Research, *Competition Act*, 1992).

Thus, a number of factors have resulted in the continuing existence of a monopoly mentality ideology: historical practice, public ownership, government regulatory policies, and the natural desire of business to dominate a market. It is important to recognize that the monopoly mentality is being perpetuated by businesspeople, and it is not appropriate to solely blame government for this situation.

The Mixed Economy

What may be occurring in the Canadian business system is a blend between collectivism and conservatism, often referred to as a "mixed economy." The market system is constrained, and interventionist activities by government are common. The result is an uneasy alliance between the fundamentals of a market economy and the practices of socialism, administered by bureaucrats and governed by political pragmatism. Examples of this ideological perspective are given in Exhibit 4-3.

Exhibit 4-3

Examples of the Mixed Economy Ideology

The Trudeau Proposal for a "New Society"

In a television interview in late December 1975 and in a speech to the Canadian Club of Ottawa in January 1976, Prime Minister Trudeau outlined what were referred to as his "new society" comments (Trudeau, 1976). In these comments, he suggested that Canadian society needed a change in its values and economic system to solve such problems as inflation and unemployment. More government intervention would be required in the economy as the traditional market system was inadequate to cope with modern problems. The Liberal Government had introduced price and income controls in October 1975, and the introduction of controls, along with these "new society" remarks, caused considerable debate within the business community (Hartle 1976).

Some of the main points that Trudeau made included the following:

1) There is a distinction between a free enterprise system, which he claimed existed, and a free market system, which he claimed no longer exists. There were parts of the economy that were truly competitive, such as some retail and service industries. In other industries and with labour, larger power blocks dominated the economy and Canadians wanted their governments to protect the public interest in such cases.

2) The main reason for the prosperity Canada enjoyed was the existence of a mixed economy of both private and public enterprise.

3) The business community had supported and encouraged governments to intervene in the market place in order to promote growth and stability in the economy. Also, most Canadians were convinced of the necessity of government intervention to promote steady growth, stable prices, full employment, and to make sure private industry acted in the public interest.

4) Business, labour and the public would all have to contribute to the economy in a responsible fashion given the circumstances in which Canadians found themselves. Trudeau was thus in disagreement with those who advocated the creation of a truly free market economy.

"The Way Ahead" Discussion

In October 1976, the Government of Canada issued a working paper, entitled *The Way Ahead: A Framework for Discussion* (Canada, 1976), to generate discussion of the major structural components of the economy and society in order to discover the root causes of inflation. Income and price controls had been introduced in October 1975 and the paper was to outline the government's economic and social directions after controls ended. The paper discussed some topics relevant to business ideology, in particular, the role of government.

The paper identified the following three basic views as to the role of government in the social and economic system: (1) a minimal role; (2) a continually expanding role; and (3) a middle road role. The minimal role for government asserts that the market system allocates resources most efficiently, resulting in the highest possible production and growth. The continually expanding role emphasizes the government's responsibility to support economic growth, equity, and the public provision of goods and services, and to intervene in the working of the market system to ensure socially acceptable outcomes. The middle road role rejects the previous two and attempts to strike a balance. The paper concluded that there was the necessity to increase the reliance on the market system while at the same time recognizing that market-directed economic growth had not fully served the social needs of Canadians. Business enterprises would also have to embrace a socially responsible approach in the conduct of their affairs in the market. The paper found that there was need for consultation in the decision making process. It indicated that the government's priorities would remain much the same, but that there would be less direct intervention in the economy and increased reliance on the market.

Gillies's **Where Business Fails**

The prevalence of the "mixed economy" with its middle-of-the-road position relating to the participation of the private and public sectors is summarized by Gillies in his book *Where Business Fails*. Gillies feels that decisions on the production of goods and services in Canada were made by more or less mutual agreement between business and government. According to Gillies, "Such agreement was forged from the input of all sectors affected by the decision, and in this way, through the years, the public and private sectors were able to function successfully in what has come to be known as a 'mixed economy'" (Gillies, 1981, p. 137).

Down With Laissez-faire

In a letter to the editor of *The Financial Post* (November 14, 1992, p. 55), Charles P. Mooney of Vancouver, B.C. expresses relief that with the election of President Clinton, the U.S. would be giving up the laissez-faire, leave-it-to-the-private-sector approach to government. He states that "right-wing leadership is not working" as demonstrated by the weak economies of the U.S., Britain, and Canada. He concludes his letter by stating that "... steps must be taken to re-establish the government's role" in Canada's economy and that "A well-balanced mixed economy should be the course for us now as it surely will be for the U.S."

A Thing of the Past

William Thorsell, a columnist for the *Report on Business Magazine*, believes that the mixed economy is a thing of the past. In a column in the May 1990 issue (p. 109), Thorsell states that the 1988 election over free trade forced Canadians to "face up to the myths of economic nationalism — something that was necessary if Canadian business was to compete in the global economy. He states that "the death of the mixed economy in fact, and the acceptance of economic continentalism through free trade by treaty, are still causing a crisis of identity among many Canadians and nostalgia for a Canada we thought we knew just 10 years ago."

It is argued that the best of both worlds exists in the mixed economy ideology. Government intervention is designed to encourage business growth and, if possible, not to hamper business activity. It is a blend of the influence of government and the knowledge and expertise of business. Cooperation is essential for a prosperous country because if either side is cut out of the process, they may work at cross purposes with disastrous results. The National Energy Policy of the 1980's is often given as an example of the disaster that can occur when business is not consulted in the formulation of policy.

The potential cooperation between business and government in the mixed economy can create a potent combination to benefit society. It is argued that such cooperation is even more important in an environment of global competition. Some argue that the cooperation should be formalized into a stated national industrial strategy. Nevertheless, there is a drawback to the ideology as it involves a loss of market forces to some degree. Government involvement influences business decision making, often leading to corporate failures or inefficient operations sustained through government assistance.

The cooperation between government and business in the mixed economy is on an ad hoc basis and is not formalized by any mechanisms or institutions. Where the management is more orchestrated, and formalized, another ideological perspective — corporatism — is involved.

Corporatism

Corporatism, sometimes referred to as "tripartitism" or "statism," involves a partnership of business, labour, and government in all the important economic decision making in society. Pure corporatism is a system in which unions and corporations are required by law to participate in national tripartite bodies dominated by government. If the involvement of the groups is voluntary, it is referred to as quasi-corporatism. Some form of corporatism is in operation in Sweden, Japan, France, and Germany.

Corporatism is considered desirable as governments cannot win in conflicts with big business and big labour. Therefore, these institutions are absorbed into the apparatus of government. The following quotation is a good summary of the concept:

> The essence of corporatism is private or capitalist ownership coupled with state control. The characteristic objective of the corporate state is to avoid — as much as possible — adversarial confrontation between business and labour, or business and government. Private ownership is left undisturbed. The strategy is for government to enforce an incomes policy for all of the "functional" groups within the society, while calling for increased partnership or collaboration between the state and all major producers. Instead of confrontation between classes or aggressive competition between economic groups, corporatism seeks to substitute the principal of social harmony or unity through negotiation and direct cooperative interaction among business, labour and state. To achieve this collaboration, the various industrial groups are made agencies of the state or co-opted within the apparatus of government, usually within tripartite structures. Emphatically, the state becomes dominant. In place of market competition, corporatism would substitute state control. Cooperation must replace competition; if not, cooperation will be commanded and imposed by the state. (McLeod, 1976)

Some argue that corporatism will assist in resolving conflicts in the economic system, and that it involves a sound and non-adversarial deliberation of economic issues leading to a compromise solution vital to the nation. It is assumed that "big" institutions, that is, big business, big labour, and big government, are capable of deciding the economic future of society. It is argued that big corporations can generate sufficient jobs to employ all except a small portion of workers. However, to accomplish this end the corporations need government help. Capitalists usually oppose state planning, but corporatism enables corporations to plan more efficiently. It insures adherence to internal plans, controls competition, facilitates the passage of appropriate legislation, and reduces risks. Also, it is argued that if business, labour, and government together allocate incomes, the economy will be subject to less pressure from inflation.

There are drawbacks to the corporatism model. It leads to the emergence of elite groups in business, labour, and government who decide what is best for society. Furthermore, not all groups in society are represented and policy is determined without the pluralistic and democratic checks and balances of a decentralized decision-making system. It is also doubtful that the three groups will decide upon how the incomes "pie" will be divided. It is suggested that business and labour might even conspire to secure higher incomes at the expense of the rest of society. Members of society must decide whether the loss of individual freedoms is worth the promise of employment, lower inflation, and less labour-management strife. The impact of individuals in the corporatism model is limited, except in the voting process.

There is some evidence that aspects of the corporatism ideology operate in Canada. Examples are provided in Exhibit 4-4. The prevalence of the corporatism view varies over time, yet there are tendencies in the Canadian economy that enforce its existence.

Exhibit 4-4

Examples of the Corporatism Ideology

The Canadian Labour Market and Productivity Centre (CLMPC)

The CLMPC is a research and consultative body involving the government, labour and business. In January 1984, the federal government launched the CLMPC by providing the necessary financing. The CLMPC is operated jointly by labour and business, and governed by a 40 member board comprising 12 voting members nominated by the Business Council on National Issues, the Canadian Chamber of Commerce, and the Canadian Manufacturers' Association, 12 voting members nominated by the Canadian Labour Congress and the Canadian Federation of Labour; and 16 non-voting members acceptable to both sides. The CLMPC maintains an important link to the federal and provincial governments and academia through its non-voting membership.

The CLMPC's mandate is to promote dialogue between Canada's economic stakeholders and to develop joint business/labour recommendations on approaches to improving the operation of the labour market and Canada's productivity performance. On the basis of its consultation and research, the CLMPC is in a unique position to influence public policy, as well as the programs and practices of business and labour (CLMPC, 1992).

The "Quebec Inc." Model

According to many financial writers, the corporatism ideology is being applied in the Province of Quebec. The term "Quebec Inc." is used to represent the interrelationship amongst business, labour and government organizations. The following are cited as examples of corporatism in Quebec:

- the national interest is considered supreme, individual interests being subordinate
- the business sector is organized into large diversified conglomerates, such as Power Corporation of Canada, Unigesco Inc., and Bombardier Inc.
- through consultation, organized labour is a part of the provincial business consensus
- the government assists business in various ways, including ownership (whole or part), subsidies, and loans

- there is an active exchange of executives between business and the public sector
- Quebec's financial institutions finance provincial business activity, for example, the *caisse populaire*, and the chartered banks, National Bank and Laurentian Bank
- the government pension fund, the Caisse de depot et placement du Quebec, invests in Quebec business sometimes with the encouragement of the government
- provincial barriers to trade protect Quebec business enterprises
- the provincial government developed a stock ownership plan to encourage investment in Quebec.

Taken together, these activities are seen as a corporatist approach to business.

References to further materials on corporatism

For background on corporations in Canada, refer to the following:

Panitch, Leo. (1979, Spring). Corporatism in Canada. *Studies in Political Economy*, pp.43–92.

For calls for "closer" relationships amongst government, labour, and business, refer to the following:

Gillies, James. (1989, October 21). Close cooperation between government and business is essential. *The Globe and Mail*, p. B2.

Godfrey, John. (1991, Summer). A call for national unity. *The Financial Post Magazine*, pp. 69–71.

Lortie, Pierre. (1985). Comments about the tripartite consultative process. In Rea and Wiseman (Eds.) *Government and Enterprise in Canada* (pp. 351–358). Toronto: Methuen.

Lortie, Pierre. (1990, December 3). Society's key players must put it all together. *The Globe and Mail*, p. B8.

For counterviews claiming that corporatism does not exist in Canada, see the following:

Corcoran, Terence. (1986, May 5). CLC war drums signal death of tripartism. *The Financial Times*, pp. 1–2.

Taylor, Wayne. (1990, Winter). Tripartism in Canada and the socio-historical determinants of industrial relations systems. *Business in the Contemporary World*, pp .55–62.

The Managerial Approach

The "managerial" approach assumes that the owners and professional managers attempt not only to act in the best interests of shareholders but also to take into account the positions of other stakeholders, for example employees, consumers, and interest groups. Government involvement in the business system is recognized, and the assumption is made that corporations act in the public good, that is, that they are socially responsible.

This particular ideology of business is illustrated by a large portion of the business community, and one of its principal supporters is the Canadian Chamber of Commerce. The business system advocated by this ideology is referred to as the "competitive enterprise system" or the "competitive market economy" (Canadian Chamber of Commerce). The managerial approach is discussed as a separate ideology as (1) it does not support the level of government involvement upheld in the corporatism view, and (2) it does not fit with the neoconservatism view since government involvement is recognized as existing and necessary to some degree.

Many arguments are advanced in support of the enterprise system advocated by the managerial approach. Some suggest that it produces more for everyone by encouraging individual initiative, allocating resources most economically, and promoting dynamic economic growth. Under a competitive system, individuals are motivated by the opportunity for profits and the dangers of losses: competition develops the maximum managerial capabilities, technical knowledge, and operating skills necessary for growth. Supporters of this enterprise system also argue that society has benefited from the ideology by achieving a high standard of living.

Another argument is that, under a competitive system, business responds to the "democracy" of the marketplace by providing what society wants. This implies a broad dispersal of decision-making power as individuals make decisions to purchase, or not to purchase, a particular good and service from the selection available. A competitive system fosters "freedom," which in turn provides an incentive for efficiency, hard work, and innovation. Profits are put to work under this system. Profits determine the use of resources, the level of savings, the volume of investment, and the drive to greater efficiency.

The managerial approach recognizes the role of government in providing goods and services beyond the supply of infrastructure, but suggests that it should be a secondary role. Government involvement is not the issue so much as is the degree of involvement. Supporters of the managerial approach advocate a reduction in public spending, as a percentage of Gross National Product, from 50 percent to approximately 40 percent. They believe that government should support the private competitive enterprise system by maintaining an equitable and favorable climate for private action and that the role of government is to establish, promote, and enforce the role of law, and to maintain personal freedom in society. Supporters of this ideological view argue that individuals should not turn to government to solve all problems, but should rely on the private sector.

In Canada today, supporters of the managerial approach are willing to accept government assistance in many forms, and frequently argue for more government involvement. The government involvement advocated usually focuses on such things as restrictions on imports; tax and investment incentives; outright grants; preferential purchasing policies; and restrictions on competition, for example, limits on shopping centre development. They feel that social programs

— such as unemployment insurance, Medicare, and social assistance — should be reduced or not extended, and certainly administered more efficiently. A negative tax should be considered to replace most social programs, and universality of benefits should be abandoned with pension and family allowance programs.

Managers who endorse a managerial ideology are usually progressive in their thinking about business' role in society. Exhibit 4-5 contains four examples of such thinking in the areas of stakeholder management, social responsibility, business ethics, and concern for the environment.

Exhibit 4-5

Examples of the Managerial Approach

Managers practicing business according to a managerial ideology focus on stakeholder management, social responsibility, business ethics, and concern for the environment. The following quotations reflect these topics.

Stakeholder Management

R.D. Fullerton (1990), Chaiman of the Canadian Imperial Bank of Commerce, states that business and management is not solely focused on making money as expressed by return on investment. He compares the managing of modern corporations to the art of juggling, with a manager having several balls in the air at once. Fullerton states that "these balls have labels like shareholders, employees, customers, environment, community and country." He goes on to say that "... its a question of balance: the need to balance the company's social responsibilities with the expectations of the shareholders; the balance between protecting the environment and treating employees fairly; the balance between a constructive contribution to the public policy process and the organization's financial health." Fullerton concludes that, in order to be a successful corporation, the manager must juggle in such a way that all stakeholders are satisfied.

Social Responsibility

An annual report by Alcan Aluminum Limited (1989) provides the following perspective on social responsibility:

> What is corporate responsibility?

> There are as many answers as there are human interests. Like beauty, it lies in the eye of the beholder, and like beauty its standards change with time. But if there is one constant in the shifting views of corporate responsibility, it is humanity. Both the community and the company which serves it are each a collection of human needs and concerns. It is the extent to which the company addresses those needs and concerns that measures its corporate responsibility. (p.4)

Business Ethics

Arden Haynes (1988), Chairman of Imperial Oil Limited, states that "The issue of ethical behaviour is one of the most critical issues facing the business community today." Confidence and trust are basic ingredients of the economic, political, and social system in this country. He comments that "People expect the institutions that make up the system, and the people responsible for them, to comply not only with the law, but also with certain unwritten standards of honesty, integrity, fairness and good faith." If society's expectations regarding confidence and trust are not met, the foundations of the system will start to crumble.

The Environment

John Barr, vice-president of Burson-Marsteller, states that in addition to thinking about markets, prices, and making deals, Canadian managers have to deal with another imponderable — the environment. Although a concern for the environment had been showing up in opinion surveys for some time, in the late 1980s it ranked much higher as Canadians recognized the relationship between a clean environment and their personal health. Today, according to Barr, "... this social issue has become, for Canadians, a deeply felt national concern that cuts across income, age, educational and other lines. And because we are frightened, we are looking to government, and business to fix the problem — or else! Environmentalism, I believe, will endure as a central reality of doing business in Canada."

Neoconservatism

Neoconservatism is the most "right wing" ideology discussed in Canada: it is more conservative than the managerial position. Advocates of this ideology do not believe that the dominant role government has come to play in society is desirable. Big government is considered evil and undesirable as it increases costs and provides lower quality products or services. Traditional conservatives argue that no government is the best government, but some are willing to admit that laissez-faire capitalism is not practical.

However, it is argued that free enterprise — based on private ownership, individual economic decision making, and competition — should be the basis of the economic system to the maximum possible extent. Neoconservatives believe that society demands a smaller and less powerful government. Social security is viewed as violating the foundations of Canadian heritage, namely progress and freedom. Individuals should not surrender to government their right to make decisions concerning their daily lives. By expecting government to do things for them, individuals become too dependent on government: they surrender some control over their lives, retaining less freedom for themselves. This surrender and loss of freedom occurs even with the democratically elected governments advocated by socialists.

According to the neoconservative ideology, competition is required as an incentive; without it there is less improvement in prices and products and a retarded rate of economic progress. Governments exist to provide an appropriate economic climate in which individual enterprises can achieve progress and create prosperity. The state, or government, is still responsible for dividing a nation's wealth, but the private sector — rather than a govenment bureaucracy — provides the mechanism.

The rights of individuals are also of concern to neoconservatives. Government regulation restricts the rights of individuals, including the right to be left alone. Some supporters of neoconservatism even argue that Human Rights Commissions are coercive tools of the state (Amiel, 1979, 1980). Advocates of neoconservatism reject the equalitarianism of socialism and expect individuals to look out for themselves.

Neoconservatives would like to deregulate, decentralize, and reduce the scope of government involvement in the business system. The actions they would take to do so include privatizating Crown corporations; freeing interest rates from control; ending government control over the sale of farm products, currencies, and metals (especially gold); removing direct control over prices and incomes; phasing out tariffs and farm subsidies; and subjecting labour unions to the law of contract enforced by the courts.

Under neoconservative control, the approach to social programs would be revamped by introducing a competitive structure. Supporters of this ideology claim that the existing welfare system is administered by a massive and costly bureaucracy, encourages free loaders, provides disincentives to work, and creates a child-like dependence. The alternatives they propose include systems of negative income taxation and vouchers. Under the present income tax system, some earnings are tax free but individuals are taxed on earnings exceeding the basic personal allowance at rates graduated according to the size of the excess earnings. Under a negative taxation system, individuals would receive a cash subsidy if they earned less than the designated personal allowance. In order to preserve the incentive to work, the subsidies would be graduated according to the size of the unused portion of the allowance but would not bring earnings to the basic allowance. For the negative taxation system to work, the existing welfare system would have to be eliminated.

A voucher system would involve the distribution of vouchers to individuals for such services as medical care and education. Medical and educational institutions would not be given funds, or even operated, by government. Instead, the funds formerly distributed to these institutions would be distributed to individuals in voucher form, allowing them to purchase services from privately- or publicly-operated institutions. Through this system, competition would be introduced, resulting in more efficiently provided services.

The neoconservative view began to receive increased attention in the 1980's with the ideological shift to the right that reshaped some government policies.

The linkage between neoconservatism and a range of policy issues was studied by Nevitte and Gibbins (1984) who concluded that the ideology can be quite influential over public policies in economic and social areas. Exhibit 4-6 identifies some organizations and individuals that advocate this ideology.

Exhibit 4-6

Examples of the Neoconservatism Ideology

Neoconservative Organizations

Organizations that advocate (or have advocated in the past) neoconservatism include:

- *The Charlottetown Society, Toronto*   A group of influential conservative intellectuals formed to stimulate discussion of public policy from a conservative viewpoint.
- *The Canadian Conservative Centre, Vancouver*   An independent research organization that advocates public policy based on the principles of free enterprise, limited government and individual liability, and on effective national defense.
- *The National Foundation for Public Policy Development*   A neoconservative think tank started by some members of the Federal Progressive Conservative Party. In October 8, 1986, a group called the Back Bench Committee was formed by right-wing Tory backbenchers in an effort to influence cabinet and create legislation reflecting their "conservative" philosophy.
- *The Northern Foundation*   A coalition of righteous political action groups formed in 1988 to act as a clearinghouse for the conservative movement. The groups involved include REAL Women, various English rights groups, various conservative think tanks, and the Reform and Confederation of Regions parties.
- *The National Citizens Coalition, Toronto*   A public interest group advocating "more freedom through less government." It claims to defend our basic political and economic freedoms, and to prompt free markets, individual freedom, and responsibility under limited government and a strong defence.
- *The Fraser Institute*   An organization created to redirect attention to the use of competitive markets as the best mechanism for providing for the economic and social well-being of all Canadians. It is funded by business and is involved in research, publishing, and in advocating free enterprise through a variety of initiatives.

Neoconservative Individuals

The neoconservatism ideology is advocated by such individuals as:

- Barbara Amiel, journalist
- Peter Worthington, columnist for *The Financial Post* and editor of *Influence*
- Michael A. Walker, Executive Director, The Fraser Institute
- Donald Coxe, chairman of the Toronto-based Charlottetown Society
- David Somerville, President, The National Citizens' Coalition.

THE EXISTENCE OF A BUSINESS IDEOLOGY

After identifying and examining the six ideological views, it is difficult to ascertain whether Canadian business has no ideology, a dominant ideology, or many ideologies of business. It appears that each ideological view has advocates and that aspects of each exist in the Canadian enterprise system.

The definition and characteristics of ideology provided at the beginning of this chapter might provide some insights. The ideological views discussed in this chapter certainly provide a "collection of ideas, beliefs, values and attitudes" that are publicly expressed. However, since there is a diversity of views, the ideas may not influence the "sentiment and action of others" toward one particular end. Instead of one scheme of thinking that represents society's views towards business, there are several. As business itself does not provide a concise ideology, it is doubtful that society's thoughts and actions relating to business can be influenced in any one particular direction. In other words, there is no vision for the future based on a single ideological view.

Some ideological views do provide a rationalization as to why business should exist and a justification for business actions and behaviour. All views, except collectivism, provide a frame of reference to explain the conditions under which a business can operate. However, none of the views make a case sufficient to prove that business has a single, clearly defined ideological position within Canadian society. The ideological views at the extreme ends of the spectrum from least to most conservative (that is, collectivism and neoconservatism) provide the most clearly defined ideals and objectives, but all six views advocate different means and ends. The diversity of views suggests too great a flexibility in ideological attitudes toward business to achieve the characteristics or criteria, listed that the beginning of the chapter, of a working ideology.

The existence of a business ideology in Canada has been overwhelmed by the closeness of government and business, and the lack of a clear mutual understanding of the role government intervention should play in the business system.

Closeness of Government and Business

Rea and McLeod (1976) suggest that there are several reasons business has consented to an increasingly interrelated relationship with government or, as they refer to it, a "public-private symbiosis" (p. 335). First, they argue that Canadian business never really desired competition and encouraged government involvement in order to escape the rigors of market competition. To support this position, they refer to business historians who argue that Canadian capitalists have been wary in their practice of competition (Bliss, 1973; Brady, 1950; Naylor, 1975). Second, Canada has never experienced laissez-faire as has Britain or the

United States, and therefore has "no background or tradition of unadulterated liberal capitalism" (Rea and McLeod, 1976, p. 335). There has always been a relative absence of competition and a substantial presence of the state.

A third reason for the relationship is that "the inextricable intervening of the state and commercial enterprise may be the result of our national instinct toward defensiveness" (Rea and McLeod, 1976, p. 336). This defensiveness was caused by a fear of the loss of the British market after Britain embarked on free trade and by the presence of a larger American industrial economy whose multinational corporations owned the larger portion of the Canadian economy. A fourth reason is the trend to bigness in the business system, a trend occurring in the United States but that may be even more pronounced in Canada. Finally, Rea and McLeod argue that Canadian tradition lacks the individualist-liberal goals of American society. There has always been a willingness to let the state shape and protect the national economy, and in this view the state takes precedence over the individual (1976, pp. 336–37).

This closeness of government and business means that the relationship between the two is bound to be complicated and at times adversarial. There is simply a lot at stake. Also, the closeness of government and business, in the past and now, suggests that any statement of business ideology will recognize a substantial role for government in the business system.

Pragmatism of Business

The closeness of the relationship between government and business has led to a "pragmatism" on the part of business that is difficult to reconcile with a business ideology. It might be argued that a "dual ideology" has emerged.

According to Davis and Blomstrom (1971, pp. 171–72), businesspersons are happily inconsistent in their view of government. On the one hand, they advocate a pure or free enterprise, while on the other, they decry unrestricted competition. Modern business philosophies are a blend of those aspects of the classical, or traditional, model and those of a contemporary model that best suit a person's needs at a given point.

As a result, business has a schizophrenic philosophy towards the role of government in the business system. Government legislation, or regulation, is viewed differently depending upon how it impacts business in general, or how it impacts particular industries or enterprises. If the government involvement is desirable in business's perception, financial interests take precedence over the value of free enterprise.

Pragmatism in Governments

According to Gillies (1981), government involvement in the private sector has grown for pragmatic reasons rather than for reasons based on any ideology. He claims that there has never been a broad acceptance of a political philosophy representing either left or right extremes of the ideologies discussed. He says that the government's role has grown and impacted the business enterprise system because Canadians believe that government is capable of doing many things better than can the private sector (1981, p. 7). Gillies also claims that there is no fundamental support for business as in the United States, and that Canadian business finds it difficult to influence government decision making. This is especially the case when many persons in government have little appreciation of the role of business in society and of how the market system works (1981, p. 52). Governments may resort to more pragmatic solutions as requested by other sectors of society, and in so doing neglect business interests.

However, there is another aspect of pragmatism that must be remembered when attempting to understand the relations between government and business. Political parties themselves may not have an ideology that they follow. The following quotation illustrates this view:

> ... The two governing parties—the Liberals and the Progressive Conservatives—are, in fact, essentially non-ideological, seeking instead to encompass the philosophical pluralism of Canadian society. Their membership covers the ideological spectrum—on the role of government and just about everything else—and their emphasis at any time is more a reflection of what particular wing or group is ascendant within the Party rather than of any overriding party ideology. In fact, inasmuch as there is an ideological element in Canadian politics influencing perceptions of the size and role of government, it is supplied by the New Democratic Party who continually press for more government. (Neville, 1984, p. 31)

Despite Neville's claim, even NDP governments have tended to the centre of political philosophy once in power. All political parties appear to become more pragmatic when governing.

The relations between government and business are impacted by two aspects of pragmatism: government decision makers are pragmatic and ignore business ideology, and there appears to be no political ideology on the role of the private sector.

No Dominant Ideology

If a dominant ideology is not evident, another explanation might be one of pragmatism. With pragmatism, it is assumed that no explicit formulation of ideas is necessary for determining good and right action. The attitude exists that what works is good. It is argued that individuals or groups can apply values almost intuitively by experimenting, testing, and modifying until a proper fit is found. This pragmatism has caused problems. For business, it has resulted in a conflict between any traditional ideology and what actually exists. For government, pragmatism has resulted in warped activities. Business ideology in Canada has remained largely implicit and our pragmatic nature has caused business to avoid any rigorous or continuing formulation of an ideology.

No dominant ideology of business appears to exist in Canada. Instead some sort of pragmatic compromise exists based on pluralism or a spectrum of ideological views. This situation is similar to that existing in the United States. Without a consensus on an ideology, it is not possible to rely upon an ideology to guide or explain the behaviour of business. The lack of a clear ideology makes it difficult to look to the future and to ascertain and achieve patterns of business and government action that are in the best economic and social interests of Canadians. It may also influence the mixed feelings Canadians have towards business, as discussed in Chapter 6.

SUMMARY

Six ideological perspectives were described in an attempt to identify a Canadian business ideology as follows: collectivism, the monopoly mentality, the mixed economy, corporatism, the managerial approach, and neoconservatism. None are satisfactory descriptions of how things are, but each exists in some form.

With evidence of the existence of aspects of all ideologies, it is difficult, and maybe impossible, to identify one ideology. The identification is further complicated by the ideological shifting that occurs over time: for example, the past few years have witnessed a movement toward neoconservatism. Any description of Canadian business ideology is influenced by the prominent role played by government as a stakeholder in the business enterprise system. Business and government have been closely associated throughout Canadian history. Pragmatism is an explanation for this relationship from both perspectives. No dominant ideology appears to exist that can explain the Canadian business enterprise system. However, descriptions of the six ideologies assist in understanding the complexity of the system as it exists today.

REFERENCES

Adler-Karlsson, Gunnar. (1970). *Reclaiming the Canadian Economy.* Toronto: Anansi.

Alcan Aluminum Limited. (1989). *Annual Report*, p. 4

Amiel, Barbara. (1979, August 13). A bridge over the tricky waters of neoconservatism. *Maclean's*, p. 49.

Amiel, Barbara. (1980). *Confessions.* Toronto: Macmillan.

Avakumovic, Ivan. (1978). *Socialism in Canada: A Study of the CCF-NDP in Federal and Provincial Politics.* Toronto: McClelland and Stewart.

Barr, John. (1990, March 2). In Worth Repeating, *The Globe and Mail*, p. B2.

Baum, Gregory and Duncan Cameron. (1984). *Ethics and Economics: Canada's Catholic Bishops on the Economic Crisis.* Toronto: James Lorimer.

The Bishops take on Conservative economics. (1983, December 19). *Business Week*, pp. 79–80.

Bliss, Michael. (1973). *A Living Profit.* Toronto: McClelland and Stewart.

Bliss, Michael. (1985). Forcing the pace. In V.V. Murray (Ed.), *Theories of Business-Government Relations* (pp. 105–119). Toronto: Trans-Canada Press.

Brady, Alexander. (1950). The state and economic life in Canada. In Rea and McLeod (Eds.), *Business and Government in Canada: Selected Readings* (2nd ed., pp. 28–42). Toronto: Methuen.

Canada. (1976, October). *The Way Ahead: A Framework for Discussion.* Working Paper.

Canadian Chamber of Commerce. (No date.) *Competitive Enterprise System: Myth and Response...* Montreal.

Canadian Labour Market and Productivity Centre. (1992). *1991–1992 Annual Review.* Ottawa; pp. 9–10.

Cavanagh, Gerald F. (1976). *American Business Values in Transition.* Englewood Cliffs, NJ: Prentice Hall.

The Church and Capitalism. (1984, November 12). *Business Week*, pp.104–112.

Chandler, Marsha A. (1982). State enterprise and partisanship in provincial politics. *Canadian Journal of Political Science*, 15, pp. 711–740.

Clement, Wallace. (1983). Class, Power and Property: Essays on Canadian Society. Toronto: Methuen.

Cunningham, Frank A. (1978). *Understanding Marxism: A Canadian Introduction.* Toronto: Progress Books.

Davis, Keith and Robert L. Blomstrom. (1971). *Business: Society and Environment*, (2nd ed.). New York: McGraw-Hill.

Director of Investigation and Research, Competition Act. (1992). *Annual Report for the Year Ended March 31, 1992* (Catalogue No. RG51-1992). Ottawa: Supply and Services Canada.

Dolbearne, Kenneth M. and Patricia Dolbearne. (1971). *American Ideologies: The Competing Beliefs of the 1970's.* Chicago: Markham.

Essays on the Left: Essays in Hour of Honour of T.C. Douglas. (1971). Toronto: McClelland & Stewart.

Fullerton, R. D. (1990, November 29). In Worth Repeating, *The Globe and Mail*, p. B10.

Gillies, James. (1981). *Where Business Fails.* Montreal: The Institute for Research in Public Policy.

Gillies, James. (1989, October 21). Close cooperation between government and business is essential," *The Globe and Mail*, p. B2.

Godfrey, Dave (Ed.). (1970). *Gordon to Watkins to You.* Toronto: New Press.

Hardin, Herschel. (1974). *A Nation Unaware: The Canadian Economic Culture.* Vancouver: J.J. Douglas.

Hartle, Douglas G. (1976, January 17). How to assess—and deal with—Pierre Trudeau's revelations. *The Financial Post*, p. 7.

Haynes, Arden. (1988, March 11). In Worth Repeating. *The Globe and Mail*, p. B4.

Heenan, David A. (1982, Winter). Ideology revisited: America looks ahead. *Sloan Management Review*, pp. 35–46.

Hutcheson, John. (1976, Winter). The capitalist state in Canada. In Rea and McLeod (Eds.) *Business and Government in Canada: Selected Readings* (2nd ed., pp. 43–59). Toronto: Methuen.

Laxer, Robert (Ed.). (1973). *[Canada], Ltd.: The Political Economy of Dependency.* Toronto: McClelland and Stewart.

League for Social Reconstruction. (1975). *Social Planning in Canada.* Toronto: T. Nelson & Sons. (Original work published 1935)

Lewis, David. (1972). *Louder Voices: The Corporate Welfare Bums.* Toronto: James, Lewis and Samuel.

Lind, Christopher. (1983). Ethics, Economics and Canada's Catholic Bishops. *Canadian Journal of Political and Social Theory*, 7(3), pp. 150–166.

Lodge, George Cabot. (1970). Top Priority: Renovating our ideology. *Harvard Business Review*, pp. 33–45.

Lodge, George Cabot. (1975). *The New American Ideology.* New York: Knopf.

Martin, William F. and George Cabot Lodge. (1975, November-December). Our society in 1985 — Business may not like it. *Harvard Business Review*, pp. 143–152.

McEwen, Thomas Alexander. (1974). *The Forge Glows Red: From Blacksmith to Revolutionary.* Toronto: Progess Books.

McLeod, J.T. (1976, August). The free enterprise dodo is no phoenix. *Canadian Forum*, p. 8.

Monopolists collide [Editorial]. (1992, May 4). *Financial Times of Canada*, p. 22.

Monsen, R. Joseph, Jr. (1963). *Modern American Capitalism: Ideologies and Issues.* Boston: Houghton Mifflin.

Mooney, Charles P. (1992, November 14). [letter to the editor]. *The Financial Post*, p. 55.

Naylor, Tom. (1975). *The History of Canadian Business 1867–1914* (Vols. 1-2). Toronto: James Lorimer.

Newman, Peter C. (1992). Airline message: merge or die. [Business Watch Column]. *Macleans*, p. 38.

Neville, William. (1984). How government decides. In James D. Fleck and Isiah A. Litvak (Eds.), *Business Can Succeed! Understanding the Political Environment* (pp. 28–45). Toronto: Gage.

Nevitte, Neil and Roger Gibbins. (1984). Neoconservatism: Canadian variations on an ideological theme?. *Canadian Public Policy*, 10(4), pp. 384–394.

O'Toole, James. (1979, March-April). What's ahead for the business-government relationship. *Harvard Business Review*, pp. 94–105.

Penner, Norman. (1977). *The Canadian Left: A Critical Analysis.* Scarborough, ON: Prentice-Hall.

Rankin, Harry. (1975). *Rankin's Law: Recollections of a Radical.* Vancouver: November House.

Rea, K.J. and J.T. McLeod (Eds.). (1976). *Business and Government in Canada: Selected Readings.* (2nd ed.). Toronto: Methuen.

Riddell, John and Art Young (Eds.). (1977). *Prospects for a Socialist Canada.* Toronto: Vanguard Publications.

Schaefer, N.V. (1983). The U.S. business ideology in the 1980's. Administrative Sciences Association of Canada *Proceedings*, 4(6), pp. 114–124.

Slotnick, Lorne. (1986, April 29). Support for unions urged by Bishops. *The Globe and Mail*, p. A11.

Stanbury, W.T. (1985). Government as leviathan: Implications for business-government relations. In V.V. Murray (Ed.), *Theories of Business-Government Relations* (pp. 15–55). Toronto: Trans-Canada Press.

Sutton, Francis X., Seymour E. Harris, Carl Kaysen, and James Tobin. (1956). *The American Business Creed.* Cambridge, MA: Harvard Business Press.

Teeple, Gary (Ed.). (1972). *Capitalism and the National Question in Canada.* Toronto: University of Toronto Press.

Thorsell, William. (1990, May). Let us compare mythologies. *Report on Business Magazine*, p. 109.

Trudeau, Pierre E. (1976, January 23). Speech as reprinted in *The Daily News* (St. John's, Nfld), pp. 1, 9, 16.

Vining, Aidan R. (1983, March). Provincial ownership of government enterprise in Canada. *Annals of Public and Co-operative Economy*, pp. 35–55.

Williams, John R. (Ed.). (1984). *Canadian Churches and Social Justice*. Toronto: Anglican Book Centre and James Lorimer.

Working man is being assaulted by economic order, says Bishop. (1986, November 12). *The Evening Telegram* (St. John's, Nfld), p. 3.

THE DECISION MAKERS: OWNERS, DIRECTORS, AND MANAGERS

INTRODUCTION

In the past, business initiatives were largely driven by economic or profit considerations. The key stakeholders of the business system were owners, directors, and managers, and they influenced the relationship between business and society. Owners are discussed at some length in this chapter as they were the source of capital, and still are, for the system. But, their influence may be shared in the future, as other stakeholders obtain power.

In Canadian society, these business decision makers are very prominent and may be considered an elite. Elitism, and the business elite, are discussed in the first section, followed by an identification of the owners of business. The final two sections of this chaper briefly discuss the roles of directors and managers as they have been traditionally, and still are for the most part, performed.

THE PROMINENCE OF BUSINESS DECISION MAKERS

Together, the owners, directors, and managers comprise an elite in Canadian society. In order to understand more about the business elite, it is first necessary to review the roles of elites in society before looking at the business elite in particular.

Elitism Theory

Rather than provide a definition of an elite, it is preferable to identify the important aspects of an elite: size, power, organization, and identity. An elite is always a small group or minority in society that is acknowledged as being superior, or the best, because the members of the group possess some valued characteristic or position. The elite group, though small, exercises influence, power, or control in larger society. This influence results from an ordered system of power—the members of an elite are organized in a definite hierarchy. The persons in the uppermost decision-making positions in any powerful activity are usually identifiable and visible as an "establishment" about which members of society are usually curious to learn (Clement, 1985, p. 562; McMenemy, 1980, pp. 95–96; Mitchell, 1968, pp. 64–66; Plano and Riggs, 1973, p. 25). Elitism theory is the study of the body of thought aimed at explaining the nature and role of these small groups and how they exercise influence or power.

Elites are inevitable within a democracy and it is important to understand them for several reasons. The study of elites locates the most powerful activities within society, identifies the uppermost or decision-making positions within activities, and specifies the characteristics of the people holding those positions (Clement, 1985, p. 562). There is not a single elite in a society, but a variety of elites usually referred to by such categories as political, bureaucratic, economic, artistic, military, religious, media, legal, and union. There is competition amongst them, for the influence and power held by any particular elite varies over time. Elites also cooperate to keep society working—there are linkages, and even overlaps, between elites and society (McMenemy, 1980, p. 98). Although elites are viewed in pejorative terms, as they promote the interests of a small group, society is dominated by such groups and they cannot be ignored.

Elites maintain power for several reasons. In extreme cases, an elite maintains power through domination by coercion and manipulation. Their compact size enables members to act together in a conscious manner (Miller, 1987, p. 131). This cohesiveness is possible because of similarity of social background, of attitudes and values, of power skills, and of personal and family contacts (Mitchell, 1968, p. 64). It is simply easier to communicate within the small, cohesive groups than it is in larger society, enabling the elite to be unified in action.

Elites do run the risk of alienating society and thus reducing their power. A skilled elite will maintain links with society and will be prepared to absorb new interests, policies, and persons. Loss of power or influence occurs when an elite group becomes too closed, its values clash with those of society, and a counter-elite emerges to dilute its power (Miller, 1987, p. 132).

There are challenges to elitist theory. Advocates of Marxism claim that elitism fails to explain the fundamental basis of elite domination of economic class relations. Marxism included belief in a dominant or ruling class, and emphasized economic power as the sole focus of power (Mitchell, 1968, p. 64). A more serious challenge to elitist theory emerged from pluralism. The pluralist model characterizes modern societies by many interests, all of them competing for power and influence: a small, unified elite seldom achieves overall dominance. Instead, different and changing groups hold influence in different areas of decision making, and pluralists claim the elitist theory fails to appreciate the multiple policies of decision-making centres in society (Miller, 1987, p. 132).

Porter (1965) and Presthus (1974) have written two comprehensive studies of elites and elitism theory in Canada. Both conclude that political and bureaucratic elites dominate decision making in society, along with the private economic sector as represented by large business and financial institutions. The next section discusses the Canadian business elite.

The Business Elite

The following three quotations from Clement's (1985) discussion of elites in *The Canadian Encyclopedia* highlight the prominence of the business elite: "those who control the economy are a powerful elite within any modern society"; "of all the elites in Canada, the economic elite is the most exclusive"; and "the most powerful elites, those that command the greatest resources in Canada today, are the corporate and state elites" (1985b, pp. 562–563). Furthermore, the dominant corporations, and their Boards of Directors, CEOs, and other executives are the power bases for the economic elite, according to Clement's *The Canadian Corporate Elite* (1975).

Clement was not alone in writing about the Canadian business elites. Peter Newman has written extensively on the business elite: of particular note is *The Canadian Establishment* (1975). Other comprehensive accounts are provided in *Corporate Power and Canadian Capitalism* (Carroll, 1986), *Controlling Interest: Who Owns Canada?* (Francis, 1986), *Canadian Capitalism* (Niosi, 1981), and *Circles of Power* (Fleming, 1991). Other books have examined business elites in various regions, for example, *Prairie Capitalism* (Richards and Pratt, 1979) and *Quebec Inc.* (Fraser, 1987). Business publications often provide listings of the business elite, for example, *The Financial Post Magazine's* "Canada's Corporate Elite" (1992). *Who's Who in Canadian Business* is published annually and serves as a reference volume by providing about 5000 business and financial executive biographies, listing about 100 professional bodies and associations, reproducing the Canadian Business Corporation 500 from *Canadian Business* magazine, and listing all laureates of the Junior Achievements Canadian Business Hall of Fame.

A listing of Canadian business elite is not given in this book but is readily available in sources such as those listed above. What is important is to recognize the characteristics of the business elite. Its members are identifiable, and it appears to be a fairly cohesive group. The business elite appears to be better organized and financed than others. For this reason, it has an impact on Canadian society, the government, and other elites. Critics of Canadian business claim that it has too much power—especially since it cooperates and has close linkages with other elites, in particular the political and media elites. Although the business elite has considerable power, it is not the sole form of power in society. Business influence has fluctuated, and the business elite must always be sensitive to not alienating society if it wishes to retain its power. The current emphasis on the stakeholder concept is a manifestation of pluralism. To date, the stakeholder concept does not appear to have eroded the power of the business elite, but it will be interesting to watch if it does in the future.

As the business elite is largely comprised of owners and managers, the following sections identify the owners of Canadian business and discuss the roles of managers and directors.

THE OWNERS OF CANADIAN BUSINESS

Who owns Canadian business? A quick response would be "shareholders." The list of owners in Figure 5-1 suggests that the answer is not as straightforward as this. The owners of Canadian business enterprises have been grouped into four categories: individual, corporate, nonprofit organizations, and government. In turn, individual owners can be subdivided into direct and indirect owners. Each of these categories requires some explanation.

Individual, Direct Owners

Owners in this category personally own equity in the corporation either as investors, entrepreneurs, managers, employees, customers, or producers. This breakdown is important as different issues relating to ownership arise with each type. The following describes these owners, and their prevalence in Canada.

Figure 5-1 Owners of Canadian Business

Individual Owners

DIRECT	INDIRECT
Investors	Mutual Funds
Entrepreneurs	Pension Funds
Managers	Trusts
Employees	Stock Brokers
Customers	Unions
Producers	

Corporate Owners

Corporations
Common Share
Portfolio Companies
Banks
Venture Capitalists

Nonprofit Organization Owners

Churches
Foundations
Universities

Government Owners

Federal
Provincial
Municipal

Investors

Individuals who personally hold equity interests for investment purposes, and are not involved in the corporation as entrepreneurs or managers, are referred to as investors. Those individuals who have purchased shares in corporations listed on a stock exchange are an example of this type of owner. There is some evidence of the extent of this type of ownership. A study conducted by the Toronto Stock Exchange in 1986, *Canadian Shareowners: Their Profile and Attitudes,* shows that in that year 13.4 percent of adult Canadians were shareholders, while the comparable figure for 1983 was 9.4 percent. However, a large portion of these shareholders are not viewed as active shareholders. These are individuals whose sole stock holdings are shares in the British Columbia Resources Investment Corporation (BCRIC) and who received their shares through a free distribution to the general B.C. population in 1979. When these individuals are removed from the equation, the percentages are 10.5 for 1986 and 7.5 for 1983. Included in these percentages are individuals owning shares through an Employee Share Ownership Plan (ESOP) at their place of employment (as discussed in the later section, "Employees"), and individuals holding self-directed Registered Retirement Savings Plans (RRSPs) whose contents include the shares of publicly-traded companies.

The Toronto Stock Exchange study found that in 1986 about 18 percent of the adult Canadian population participated in the stock market, compared to 13 percent in 1983 (the difference between these percentages and those stated in the previous paragraph can be attributed to ownership in equity mutual funds, which will be discussed in a later section). The increase in share ownership was attributed to many factors, including the growth in the economy since the 1982 recession, increased consumer confidence, and declining interest rates (*Canadian Shareowners*, 1986, p. 7). However, these participation rates are below those in the United States.

There is another observation that should be made, relating to investor ownership. The number of shareholders in many major Canadian companies has declined, for example, in 1986 BCE Inc. had 338 528 shareholders and in 1990 it had 277 295. Inco Limited had 84 320 shareholders in 1970 versus 37 565 by 1990. TransCanada Pipelines Limited had 24 259 shareholders in 1986 and 17 733 in 1990. There are probably two main explanations for this phenomenon: the growth of mutual and pension funds participation in the equity markets; and the continuation of merger and/or takeover activity. However, at the same time, Canadian investors have had a greater opportunity to participate in stock ownership as the number of listings on stock exchanges has increased. During 1986, there were 175, 214, and 182 new listings on the Toronto, Montreal, and Vancouver Stock Exchanges respectively. New listings continued to appear throughout 1987 before the sudden decline experienced by world stock markets in October, but new listings dropped drastically after that as the recession took hold. The number of new listings increased again during 1993 and the first part of 1994.

Entrepreneurs

Ownership of business by individuals, that is entrepreneurs, is a common form of ownership and has become increasingly so in recent years. According to Statistics Canada, small entrepreneur-owned business enterprises account for about 98 percent of the approximately 900 000 enterprises in Canada. Although larger in numbers, such business enterprises account for less than 20 percent of total business revenue.

Managers

Managers of "owner-manager" business enterprises that are larger than typical may also be owners. They fall into the "employee" category of direct owners, but have been identified separately because of the influence they exert. Like other employees, managers also participate in stock purchase plans as discussed in the employee category, but they may also have access to optional arrangements that enable them to acquire larger blocks of stock.

Management groups are often involved in a "management buyout"—the purchase of a business enterprise by its current management. Often the approach used is a leveraged buyout, which involves borrowing against the assets of the company being purchased. According to Anderson (1985), the leveraged buyout is the most common mechanism for turning managers into owners. He claims that there are no statistics to show the prevalence of management buyouts, but indicates that financial intermediators are offering an increasing number of financing packages to bring ownership within financial reach of competent managers. There are several reasons management buyouts may occur, including the desire of foreign or conglomerate owners to divest businesses that no longer fit their corporate strategies; the decision by existing owner-managers to retire or pursue other interests; the offer by an estate to sell the enterprise; and the existence of a conflict between business partners resulting in a decision to sell.

Employees

Employees are listed separately to indicate that workers, in addition to managers, may own all or parts of enterprises. Employee ownership can take several forms, including participation in an employee stock purchase plan (or employee share ownership plans—ESOPs); cooperation with an entrepreneur to refinance an enterprise and operate it as a going concern; and establishment of a worker cooperative.

Data on employee share ownership is available from a Toronto Stock Exchange (TSE) study entitled *Employee Share Ownership at Canada's Public Corporations* (1987). The study found that 63.3 percent of the 1011 listed companies had ESOPs. Two types of plans existed as follows: (1) share purchase plans, where employees were allowed to make voluntary purchases of employer's stock, and most plans provided some form of financial assistance for employee purchases; and (2) stock option plans, where employees were granted the right to buy a certain quantity of the employer's stock at a stipulated price and within a predetermined period. Of the TSE companies, 23 percent had share purchase plans and 53.6 percent had stock option plans. There was a total of 877 plans in the 640 companies involved (pp. 12–13). About one half of all plans were available to officers, directors, and other selected senior personnel, while the remaining half of all plans offered were open to most or all employees. Of stock option plans, 62 percent were geared to officers, directors, and senior personnel and 72 percent of share purchase plans were designed to include most or all employees (pp. 17–18). There are some interesting findings in the TSE report, including the following: companies with ESOPs were outperforming most other TSE-listed companies in their sector (p. 44); larger companies were more likely to offer share purchase plans to all employees (p. 16); and roughly 80 percent of all employee share ownership plans were introduced in the 1980's (p. 20).

Employees sometimes participate in ownership as a result of a buyout of the enterprise. Such buyouts are usually coordinated by an entrepreneur. There is no known compiled list of these buyouts, but examples obtained from the financial press include Beef Terminal Ltd., Toronto; Lar Machinerie Inc., Metabetchouan, PQ; Britex Ltd., Bridgetown, NS; National Hardware Specialties, Dresden, ON; Tembec Inc., Temiscaminque, PQ; Algoma Steel Corp., Sault Ste. Marie, ON; and Spruce Falls Power and Paper Co., Kapuskasing, ON. The buyout is usually triggered by the closing of a plant or enterprise for some reason. An entrepreneur usually manages the process as either an outsider or a member of internal management. The entrepreneur arranges refinancing, which includes contributions from some or most employees and almost always involves some form of government assistance.

The third type of employee ownership is the formation of a worker cooperative. The governments of Manitoba and Quebec assist workers in the formation of such cooperatives. Government support includes assistance in paying for a feasibility study and loans or loan guarantees of up to 25 percent of the capital cost to start the cooperative. According to the Worker Ownership Development Foundation of Toronto, there were about 500 such cooperatives in 1987 and the number was expected to double in two years ("Worker-Owned Plant," 1987).

Customers

There are two commonly known enterprises that customers, in effect, own: mutual insurance companies, and cooperatives. Holders of insurance policies from firms such as Sun Life Assurance of Canada, Manufacturers Life Insurance, and North American Life Assurance are also owners of the company. The extent and influence of this type of ownership has not been established.

There is more data on cooperatives. The revenue of non-financial cooperatives (excluding credit unions and insurance cooperatives) is about $16 billion, with a membership of 3.4 million (Sullivan, 1992, p. 4). Credit unions have assets in excess of $45 billion and a membership of 4.4 million (Hopkins, 1992).

Members of a cooperative are owners and vote for directors at annual meetings, thus claiming that they control the enterprise.

Occasionally other enterprises will offer shares to customers. Two examples are the daily Moncton *Le Matin* which offered shares in the newspaper to its readers; and the Newfoundland Power Co. Limited which offers a "Consumer Share Purchase Plan" to its customers. However, these enterprises are exceptions.

Producers

Producer ownership is through cooperatives in industries such as agriculture and fisheries. The cooperative share of the grain trade is estimated to be 70 percent; of the dairy industry, 50 percent; and of the fertilizer and feed industries, 30 percent. About 350 000 producers participate in the grain-handling, dairy, and fisheries cooperatives.

Individual, Indirect Owners

With "direct" individual owners, the ownership rights are held by those individuals. With "indirect" individual ownership, the ownership relationship is not as clear and straightforward because an intermediary institution exists between the individual owners and the enterprise in which investments are made. The indirect" owners in this category include mutual and pension funds, trusts, stock brokers, and unions.

Mutual Funds

Money contributed to equity mutual funds is invested, by fund managers, in a portfolio of shares in enterprises. It is estimated that Canadian common share funds represent 20 percent of all mutual fund assets. Ownership via mutual funds appeals to some investors as it allows them to participate in the stock market without having to make separate decisions about each purchase or sale of stocks.

Pension Funds

About 28 percent of the approximately $180 billion assets in pension funds is invested in corporate stock. Included in this total for 1991 are some major funds, such as those at Canadian National, with assets of $6.9 billion; Bell Canada, with $6.0 billion; the Ontario Municipal Employees Retirement Board (OMERS), with $12.5 billion; and the Quebec Pension Plan, with $41.1 billion. Also, a pension fund may own a substantial portion of a corporation's shares—as, for example, when the Canadian National fund owned 20 percent of Cambridge Shopping Centers Ltd. Equity held by pension funds and professionally managed on behalf of contributors represents a substantial ownership share.

Trust Funds

The number of trust funds managed on behalf of individuals is not known, but trust owners may participate in investment decisions, depending on the terms of the trust fund and its owner's preferences.

Stock Brokers

Stock brokers are listed as indirect owners even though, technically, they do not own shares. The Canadian Depository for Securities Limited (CDS) serves as a nominee holder for millions of securities on behalf of intermediaries. Ownership is recorded in a "book-based system" and no share certificate is issued to the owner. This system facilitates transfers of ownership as it only requires an entry in the records of the depository and the stock broker. The system speeds the transfer process and reduces costs. Until recently, these shares were not voted, and owners did not receive annual reports and other information from the company. Because of this system, it was difficult to ascertain the actual owners of shares as the owners' names did not appear on the enterprise shareholder lists.

Unions

A recent development has been the involvement of unions in the financing of business enterprises. An example is the investment fund created by the Quebec Federation of Labor. It has invested more than $245 million in Quebec companies over seven years. The fund has about 110 000 shareholders, and the purpose of the fund is to create new jobs and to preserve endangered jobs. It is estimated that 23 000 jobs have been created or saved.

An issue relating to this indirect ownership is whether or not the persons who manage these funds should play a passive or active role in influencing the corporation. This issue will be examined when the matter of who controls the enterprise is discussed in Chapter 11.

Corporate Owners

There are several owners who can be categorized as "corporate": corporations, common share portfolio companies, banks, and venture capitalists.

Corporations

Corporations often own shares in other enterprises. This inter-corporate ownership is widespread. A main source for assessing such ownership relationships is the annual publication, *Inter-Corporate Ownership* (Statistics Canada). This book lists over 65 000 corporations and contains information on the percentage of voting rights each corporation holds in others. This inter-corporate ownership leads to considerable concentration of ownership, an issue that has been extensively documented (a good summary is provided by Beck, 1985). One indication of this concentration is provided by statistics from the *Annual Corporation and Labour Unions Returns Act Report* (Statistics Canada).

Corporate control over the Canadian business system is also expressed in relation to the proportion of stocks owned and/or controlled by a limited number of family "conglomerates." Some indication of this control is provided by the fact that nine families dominate a large proportion of the companies that make up the Toronto Stock Exchange (TSE) 300 Composite Index. One estimate is that these families own more than 10 percent of the total value of the index, another calculated that they controlled stock worth 46 percent of the value of the TSE 300. About 20 of the TSE 300 companies are widely held, the remainder having at least 20 percent of their voting stock held by a single shareholder. These figures are much higher than those reported for the Standard and Poor's Index of 500 companies on the New York Stock Exchange, meaning that large corporations are more widely held in the United States.

Common Share Portfolio Companies

This type of company is a recent development in the Canadian financial industry. The company is established by an investment dealer or group of dealers for the purpose of holding shares in one or a few corporations. The first such company was established by McLeod Young Weir Ltd., a stockbroker, to hold Bell Canada Enterprise Inc. (BCE) shares. As this was the first venture to use this approach, similar firms are sometimes called "B. Corps."

The shares purchased are usually acquired through a private placement by a firm such as BCE or a bank. The advantage is that issue costs and risks to the corporation are reduced when selling the total issue to one purchaser. In turn the purchaser offers the public preferred shares and instalment receipts (or capital shares that resemble warrants) both of which are listed on the stock exchange.

This approach is attractive to investors. The preferred shares are issued at about three quarters of the market price of the underlying shares, and all dividends are received by the investors. The plan is to wind down this type of firm in a specified time, say six years, and the instalment receipt holders receive capital gains for the value of the shares in excess of the 75 percent original value.

Banks

Banks normally do not own business enterprises as they are interested in lending funds rather than taking an equity position, and the Canada Bank Act limits a bank's shareholding to less than 10 percent. As a result of financial restructuring following the business downturn in the early 1980's, however, many banks acquired equity in enterprises to which they had lent money. Debt investments were converted to equity ones in the hope that the banks could recover their money by selling the shares sometime in the future.

Most of this type of ownership is forced on the banks and, where the investments were greater than 10 percent, requires special permission from the Inspector General of Banks. Generally the conversions are from debt to new, usually nonvoting, preferred shares yielding something above the prime bank rate. Seldom do banks invest directly by cash purchases of shares. Banks are included in the list of owners of Canadian business as they now have substantial holdings, especially in the resource based industries, and in many cases play an active role in managing business enterprises. Corporate ownership by banks is expected to decline with improved economic conditions.

Venture Capitalists

Venture capital companies usually acquire part ownership of business enterprises for which they provide financial and management assistance. There are dozens of venture capital companies in Canada, and they invest in new, or established enterprises with growth potential that are unable to obtain needed financing from conventional sources. Venture capital investments are made at every stage in business growth, but often are made in speculative and higher risk ventures. The role a venture capitalist plays varies depending on the success and needs of the enterprise, and is minimized by the successful operation of the firm.

Nonprofit Organization Owners

Examples of nonprofit organization owners are churches, foundations, and universities. Investment or endowment funds in these organizations sometimes own stock in business enterprises. The extent of this ownership is not great, and any one organization seldom owns a large portion of a particular enterprise. However, the influence of these owners may be greater than their small holdings indicate. In particular, church groups have achieved a high profile by questioning aspects of an enterprise's operations at annual meetings and other public forums. The portfolios of universities are carefully scrutinized for any enterprises involved in what the university community considers to be unethical activities.

Government Owners

Canadian federal, provincial, and municipal governments all operate a large number of business enterprises, usually referred to as Crown corporations. Government owned corporations have been used extensively as instruments of public policy implementation, and are considered by some to be part of the

Canadian economic culture (Hardin, 1974). Crown corporations have been utilized by all political parties and have played a major role in public policy relating to transportation, financial services, trade, research, communication, agriculture, fisheries, energy, and culture and recreation.

The influence of government ownership of business enterprises peaked in the 1980's. During the latter half of the decade, several government owned corporations were privatized, for example, Air Canada and Alberta Government Telephones. In addition, governments relied less on the Crown corporation as a mechanism for implementing public policy.

Ownership Patterns

From the discussion of owners, a categorization of ownership patterns can be developed. Some corporations are widely held, meaning that shares are held by thousands of individual investors with no one investor owning a block of shares large enough to influence Board decision making. The five large Canadian banks and many utility companies are examples of corporations in this category.

Another group of corporations are controlled by one owner, either an individual, an institutional investor, or another corporation. One or more owners control sufficient shares to influence the operations of the enterprise. This type of pattern can occur with as little as 5 percent ownership, with influence increasing as ownership share rises. A third category of ownership is the 100 percent ownership of a corporation by one individual or entrepreneur, a family, or another corporation. Government ownership is identified as a separate category, usually involving complete ownership. The last ownership category pattern is one in which stakeholders other than shareholders exert influence, as with employee ownership. Figure 5-2 divides the owners identified in this chapter according to these five categories. The categorization is not perfect, but emphasizes the differences in ownership patterns that exist in the Canadian business enterprise system.

The Traditional View of Owners

This chapter outlines the extent of ownership of the business system for two reasons: to emphasize the different categories of owners, and to establish a context in which to examine changes in ownership in a later chapter. The main objective of owners, in the past, has been an economic one, that is, a return on their investment. Business was conducted with an emphasis on that objective. There was some logic to this in that owners provided the essential ingredient to the system, capital, and were the principal stakeholder, and the driving force, in the business system. This emphasis has changed and will be discussed in Chapter 11, Issues of Ownership and Control. Two other stakeholders represent the traditional view of business: directors and managers.

Figure 5-2 Patterns of Ownership and Categorization of Owners

Widely-Held Enterprises

> Investors
> Mutual/Pension Funds (if holdings small)

Control by One or More Owners

> Corporations
> Mutual/Pension Funds (if holdings substantial)
> Common Share Portfolio Companies
> Banks
> Venture Capitalists
> Managers

100% Owned

> Entrepreneurs (or Family)
> Managers
> Corporations

Government Owned

> Federal/Provincial/Municipal Governments

Stakeholders (Other than Shareholders) with Influence

> Employees
> Customers
> Producers
> Unions
> Trusts
> Churches

THE BOARD OF DIRECTORS

Owners, or shareholders, are represented by a Board of Directors, which—according to Section 97(1) of the *Canadian Business Corporations Act*—"shall manage the business and affairs of a corporation." The Board has the power to select, evaluate, and terminate employment of top management personnel (Section 116). The directors are required to provide shareholders with financial statements and an auditor's statement [Section 149(1)], and other financial and operational information required by the incorporation articles or bylaws, or a shareholder agreement. This information is usually presented as an Annual Report. Information on Canadian Boards of Directors is presented in Exhibit 5-1.

The role of the Board is to monitor and evaluate the corporation's activities, performance, and management in the best interests of the shareholders. The Board members are elected by shareholders and are thus concerned with the shareholders' primary objective, return on investment. Thain and Leighton (1992, Summer) identified the following five basic tasks of a board:

1) The appointment and supervision of the CEO and other officers. This task should include plans for management succession and removal of corporate officers, if necessary.

2) The direction and evaluation of strategic planning. This task involves participation in formulating plans, but also keeping management accountable for implementing plans and monitoring performance.

3) The representation of shareholders and maintenance of shareholder relations. This task involves not only representing shareholder interests but also reporting to shareholders.

4) The protection and enhancement of corporate assets. The board will be involved in major decisions relating to ownership, investments, acquisitions, divestments, takeovers, or insolvency.

5) The fulfilment of fiduciary and legal requirements as outlined in the *Canadian Business Corporations Act* (p. 21).

These tasks are performed differently depending on the pattern of ownership. In widely held ownership patterns, the directors' roles can be described as those of a fiduciary or trusteeship. As there is a tendency in such corporations for management to predominate, directors must strive to keep the shareholders' interests before the Board. At the other extreme, where one corporation is the single owner, directors will tend to act in an advisory capacity largely reflecting the shareholder's wishes. The role of directors in other ownership patterns is somewhere in between (1992, Summer, pp. 21–2). The effectiveness of Boards has been seriously questioned in recent years.

Issues Related to Corporate Boards

Boards of Directors and their operation have been confronted by several criticisms. The types of concerns expressed include the following:

- the selection process. In many corporations, management controls the selection of directors who as result may feel more obligation to managers than to shareholders.

- a relatively small number of persons serve as directors in several boards, thus giving rise to interlocking directorship conflicts. Managers in one corporation serve as directors in another, and the selection process for new directors is limited to a small circle.

- in some cases, corporate management also serves as the board, or dominates the board. This practice of "internal" board membership is considered undesirable.

- few women are appointed as directors, and representatives of other stakeholders (for example, customers, employees, interest groups) are rarely appointed.

- few Boards specify membership qualifications and duties, terms of office, and evaluation procedures.

In general, the effectiveness of directors in representing shareholders' interests has been questioned as they are often far removed from shareholder influence especially in widely held corporations.

Exhibit 5-1

Information on Canadian Boards and Directors

The following facts provide some understanding of the features of Boards and the characteristics of directors.

- There are about 16 000 directors of Canadian companies residing in Canada.

- The median size of a board is 11, but ranges from 3 to 38.

- A median of five meetings are held each year.

- Of directors, 62 percent are independent outsiders, that is, not members of management.

- The occupations most frequently mentioned for outside directors were independent businesspersons, financiers, or consultants; lawyers; and owners or managers of merchandise or trading companies.

- Women make up almost 6 percent of all directors.

- In 45 percent of all companies, the CEO and Chairman of the Board positions are held by one person.

SOURCE: Adapted from John Longair. (1990, March) *Canadian Directorship Practices: A Profile 1990* (Report 51-90). Ottawa: Conference Board of Canada; *The Financial Post Directory of Directors.* (1992). Toronto: The Financial Post.

The Traditional View of Directors

The traditional view of directors is not a very favourable one. Although they are required to represent the owner or shareholder interest, they appear to fall down at that task. Directors seldom own substantial shares in a corporation, and sometimes none, and are thus not motivated in their own financial interest. Directors who represent majority owners, usually corporate, are most likely to aggressively represent the owner's interests, perhaps at the expense of minority shareholders.

The traditional view of Board operation is also reflected in Thain and Leighton's (1992, Spring) discussion of the "old code" of Board member behaviour. The authors claim that in the past the following behavioural codes were widely accepted as standard practice for directors:

- display total loyalty to the chairman
- support management at all times
- be compatible, always trying to get along well and never letting differences surface
- be legally correct
- participate correctly and constructively, but within limits so as not to upset the chairman or your colleagues
- do not take the job too seriously
- go through the right channels
- be discreet by watching what you say and to whom you say it
- take your perks and keep quiet
- do not rock the boat.

The result was many Boards that were ineffective and did not adequately represent shareholder interests. James Gillies puts forth criticisms along a similar theme in his book, *Boardroom Renaissance* (1992a), and in an article, "The New, Improved Board Game" (1992b). Overall, the traditional view of the Board of Directors is not flattering. Many changes have been proposed, and will be discussed in Chapter 12, Reforming Corporate Governance.

CORPORATE MANAGEMENT

Corporate managers have been delegated authority by the Board to conduct all the day-to-day operations. Their mandate is broad and not overly restricted by the Board of Directors. A hierarchy exists in management, starting with a top manager of some type who may carry one or more titles such as chief executive officer, president, or managing director. Under this position are several lower-level managers, including vice-presidents, directors, and supervisors.

The Traditional View of Management

These managers have, in the past, been primarily concerned with economic objectives that ultimately lead to a sufficient return on investment for shareholders. The pressure may come directly from individual owners, but the decisions of owners through the mechanism of the stock market also influence management actions. Thus, managers have been driven by the need to make profits, especially in the short term. As a result, it has been difficult to get some managers to be as socially sensitive or as responsive to society as they should be for the long term well-being of the corporation and the business enterprise system.

Managers have also focused on one stakeholder, owners. In the past, most business decisions were made with the interests of this stakeholder receiving uppermost attention. Other stakeholders' interests—for example, those of suppliers, dealers, employees, consumers or interest groups—received less attention. Changes to this approach have slowly been taking place: they will be examined in Chapters 7, Social Responsibility; Chapter 8, Business Ethics; and Chapter 9, Issues and Stakeholder Management.

SUMMARY

This chapter has focused on the stakeholder who has, in the past, influenced the responses of business to society the most: the owner or shareholder. This stakeholder is the source of the business elite, discussed at the beginning of the chapter, and most likely advocates a neoconservative business ideology. Examining owners, directors, and managers helps explain the past behaviour of business enterprises— the interests of one stakeholder, the owner or shareholder, were emphasized.

But, the emphasis of decision makers has been changing and will continue to change in the future. The desire for profits has not lessened, but noneconomic factors are increasingly being considered in business decisions. Ownership is shifting, and some new owners are concerned about the role of the corporation. The attitudes of some managers are changing as they recognize that noneconomic objectives are important for the long-term survival of their enterprises.

Other stakeholders are increasingly being considered, as discussed in the following chapters on social responsibility, business ethics, and issues and stakeholder management. In Part III, the challenges to business from other stakeholders is examined. All of these concerns reflect changes in business's response to society.

REFERENCES

Anderson, Ronald. (1985, November 7). Managers moving into buyout boom. *The Globe and Mail*, p. B2.

Beck, Stanley. (1985). Corporate power and public policy. In *Consumer Protection, Environmental Law and Corporate Power, a Background Report for the Royal Commission on Economic Union and Development Prospects for Canada* (Catalogue No. 21-1983/1-41-50, pp. 152–219). Ottawa: Supply and Services Canada.

Biggar, Kimberley (Ed.). (1992). *Who's Who in Canadian Business* (13th ed.). Toronto: Trans-Canada Press.

Canada's Corporate Elite. (1992, November). *The Financial Post Magazine*, pp. 23–73.

Carroll, William K. (1986). *Corporate Power and Canadian Capitalism.* Vancouver: University of British Columbia Press.

Clement, Wallace. (1975). *The Canadian Corporate Elite: An Analysis of Economic Power.* Toronto: McClelland and Stewart.

Clement, Wallace (1985). Elites. *The Canadian Encyclopedia: Vol. 1. A–F* (pp. 562–563). Edmonton: Hurtig.

Fleming, James. (1991). *Circles of Power: The Most Influential People in Canada.* Toronto: Doubleday Canada.

Fortis Advertisement. (1988, February 21). *The Sunday Express* (St. John's, Nfld), p. 12.

Francis, Diane. (1986). *Controlling Interest: Who Owns Canada?* Toronto: Macmillan of Canada.

Fraser, Matthew. (1987). *Quebec Inc.: French Canadian Entrepreneurs and the New Business Elite.* Toronto: Key Porter Books.

Gillies, James. (1992a). *Boardroom Renaissance: Power, Morality and Performance in the Modern Corporation.* Toronto: McGraw-Hill Ryerson Limited.

Gillies, James. (1992b, April). The new improved board game. *Canadian Business*, pp. 74–78.

Hardin, Herschel. (1974). *A Nation Unaware: The Canadian Economic Culture.* Vancouver: J.J. Douglas.

Hopkins, Raymond F. (1992). Credit unions controlled by the people they serve. *The Evening Telegram* (St. John's, Nfld), p. 19.

Kitchen, Harry M. (1986). *Local Government Enterprise in Canada.* (Discussion Paper No. 300). Ottawa: Economic Council of Canada.

McMenemy, John. (1980). *The Language of Canadian Politics.* Toronto: John Wiley & Sons.

Miller, David (Ed.). (1987). *The Blackwell Encyclopedia of Political Thought.* London: Blackwell.

Mitchell, G. Duncan (Ed.). *A Dictionary of Sociology.* Chicago: Ardine Publishing Co.

Newman, Peter C. (1975). *The Canadian Establishment* (Vol. 1). Toronto: McClelland and Stewart.

Niosi, Jorge. (1981). *Canadian Capitalism: A Study of Power in the Canadian Business Establishment.* Toronto: James Lorimer.

Plano, Jack C. and Robert E. Riggs. (1973). *Dictionary of Political Analysis.* Hinsdale, IL; Dryden Press.

Porter, John. (1965). *The Vertical Mosaic: An Analysis of Social Class and Power in Canada.* Toronto: University of Toronto Press.

Presthus, Robert. (1974). *Elite Accommodation in Canada.* Toronto: Macmillan of Canada.

Richards, John and Larry Pratt. (1979). *Prairie Capitalism: Power and Influence in the New West.* Toronto: McClelland and Stewart.

Statistics Canada. *Annual Corporation and Labour Unions Returns Act Report, Part I - Corporations* (Catalogue No. 61-210). Ottawa: Supply and Services Canada.

Statistics Canada. (1992). *Inter-Corporate Ownership* (Cat. No. 61-517). Ottawa: Supply and Services Canada.

Sullivan, Jim. (1992). *Co-operation in Canada* (1990). Ottawa: Co-operatives Secretariat, Government of Canada.

Thain, Donald H. and David S. R. Leighton. (1992, Spring). The director's dilemma: What's my job? *Business Quarterly*, pp. 75–87.

Thain, Donald H. and David S. R. Leighton. (1992, Summer). Improving board effectiveness. *Business Quarterly*, pp. 19–33.

The Toronto Stock Exchange. (1986, December). *Canadian Shareowners: Their Profile and Attitudes.* Toronto.

The Toronto Stock Exchange. (1987). *Employee Share Ownership at Canada's Public Corporations.* Toronto.

Worker-owned plant thrives in Winnipeg after nearly folding. (1987, July 28). *The Evening Telegram* (St. John's, Nfld), p. 21.

CHAPTER 6

SOCIETY'S ATTITUDES TOWARD BUSINESS

INTRODUCTION

In this chapter, the attitudes of Canadians toward business are identified along with some of their underlying causes and particular criticisms. Business must be sensitive to attitudes towards it because if a strong anti-business mood prevails, there is a threat to the legitimacy of the business enterprise system. Finally, the point is made that attitudes toward business are constantly changing and managers must be aware of such changes.

SOME RECENT EVIDENCE OF SOCIETAL ATTITUDES

Attitudes toward business are indicated in a variety of ways. Some examples from the print media, polling results, and a government study follow. The *Maclean's*/CTV poll conducted annually provides some insight into how Canadians feel about business. In 1992, when asked "Who do you look to, to look after your best economic interests?," 27 percent of respondents said government; 53 percent, business; 13

percent, unions; and 7 percent did not know. Over the previous seven years, the number of respondents answering business has varied from 31 to 53 percent, indicating quite a strong commitment to the business enterprise system. When Canadians were asked "From your point of view, which of the following groups has the most honesty and integrity?," business executives did not do well. They were chosen by 12 percent of the respondents, while doctors were chosen by 24 percent, scientists by 21 percent, and university professors by 21 percent. However, business executives ranked better than some other prominent groups: journalists were chosen by 10 percent, lawyers by 4 percent, and politicians, by 2 percent ("Voices of Canada," 1993).

Decima Research surveyed Canadians' opinions of the competence of business leaders. In 1990, 45 percent of those surveyed felt that business leaders were unprincipled, versus 27 percent in 1980. In terms of ability, 59 percent felt business leaders were competent, down from 73 percent in 1980. This survey concludes that business leaders must take a look at their corporate image if they want to have any credibility (Strauss, 1990). Diane Maley, Business Analyst at Thomson News Services, responds in her column that business leaders don't deserve this poor image as most are honest, hardworking, intelligent men and women. She says the problem is that many business people come across as double-talking, self-serving, and ruthless. This perception has resulted because some business people have not been completely honest about the actual financial circumstances of their enterprises, have used annual reports to promote rather than inform, have not held employees or customers in sufficiently high regard, and have failed to handle the media appropriately (Maley, 1990).

A Yankelovich study, also done in 1990, concludes that consumers' confidence in the ethics of business leaders is softening. About three quarters of the respondents agreed with the suggestion that even well-known companies are not to be trusted without some type of consumer advocate monitoring them. Eighty-three percent of respondents felt that the larger enterprises in Canada need to learn to respect consumers. Overall, consumers felt that business communication was not always truthful, and that business was especially guilty of saying something just to make a sale (Strauss, 1990).

In 1992, the Department of Industry Science and Technology released a report entitled *Canadian Attitudes Toward Competitiveness and Entrepreneurship* (Fletcher, 1992), that documented the results of a survey of Canadian attitudes along with a comparison to American attitudes. It has been argued that Americans are more favourably disposed to business and capitalist fundamentals than are Canadians. Exhibit 6-1 presents some of the findings relative to the attitudes of Canadians, and Table 6-2 provides a comparison of Canadian and American attitudes.

Fletcher identifies three major findings:

1) Canadians greatly value achievement, believe in rewarding merit, and welcome the benefits of competition.

2) When comparing Canadian attitudes with those of Americans, Canadians compare favourably in the emphasis they place upon excellence, merit, and competition.

3) The high value that Canadians place upon the values of merit and competition enjoy relatively widespread support across most demographic categories (1992, pp. 38–39).

Overall, the study indicates that Canadians feel fairly positive about the business enterprise system.

Exhibit 6-1

Canadian Attitudes Toward Achievement and Merit in Canada, in Percentages

In a fair economic system:
1. all people should earn about the same (12).
2. people with more ability should earn higher salaries (71).
3. neither or undecided (17).

The profit system:
1. brings out the worst in human nature (17).
2. usually teaches people the value of hard work and personal achievement (61).
3. neither or undecided (22).

Competition, whether in schools, work, or business:
1. leads to better performance and a basis for excellence (73).
2. is often wasteful and destructive (15).
3. neither or undecided (11).

When businesses are allowed to make as much money as they can:
1. everyone profits in the long run (35).
2. workers and the poor are bound to get less (34).
3. neither or undecided (31).

Government regulation of business:
1. usually does more harm than good (27).
2. is necessary to keep industry from becoming too powerful (35).
3. neither or undecided (38).

SOURCE: Joseph F. Fletcher. (1992). *Canadian Attitudes Toward Competitiveness and Entrepreneurship* (Catalogue No. C2-199/2-1992E, pp. 4–25). Ottawa: Supply and Services Canada.

Overall, the above evidence doesn't clearly signal whether positive or negative attitudes towards business prevail in Canada. No doubt both types of attitudes exist in society. What is important to appreciate is that people's attitudes or

Table 6-2 Comparison of Canadian and American Attitudes Toward Achievement and Merit

Question	% in agreement with questions	
	Canadians	Americans
1) In a fair economic system people with more ability should earn more.	71	78
2) The profit system usually teaches people the value of hard work and personal achievement.	61	54
3) Competition leads to better performance and a drive for excellence.	73	81
4) When businesses are allowed to make as much money as they can everyone gains.	35	42
5) Government regulation of business usually does more harm than good.	27	28

SOURCE: Joseph F. Fletcher. (1992). *Canadian Attitudes Toward Competitiveness and Entrepreneurship* (Catalogue No. C2-199/2-1992E, pp. 25–34). Ottawa: Supply and Services Canada.

perceptions of the business enterprise system are influenced by many factors. The purpose of the following section is to discuss both those factors that create favourable perceptions and those that create less desirable perceptions.

FACTORS THAT INFLUENCE ATTITUDES

Many factors influence attitudes toward the Canadian business enterprise system. The following list discusses some of the more commonly identified factors that can lead to negative or hostile attitudes.

Standard of Living

A prominent argument used in justifying or supporting the business enterprise system is the standard of living that it provides. Most of the countries with a high standard of living have some type of market economy and are the wealthier nations of the world. The criticism that accompanies this argument is that societies with a business enterprise system are based on consumption. Business, critics claim, forces people to desire things they do not need in order to sustain themselves. Advertising, the manufacture of frivolous products, and planned obsolescence are particularly disapproved. The counterargument is that no one is forced to consume in such a system, and that it is up to individuals to resist social pressures to consume.

Decentralized Decision Making

Another factor of the business enterprise system that is considered to be desirable is the decentralized decision-making process involved. According to

Canadian values, the process compares favourably to a centralized system in which economic decisions are made by a few or a centralized agency. The bases for a decentralized system are individualism and pluralism: it is considered more desirable for many individuals to make decisions about the economy, rather than a centralized body or one individual. It is argued that decentralization allows for a quicker response to particular challenges in an economy. Pluralism ensures that a variety of interest groups have some input and can influence economic decisions made by business enterprises.

Allocation of Resources

Some argue that the efficient allocation of resources is more likely to occur with a business enterprise system as allocation is based on the price and availability of resources. However, critics of the business system challenge the efficiency claim. They argue that enterprises control prices, for example in oligopolistic industries, or that business enterprises control the availability of resources, creating artificial scarcities. In a business system, some of the costs of obtaining resources are not necessarily incorporated into the decision-making process—for example, in the past, the costs associated with pollution or planned obsolescence were not accounted for. Whether or not an efficient allocation of resources has always occurred can be questioned.

Self-interest

In a business enterprise system, the individual can behave in his or her own self-interest. Self-interest acts as a motivator, and provides the drive for profit that encourages individuals to get things done. In a competitive business enterprise system, consumers choose between businesses that provide basically the same good and service. Everyone working in his or her own self-interest provides a stimulus to the operation of the economy, even though it is referred to by some as "greed." Positive self-interest is intended to produce intelligent and informed pursuit of wealth. However, some claim that self-interest sometimes becomes cruel and malicious and at other times, dumb and hysterical, and that this is appropriately referred to as "greed." Self-interest appeals to many as a motivating force, but to others it is a source of negative attitudes toward the business system.

Inequities in Society

Some critics of the business enterprise system claim that a system based on a capitalistic market leads to inequities. Supporters of the system say that inequities are inevitable and necessary in a dynamic economy to provide incentive and prevent the regimentation of equality. The issue is deciding how much inequality is necessary to provide incentive, and how much inequality will be tolerated in society. A problem arises when particular groups in society are discriminated against economically to an extent that cannot be tolerated. Society's expectation may be for the "poor to get richer," which may not be satisfied in a system that, by its very nature, is not based on equal economic treatment of all members of society. A similar situation involving inequities comes about among regions of a country. This is particularly the case in Canada, where the market system has resulted in greater prosperity in Western Canada than in the Atlantic Region.

Class System Based on Economics

Inequities are associated with the issue of a class structure in society. One class structure in Canadian society may be based on monetary wealth, that is, persons with high incomes are of higher class. However, it should be pointed out that the business enterprise system is capable of disrupting existing class barriers and official hierarchies. Successful entrepreneurs and businessmen can rise to higher classes in society because of economic or business achievements.

Business Cycle

Business cycles are natural in a market system and probably are more accentuated in a business enterprise system than in a centralized economy. With periods of prosperity followed by recessions, the business enterprise system is vulnerable to criticisms because of the hardships imposed upon particular individuals and types of businesses at various times. On the other hand, it can be argued that business cycles are not completely undesirable. Recessions tend to flush unwanted products and mismanaged companies out of the system. It is unlikely that business cycles can be avoided in a market system as private and public decision makers have limited capabilities to predict and/or respond to economic signals.

Inflation and Unemployment

Two hardships associated with the economy and business cycles are inflation and unemployment. The cause of inflation is difficult to ascertain, and placing blame with government, business, or labour accomplishes little. Unemployment has also been higher in recent years. Both inflation and unemployment are blamed on the business enterprise system that operates in this country; however, it should be remembered that both inflation and unemployment occur in all types of economic systems.

Innovation

The business enterprise system is designed to constantly seek innovation. A large portion of technological developments has been the result of the efforts of business enterprises. This is especially true of the application of technological innovations. Some people criticize continuous and accelerating technology and social change, while conceding that technology has improved their material well-being.

A problem associated with this rapid technological change is alienation, particularly alienation in the work place. People are frequently bored, finding their jobs monotonous and unrewarding. It must be pointed out that this alienation may not arise from the economic system itself as much as from the particular stage of industrial and technological development. Work alienation is evident in all types of economic systems. At least in a business enterprise system citizens do have a choice, most of the time, to seek other employment—even if they have to accept less pay.

At any time, one or a combination of the above factors influences attitudes. Even though the factors can be listed, it is unlikely that there will be a consensus on which factors are the most influential. The list identifies factors that are included in any assessment of attitudes towards business.

CRITICISMS OF BUSINESS

Business is confronted with substantial criticisms. The sources of this criticism include business itself; government civil servants and politicians; some consumer activists and environmentalists; trade union leadership; some portions of the university community; and some members of the media. Various aspects of business are criticized, and the criticisms are wide-ranging and may, or may not, be justified. These include criticisms of the maltreatment of minority shareholders in takeovers; worker health and safety hazards; mistreatment of the consumer; pollution of the environment; demands for preferential subsidies that burden small taxpayers; and lobbying for preferential tax treatment.

The public may have too high an expectation of what can be done by this business, and this may lead to disappointment and criticism. The purpose of this section is to summarize the major criticisms even if they may be unfounded or incorrect, as they do exist in the minds of the public. Some criticism of business stems from current events such as corporate crimes, scandals, or alleged wrongdoing. Exhibit 6-2 provides examples of such wrongdoings. In reality, such wrongdoings represent a very small portion of all the activities conducted by business, but they receive substantial attention and are sometimes generalized to all business.

Critics claim that business is sometimes unresponsive to consumers, employees, its own shareholders, and the public, and are concerned with the plundering of natural resources. They claim that as business is motivated by profits, natural resources are wasted, and in the case of renewable resources, businesses are guilty of poor practices to insure future supply. Business is criticised for enjoying a symbiotic relationship with government that gives it inordinate power to serve its own interests. Some people feel that business enterprises abuse the power they exercise over economic, political, and social aspects of society. Some members of society have difficulty reconciling business's demands for less government

---

Exhibit 6-2

Examples of Corporate Wrongdoing

Kickbacks — These are payments or gifts by a seller to executives who were instrumental in awarding a contract or buying a product. Offering or receiving a kickback is a violation of the Criminal Code of Canada. According to one executive, kickbacks are "a way of life."

Stakeholder most affected: suppliers.

Insider Trading — Insiders are directors, senior officers, and shareholders holding more than 10 percent of a company. These insiders must report all of their company's stock market trades of securities within 10 days of the end of the month in which the trade is made. In addition, any person or company in a special relationship with a company listed on a stock exchange is prohibited from trading on the basis of undisclosed material information. Those having a "special relationship" include any insiders, employees of the company or of another company that is an insider and any person or company that has engaged in, is engaged in, or will engage in any business or professional activities with the listed company. This last group includes underwriters, lawyers, engineers, accountants, printers, public relations advisers, research analysts, and merger and acquisition teams in financial institutions. Insider trading is regulated under the Canada Business Corporations Act and provincial securities laws. Basically, it is illegal for insiders or those with a special relationship to profit from buying and selling company shares while processing information that has not also been provided to the public.

Stakeholder most affected: shareholders who are not insiders.

Stock Manipulation — This activity involves cooperating to buy and/or sell shares of a company so as to mislead the public into thinking there is genuine market interest in a company's shares. Active trading can persuade investors to buy shares, pushing the price higher. The stock manipulators then sell their shares for large profits. Manipulation also involves releasing misleading information, about a company and its prospects, that might affect share profits. It is illegal under the Criminal Code of Canada.

Stakeholder most affected: prospective shareholders.

Bid Rigging — Instead of submitting bids independently of one another, competitors consult and act in concert to prepare and submit bids for construction and other contracts. A variety of arrangements can be made among the conspirators. One possibility is for the company that puts in the lowest and winning bid to pay off the other bidders.

Stakeholder most affected: the business enterprises or government soliciting bids.

Violation of Copyrights, Trademarks, and Patents — Many possible variations of this type of wrongdoing exist, including unauthorized duplication of records, compact disks, videotapes, and audio tapes; copying computer hard- and software; counterfeiting consumer products such as designer fashions; and using a production process or technology patented by someone else.

Stakeholders most affected: the individual or enterprise who was the original/legal owner; sometimes consumers.

Embezzlement — This activity involves someone fraudulently taking money, securities, or other assets entrusted to his or her care and using them for personal gain. This form of wrongdoing is usually committed by lawyers, bank managers, or others who have been hired to manage funds. An employee may embezzle from his or her employer, and possibly through sophisticated manipulation of computer data files.

Stakeholder most affected: the business or individual embezzled.

Taxation Evasion — This example of wrongdoing involves deliberate action to deceive the government on some taxation matter. This action can range from submitting fraudulent personal income tax returns, to cheating on corporate taxes, to evading customs duties.

Stakeholder most affected: government.

Real Estate Fraud — Fraud in real estate transactions occurs when some misrepresentation takes place. Examples include falsifying documents, and misrepresenting the value, quality or state of readiness of a property.

Stakeholder most affected: customer or consumer.

Bankruptcy Frauds — Fraud occurs when the owners or the managers of a company disclose financial insolvency, and through their actions, are able to gain from the bankruptcy. Fraud of this type occurs, for example, when owners somehow remove the assets of the enterprise prior to declaring bankruptcy; when owners repurchase the viable enterprise after the goods obtained on credit from suppliers have been sold and creditors paid off.

Stakeholder most affected: creditors.

Insurance Frauds — These frauds sometimes involve submitting false claims on property and casualty insurance policies, or claiming the same loss with a number of different insurance companies.

Stakeholder most affected: supplier, i.e., insurance company.

Franchising Frauds — Franchisers sometimes fail to deliver on promised goods or services to the franchisee. The most serious incident of this type occurs when a franchiser steals the money paid as a downpayment for the franchise.

Stakeholder most affected: small, independent businesspersons.

---

involvement on the one hand, and its requests for preferential tax treatment, subsidies, or protection on the other.

More specifically, some in society criticize business for failing to provide employment for all who want to work, for promoting a biased distribution of income, and for providing a minimum standard of living for many. The failure of the business system to achieve equal results or conditions, and its inability to insure equality of opportunity concerns many. It is perceived that business has resulted in the formation of an "elite," a capitalist ruling class, that dominates economic decision making in society (Clement 1975, 1985). The corporation is the instrument used by this ruling class to achieve power. The increasing size of corporations has lead to the association of power with bigness. Critics of business argue that the bigness of corporations is inconsistent with capitalist ideology, which is premised on the existence of many competing, small business units.

The fear is expressed that corporations have become so large and powerful that they are not as responsible or accountable to society as they should be. Some claim that a "private" government exists that does not necessarily respond to society's concerns. This perception leads to a "legitimacy crisis" in that some members of society no longer trust business corporations to act in anyone's interest but their own. As some argue that business exists at the pleasure of society, they feel that limits should be placed on business to force it to be responsive.

In addition to realizing that only some of these criticisms may be valid, it must be recognized that all institutions in society are subject to criticism of some sort at some time. For example, churches, schools, the press, charitable organizations, the professions, and hospitals are all criticized, but few advocate their elimination. Over time, most institutions respond to legitimate criticisms and institute changes. Business—and its main institution, the corporation—behave in much the same way, as is examined in later chapters.

BUSINESS LEGITIMACY

Legitimacy is the belief in the rightness of an institution, in this case, the appropriateness of our business enterprise system to supply the goods and services required in Canadian society. Legitimacy is a difficult concept because it is something that either is or is not believed in; it is not necessarily a question of ethics or legality; it is normative and concerned with what ought to be rather than what is; and it has to be plausible yet is artificial because it constantly changes. Finlay (1979) discusses legitimacy when he refers to corporate credibility. He considers there to be two aspects of corporate credibility: (1) the co-efficient of aggregate believability, which involves the trust and confidence of society in the business enterprise system; and (2) the legitimizing function, which is concerned with the extent to which non-democratic concentration of economic and social power is perceived to operate in the public interest.

There are several important challenges to the legitimacy of the business enterprise system. The first involves the implications of a class system. Members of the upper class often have positions in business, the middle class generally supports business, and the working class tends to challenge the business enterprise system, especially during times of economic hardship—for example, during the 1930's depression. Some members of the lower class challenge the business system because of the bad feelings resulting from inequities and from excesses in the system, such as alleged excessive profits and corruption. Another implication of the class system is the adversarial relationship between business and the trade unions to which greater numbers of working-class persons belong. Trade unions are used as a mechanism to extract more from the business enterprise system for a particular group of employees. Despite working class reliance on trade unions and resentment of the system, the lower classes are not out to destroy the system as much as they are out to get their share.

Canadian society has been based on Judeo-Christian values and society, which have traditionally been suspicious of materialism. According to Bliss (1980), most Christian religions argued that there are nobler goals than the pursuit of wealth or material things in society. Bliss argues that many of the challenges to the legitimacy of the business system are based on economic ignorance. Finlay (1979) claims that the reasons for lack of corporate credibility are based on the public's failure to understand how business works. He goes on to explain that efforts by business to overcome this economic ignorance have not been successful, and elaborates on the failures of economic education programs, "telling our story" campaigns or advocacy advertising, and public relations efforts.

Bliss (1980) claims that the hypocritical attitudes business has taken toward government lead society to question the legitimacy of the system. He claims, and this argument is used frequently, that businesses have asked for government assistance in a great variety of ways—through tax concessions, grants, and tariff protection—and have requested that the free enterprise system be rescued when it got into particular difficulties in such areas as the automobile, textile, farm implement, and fishing industries. Although businesspersons speak highly of the free enterprise system and competition, most are reluctant to live in an unregulated competitive environment. Bliss argues that businesspersons are unwilling to criticize these assaults on free enterprise, launched from within the business enterprise system in the form of calls for government support. He claims that there is a conflict between support for the competitive market system and the interest in maximizing business profit as a result of government involvement. This inconsistency in attitude toward government confuses the public.

Other challenges include the argument that businesspersons do not set good examples in society. For example, some claim that businesspersons are rather aloof from the media, and thus their opinions are not publicly expressed for members of society to consider. The recent rash of takeovers and the trend toward bigness has been alarming to many in society. The trappings of power associated with chief executives alienate many people. Recently, the failure of many corporations—resulting in bankruptcy, shutdown, or downsizing—and the subsequent loss of jobs have soured the attitudes of many Canadians.

When one is referring to the legitimacy of the business system, the concept of power emerges. If the power of the business system is to endure, the general population must believe that the business enterprise system is using its power appropriately. Finlay (1979) argues that there is now a new set of standards for the public consent to the system, or belief in the legitimacy of the system. He argues that there is a very fragile interdependence between business and society, and that society's values shift. People are now more socially sensitive and more community-minded, and have values and ideals that transcend profits and economics. Finlay claims that the corporation's legitimacy and the public's approval of the system will be increasingly shaped by a broader sense of values that includes the treatment of employees, respect for the environment, commitment to product safety and public health, perceived openness and honesty, enlightened recognition of the public interest, and overall contribution to community, society, and the quality of life. The conclusion is that, to be legitimate, the business enterprise system must respond to the changing values and expectations in society. Therefore, society's attitudes toward business and the criticisms of business should be monitored.

CONSTANTLY CHANGING ATTITUDES TOWARD BUSINESS

The necessary monitoring may not be easy as attitudes are always changing. Olive (1987, p. 58) identifies the popular attitudes toward business between 1880 and 1987. He portrays the attitudes as shifting between positive and negative ones. The positive periods were the "Roaring Twenties" and the era of "Rampant Consumerism" (the 1950's and 1960's), while the negative periods were the "Robber Baron Era" (late 1800's), The Depression, and the "Psychedelic Sixties/Cynical Seventies." His observations are largely based on American events, but there no doubt is some application to Canada. The important point is that attitudes toward business likely do fluctuate, and recent experience provides some evidence of this.

The 1980's appeared to be a period favourable to business. Governments more receptive to business views were in power in Canada, the United States, and the United Kingdom. It was a period of some prosperity and materialism was in vogue. The watchwords of the 1980's were big bucks, borrowing, spending, and flaunting. Takeovers were common—often through leverage buyouts financed by junk bonds. Green mail circulated and executives were equipped with golden parachutes. Donald Trump exemplified spending and flaunting with his marriage, luxurious possessions, and corporate empire.

By 1990, the go-go positive attitude toward business altered as society recognized the greed mentality existing and the reputation of business was harmed. In addition, the recession exposed the instable financial basis for much of the expansion that occurred in the 1980's. Real estate prices dropped and lenders realized that many loans were made with insufficient, or maybe even no, security. Society became even more concerned with environmental problems, global competition, and market declines resulting in employee layoffs. Confidence in financial institutions declined as major trust companies failed (Central and Royal Trust), old and reputable firms went bankrupt (Birks, Imperial Optical), and major corporations suffered losses and downsized (General Motors, IBM). The "greed" attitude of the 1980's was overtaken by the "value" attitude of the 1990's. In other words, society is now less materialistic and more concerned with the environment, worried about jobs and financial security, and insistent on the quality of goods and services purchased. This is quite a shift from the go-go, greed attitude of the 1980's when business was allowed more freedom of action.

Several headlines from various sources illustrate this change of attitude toward business.

- "A backlash against business? Washington's tough talk about the market reflects the public mood" (*Business Week*, February 6, 1989, pp. 30–31)
- "Backlash against business" (*The Economist*, April 15, 1989, pp. 11–12)
- "Fighting back: The resurgence of social activism" (*Business Week*, May 22, 1989, pp. 34–35).
- "Cozy honeymoon with consuming public likely soon over for business community" (Thomson News Service, May 23, 1989)
- "Is greed dead? The party may be over for the money society of the 1980's. Flashy spending is out, saving and family are in, and helping has become hip. Credit yuppies in part" (*Fortune*, August 14, 1989, pp. 40–49).
- "Board takes on greed" (*The Economist*, February 17, 1990, pp. 71–72)
- "What comes after greed?" (*Fortune*, January 14, 1991, pp. 43).

Trends in the attitudes Canadians hold toward business change. Business people should always be aware of this phenomenon and be prepared to do something about it if it ever threats the legitimacy of the business enterprise system.

SUMMARY

The attitudes held by Canadians about business vary over time, and evidence is presented to illustrate this variation. A report entitled *Canadian Attitudes Toward Competitiveness and Entrepreneurship* finds that Canadians view business and the fundamentals on which it is based favorably even when compared to findings for American attitudes.

Several factors influence attitudes, including the standard of living largely attributable to the business system; the business practice of making economic decisions on a decentralized basis; the resultant efficient allocation of resources; the flexibility provided individuals to operate in their own self-interest; the inequities in society that result; the existence of a class system based on economics; the fluctuations created by business cycles; the occurrence of inflation and unemployment; and the amount of innovative activity generated.

The influencing factors can be positive or negative, with the latter forming a list of criticisms of business. It should not be surprising that business is criticized as it plays a significant economic role in the lives of all Canadians. The list of stakeholders of the business system encompasses any Canadian, for example, as an employee, shareholder, consumer, and so on.

The attitudes of Canadians toward business are important as they can undermine the legitimacy of business as an institution in society. Thus, businesspersons and managers must monitor attitudes and attempt to influence them, directly or indirectly. It is unfortunate that some corporate wrongdoing—for example, kickbacks, stock manipulation, bid rigging, and other practices overshadows the good practices of business and the suitable behaviour of managers. One thing is certain, the attitudes of Canadians toward business are constantly changing.

With the background provided in the six chapters of Part I, it is now appropriate to examine some general responses business has made to its role in society.

REFERENCES

Bliss, Michael. (1980, September). "Singing the subsidy blues," *Canadian Business*, pp. 128–132.

Clement, Wallace. (1975). *The Canadian Corporate Elite: An Analysis of Economic Power.* Toronto: McClelland and Stewart.

Clement, Wallce. (1985). Elites. *The Canadian Encyclopedia*, Vol. 1, A-F (pp. 562–563). Edmonton: Hurtig.

Finlay, J. Richard. (1979, Summer). De-coding the corporate creditability dilemma," *The Business Quarterly*, pp. 43–45.

Fletcher, Joseph F. (1992). *Canadian Attitudes Toward Competitiveness and Entrepreneurship* (Catalogue No. C2-199/2 - 1992E). Ottawa: Supply and Services Canada.

Maley, Diane. (1990, October 3). Businessmen also reflecting a bad image, poll shows. *The Evening Telegram* (St. John's, Nfld), p. 35.

Olive, David. (1987). *Just Rewards: The Case for Ethical Reform in Business.* Toronto: Key Porter Books.

Strauss, Marina. (1990, October 1). Public cynicism growing. *The Globe and Mail*, p. B3.

Voices of Canada. (1993, January 4). *Maclean's*, pp.42-45.

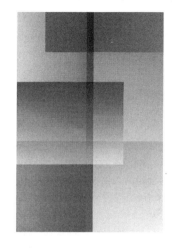

PART **II**

CORPORATE SOCIAL RESPONSIBILITY, RESPONSIVENESS, AND PERFORMANCE

Chapter

The four chapters in Part II cover some of the theoretical and conceptual developments in the areas of corporate social responsibility, social responsiveness, and social performance. The term presently used to capture all three areas is "corporate social performance" (CSP). One of the first comprehensive definitions of the term was presented by Wartick and Cochran (1985), who built on the works of several researchers. They defined the CSP model as "the underlying interaction among the principles of social responsibility, the process of social responsiveness, and the policies developed to address issues" (1985, p. 758). Wood (1991) felt this definition was incomplete and had drawbacks, and revised it to produce a new definition of CSP as "a business organization's configuration of principles of social responsibility, processes of social responsiveness, and policies, programs, and observable outcomes as they relate to the firm's societal relationships" (1991, p. 693). A framework for the corporate social performance model was outlined and is presented in Figure II-1 below. This model captures most of the developments providing a good overview. This table is briefly explained along with indications of where the topics will be discussed in this part or following parts.

Business and society are interwoven, and society has certain expectations of business behaviour and outcomes. These expectations are placed on all businesses because of their roles as economic institutions (legitimacy of the institution is discussed in Chapter 6). The expectations placed on particular firms (public responsibility of the organization) and the expectations placed on managers (individual or managerial discretion) are discussed in Chapters 7 and 8.

The process of corporate social responsiveness is dealt with in Chapter 9. The final chapter in this part examines corporate social performance, or the outcomes of corporate behaviour.

Figure II-1 The Corporate Social Performance Model

Principles of corporate social responsibility

> Institutional principle: Legitimacy
> Organizational principle: public responsibility
> Individual principle: managerial discretion

Processes of corporate social responsiveness

> Environmental assessment
> Stakeholder management
> Issues management

Outcomes of corporate behaviour

> Social impacts
> Social programs
> Social policies

SOURCE: Donna J. Wood. (1991). Corporate Social Performance revisited. *The Academy of Management Review* 16, p. 694.

REFERENCES

Wartick, Steven L. and Philip L. Cochran. (1985). The evolution of the corporate social performance model," *The Academy of Management Review* 10, pp. 758–769.

Wood, Donna J. (1991). Corporate Social Performance revisited. *The Academy of Management Review* 16, pp. 691–718.

SOCIAL RESPONSIBILITY

INTRODUCTION

The business enterprise system is the mechanism selected by society to produce and distribute goods and services. Originally, people felt that a business enterprise had fulfilled its social responsibility by surviving and realizing the maximum profit possible. The resources of society could be used by the business enterprise to make profits as long as the enterprise complied with the few rules imposed by governments to check abusive practices. The market system provided the regulation necessary to police the system, and profits provided incentive and insured efficiency. The work ethic and self-interest were the guiding principles of the system. By making a profit, business enterprises contributed to a growing, healthy economic system that provided employment and adequate incomes for all. In other words, corporate social responsibility was to operate profitably, and the corporation could not survive without profits, much less play a social role.

More recently there has been a belief that business exists for more than profits (or economic goals), with the public expecting something else from business. As a result, the original concept of social responsibility involving the maximization of profits has been modified. Although profits are to be made, social, as well as economic, goals are to receive attention. Society depends on business to achieve social as well as economic goals, that is, social responsibilities are placed on business.

The issue of social responsibility cannot be easily resolved. To illustrate, consider the following questions: How should corporate performance in society be judged apart from traditional economic standards? Are there goals and measures that individuals inside and outside the corporation can use for guidance? Given the relationship between the corporation and its social environment, what is the scope of managerial responsibility? To what extent should the corporation involve itself in social concerns? How do corporations typically respond to social involvement issues? Is there a common process that will enhance the corporation's understanding of corporate social performance?

It must be appreciated that corporate social responsibility and a corporation's social performance are two of many factors in an extremely complex business environment in which the corporate manager is called upon to operate the business. Various stakeholders are constantly seeking a different role for business in society. Government continues to influence the business enterprise system and to change the forms and manner of this influence. Technological change is occurring at a very rapid pace. The public media advises citizens quickly of events in the business world, allowing for quick public reaction.

This chapter defines social responsibility, reviews the case for business social involvement, reviews the arguments against involvement, and concludes with some business reactions to corporate social responsibility.

DEFINING SOCIAL RESPONSIBILITY

There have been many definitions of corporate social responsibility, and rather than giving one, listing the key elements found in various definitions may be more insightful. Buchholz (1991, p. 19) identified five key elements found in most, if not all, definitions.

1) Corporations have responsibilities that go beyond the production of goods and services at a profit.
2) These responsibilities involve helping to solve important social problems, especially those they have helped create.
3) Corporations have a broader constituency than stockholders alone.
4) Corporations have impacts that go beyond simple marketplace transactions.
5) Corporations serve a wider range of human values than can be captured by a sole focus on economic values.

According to Wood (1991, p. 695), the "basic idea of corporate social responsibility is that business and society are interwoven rather than distinct entities" and that expectations are placed on business due to its three roles: as an institution in society, as a particular corporation or organization in society, and as individual managers who are moral actors within the corporation. These roles result in three levels of analysis—institutional, organizational, and individual—and can be expressed in terms of three principles of corporate social responsibility—legitimacy, public responsibility, and managerial discretion (refer to Figure II-1).

The principle of *legitimacy* refers to society's granting of legitimacy and power to business, and business's appropriate use of that power and the possibility of losing that power. Corporate social responsibility defines the institutional relationship between business and society that is expected of any corporation. Society has the right to grant this power, to impose a balance of power among its institutions, and to define their legitimate functions. The focus is on business's obligations as a social institution, and society takes away power or imposes some sort of sanction on business if expectations are not met.

The principle of *public responsibility* means that business is responsible for outcomes related to its areas of involvement with society. The level of application is organizational, that is the corporation, and confines business's responsibility to those problems related to a firm's activities and interest. This principle includes the view that firms are responsible for solving the problems they create. The nature of social responsiblity will vary from corporation to corporation as each firm impacts society's resources in different ways or creates different problems. The principle involves emphasizing each corporation's relationship to its specific social, ethical and political environment.

Last, the principle of *managerial discretion* refers to managers as moral actors who are obliged to exercise such discretion as is available to them to achieve socially responsible outcomes. Discretion is involved as the actions of managers are not totally prescribed by corporate procedures. The level of application is the individual who has the choices, opportunities, and personal responsibility to achieve the corporation's social responsibility (Wood, 1991, pp. 695–700).

This discussion of definitions could be extensive, but the purpose is to provide an appreciation for social responsibility. Further understanding of the concept, its origins, and its interpretations is achieved by summarizing some of the debate over social responsibility.

THE SOCIAL RESPONSIBILITY DEBATE

The discussion of the appropriateness and meaning of social responsibility continues. This debate is treated in two ways in this chapter: through a listing of the arguments for and against social responsibility, and through a summary of the theories used to represent the variety of views toward social responsibility.

The Case For Involvement

There are many arguments in support of business involvement in society, that is, in support of the social responsibility or social responsiveness of business. These arguments are summarized below.

1) Business should operate in such a way as to fulfil the public needs, or expectations. It should do so for a very pragmatic reason: it is believed in some quarters that business functions by the consent of society and therefore must be sure to satisfy the needs of society. In other words, the existence of the business enterprise system depends on its acceptance by society. If business is to prevent criticisms or mutinous behaviour, it must be receptive to what is happening in society and respond in some way.

2) A social responsibility role should be undertaken in order to prevent some public criticism and discourage further government involvement or regulation. This is a defensive approach designed to offset possible government action against those in the business system who use their power irresponsibly. The threat of nationalization of business enterprises is sufficient to motivate some businesses to become involved in social responsibility endeavours.

3) Business must realize that society is a "system" of which corporations are a part, and that the system is interdependent. Therefore, if business institutions interact with others in society, there is a need for social involvement—along with increasing interdependence comes the need to participate in the complex system that exists in society. There are many mutual involvements among individuals, groups, and organizations in society, or among subsectors of society. Business is vulnerable to the actions or events that occur in other subsectors.

4) Social responsibility is in the stockholder's interest—that is, being socially responsible will simply be profitable—especially in the long term.

5) A poor social responsibility role on the part of the corporation means poor management to some investors. They view failure to perform in society's interest in much the same way as they view the corporation's failure to perform in financial matters.

6) Business must realize that social problems can become opportunities, or can lead to profits. Expenditures on pollution abatement may result in the retrieval of materials that were formerly disposed of as waste, or may allow for equipment to operate more efficiently, therefore generating more profits on future operations.

7) With regard to social responsibility matters, business should take a long-run as opposed to a short-run view. Profits may increase in the long run as a result of actions taken at the present time. Judging the benefits of social responsiblity becomes a simple matter of ascertaining whether or not it is in the corporation's longest-term self-interest to be conscious of social responsibility matters.

8) Business enterprises must be concerned with the public image and the good-will generated by responsible social actions.

9) Business should be given an opportunity to solve some social problems. The logic behind this argument is that business can solve problems as well as government can and that it certainly cannot do any worse than government has in the past: business possesses the expertise, in its managers and executives, to develop plans to overcome social problems.

10) Preventing is better than curing. It is better to take a proactive stance than a reactive one.

11) Businesspeople are also concerned citizens and humans who are interested in social matters. It is not appropriate for them to ignore social matters.

The Counterargument

Although there are several arguments for social involvement by business corporations, there are many arguments against business social involvement, including the following.

1) Profit maximization is the primary purpose of business and to have any *NEO LIBERAL* other purpose is not socially responsible. To have other than a profit maximizing goal is to sabotage the market mechanism and distort the allocation of resources. Generally then, it is contrary to the basic function of business to become involved in social matters. It should not be forgotten that business is an economic institution, not a social one, and its only responsibility is to manage efficiently within the law. The company would be irresponsible if it did not pursue profits and operate in the efficient market.

2) Business corporations are responsible to the shareholders and, in effect, *NEO-LIBERAL* have no authority to operate in the social area. When a corporation becomes involved in social matters, there is a question of legitimacy. Even if corporations are sufficiently competent and powerful to bring about social changes in matters considered beyond the range of their immediate involvement, there is a real question as to whether such endeavours are appropriate.

3) Social policy is the jurisdiction of governments, not business. *Collectivism*

4) Business lacks training in social issues, and lacks social skills necessary to carry out social programs. In other words, business is not competent to undertake social responsibility tasks.

5) Social responsibility is viewed by some as another excuse to let big business *Neo Liberal* increase its power. The increase in power comes as a result of business becoming involved in social as well as economic matters. Imposing business values on social issues may lead to inappropriate domination: Business already has sufficient power, and it would be inappropriate to extend that power to other matters.

N-L

6) Business involvement in social matters increases costs—not only costs to the organization but possibly even social costs—instead of decreasing them. This in turn may lead to business failures.

7) There is no acknowledged source of reliable guidance or policy for business in social responsibility questions, and it is not easy to make the choice between responsible and selfish action in social issues. Social responsibility is an elusive concept for which few standards are available to evaluate and control the actions of corporations.

8) As institutions in society, business corporations cannot be held accountable for their actions in a way sufficient to satisfy demands for social involvement. Institutions involved in social matters should be accountable to society for that involvement. At the present time, there are few mechanisms available to ensure business corporations are accountable for their social actions.

9) There is divided support in the business community for social involvement, and as a result there is unlikely to be a very satisfactory treatment of social issues by business.

These listings summarize the reasons for and against corporations assuming social responsibility for their activities. The following section also addresses this debate but from a different perspective, summarizing the different corporate social responsibility theories that exist.

Social Responsibility Theories

Klonoski (1991, p. 16) sets out to address a fundamental question: "Does business and the corporation have a social nature, or not?" The answer given by any stakeholder can be associated with a theory of corporate social responsibility, and these theories fall into three categories: amoral, personal, and social. Table 7-1 lists the categories and briefly describes the theories in each.

The Amoral View

This category represents a traditional view of business and the role of the corporation, that is, the corporation is seen as "a highly individualized rights-bearing economic entity designed for profit making and legitimatized by the laws governing incorporated businesses" (Klonoski, 1991, p. 16). Free market defenders and legal recognition theorists are among those holding this view including some who believe there is no such thing as corporate social responsibility.

The "amoral" view should be carefully defined and not confused with an "immoral" view. Amoral refers to an activity without a moral quality, that is,

Table 7-1 Summary of the Corporate Social Responsibility Debate

Alternate View of the Corporation	Theory	Description
AMORAL	Fundamentalism	The corporation has no or very little social responsibility.
	Legal Recognition	The corporation is an autonomous entity and not the creation of society.
	Functionalism	Groups in society should not encroach on each other's provinces of behaviour.
	Individual Agreement	Corporations can be socially responsible, but only within the limits of a prior contractual agreement with stockholders.
	Traditional Stockholders Model	Beyond individual agreements, corporations are not ethically required to be socially responsible; they are responsibe only to monies and to maximize profits.
	Role-Based Approach	The role of the corporation determines its responsibilities.
PERSONAL	Moral Person/ Moral Agents	Corporations are collectives that act like individuals; they exist as legal persons and can be held responsible for their actions.
SOCIAL	Social Contract	An implicit social agreement exists between business and society that determines the social nature of the corporation, identifies its duties and rights, and is considered to be an evolving document.
	Ideological/Historical	Society evolves and history gives rise to new social needs, societal demands, and changes in social values to which business is expected to contribute.
	Stakeholder	There is a social responsibility function of the interrelationships developed by the corporation with groups that have a stake. Also referred to as "constituency theory."
	Legal Creator	The corporation is a creature of law, existing only in contemplation of law, and is thus made by society for the common good of society. A similar view is referred to as "legal framework."

Table 7-1 Summary of the Corporate Social Responsibility Debate (cont.)

Alternate View of the Corporation	Theory	Description
	Social Permission	Society can legitimately demand that the corporation do certain kinds of activities and if the corporation is harming the public good, can restrict or eliminate its activities.
	Corporate Citizenship	With the charter, corporation becomes a legal entity with standing as a citizen similar to that of the individual and has duties as well as rights and privileges.
	Property-Based	Corporations legitimize themselves as common property with responsibilities expected to extend to the common good. The corporation as a privately held good should be used in a socially responsible way because it is also public or common property.
	Social Impact	Business has the power to change society and must consider social responsibilities.
	Interpenetration	Business is so intertwined with society that it cannot avoid social responsibilities.
	Moral Gratitude/ Reciprocity-Based	As business operates within a social system, it should be socially responsible out of "gratitude" or have a moral responsibility to "reciprocate." Corporations benefit from and thus owe society.
	Utilitarian	It is to the benefit of society or "for the greatest good for the greatest number of people" that corporations are socially responsible; social responsibility is in business's best interest.
	Virtue-Based	This view focuses on the development of good or morally virtuous people instead of principles or contracts. A morally responsible business is one in which good people make decisions based on generally developed moral character, self-discipline, moderation, hard work, courage, creativity, good humour, and intelligence.

SOURCE: Summarized from Richard J. Klonoski. (1991, July/August). Foundational considerations in the corporate social responsibility debate. *Business Horizons*, pp. 9–16.

something that is neither moral nor immoral: moral standards, restraints, or principles do not exist. This is quite different from immoral, which denotes activities that are not moral and do not conform to usually accepted or established patterns of conduct. Amoral means lacking in morals, good or bad, while immoral connotes evil or licentious behaviour. Although in some contexts being amoral is considered as reprehensible as being immoral, that is not the position taken by most advocates of the theories listed in this category.

The Personal View

This view discusses the nature of the corporation in ascertaining whether or not it can be held accountable. The question involved is whether corporations are "moral agents" or "full-fledged" moral persons. This question has been extensively discussed in the literature and Klonoski (1991) provides a brief summary.

Those arguing that corporations are persons claim that corporations are responsible for their actions in a way comparable to the actions taken by natural persons or individuals. Therefore, the corporation can be morally blamed in a way identical or very similar to natural persons. Goodpaster and Matthew (1982) pose the question "Can a corporation have a conscience?" in a *Harvard Business Review* article, and conclude that conscience can reside in the organization. Others supporting the view that corporations should be considered as persons and be held morally responsible include French (1979), DeGeorge (1990), Hoffman and Frederick (1986), and Donaldson (1985).

A strong counterargument in the literature claims that corporations are not persons (Gibson, 1986; Danley, 1990; Velasquez, 1990). Supporters of this view argue that it is not possible to impose moral sanctions or punishments on corporations as corporations. It is possible to blame or punish the people who work for or manage the corporation but not the corporation itself. Some punishments, such as fines, are in effect paid by shareholders or passed on as costs to consumers. An argument is that corporations lack the capacity to reciprocate morally. They may be made to respond to social harms but because of their structure and function, they will do so in a self-interested way (Klonoski, 1991).

The debate over whether or not the corporation can be seen as a moral person does not provide an answer as to whether or not the corporation is a social institution. Those claiming that the corporation is a person believe that it is socially responsible for its impact on society, and that it can be held morally accountable for its actions in the social sphere. Those who do not consider the corporation to be a person say that claims against the corporation by society need a different basis than that provided by the moral person or agency theory. To complicate the discussion there is a position between these two: the "personal" view fits between the amoral and social views. For an example of this type of view, Ewin (1991) claims that corporations are moral persons in that they have rights and duties, but their moral personality is severely limited. The following quotation summarizes Ewin's position:

> Because they are artificial people and not "natural" people, corporations lack the emotional makeup necessary to the possession of virtues and vices. Their moral personality is exhausted by their legal personality. Corporations can have rights and duties; they can exercise the rights through their agents, and they can in the same way fulfil their duties. If necessary, they can be forced to fulfil their duties. The moral personality of a corporation would be at best a Kantian sort of moral personality, one restricted to issues of requirement, rights, and duties. It could not be the richer moral life of virtues and vices that is lived by the shareholders, the executives, the shopfloor workers, the unemployed, and "natural" people in general. (Ewin, 1991, p. 755)

The personal view leaves the debate unresolved. However, the arguments favouring the treatment of corporations as persons lead to the next theoretical view of corporate social responsibility: the social view.

The "Social" View

This view holds that the activities of corporations occur within an interpersonal and, most likely, social context. The corporation is considered a social institution in society, with social responsibilities. But, the social nature of business can rest in many different theories, as outlined in Table 7-1. The extent of corporate social responsibility depends on the theoretical foundation used to support the view (Klonoski, 1991, pp. 11–12).

It is argued that the corporation should be considered a social institution as it exists because individuals come together to achieve some objective related to the provision of goods and services. Today, corporations exist because society implicitly sanctions them to operate in that form. Many in society believe that corporations now operate within the "social" view of corporate social responsibility despite the continuing claims of those who argue the "amoral" view, with its incomplete vision of the corporation operating as a private institution with a solely economic purpose.

Many theories and frameworks have been presented to describe corporate social responsibility. Some of them overlap and some parallel the arguments for and against corporate social involvement. The existence of numerous theories supporting corporate social responsibility makes it difficult to find a comprehensive and definitive definition, as mentioned in the Defining Social Responsibility section.

The literature contains numerous models of social responsibility, and one has been selected for presentation. Carroll's (1991) pyramid of corporate social responsibility is a practical framework for managers: it incorporates economic, legal, social, and ethical responsibilities.

THE PYRAMID OF CORPORATE SOCIAL RESPONSIBILITY

One way to view corporate social responsibility is through Carroll's Pyramid (1991) which he claims presents the concept such that social responsibility will be accepted by a conscientious business person. There are four kinds of social responsibility—economic, legal, ethical, and philanthropic—that can be depicted in a pyramid, as presented in Figure 7-1. Carroll contends that all of these responsibilities have always existed to some degree, but ethical and philanthropic responsibilities have only become significant in recent years.

Economic responsibilities relate to business's provision of goods and services in society. Profits result from this activity and are necessary for any other responsibilities to be carried out. It is assumed that corporations will be as profitable as possible, maintain a strong competitive position, and maintain a high level of operating efficiency.

Society expects business to conform to laws and regulations, formulated by governments that act as the ground rules under which business must operate. Corporations are expected to pursue profits within the framework of the law, which establishes what are considered fair operations. Society expects that all goods and services and relationships with stakeholders will meet at least minimal legal requirements.

Ethical responsibilities include those activities that are not expected or prohibited by society as economic or legal responsibilities. Standards, norms, or expectations that reflect concern for select stakeholder input is fair, just, or in keeping with their moral rights. Ethics or values may be reflected in laws or regulations, but ethical responsibilities are seen as embracing the emerging values and norms that society expects of business even if not required by law presently. These responsibilities are more difficult for business to deal with as they are often ill-defined or continually under public debate. Ethical responsibilities also involve the fundamental ethical principles of moral philosophy, such as justice, human rights, and utilitarianism. The changing or emerging ethical responsibilities are constantly pushing legal responsibilities to broaden or expand, while at the same time expecting business's ethical behaviour to go beyond mere compliance with laws and regulations.

Philanthropic responsibilities involve being a good corporate citizen and include active participation in acts or programs to promote human welfare or goodwill. Examples are contributions to the arts, charities, and education. Such responsibilities are not expected in an ethical or moral sense, making philanthropy more discretionary or voluntary on the part of business even though society may have some such expectations of business.

Carroll views the pyramid as a basic building block structure with economic performance as a foundation. At the same time, business is expected to obey the law, behave ethically, and be a good corporate citizen. Although the responsibilities are portrayed as separate elements, in practice they are not mutually exclusive;

Figure 7-1 Carroll's Pyramid of Corporate Social Responsibility

**PHILANTHROPIC
Responsibilities**
Be a good corporate citizen
Contribute resources
to the community;
improved quality
of life.

**ETHICAL
Responsibilities**
Be ethical
Obligation to do what is
right, just, and fair.
Avoid harm.

**LEGAL
Responsibilities**
Obey the law
Law is society's codification
of right and wrong.
Play by the rules of the game.

**ECONOMIC
Responsibilities**
Be profitable
The foundation upon which all others rest.

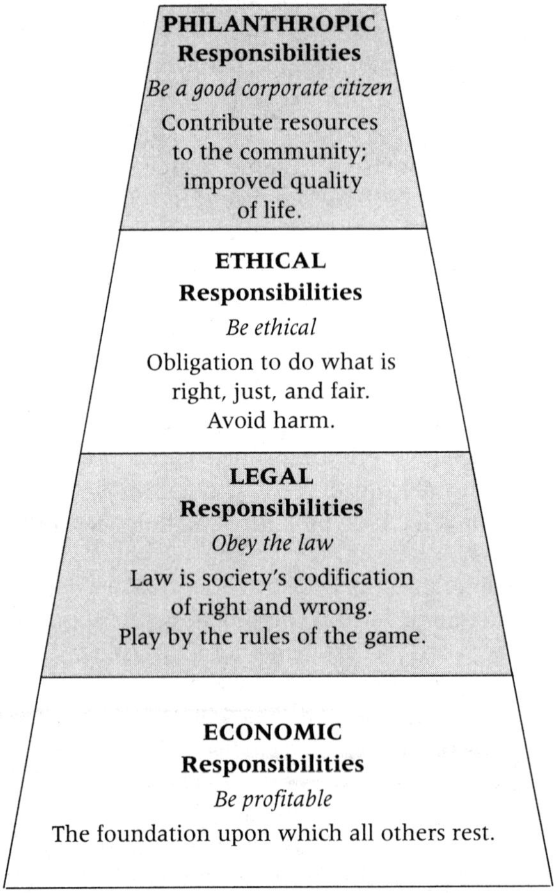

SOURCE: Archie Carroll. The pyramid of corporate social responsiblity: toward the moral management of organizational stakeholders. Reprinted from *Business Horizons*, July/August 1991,
p. 42. Copyright © 1991 by the Foundation for the School of Business at Indiana
University. Used with permission.

however, the separation aids managers to appreciate the different obligations that
are in a constant but dynamic tension with one another. For example, there are
particular tensions between economic and ethical responsibilities. In summary,
Carroll views the total social responsibility of business as involving the simultane-
ous fulfilment of the four responsibilities, which—stated in pragmatic terms—
means that the corporation should strive to make a profit, obey the law, be ethical,
and be a good corporate citizen (1991, pp. 39–43).

AN ALTERNATIVE APPROACH

The concept of corporate social responsibility has been challenged recently, by Freeman and Liedtka (1991, p. 92), as one that has failed to help create a good society. They claim that conversations about corporations and the good life have been hampered by the concept, and a new form of conversation is necessary.

Freeman and Liedtka's reasons for abandoning the concept of corporate social responsibility are summarized in Exhibit 7-1. After presenting these reasons, they suggest three avenues to replacing the worn-out language of corporate social responsibility with richer, and more useful conversations (1991, p.96). Their proposals are summarized in Exhibit 7-2. It is too early to ascertain whether these proposals will gain acceptance with academics or practitioners. But, these proposals do emphasize the fact that the corporate social responsibility concept is still evolving.

EXHIBIT 7-1

Seven Reasons to Abandon the Concept of Corporate Social Responsibility

1. The origins of the concept are suspect, as they derive primarily from the field of economics, and fail to include, among others, history, religion, and culture.

2. The different models of corporate social responsibility all accept the terms of the debate as set forth by Milton Friedman's argument that sees corporations only as profit maximizers.

3. Corporate social responsibility accepts the prevailing business rhetoric of "capitalism: love it or leave it."

4. Corporate social responsibility is inherently conservative—it starts with the standard received wisdom and then attempts to "fix" its unintended consequences.

5. Corporate social responsibility promotes incompetence by leading managers to involve themselves in areas beyond their expertise—that is, repairing society's ills.

6. Corporate social responsibility accepts a view of business and society as separable from each other, each with a distinct ethic, linked by a set of responsibilities.

7. The language of rights and responsibilities is, itself, both limiting and often irrelevant to the world of the practising manager.

SOURCE: R. Edward Freeman and Jeanne Liedtka. Corporate social responsibility: a critical approach. Reprinted from *Business Horizons*, July/August 1991, p. 93. Copyright © 1991 by the Foundation for the School of Business at Indiana University. Used with permission.

EXHIBIT 7-2

Three Propositions for New Conversations

PROPOSITION 1: **Corporations are connected networks of stakeholder interests.**

> This proposition expands the conversation to include suppliers, employees, and customers, among others, making them legitimate partners in the dialogue.

PROPOSITION 2: **Corporations are places in which both individual human beings and human communities engage in caring activities that are aimed at mutual support and unparalleled human achievement.**

> This proposition pushes us beyond the language of rights and responsibilities to a focus on the ethic of care, which recognizes needs and affirms the self and its linkage with others.

PROPOSITION 3: **Corporations are mere means through which human beings are able to create and recreate, describe and redescribe, their visions for self and community.**

> This proposition urges us to see the projects of "self-creation" and "community creation" as two sides of the same coin, and see in institutions many possibilities for different ways of living together to pursue the joint ends of individual and collective good.

SOURCE: R. Edward Freeman and Jeanne Liedtka. Corporate social responsibility: a critical approach. Reprinted from *Business Horizons*, July/August 1991, p. 96. Copyright © 1991 by the Foundation for the School of Business at Indiana University. Used with permission.

SUMMARY

This is the first of four chapters discussing aspects of the corporate performance model outlined in the overview to Part II. It begins by defining social responsibility not with a specific definition, but by pointing out that most definitions contain five key elements. Corporate social responsibility is a reflection of the fact that business and society are interwoven and can be expressed in terms of three principles: legitimacy, public responsibility, and managerial discretion. The Principle of Legitimacy refers to society's granting of legitimacy and authority to business, along with business's appropriate use of that power; the Principle of Public Responsibility means business is responsible for outcomes related to its areas of involvement with society; and the Principle of Managerial Discretion refers to managers as moral actors who are obligated to exercise such discretion as is available to them to achieve socially responsible outcomes.

The debate as to whether or not social responsibility is an appropriate concept is summarized in a list of arguments for and against corporate social involvement. These arguments are reflected in Klonoski's summary of social responsibility theories, categorized according to three alternative views of the corporation as amoral, personal, and social. The arguments and theories are not presented to provide a definitive answer to the question of corporate social responsibility but to review the background to the debate. In fact, the debate has not been resolved to date!

A pyramid of corporate social responsibilities is presented, based on economic, legal, ethical, and philanthropic responsibilities. A hierarchy of responsibilities exists—economic and legal obligations are primary and basic. In recent years, the ethical and philanthropic responsibilities have received more attention.

The final section presents an alternative approach to or view of corporate social responsibility. The traditional discussions (as represented by the arguments for and against corporate involvement) have hampered the achievement of a clear understanding of social responsibility, and a new approach to conversation with business is necessary. Propositions for the new conversations are presented.

Now that a basis for corporate social responsibility has been established, the following chapter reviews "business ethics" as one dimension of social responsibility that has been the focus of recent discussion.

REFERENCES

Buchholz, Rogene A. (1991, July/August). Corporate responsibility and the good society: from economics to ecology. *Business Horizons*, pp. 19–31.

Carroll, Archie. (1991, July/August). The pyramid of corporate social responsibility: toward the moral management of organizational stakeholders. *Business Horizons*, pp. 39-48.

Danley, John R. (1990). Corporation moral agency: the case for anthropological bigotry. In W. Michael Hoffman and Jennifer Mills Moore (Eds), *Business Ethics: Readings and Cases in Corporate Morality* (pp. 202–208). New York: McGraw-Hill Publishing Co.

DeGeorge, Richard. (1990). *Business Ethics* (3rd ed.). New York: MacMillan Publishing Co.

Donaldson, Thomas. (1985). Fact, fiction and the social contract: a reply to Kultgen. *Business and Professional Ethics Journal*, 5, pp. 40–46.

Ewin, R. E. (1991). The moral status of the corporation, *Journal of Business Ethics*, 10, pp. 749–-756.

Freeman, R. Edward and Jeanne Liedtka. (1991, July/August). Corporate social responsibility: a critical approach. *Business Horizons*, pp. 92–98.

French, P. A. (1979, July). The corporation as a moral person. *American Philosophical Quarterly*, pp. 207–215.

Gibson, Roger. (1986, Summer). Corporations, persons and moral responsibility , *Journal of Thought*, pp. 17–27.

Goodpaster, Kenneth E. and John B. Matthews, Jr. (1982, January-February). Can a corporation have a conscience? *Harvard Business Review*, pp. 132–141.

Hoffman, W. Michael and Robert E. Frederick. (1986, Summer). Corporate moral responsibility: a reply to Professor Gibson. *Journal of Thought*, pp. 27–39.

Klonoski, Richard J. (1991, July/August). Foundational considerations in the corporate social responsibility debate. *Business Horizons*, pp. 9–18.

Velasquez, Manuel. (1990). Why corporations are not morally responsible for anything they do. In Joseph R. Desjardens and John J. McCall (Eds.), *Contemporary Issues in Business Ethics* (pp. 114–125). Belmont, CA: Wadsworth Publishing.

Wood, Donna J. (1991). Corporate social performance revisited. *The Academy of Management Review*, pp. 16, pp. 691–718.

BUSINESS ETHICS

INTRODUCTION

Ethics have always been a concern for society and its various institutions. Business corporations, and their management, have been no different, despite the view held by many that businesspersons are somehow less ethical than others. To some extent, this view has been a product of the traditional view of the free enterprise system that alleges that profits are the only motivating force for business, business activity requires and rewards deception, business evades the law, businesspersons and managers manipulate others, and business activity leads to materialism.

During the 1980's, especially in the latter half of the decade, business ethics became the focus for discussion in society and with managers. This chapter examines the business ethics "fad," defines business ethics, identifies sources of ethics, and lists initiatives taken by management to enforce ethical behaviour. In order to give you some appreciation for the extent of ethical issues, Exhibit 8-1 is a list of some ethical issues that confront a manager.

BUSINESS ETHICS—THE "IN" THING

Few Canadians can avoid the discussion of business ethics in newspapers, magazines, and on the the radio and television. The following is a list of some Canadian contributions to this discussion.

- *Books*   Olive's *Just Rewards* (1987) advocates ethical reform of Canadian business. Olive is a journalist and the book is written in a readable style. A more serious approach is taken by Poff and Waluchow in *Business Ethics in Canada* (1991), a book of readings on ethical theory that discusses business ethics in the context of such issues as employment equity, health and safety in the workplace, and advertising. A textbook with an applied discussion of business ethics plus cases was published in 1991 (Bird and Gandz, 1991). Numerous other business books touch on business ethics, including Francis's *Controlling Interest* (1986) and *Contrepreneurs* (1988), and the accounts of various business failures or misdoings—for example, Clement's *Hardrock Miners* (1980) deals with the treatment of miners by Inco, and Fleming's *Merchants of Fear* (1986) deals with the practices of Canada's insurance industry.

- *Journals*   Many academic journals contain articles on business ethics, and some are completely devoted to the topic—for example, the *Business and Professional Ethics Journal, Business Ethics Quarterly*, and the *Journal of Business Ethics*. The last journal's editor-in-chief, Alex C. Michalos, is from the University of Guelph, and other editors are also Canadian, although the journal is published by Kluwer Academic Publishers of the Netherlands. Many Canadians author articles for the journal.

- *Articles*   Ethics has been the topic of hundreds of newspaper and magazine articles. Brooks (1989) discusses why individuals, business, and government are taking a more proactive role in the ethical dimension of Canadian society in an article entitled "Corporate ethical performance: trends, forecasts and outlooks." The *Business Quarterly* regularly carries articles on business ethics—for example, "Ethics come out of the closet" (Gandz, 1988) in which the author claims that business is no more ethical or unethical than in the past, but that business ethics issues are being talked about much more openly now; and "Survival ethics" (Finlay, 1990) in which the author wonders if the lessons that society learned from the 1980's will be reflected in business behaviour in the future. A sample listing of the titles of articles that have appeared in the financial press gives an indication of what is being discussed in the medium:

Exhibit 8-1

Potential Ethical Issues in Business Enterprises

The list below identifies some of the ethical problems that exist in business enterprises. The problems are listed by the stakeholder they most involve or affect, but they can be attributed to, or influence, more than one stakeholder. It should be noted that the items listed do not always involve ethical problems, but the potential exists.

OWNERS
- Reporting to shareholders fairly (disclosure)
- Treatment of minority shareholders
- Paying fair dividends
- Appropriateness of diversification

EMPLOYEES
- Hiring practices
  - preferential treatment
  - nepotism
  - promotion
  - training
  - evaluation and appraisal
  - testing (integrity tests)
- Firing practices
  - employment security
  - just cause
  - dismissal procedures
  - layoffs
  - downsizing procedures
- Wages and working conditions
  - fair wages
  - profit sharing
  - stability of work
  - feedback on performance
- Private lives versus company lives
  - control over personal time/activities
- Discrimination
  - sex
  - age
  - minorities
  - race and social origin
- Honesty
  - calling in sick to take a day off

- using company services for personal use
- conducting personal business on company time
- claiming credit for someone else's work
- passing blame for mistakes to others
- pilfering materials and supplies
- padding expense accounts
- Unions
  - bargaining with in good faith
  - allowing unions to form and operate
- Conflicts of interest
  - bribery
  - payola
  - extortion and gifts
  - moonlighting
  - kickbacks
  - whistle-blowing
- Secrecy and espionage
  - insider information
  - obligations to former employers
  - secrecy and the public interest
  - saboteurs/hackers

CONSUMERS AND CUSTOMERS
- Business practices
  - fraud, lying, and deception
  - disclosure in credit sales
  - advertising—dishonest
  - publicity and public relations
  - packaging and liability
  - product safety
  - overselling and other questionable selling practices
- Pricing practices

- price fixing
- price leadership
- resale price maintenance
- discriminatory pricing
- bait and switch pricing
- gimmicks
• Collusion with competitors

CREDITORS/LENDERS
• Disclosure of information
• Valuation of inventory

COMPETITORS
• Non-competitive behaviour
  - price-fixing
  - cooperation with competitors
• Unfair practices
  - unfair competition
  - restraint of trade
  - pricing below cost
  - stealing personnel
  - industrial espionage

SUPPLIERS
• Maintaining a balanced, professional relationship
  - respect for efforts and costs
• Exploitation of captive suppliers
  - unfair pressure tactics
• Questionable practices
  - kickbacks
  - gifts, bribes
  - receiving stolen goods

GOVERNMENT
• Political contributions in return for favours
• Lobbying
• Honesty in tax returns
• Accurate reporting

SOCIETY AT LARGE
• Damaging environment
• Discrimination in employment practices
• Conditions to corporate giving

SOURCE: Robert W. Sexty. (1991). *Canadian Business: Issues and Stakeholders*. Scarborough, Ontario: Prentice-Hall Canada, pp. 534–535.

- "Corporate ethics a concern for all" (Anderson, 1986)
- "Canadian chartered banks taking their corporate ethics seriously" (Roseman, 1988)
- "Outstanding ethical issues pose problems for all business people" (Mathias, 1989)
- "Working on expressing emotions" (Gibb-Clark, 1990)
- "Ethical standards begin at the top" (Stern, 1991)
- "OSC chief calls for better corporate ethics" (Howlett, 1993)
- "To bribe or not to bribe" (Drohan, 1994).

• *Films* The National Film Board has produced many films on social issues related to business. Two that address business ethics are *A Choice of Two*, a portrayal of the unethical and illegal practices that occurred because of one executive's greed; and *After the Axe*, a film about the firing of a senior executive after years of service. Ethical issues in business organizations are also the basis for movie plots. Examples include *Broadcast News*, set in a television newsroom; *Wall Street*, based on behind the scenes wheeling and dealing in the stock market; *Glengarry Glen Ross* which investigates the moral dilemmas faced by salesmen in an industrial real-estate firm; and *Pretty Woman* which combines questionable business dealings with a love story.

- *Ethics Centres and Interest Groups*   Exhibit 8-2 lists and describes several organizations that have been established to monitor the ethical behaviour of Canadian business.

- *Teaching*   Business ethics courses are now being taught at universities. One of the most widely publicized courses is taught by Professor Max Clarkson at the University of Toronto. The teaching of business ethics is discussed later in this chapter.

The discussion of ethics in this chapter is divided into various topics relating to business and its dealings with other issues and stakeholders.

Exhibit 8-2

Ethics Centres and Interest Groups

The following is a description of some organizations in Canada that monitor the social responsibilities of business.

Canadian Centre for Ethics and Corporate Policy

The Canadian Centre for Ethics and Corporate Policy is a nonprofit organization formed in 1988 to raise the ethical awareness of Canadian managers. It comprises persons from business, academia, the clergy, and the media and provides resources for business, government, labour, and other groups that are concerned with ethical issues in management. The Centre's activities include publishing a quarterly newsletter, *Management Ethics*; organizing luncheons at which prominent speakers address contemporary ethical issues; organizing conferences; and conducting in-house management seminars.

EthicScan Canada Ltd. and Canadian Clearinghouse for Consumer and Corporate Ethics

These organizations are building a database of corporate ethical conduct in Canada. The data is used in a for-profit business in ethics newsletters, consulting services, and seminars.

Project Ploughshares

Project Ploughshares is a church-sponsored advocacy group concerned with the problems of disarmament and Third World underdevelopment. It also acts as a consultant on business ethics issues to groups advocating social responsibility.

Taskforce on the Churches and Corporate Responsibility

The Taskforce was formed in 1975 and is a national ecumenical coalition of major churches in Canada advocating corporate social reform. The Taskforce often attends corporate annual meetings at which it presents shareholder resolutions and questions executives. It also approaches corporations on a private basis to secure changes in corporate policies.

SOURCE: Leonard James Brooks. (1990, Spring). Business ethics: directions for the 1990's. *Canadian Business Review*, pp. 38–41; and David Olive. (1987). *Just Rewards: The Case for Ethical Reform in Business.* Toronto: Key Porter Books.

ETHICAL CONTEXTS

Ethics is "in" and is being discussed in many contexts associated with business. The following are examples, with references:

- *Government (Public Sector)*
  "A special issue on ethics and the public sector" (Jabes, 1991)
  "Do unto others: ethics in government and business" (Wilson, 1991)

- *Environment*
  "Ethics and the environment: beyond self-interest" (Richardson, 1991)
  "Ethics and the environment: a business perspective" (Thoburn, 1991)

- *Energy*
  "Ethics and energy supplement" (Stevenson, 1991)

- *Lobbying*
  "Ethics and lobbying: a government's perspective" (Post, 1991)
  "Ethics and lobbying: a business perspective" (Erola, 1991)
  "The ethical dimension in business and government" (Haynes, 1991)

- *Films*
  "Ethical issues central to two films" (Jefferson, 1988)

- *Multinational Corporations*
  "Ethics and multinational corporations vis-à-vis developing nations" (Simpson, 1982)

- *Banking*
  "Business ethics in banking" (Green, 1989)

- *Competitiveness*
  "Ethics and competitiveness — putting first things first" (Akers, 1989)

- *Industrial Relations*
  "Contemporary ethical issues in labour–management relations" (Adler and Bigoness, 1992)

This illustrates the abundance of materials available on ethics. This chapter cannot begin to reference all these materials but readers should be aware of the vastness of the literature.

DEFINING ETHICS

Many definitions of business ethics exist. The definitions include words such as moral principles, morality of human actions, standards of conduct, rights and wrongs, truth, honesty and fairness, values, customs, the Golden Rule, and philosophy. One researcher has developed a definition that synthesizes what he found to be the four most mentioned concepts in existing definitions: "Business ethics is rules, standards, codes or principles which provide guidelines for morally right behaviour and truthfulness in specific situations" (Lewis, 1985, p. 381).

This definition indicates that moral guidelines, such as rules or codes, exist to prevent unethical behaviour. An example of these guidelines are rules governing the behaviour of chartered accountants established by the Canadian Institute of Chartered Accountants. "Morally right behaviour" consists of the actions of businesspersons that conform to justice, law, or another standard so that their integrity is maintained. Thus, a clause the in *Association of Canadian Franchisers, Code of Ethics* states that "all advertisements shall comply, in letter and spirit, with all applicable rules, regulations, directions, guides and laws of any governmental body or agency having jurisdiction" (Association of Canadian Franchisers, *Code of Ethics*, 1987, p. 42).

"Truthfulness" in the definition of business ethics suggests that ethical statements and actions will at least have the appearance of truth. For example, Canadian Pacific's *Code of Business Conduct* includes a clause that requires employees to maintain the company's books and records in an accurate manner, and it forbids undisclosed or unrecorded funds or assets. Finally, occasions of personal moral dilemma that call for ethical decisions are the "specific situations." For example, codes of conduct specify behaviour appropriate when dealing with the media, suppliers, labour unions, and so on.

Lewis (1985) and others argue that business ethics is difficult to define as it apparently means different things to different managers. However, the definition given above and the discussion of its main components provide a basis for understanding the concept.

SOURCES OF ETHICAL STANDARDS

There is no definitive source of ethical behaviour. One reason for this is that ethics are not absolute and can vary from one situation to another. Some of the fundamental sources of ethical guidelines for all managers include the following:

- *Individual Morals* Managers often make ethical decisions based on the morals they acquire while growing up. The family or home environment is a major influence, making the personal convictions of individual managers a source of ethical standards.

- *Government Legislation and Regulation* Government legislation does influence ethical decisions. For example, the Competition Act makes some questionable market practices illegal and thus discourages some managers from becoming involved in such practices. Certain government and industry regulations require the disclosure of certain information to protect the interests of stakeholders. For example, when selling shares to the public, a corporation must clearly state certain information about its finances and operations.

- *The Legal System*   The law makes some behaviour illegal and most managers are sensitive to maintaining behaviour that is within the law. It is claimed that moral judgements are contained in judicial decisions relating to business transactions. According to the financial press, the Supreme Court of Canada set a new ethics standard in its ruling on a case between Lac Minerals Ltd. and Corona Corp. The dispute was over the ownership of the Page-Williams gold mine in Northern Ontario. In 1981, two geologists discussed the possibility of a joint venture to develop the mine. Lac Minerals used the confidential information obtained to go ahead on their own with the mine. The Court found that the information exchange created an obligation, or trust, on Lac's part not to use the information to their advantage. Trust, or fiduciary duty, implies an obligation to act selflessly. The Court found that Lac had not done so. Fiduciary duty has always existed in professional relationships, such as that between lawyers and clients. The Court's decision extends the concept to the business world. The Court's decision awarded the mine, estimated to be worth $3 to 4 billion, to Corona Corp.

- *Religion*   For some managers, religious upbringing and contact with religious organizations as an adult provide a basis when confronted with ethical decisions.

- *Colleagues or Peers*   The moral standards set by other businesspersons may become the basis on which an individual manager considers ethical issues.

- *Education*   The educational process that a manager is exposed to may become a reference point. Ethical matters in general are examined in schools, and some managers may even have university education in ethics or philosophy.

The above list attempts to identify sources of ethical standards. It must be recognized that there are other things in society and the business system that have an influence over the ethical behaviour of management. Influences that lead to higher ethical standards in business include the following:

- *Media*   The possibility of exposure influences decisions. In fact, one test of ethical behaviour is whether or not the manager can defend the decision if it becomes known.

- *Corporate Missions, Objectives, and Culture* A mission statement usually involves identification of the values held by the organization, and these values are reflected in culture. Objectives that are socially oriented emphasize values or moral considerations.

- *Union Contracts*   Union contracts often specify the type of action that can or cannot be taken by managers. For example, if there is to be a layoff, managers cannot retain their favourites but must release employees according to seniority.

- *Competitive Behaviour*   The behaviour of others in the same industry affects a manager. For example, if one soft drink manufacturer decides to mount an advertising campaign based on attacking the competitor's product rather than on emphasizing the qualities of his or her own product, it is more likely that the attacked soft drink manufacturer will respond with a similar campaign.

- *Activist or Advocacy Groups*   The numerous activist or advocacy groups existing in society can have an impact on business decisions. An example is the Taskforce on the Churches and Corporate Responsibility, described in Table 8-2. This group was instrumental in getting some Canadian corporations to withdraw from South Africa.
- *Business or Industry Organizations*   Many business or industry organizations encourage members to act ethically. For example, the Better Business Bureau (BBB) is comprised of "businesses, organizations and individuals who believe that it is in the interests of good business to be honest and fair to their customers and clients" (Better Business Bureau materials). BBB services are designed to promote and insure more ethical business practices.
- *Professional Associations*   Business employs professionals such as lawyers, architects, engineers, and doctors. Ethical codes or guidelines have been developed by the professional associations and must be adhered to by their members.

These fundamental sources of ethical standards and other influences affect the decisions of managers and how ethical they are. But, by themselves, these sources or influences do not insure any type of standardized or uniform behaviour. Managements of business enterprises are now taking initiatives that they anticipate will reinforce ethical behaviour in their organizations.

THE THEORETICAL BASIS FOR ETHICAL CONDUCT

Managers often seek some standard for ethical conduct in theory, that is, a set of principles, theories, maxims, or beliefs that can be used as a foundation for ethics. There are numerous sources for such a foundation and many are briefly described below. These theoretical bases for ethical conduct were compiled from Hosmer (1991, Chapter 4), Lewis (1989), Steiner and Steiner (1991, Chapter 8), and Walton (1992, Chapter 3).

- *Categorical Imperative*   The managers should behave in such a way that the action they take under the circumstances can be an appropriate decision or rule of behaviour for others in a similar situation. A way to express this principle is "what individuals believe is right for themselves, they should believe is right for all others."
- *Conventionalist Ethic*   In this view of ethics, managers should act to further their own interests so long as laws are not broken. Under this principle, managers are allowed to bluff or lie, and to take advantage of all legal opportunities and widespread practices or customs. Business is considered a game, like poker, and the rules are different from those that individuals use in their personal lives.

- *Disclosure Rule*   According to this code of conduct, managers should ask themselves how they would feel if the bases and details of an ethics-related decision became known. For example, the manager should ask, "Would I feel comfortable explaining to a national television audience why I made the decision?" However, the disclosure audience can also be colleagues, friends, partners, or family. This rule is also referred to as the "TV Test" or the "Light of Day Test."

- *Distributive Justice*   This view involves the belief that moral standards are based on the primacy of a single value: justice. Managers should act to insure a more equitable distribution of benefits so that all individuals are better off.

- *Ego Ethic*   The manager should do whatever is in his or her own self-interest. The ethic suggests that individuals love themselves so much that conventional ethical behaviours of religion or society are irrelevant to life. This view is also referred to as the "Hedonistic Ethic." Since there are no moral absolutes, no blame is attached to such self-interested behaviour.

- *Eternal Law*   The principles to be followed by managers are revealed in Scripture or are apparent in nature as interpreted by religious leaders or humanist philosophers.

- *Expediency Ethic*   Managers should learn to be cunning, cruel, manipulative, and calculating when making decisions or taking action. This ethic involves the use of power to accomplish what one wants or what is required for success.

- *The Golden Rule*   This popularly quoted ethic suggests that managers should act towards others in way that they expect others to act toward them. Managers should examine a problem from the perspective of other parties involved or affected by the decision, and try to determine what response the other parties see as the most ethical. This ethic is often referred to by the phrase "Do unto others as you would have them do unto you."

- *Intuition Ethic*   Managers are to act according to their "gut feeling" of what is right in the circumstances. It is assumed that people are endowed with a kind of moral sense of right and wrong. Another expression exemplifying this ethic is "Flying by the seat of your pants."

- *Market Ethic*   Adam Smith's *Wealth of Nations* (1776) is held up as the foundation for this ethic according to which managers may take selfish actions and be motivated by personal gains in their business dealings. Selfish actions in the marketplace are justified as they contribute to the efficient operation of the economy, which in turn results in prosperity and the optimum use of society's resources.

- *Means-End Ethic*   The guideline here is that worthwhile ends justify efficient, and even unscrupulous, means to reach them. When faced with an ethical decision, managers should ask themselves whether or not the desired end justifies any moral transgression.

- *Might-Equals-Right Ethic* Strength is considered important with this ethic: what is ethical is what a manager has the strength and power to accomplish. Managers should seize any advantage that they are strong enough to have, and ignore normal social conventions and laws.

- *Natural Law Theory* It is assumed that there is a known and absolute correctness or good that enlightened or thoughtful persons can identify. This ethic assumes that a known, absolute, correct—or good—code of behaviour exists, and can be recognized by enlightened or thoughtful persons. This behavioural code is inalienable and natural, and cannot be denied: the manager who behaves according to natural law behaves ethically.

- *Organizational Ethic* The manager should base decisions on whether or not he or she is being consistent with the organization's goals and on what is good for the organization. The ethic implies that the desires and needs of individuals should be subordinated to the greater good of the corporation. Simply stated, the ethic means "Be loyal to the organization."

- *Personal Liberty* A manager's ethical decisions should be based upon the primacy of a single value: liberty. This ethic assumes that everyone should act to ensure greater freedom of choice as this promotes the market exchange that is essential for the well-being of all in society.

- *The Principle of Proportionality* Managers should assume responsibility for whatever they decide on as a means or an end, and if the means and the end are good in and of themselves, managers may ethically permit or risk the foreseen but undesirable side effects if, and only if, there is a proportionate reason for doing so. There are five measures of proportionality: the type of good or evil involved; the probability of effect; the urgency of the situation; the intensity of one's influence over effects; and the availability of alternative means.

- *The Professional Ethic* Managers should only take those actions that would be viewed as proper by a disinterested panel of their professional colleagues. In particular, this approach to ethics applies where managers are accountants, engineers, architects, or lawyers. Codes of ethics usually exist in such professions, and the codes serve as the bases for making ethics-related decisions.

- *The Revelation Ethic* Managers supporting this ethic whould be very religious, and believe prayer, meditation, or contact with transcendent beings and forces provide answers. In effect, according to this ethic guidance should be sought from God. This ethic is close to the intuition ethic, but the Revelation Ethic assumes some divine presence.

- *Survival Ethic* This ethic assumes that the fittest will survive, and that this justifies dog-eat-dog behaviour. Things should happen according to a law of nature or a law of God. In business, there are struggles between competitors, business and government, and labour and management, and decisions should be made to ensure the survival of the corporation.

- *Utilitarianism* In simple terms, this principle means "the greatest good for the greatest number." When managers make decisions, they should consider whether the harm in an action is outweighed by the good. If the action maximizes benefit, then it is the optimum course to take among alternatives that provide less benefit.

The manager is confronted with quite an array of ethical alternatives although there is some overlap among those in the above list. There is most likely some truth in most of the principles, but some are not acceptable in society today. Some of the principles are self-centred while others are socially-oriented, to the common well-being. It should be noted that for all the principles listed above there are drawbacks or downsides. In a study of a similar listing of principles, Lewis (1989) finds that some of the principles are seen as standards that can be applied with no further thought or research necessary by the manager—namely, the categorical imperative, the disclosure rule, the Golden Rule, and the organizational ethic. Although variations exist among the groups studied, the following principles have been rejected as guides to ethical decision making: the conventionalist ethic, the hedonistic ethic, the market ethic, the might-equals-right ethic, and the revelation ethic.

The theories of ethical conduct should not be viewed by businesspersons and managers as sources that will clearly establish right from wrong, or good from bad. The study of these theories can leave managers confused, and seldom are theories of ethics directly relied upon when making business decisions. As a result, business relies upon a variety of "initiatives" to reinforce ethical behaviour.

MANAGEMENT INITIATIVES TO REINFORCE ETHICAL BEHAVIOUR

The managements of business enterprises have responded to the increased concern over ethics. Various initiatives have been taken to institutionalize ethics, that is, to implement policies or programs that increase the awareness of ethics in the organization. Some of the initiatives taken are discussed below.

Statement of Values or Philosophy

Some business enterprises prepare statements of their "core values" or "philosophy" that will serve as a guide for ethical decision making and indicate what the corporation's beliefs are. An example of one corporation's values is provided in Exhibit 8-3. A statement of values also becomes the basis for a code of ethics.

Codes of Ethics

A code of ethics or conduct is a statement of ethical principles, acceptable behaviour, or rules and policies that describes the general value system within which a

---

Exhibit 8-3

Corporate Values of NOVA Corp.

NOVA values its international scope of operations and its ability to compete worldwide from its Canadian base. Corporate values create the base for long-term prosperity and growth.

Human Resources

The NOVA workforce is highly-trained and productive. Employees share and support an entrepreneurial business style that values leadership, innovation, planning and hard work.

NOVA practices non-discriminatory hiring, compensation and employee development policies that reinforce performance as the key to career development.

Reflecting these values, an innovative employee compensation program was implemented in January 1990 to provide a competitive package that rewards performance. It includes a savings and profit sharing plan and flexible benefits package that allows employees to tailor compensation programs.

Health, Safety and Envirnoment

NOVA is committed to the operation of its businesses at a standard that will establish the Corporation as an industry leader.

All employees practise and encourage safe work habits and environmental responsibility as integral conditions of work. Through policies and routine audits, NOVA ensures that operating units aim to meet or exceed all applicable laws and standards, while continuing to work in a productive manner. NOVA supports the environmental codes of practice as established by groups such as the Canadian Chemical Producers Association, the Canadian Petroleum Association and the Chemical Manufacturers Association in the United States.

In 1989, Nova had capital expenditures of $30 million and operating expenditures of $21 million related to pollution abatement

and control measurers. In addition, NOVA expends substantial efforts in the areas of occupational health, product and process toxicology, industrial hygiene and safety, to protect NOVA's employees and the public.

Research and Technology

NOVA's business objectives are supported by a commitment to applied research and technology development.

Research allows development of value-added products that meet specific customer needs. This is an essential component of NOVA's ability to achieve and maintain its position as a preferred supplier of goods and services. Unified activities are conducted at three major research facilities in Canada and the United States to provide a comprehensive approach to specific research projects for all NOVA operations. The research group employs about 400 scientists, engineers and technical support staff.

In 1989, NOVA spent approximately $48 million on research and development activities and an additional $17 million on product support research activities related to the improvements of existing products, services and processes.

Corporate Contributions

NOVA supports non-profit activities designed to support the quality of life in the communities in which it operates.

Contributions support national organizations and reflect NOVA's international business activities. Emphasis is directed to health and welfare, education, the environment, arts and culture and recreation.

In 1989, major initiatives included a program to match employee contributions to charities such as the United Way, support for litter clean-up campaigns and donations to universities.

SOURCE: NOVA Corporation of Alberta. *Annual Report 1989*, p. 17.

corporation attempts to operate in a given environment. Many business enter-prises, business associations, and professional organizations have established codes of ethics: it is the most common approach to institutionalizing ethical behaviour. There are several reasons for the development of codes, as follows:

- They can improve customer confidence in the quality of a product or the level of service, and also help insure ethical and fair treatment of customers.

- Codes simplify the detection of unethical behaviour in competitors and employees by standardizing norms of behaviour.

- The reputation of the business enterprise or organization that develops codes is improved and attracts high-calibre employees and customers.

- Codes provide for self-regulation, which is preferable to external control.

- Since codes increase awareness, they discourage ethical apathy, facilitate ethi-cal decision making, and make it easier to refuse an unethical request.

Components of Codes

The issues addressed in a typical code of ethics include:

- a general statement of ethics, values, or philosophies

- responsibility toward employees, including items such as health and safety, non-discrimination, and privacy

- conflicts of interest, their identification, and how to handle them

- protection of enterprise assets, including accurate accounting, security or property, and insider information

- appropriate business practices, including honesty, fairness, and obeying the law

- appropriate conduct on behalf of the organization, for example, relationships with customers, suppliers, competitors, creditors, and government

- responsibilities to society at large, including contribution to political parties, responses to media, treatment of communities, and concern for environmen-tal protection

- implementation procedures including familiarity with the code, reporting of violations, refusing unethical requests, and seeking help on ethical matters

- specification of enforcement/compliance procedures and the penalties for ille-gal behaviour.

The content and format of codes of ethics vary substantially among enterpris-es. There have been many studies of the contents and focus of corporate codes of ethics. Lefebvre and Singh (1992) perform a content analysis of 75 codes of *The Financial Post* 500 corporations. They find that about one-third of these firms have fairly well developed codes of ethics. The focus of Canadian corporate codes is protection of the firm rather than issues concerning conduct on behalf of the firm. The most frequently addressed issues are those policies pertaining to conflicts of interest and the integrity of books and records. Other findings include the following: very few codes mention product safety, product quality, consumer relations, or the environment; about one half are concerned with maintaining the corporation's reputation; and almost three-quarters specify enforcement or compliance procedures (1992, p. 808). Although the existence of codes is widespread, especially in larger corporations, they also have some drawbacks.

Drawbacks to Codes

Some critics claim that codes of ethics or conduct are at best a minimal but unenforceable standard and at worst a hollow pretence. An implication of this claim is that most enterprises and professionals operate at an ethical level above that specified in the codes. It is only for the less scrupulous that the codes are intended, but the guidelines may not be very effective with this group. Most codes are characterized by voluntary compliance. It is, therefore, difficult to enforce the codes and, even if they are enforced, the penalties may be insignificant. Those following a code may also be placed in a disadvantageous position because those who don't adhere to the code are not restricted in their actions. As a result, convincing everyone to comply is not easy. In business enterprises, codes are sometimes pointed to with pride but ignored in practice. Frequently, the codes are idealistic or written in meaningless generalities.

Sometimes codes of ethics are developed merely to control competitive conduct among business enterprises or individuals. They specify conduct that is considered unprofessional, such as advertising by lawyers and certain pricing practices in some industries. The code of conduct, in these cases, is really designed to reduce competition, and this kind of self-regulation is sometimes a stopgap measure of questionable intent designed merely to prevent government legislation and serves as a response to public criticism.

Brooks (1991) concludes that the use of codes and their reasons for existing are no longer issues. Codes are important devices for communicating and controlling employees' behaviour within the existing legal framework. He identifies several ways in which codes can be made more effective, including improving content, increasing commitment to the codes, and creating mechanisms that encourage employees to embrace their codes by living by them on a daily basis.

Ethics Training

Ethics training involves teaching employees about the values and policies on ethics they should follow in decision making. The teaching sessions involve an orientation on values or ethics and related policies. A code of ethics or statement of values may be used in this teaching process, in addition to handbooks or policy statements. Such teaching can be done by line managers or outside consultants, and has been addressed to all levels of employees, but more emphasis has been placed on management levels. The reasons for establishing such training programs are to develop employee awareness of ethics in business, and to draw attention to the ethical issues to which an employee may be exposed.

Ethics Audits

An ethics audit is a systematic effort to discover actual or potential unethical behaviour in an organization. They are designed not only to uncover unethical behaviour, but also to identify the opportunities for unethical behaviour that exist. They have a preventive as well as a remedial purpose. Audits are particularly useful when used in conjunction with a code of ethics as the code can be the basis for comparison to establish how well or poorly the organization is doing. Regular audits foster ethical practice.

Ethics Consultants

Consultants knowledgeable of ethics advise management on how to put "integrity" into enterprise culture. Ethics audits, or surveys, may be conducted by consultants to ascertain compliance to ethical standards, and consultants may be involved in training and code development. The consultants are persons external to the organization. The next initiative, by contrast, involves the monitoring of ethics by someone inside the corporation.

Ethics Ombudsperson (or Ethics Advocate)

The ethics advocate is an independent executive, reporting to the CEO who reviews complaints or information from anyone in the organization or any stakeholder, studies the situation, and recommends action if necessary. Toll-free telephone numbers may be provided for employees in large enterprises to report ethical problems. This approach provides a "release" mechanism for disenchanted or concerned employees. The ombudsperson or advocate must be independent of management to insure the trust of stakeholders. Such a person can alert the organization to ethical problems or issues before they become public knowledge, allowing time to prepare a defence or to take remedial actions.

According to Nitkin (1991), there are not many ombudsperson programs in Canadian corporations, but he lists examples at the Bank of Nova Scotia, Canada Trust, CIBC, IBM, Magna International, Royal Trust, and the Toronto-Dominion Bank. Five essential characteristics are necessary for ombudsperson programs to succeed: competent staff; widespread respect among and support from senior management; ironclad confidentiality; direct access to the CEO or president when necessary; and the leaving of decisions, whenever possible, to employees once they are informed of their rights (1991, p. 178).

Ethics Committees (or Business Conduct Committees)

Such committees usually are formed at the Board of Directors level to monitor ethical standards and behaviour. The formation of such a committee injects ethics at the highest level in the organization, and is a symbol to all stakeholders of the company's commitment to ethical practice. This type of committee is involved in developing a code of ethics and may monitor management and employee behaviour for ethical issues. The report of one such committee is presented in Exhibit 8-4.

Ethics committees comprising management, employees, and outside stakeholders can also exist within the organization. Present practice appears to be that ethics committees are top management focused. Such committees may also be called corporate ethics and responsibility committees, or advisory boards or councils, which are usually comprised of a variety of stakeholders.

Executive Speech Making

As business ethics became the "in" thing, many chief executives used it as a topic of their public speeches. Speeches are made to inform certain stakeholders that the business enterprise and its management are concerned about ethics and are responding to society's interest in the matter. It is not always clear to which stakeholders the speeches are directed, but they most likely address society at large, activist and advocacy groups, employees, and possibly some shareholders. The influence of these speeches is even less clear.

ETHICS PROGRAMS AND THEIR EVALUATION

The above list of management initiatives represents an explicit expression of a corporate ethics program. Just because a corporation is not involved in the initiatives mentioned does not mean that it does not have an ethics program, according to Max Clarkson, Director of the Centre for Corporate Social Performance and Ethics (1993). He argues that all corporations have programs, but that some of them are implicit. The implicit ethics programs are implemented through such things as the organization's culture, reward systems, valued behaviour, promotion policies, management example, general practice, and performance measures.

Exhibit 8-4

Report of the Business Conduct Review Committee — Royal LePage Limited

The most effective system for dealing with conflict of interest situations is a combination of strict but workable regulatory framework and appropriate self-governance mechanisms.

At Royal LePage, corporate self-governance responsibilities are honoured by adhering to certain business principals. Included are:

- a major commitment to the quality, timeliness and accuracy of board and committee reporting;

- a significant number of independent directors on the board;

- a policy which invites substantial public investment, reflected in a public shareholding of 48 percent in Royal LePage;

- substantial equity participation by senior management; and

- a high level of accountability to a major shareholder.

The Business Conduct Review Committee was constituted on October 25, 1985, and subsequently approved by shareholders. The Committee is composed of four directors of Royal LePage who are unaffiliated in any way with a major shareholder of Royal LePage.

The Committee has established a Code of Business Conduct for Royal LePage which includes policies regarding business ethics and conflicts of interests applicable to employees, directors and shareholders. It must approve all significant investments, loans or other business activities of Royal LePage, which may involve a material conflict of interest.

The Committee is provided with ready access to senior management and Royal LePage's auditors and it can, as it deems necessary, retain independent legal counsel to advise on matters which come before it. Members of the Committee are Samuel T. Paton, Lorne K. Lodge, Susan C. Bassett-Klauber and Roy MacLaren.

During the year, the Committee reviewed and approved all significant transactions and policies under its mandate. It is of the opinion that during its sixth year of existence, it continues to comply with both the spirit and the substance of its mandate.

On behalf of the Committee
Samuel T. Paton Chairman,
January 18, 1990

SOURCE: Royal LePage Lmited. *1989 Annual Report*, p. 28.

Evaluation of Ethics Programs

Clarkson (1993) identifies some criteria for evaluating the effectiveness of an ethics program: visibility, ownership, fit, and balance. Initiatives should be clearly evident in that statements such as codes should be widely distributed and communicated in a variety of formats. There should be evidence of a commitment to the ethics program, as demonstrated by awareness and usage of the initiatives, and by their integration into the organizational culture. Initiatives should be appropriate to the circumstances of the corporation, that is, programs should be complementary with the type of business or industry. Lastly, there should be a balance in the programs among rules, redress, and principles, or a balance between "imposed control" and "self-control." Clarkson also identifies criteria for evaluation of the program's implementation. Such criteria are the extent of resource commitment to the program, the CEO's involvement, the extent of communication about the program, and the training and education carried out.

Of relevance to management initiatives is the possibility that graduates of colleges and universities have received ethics education in the classrooms and are thus prepared to address critical issues when they obtain employment.

TEACHING ETHICS IN BUSINESS SCHOOLS

Colleges and universities are being pressured to teach ethics in business or management programs. In addition, short courses in ethics are being offered at management development training centres. But it is not clear that ethics can be taught, either at the post-secondary level in the education system or to adults. The arguments for and against teaching ethics at the college and university level are summarized below.

Arguments For Teaching Ethics

The following points summarize the principal arguments in favour of teaching ethics at a post-secondary level.

- There are so many immoral or unethical events taking place that it is essential to teach ethics in an attempt to increase awareness.
- Teaching ethics sends a powerful message to students, that is, "this school feels it is a priority for students to follow generally accepted rules of business when they graduate."
- Businesspersons, as well as students, suffer from ethical naivete. A course in business ethics alerts students to the existence of ethical conflicts and dilemmas. It is very important to increase awareness of actual and potential ethical issues.
- From an ethical perspective, the business environment is changing radically and students must be made aware of this. Old principles or standards do not work today, and what is acceptable today may not be in the future.
- Only a separate course in business ethics focuses on the long-term perspective and asks "what if" questions. Most courses emphasize short-term objectives and management of the "bottom line," that is, making profits. Longer-term perspectives are largely neglected in corporate planning, and courses in ethics may assist in changing this emphasis.

- Ethics courses can provide students with some tools or techniques of analysis, or with a conceptual framework for analyzing ethical issues. It is possible to teach the essential tools of moral reasoning, deliberation and justification that should be helpful to future businesspersons in explaining corporate behaviour.

- Ethics courses legitimize the consideration of ethical components as an integral part of managerial decision making.

Arguments Against Teaching Ethics

The prinicpal arguments against post-secondary ethics education are as follows.

- There is little need for it. Business ethics are not a major problem. In particular, Canada has not experienced the major problems with insider trading and stock fraud found in the United States.

- There is little likelihood that university or college professors or instructors can meaningfully alter the ethical behaviour of students. Students' underlying moral convictions are obtained throughout life—from family, peers, grade school, religious instruction, and the community—and are not likely to be altered much.

- There are few qualified teachers of ethics in business and management departments. If anything, students should be sent to philosophy departments to learn about ethics in general.

- Specific business ethics courses are unlikely to be of much help in 20 or more years when students are in positions with executive responsibility. This is particularly the case given the rapid change in the business environment.

- Many business problems involve ethical considerations that are not resolvable: managers lack any influence over many factors in the business environment.

- Offering a separate ethics course suggests to managers that ethics are a "separate" consideration in decision making. In fact, ethics are fundamental to all decision making.

- There are few formulas or techniques that can be taught to solve the ethical problems confronting business.

The debate over the usefulness of ethics education will continue until the current preoccupation with business ethics fades. Watch for discussions of ethics in your business courses!

ETHICS—WHOSE RESPONSIBILITY?

A simple answer to the questions "Who is responsible for ethics?" is everyone. But, in a corporation it is argued that the responsibility for recognizing the importance of ethical behaviour in business and doing something about it has to start at the top, that is, with the Board of Directors. Bavaria (1991) claims that directors have been remiss in this area, especially the docile outside directors who have the independence to monitor ethical behaviour. Gillies (1992, Chapter 8) states that directors have two tasks in relation to ethics: to collectively identify values that determine acceptable behaviour in the firm, and to put in place a process that assures values are reflected in action. Merely acting on the basis of one's own values is not sufficient, and it is necessary to deliberately consider the implications of unethical behaviour. Not all directors agree with this position, and the arguments for and against it reflect the general discussion of whether or not business has any social responsibility.

The reasons given for the Board's responsibility for ethical or moral behaviour include the point that it is simply good management to develop an appropriate culture, sensitive to ethics issues. In addition, the Board itself is involved in ethical questions such as conflicts of interest, compensation schemes, management buyouts, the rights of minority shareholders, and changes in management. Finally, it is easier to make decisions if the fundamental principles or values of the corporation are known and can serve as a reference point. In the past, and maybe the present, directors were often not aware that ethics were involved in a decision. They must be aware that values change over time and that their own values may not have altered. As directors are the ultimate decision makers in corporations, they must demand that decisions made by management and all employees be based on ethical standards acceptable to society.

Assistance for Managers

Numerous lists of questions, moral standards, and tests have been developed to assist managers when making ethical decisions. Three examples are provided.

First, writing in the *Harvard Business Review*, Nash (1981: pp. 79–89) argues that plainly worded questions, such as the following, should be used by managers when examining the ethics of a business decision:

1) Have you defined the problem accurately?
2) How would you define the problem if you stood on the other side of the fence?
3) How did this situation occur in the first place?
4) To whom and to what do you give your loyalty as a person and as a member of the corporation?
5) What is your intention in making this decision?
6) How does this intention compare with the probable results?

7) Whom could your decision or action injure?

8) Can you discuss the problem with the affected parties before you make your decision?

9) Are you confident that your position will be as valid over a long period of time as it seems now?

10) Could you disclose without qualm your decision or action to your boss, your CEO, the Board of Directors, your family, society as a whole?

11) What is the symbolic potential of your action if understood? If misunderstood?

12) Under what conditions would you allow exceptions to your stand?

Nash refers to this approach as "good puppy" theory as it allows corporate morality to be defined and explored halfway between the rigorous moral analogy of the corporation being the "good person" and the purely amoral definition of good. According to Nash,

> Moral capacity is perceived as present, but its potential is limited. A moral evaluation of the good puppy is possible but exists largely on concrete terms: we do not need to identify the puppy's intentions as utilitarian to understand and agree that its "ethical" fulfilment of the social contract consists of not soiling the carpet or biting the baby. (1981, p. 89).

Second, Bird and Waters (1987) analyze descriptions of how managers think about questions that come up in their work. They find that managers refer to the following moral standards as guides when making decisions.

1) *Honesty in Communication*   Managers should be committed to honest communication with stakeholders. This honesty includes candid evaluations of employees, speaking without intentional deception, and not distorting or withholding information.

2) *Fair Treatment*   Managers should act according to impartial standards, without bias, and within established procedures.

3) *Special Consideration*   Special regard should be given to particular individuals or groups because of their circumstances or contributions.

4) *Fair Competition*   Managers should avoid accepting bribes or kickbacks, treat all customers and suppliers the same, and in general follow the competitive conventions of their particular type of business.

5) *Organizational Responsibility*   The interest of the organization must be considered when making decisions.

6) *Corporate Social Responsibility*   Managers should be concerned about the impact of their decisions on the environment and various stakeholders.

7) *Respect for Law*   The law is a standard that managers should refer to when they judge an issue to be of moral concern.

The authors conclude that these normative standards assume the cultural form of social conventions, but because managers invoke them as largely private intuitions, their cultural status remains precarious and unclear.

Finally, the Pagano model uses six clear questions that serve as several tests of the ethics of a particular action. Pagano (1987) identifies six tests that he feels provide useful insights into the ethics of a business's actions. The tests are as follows:

1) *Is It Legal?*   This is a core starting point.

2) *The Benefit Cost Test*   This test employs the Utilitarian perspective of the greatest good for the greatest number.

3) *The Categorical Imperative*   Do you want this action to be a universal standard? This test takes the view that if it's good for the goose, it's good for the gander.

4) *The Light of Day Test*   What if your actions appeared on TV? Would you be proud?

5) *Do Unto Others*   This test uses the Golden Rule. Do you want the same to happen to you?

6) *The Ventilation Test*   Get a second opinion from a wise friend with no investment in the outcome (Pagano, 1987).

The author feels that this approach has the advantages of being compact and simple. Note that most of the questions represent the principles discussed earlier.

Ethical Propositions

Business ethics is identified as an "in" topic, yet it has been discussed seriously for four decades. Much of the earlier material on ethics is still applicable. An article by Laczniak (1983) contains some ethical propositions that are still appropriate.

- Ethical conflicts and choices are inherent in business decision making.
- Proper ethical behaviour exists on a plane above the law. The law merely specifies the lowest common denominator of acceptable behaviour.
- There is no single satisfactory standard of ethical action agreeable to everyone that a manager can use to make specific operational decisions.
- Managers should be familiar with a wide variety of ethical standards.
- The discussion of business cases or of situations having ethical implications can make managers more ethically sensitive.
- There are diverse and sometimes conflicting determinants of ethical action. These stem primarily from the individual, from the organization, from professional norms, and from the values of society.

- Individual values are the final standard, although not necessarily the determining reason for ethical behaviour.

- Consensus regarding what constitutes proper ethical behaviour in a decision-making situation diminishes as the level of analysis proceeds from abstract to specific.

- The moral tone of an organization is set by top management.

- The lower the organizational level of a manager, the greater the perceived pressure to act unethically.

- Individual managers perceive themselves as more ethical than their colleagues.

- Effective codes of ethics should contain meaningful and clearly stated provisions, along with enforced sanctions for noncompliance.

- Employees must have a nonpunitive, fail-safe mechanism for reporting ethical abuses in the organization.

- Every organization should appoint a top-level manager or director to be responsible for acting as an ethical advocate in the organization. (Laczniak, 1983, pp. 23–29)

The propositions summarize many of the points made in this chapter. They also indicate that, within the corporation, directors and managers are all responsible for ethical behaviour, with top management assuming leadership. Despite being compiled more than a decade ago, these propositions provide practical guidance to the institutionalization of ethical behaviour in corporations.

SUMMARY

Business ethics has been an "in" topic for the past decade. The topic has been discussed extensively in the literature, the media, and the classroom. Ethical behaviour as it relates to a variety of contexts has been examined—for example, as it relates to public administration and government, the environment, multinational corporations, banking, competitiveness, and industrial relations. There has been an extensive examination of ethical behaviour not only as it relates to business and the corporation but also as it impacts the various interrelationships among business, society, and stakeholders.

In this chapter, a definition of business ethics, considered to be appropriate for the purpose of this discussion, was selected from a review of the literature. The numerous sources and influences on ethical behaviour were identified, indicating that the ethics of businesspersons and managers are established in different ways. Several theories of ethics were listed to illustrate the difficulty of relying on theories for guidance in decision making.

Managers and corporations have used several initiatives to reinforce ethical behaviour. The effectiveness of these initiatives is questionable. Their value is measured by the extent of the resource commitment made, the involvement of top management, the extent of communication about the initiative, and the training and education undertaken. The issue of teaching ethics in business programs was examined, reaching no clear conclusion about its usefulness.

Business ethics is the responsibility of everyone in the corporation—directors, managers, and employees. Examples of guidelines or checklists for ethical conduct were presented to illustrate how managers can become more sensitive to the ethical consequences of decision making.

Chapter 7 describes the social responsibility concept, while Chapter 8 reviews business ethics. These two concepts give rise to numerous issues of a social and ethical nature that impact many stakeholders. Chapter 9 describes the management of these issues and the stakeholders involved.

REFERENCES

Adler, Robert S. and William J. Bigoness. (1992). Contemporary ethical issues in labor-management relations. *Journal of Business Ethics*, 11, pp. 351–360.

Akers, John F. (1989, Winter). Ethics and competitiveness—putting first things first, *Sloan Management Review*, pp. 69–71.

Anderson, Ronald. (1986, July 10). Corporate ethics a concern for all. *The Globe and Mail*, p. B2.

Association of Canadian Franchisors, Code of Ethics (1987) from advertisement in the *Financial Times of Canada*, February 23, 1987, p. 42.

Bavaria, Steven. (1991, January-February). Corporate ethics should start in the boardroom. *Business Horizons*, pp. 9–19.

Bird, Frederick and Jeffrey Gandz. (1991). *Good Management: Business Ethics in Action.* Scarborough, ON: Prentice-Hall Canada Inc.

Bird, Frederick and James A. Walters. (1987). The nature of managerial standards. *Journal of Business Ethics*, 8, pp. 1–13.

Brooks, L. J. (1989). Corporate ethical performance: trends, forecasts and outlooks. *Journal of Business Ethics*, 8, pp. 31–38.

Brooks, Leonard J. (1991). Codes of conduct for business: are they effective, or just window-dressing? *Canadian Public Administration*, Vol. 34, No. 1, pp. 171–176.

Clarkson, Max B. E. (1993, March 3). Ethics and profit: the changing values of business in society. Unpublished presentation to the Faculty of Business Administration, Memorial University of Newfoundland, St. John's, Nfld.

Clement, Wallace. (1980). *Hardrock Miners: Industrial Relations and Technological Changes at Inco Ltd.* Toronto: McClelland and Stewart.

Drohan, Madelaine. (1994, February 14). To bribe or not to bribe. *The Globe and Mail*, p. B7

Erola, Judy. (1991). Ethics and lobbying: a business perspective. *Canadian Public Administration*, 34, pp. 90–94.

Finlay, J. Richard. (1990, Autumn). Survival ethics. *Business Quarterly*, pp. 40–41.

Fleming, James. (1986). *Merchants of Fear: An Investigation of Canada's Insurance Industry.* Markham: Penguin Books.

Francis, Diane. (1986). *Controlling Interest: Who Owns Canada?* Toronto: Macmillan.

Francis, Diane. (1988). *Contrepreneurs.* Toronto: Macmillan.

Gandz, Jeffrey. (1988, Autumn). Ethics come out of the closet. *Business Quarterly*, pp. 61–63.

Gibb-Clark, Margot. (1990, November 15). Working on expressing emotions. *The Globe and Mail*, p. B8.

Gillies, James. (1992). *Boardroom Renaissance: Power, Morality and Performance in the Modern Corporation.* Toronto: McGraw-Hill Ryerson.

Green, C. F. (1989). Business ethics on banking. *Journal of Business Ethics*, 8, pp. 631–634.

Haynes, Arden R. (1991). The ethical dimension in business and government. *Canadian Public Administration*, 34, pp. 17–20.

Hoser, Larue Tone. (1991). *The Ethics of Management* (2nd ed.). Homewood, IL: Irwin.

Howlett, Karan. (1993, November 16). OSC chief calls for better corporate ethics. *The Globe and Mail*, p. B3.

Jabes, Jak (Ed.). (1991). A special issue on ethics and the public sector, *Optimum: The Journal of Public Sector Management*, Vol. 22, No. 1, pp. 171–176.

Jefferson, Philip. (1988, February). Ethical issues central to two films, *Canadian Churchman*, p. 26.

Laczniak, Gene. (1983, January-February). Business ethics: a manager's primer. *Business* (Georgia State University), pp. 23–29.

Lefebvre, Maurica and Jang B. Singh. (1992). The content and focus of Canadian corporate codes of ethics. *Journal of Business Ethics*, 11, pp. 799–808.

Lewis, Phillip V. (1985). Defining business ethics: like nailing jello to a wall. *Journal of Business Ethics*, 4, pp. 377–383.

Lewis, Phillip V. (1989). Ethical principles for decision makers: a longitudinal survey, *Journal of Business Ethics*, 8, pp. 271–278.

Mathias, Philip. (1989, July 24). Outstanding ethical issues pose problems for all business people. *The Financial Post*, p. 2.

Nash, Laura L. (1981, November-December). Ethics without the sermon. *Harvard Business Review*, pp. 79–89.

Nitkin, David. (1991). Corporate ombudsman programs. *Canadian Public Administration*, Vol. 34, No. 1, pp. 177–183.

Olive, David. (1987). *Just Rewards: The Case for Ethical Reform in Business.* Toronto: Key Porter Books.

Pagano, Anthony M. (1987). Criteria for ethical dcision making in managerial situations. *Proceedings*, National Academy of Management, New Orleans, pp. 1–12.

Poff, Deborah C. and Wilfrid J. Waluchow (Eds.). (1991). *Business Ethics in Canada* (2nd ed.). Scarborough, ON: Prentice-Hall Canada Inc.

Post, George. (1991). Ethics and lobbying: a government's perspective. *Canadian Public Administration*, 34, pp. 84–89.

Richardson, Dorothy. (1991). Ethics and the environment: beyond self-interest. *Canadian Public Administration*, 34, pp. 111–116.

Roseman, Ellen. (1988, December 13). Canadian chartered banks taking their corporate ethics seriously. *The Globe and Mail*, p. B5.

Simpson, James R. (1982). Ethics and multinational corporations vis-à-vis developing nations. *Journal of Business Ethics*, 1, pp. 227–237.

Smith, Adam. (1776, 1910 printing). *The Wealth of Nations.* Edinburgh: J.M. Dent and Son Ltd.

Steiner, George A. and John F. Steiner. (1991). *Business, Government and Society: A Managerial Perspective. Text and Cases.* New York: McGraw-Hill Inc.

Stern, Michael. (1991, November 11). Ethical standards begin at the top. *The Globe and Mail*, p. B4.

Stevenson, Mark. (1991). Ethics and energy supplement. *Journal of Business Ethics*, 10, pp. 641–648.

Thoburn, Weldon. (1991). Ethics and the environment: a business perspective. *Canadian Public Administration*, 34, pp. 117–120.

Walton, Clarence C. (1992). *Corporate Encounters: Ethics, Law, and the Business Environment.* Fort Worth: The Dryden Press.

Wilson, V. Seymour (Ed.). (1991). Do unto others: ethics in government and business. *Canadian Public Administration*, 34 (1), pp. 3–222.

ISSUES AND STAKEHOLDER MANAGEMENT

INTRODUCTION

Chapters 7 and 8 describe the concepts of social responsibility and business ethics, while this chapter discusses some approaches to operationalizing these concepts. Two approaches, issues management and stakeholder management, are discussed. They are treated separately even though there is some overlap between the approaches and sometimes they intertwine.

ISSUES MANAGEMENT

Issues management as a formal function has emerged during the past 15 years. It is defined as "the process by which the corporation can identify, evaluate, and respond to those social and political issues which may impact significantly upon it" (Johnson, 1983, p. 1). This definition suggests that issues management is a systematic approach to managing a particular issue or portfolio of issues that will somehow impact the accomplishment of the organization's objectives. It is assumed that the word "social" includes ethical issues. A second definition highlights another aspect of this approach: issues management is "a process to organize a company's expertise to enable it to participate effectively in the shaping and resolution of public issues that critically impinge upon its operations"

(Arrington and Sawaya, 1984, p. 148). This definition also suggests a systematic approach, but mentions "public" instead of social and political issues. Public affairs departments made early attempts to address issues and, for the purposes of this book, public issues can be interpreted to mean social and political issues.

Another aspect of both definitions is the implicit assumption that corporations can manage the issues confronting them. The term "issues management" is considered to be a misnomer as no corporation can manage or influence events to attain a desired outcome on a particular issue in all situations at all times. The second definition uses the term "shaping" to describe managment activity which probably more appropriately represents what actually occurs. Issues management does not mean that the corporation can create social change, or can control or manipulate society. Instead, the term refers to the process by which the corporation responds to social and political issues.

Components of Issues Management

Issues management is not only a systematic process but also provides a continuous focus on the relationship between business and society. There are four components of issues management usually mentioned in the literature: identification of the issues; analysis of potential impacts; development of responses; and implementation.

It is important that the corporation identify relevant issues through scanning of the environment. It should not assume that social or ethical issues will be picked up through other environmental assessments, for example, those done in the strategic planning process or marketing plans. Some argue that there should be a deliberate effort to monitor developments in the social, ethical, and political spheres. This environmental scanning provides foresight by identifying what to think about, in other words, what issues to monitor, analyze, and prioritize.

The second component involves an analysis of the potential impacts of identified issues on the corporation, and an estimation of the probabilities of occurrence. This analysis must be performed carefully to ensure that all corporate managers understand the dimensions of the issue. The analysis should carefully describe the issue and avoid discussing solutions or responses, that is, suggesting how to think about the issues. The issues must be given a meaning or interpretation that is shared by all managers so that prioritizing can be effectively accomplished.

Following the analysis, an appropriate response or policy must be formulated. In considering responses, there should be a reconciliation of internal interests or issues to insure a coherent external advocacy. Thought must be given to past, present, and emerging issues. Responses to past issues, for example, 1980's issues such as investment in South Africa, affirmative action, and deregulation—must continue to be addressed, while responses to issues of the 1990's are being formulated—for example, responses to waste management, education reform, drug abuse, AIDS in the workplace, and global competition. Managers must both lead the development of strategies to contend with past issues and be in the process of developing strategies for emerging issues.

Finally, management must implement the responses that will attempt to influence, prevent, or change the impact of social issues. This component involves pragmatic action plans, or identification of what to do.

Perspectives on Issues Management

Different perspectives have been taken on issues management (Mahon and Waddock, 1992, pp. 21–25) and focus on issues related to public policy, corporate strategy, and pressure groups. In its earlier stages, issues management focused on the impact of public, or government, policy. Courses in "Government and Business" were offered to teach managers how to cope with changes in public policy and to emphasize that business must monitor society to identify issues that might move society's views on the public agenda and lead to regulation and legislation. This perspective led to the publication of several books, the titles of which illustrate the focus of the perspective: *Government and Enterprise in Canada* (Rea and Wiseman, 1985); *Theories of Business–Government Relations* (Murray, 1985); *Government Policy Toward Business* (Brander, 1988); *Policy Analysis: Concepts and Practice* (Weimer and Vining, 1992); *Managing Business Relationships with Government* (Crookell, 1991), *Business–Government Relations in Canada* (Stanbury, 1986); and *Canadian Cases in Business–Government Relations* (Baetz and Thain, 1985).

This perspective is actually a narrow one and may, in part, be attributable to the existence of Public Affairs Departments in corporations. The focus is on identifying and responding to issues related to interactions between business and government—for example, attempting to influence legislation or policy, advocating more favourable taxation policies, seeking tariff or other protection, and acquiring loans or grants.

A second perspective is "strategic" in that the issues dealt with are critical to the success of the organization and must be addressed. An issue is a trend, threat, or opportunity that has a potentially large (positive or negative) impact on the future performance of the corporation. A strategic issue is one that affects an organization's fundamental policies or its mandate or constitution; mission; values; product or service level and mix; clients, payers or users; costs; financing; organizational design; or management. Strategic issues emerge from the way the corporation chooses or is forced to relate to its external or internal environments (Bryson, 1988, p. 56). The issues management approach is often attributed to Ansoff (1980) and focuses attention on the recognition and resolution of strategic issues which he defines as "forthcoming developments," either inside or outside the organization, that are likely to have an important impact on the ability of the enterprise to meet its objectives (1980, p. 133). Strategic issues are formulated in the external environmental assessments and in assessment of resource capabilities. This appears to be an appropriate method of capturing social and ethical issues, but as these analyses are broad and comprehensive, issues may be either missed, or, if identified, ranked low in priority, thus not receiving any substantial consideration.

Pressure or interest groups are the focus of a third perspective. Issues gain clarity and become more narrowly defined over time. They then enter into society's agenda, and thus into the attention of business. Within pressure or interest groups, visible participants, referred to as "policy entrepreneurs," bring a particular issue to the attention of society from the midst of many existing issues. Such groups exert public pressure through a variety of actions so business or government will deal with the issue (Kingdon, 1984). An example of this type of situation arises when a petroleum company must respond to the blockade on a road leading to its production facilities, located on a Native reservation. Native activists may block access to draw attention to the fact that they do not receive any or sufficient royalty revenue, or that there is a dispute over land ownership. Once again, this perspective can lead to a narrower focus than desirable, even though Kingdon does not define pressure or interest in a narrow manner. Interest groups are a stakeholder in the business system, as discussed in Chapter 2, and this perspective should not be neglected.

These three perspectives focus on three different stakeholder groups: public policy makers, managers or corporate strategists, and interest groups. Each has a different view of any particular issue, and specific issues may be of importance to one perspective but not to the others. The amount of attention paid to the issue relates to the extent to which the stakeholder accepts the need to deal with the issue, and to the way in which the issue will be dealt with if that responsibility is accepted (Mahon and Waddock, 1992, p. 25). It is argued that to gain a full understanding of the state of the issue, the position of each stakeholder group must be known. Mahon and Waddock develop an integrated issue life cycle model that captures the position of each group with regard to a particular issue, allowing them to identify how stakeholders react at various times. Their model is complex, and for our purposes it is sufficient to briefly review the concept of a life cycle as it relates to issues management.

In the above discussion, the issues addressed are generated by government or interest group stakeholders, or through the strategic management process. Any stakeholder can be the source of an issue and none should be overlooked. Rather than focusing on particular perspectives of issue management, as outlined here, managers should take a broad view and consider all stakeholders as sources of issues.

Issue Life Cycles

Issue life cycles are similar in concept to the marketing "product life cycle." The purpose of this discussion is only to introduce them. Issues can be viewed in two dimensions, over time and by degree of awareness. In Figure 9-1 the degrees of awareness at various stages of the cycle are identified as none or little, increasing, prominent, peak, and declining. Issues are often present that receive little or no attention (T1). It is also possible for an issue not to be evidence at all. Managers should be aware of these possibilities, particularly when facing the early stages of a new issue or the reemergence of an old issue.

According to Coates, Coates, Jarratt, and Heinz (1986, pp. 19–20), early indentification, in period T1, of an emerging issue having any of six characteristics is important. These characteristics are as follows.

1) The terms of the debate cannot yet be clearly defined.

2) One of the actors (stakeholders) will define the emerging issue and make it a current issue.

3) It deals with matters of conflicting values and interest.

4) It is not a problem that expert knowledge will automatically be able to resolve.

5) It is stated in value-laden terms.

6) Trade-offs are possible.

This list indicates that an emerging issue may not be easy to resolve in the short-term.

Figure 9-1 Issue Life Cycle

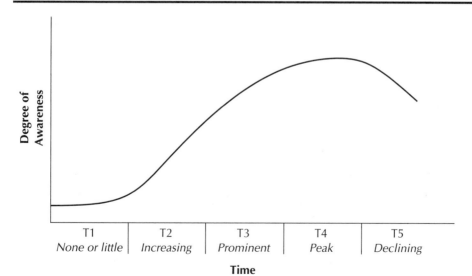

T1	T2	T3	T4	T5
None or little	*Increasing*	*Prominent*	*Peak*	*Declining*

Time

In period T2, the awareness of the issue increases, for example, as the issue receives some media attention. It is unlikely that all corporations have formulated a response by this time. In period T3, the issue is very prominent and cannot be ignored. Responses or solutions are widely discussed, and most corporations have taken a stance. The issue peaks at some point (T4), and then declines. The challenge for managers is to be sensitive to the degrees of issue awareness of society or a significant number of stakeholders. The decline stage should not necessarily be viewed with relief as issue awareness may not decline as indicated in Figure 9-1. The issue may reemerge and awareness increase, or awareness may remain constant.

There is another phenomenon that can occur as illustrated by Figure 9-2. An issue may result in a response that allows it to maintain a constant presence and then may reemerge at another time. However, the reemerged issue builds on the base created by the previous response and moves business's response and performance to yet another level. An example is society's awareness of energy usage, which has been a concern since the 1970's. Business concern for the environmental issue of the 1970's, energy conservation, has not declined, and reemerged in the 1980's due to higher energy prices. Later, in the 1980's and into the 1990's, there was another increase in concern as society pushed for conservation to reduce costs and increase awareness of environmental impacts.

Figure 9-2 Example of an Enduring Issue Life Cycle

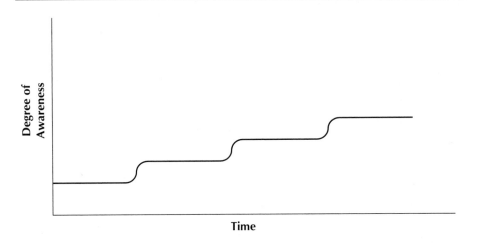

The Purposes and Benefits of Issues Management

One purpose of issues management is to minimize surprises relating to events or trends in society by serving as an early warning system. Also, it prompts managers to be more systematic in coping with issues and stakeholder concerns by using foresight to anticipate change, and by participating in the resolution of existing issues. Issues management attempts to fill a void by providing a framework for assessing matters confronting the corporation that otherwise may be overlooked. It also provides the mechanism for coordinating and integrating issues management activity throughout the corporation.

There are several benefits to practising issues management. Corporations involved in it are more likely to maintain a competitive advantage over rivals. Corporate behaviour is more likely to be consistent with societal expectations, and the corporation is less likely to make a serious social or ethical mistake. Issues management enables the corporation to detect issues earlier and develop appropriate responses much sooner, sometimes even when the issues are emerging. The corporation's vulnerability is reduced and its credibility enhanced.

Like any other management methodology or technique, issues management does not just happen and appropriate conditions must exist for success. Top management must support it and be involved. There must be broad participation at the operating and staff levels. The approach must adapt to the culture and the management dynamics of the corporation. The issues management approach should be implemented gradually, making sure that it is supported by operating units. It is important to stress output—that is, position papers, ideas, and interpretation of data—over process—that is, the techniques and mechanisms used for issues identification, issues evaluation, and response development. Decisions must be made and analysis cannot go on forever (Wartick and Rude, 1986, pp. 132–136, and Coates et al, 1986, pp. 15–16.)

The Issues Management Process

The following is a more detailed outline of the issues management process, broken into six steps: identification, analysis, ranking, response formulation, implementation, and monitoring. The description is a general one and is based on the steps outlined by Carroll (1989, pp. 479–89) and Bryson (1988). There may be variations in the overall process used, and different methodologies or techniques may be used in the steps. This description is meant to serve as a general description of the issues management process.

1) *The Identification of Issues*   This step involves the formulation of issues and in many ways, including social forecasting, futures research, environmental scanning, and public issues scanning. One person or unit can be assigned the task of identifying issues, but a more participatory approach involves a facili-

tator who assists management in formulating issues through some type of group process. Exhibit 9-1 lists some techniques that may be used to identify issues.

EXHIBIT 9-1

Techniques for Identifying Issues

Precursor Analysis
This analysis is based on trend correlation or what is happening elsewhere.

Media Analysis
This approach measures the "column inches" received by particular topics or issues. It is based on the assumption that the media represents a "national" voice, and the technique involves the identification and content analysis of the national press, national news magazines, and national radio and television.

Polls and Surveys
Business enterprises can interpret the results of public opinion polls or surveys conducted by others, or can commission their own.

Jury of Executive Opinion
This approach uses panels of senior managers to identify and evaluate issues. The assumption is that these people have extensive knowledge of the organization and have experience coping with issues.

Expert Panels
In this approach, persons very knowledgeable of societal trends, economies, and technology are assembled, and their views of emerging issues sought.

Content Analysis
This is a close reading of media content that segregates the content into predetermined categories to ascertain trends or attitudes.

Delphi
This survey technique uses a panel of experts to judge the timing, probability, importance, and implications of trends and events relating to a particular matter.

Scenario Building
Scenarios are written descriptions of how future events might unfold. Statistical techniques are sometimes used in scenario building, but usually scenarios develop a qualitative picture of how a system or organization will look at some time in the future.

SOURCE: Extracted from Coates, Joseph F., Vary T. Coates, Jennifer Jarrat, and Lisa Heinz. (1986). *Issues Management: How You Can Plan, Organize and Manage the Future.* Mt. Airy, MD: Lomond Publishers, Inc., Chapter 3. The book explains these and other techniques in more detail.

---

2) *Analysis of Issues*   In this step, issues are described and evaluated, usually in writing, so that a consensus is achieved among managers. The issues are analyzed through questions such as, What is the issue? Why is it an issue? Who (which stakeholder) says it is an issue? Which stakeholders are in a position to exert influence on the issue? Where does (did, or will) the issue confront you? How sensitive or "charged" is the issue? What is the impact on key stakeholders? What is the consequence of not addressing the issue?

3) *Ranking/or Prioritizing of the Issues*   The purpose of this step is to establish the importance of the issues identified, which should be possible after the description of each issue has been agreed to in step 2. Issues can be ranked according to many creiteria including immediacy (time pressure, urgency, long or short term); magnitude of impact; the direction of impact (plus or minus); internal or external locus; controllability; interconnectedness to other issues; whether it is an opportunity, threat, or crisis; the degree of abstractness versus concreteness of the issue; the amount of certainty versus ambiguity involved; the age of the issue (position in life cycle); complexity; level of conflict or divisiveness; the pervasiveness, scope, or specificity of the issue; and the decision-maker's interest (Dutton, Walton, and Abrahamson, 1989). Issues can be ranked by assigning probabilities and weights to their impact or importance on a number scale. The probability of the issue arising is multiplied by the assessment of its impact and the results for each issue provide the ranking. Members of management may also simply vote to identify priority items.

4) *Formulating Issue Response*   In this step, the choices available to the corporation are identified and evaluated. It is important to identify all response alternatives that may be pursued to address the issue. Only then are barriers to the implementation of these alternatives considered. From the generation of alternative responses and the analysis of each, the most feasible and appropriate option is identified.

5) *Implementing Issue Response*   At this stage, specific plans are formulated to implement the response selected. A workplan is developed to insure the implementation of the response. Such a workplan briefly describes the issue and what the response will be, who is responsible for the response and when the necessary actions will be undertaken and/or completed.

6) *Monitoring and Evaluating the Issue Response*   The status of the issue and the response is reviewed on a regular basis. Several possibilities exist: the issue may be resolved and drop from the corporation's list of issues to address, another response may have to be formulated and implemented as the current choice is ineffective for some reason; or the nature of the issue may have changed forcing managment to start the process over.

This process ensures that the most important or critical issues are addressed. The remaining issues are not dropped, but are maintained in a list of issues that is reformulated on a regular basis.

A complimentary approach to addressing social and ethical issues in the corporation is known as stakeholder management. Although this approach overlaps with issue management, it is useful to examine particular methodologies of managing relationships with stakeholders.

STAKEHOLDER MANAGEMENT

Chapter 2 discusses the stakeholder concept and identifies the generic stakeholders of a business corporation. In this chapter, stakeholder management is defined and approaches to implementing it are examined. Freeman (1984) defines stakeholder management as "the necessity for an organization to manage the relationships with its specific stakeholder groups in an action-oriented way" (p. 53). The following sections discuss basic stakeholder management approaches, and then review the approaches developed by researchers in the area.

Basic Stakeholder Management

All corporations should involve themselves in stakeholder management, even at a preliminary level. If nothing else, corporations should identify and attempt to understand the stakeholders that influence and are influenced by the corporation. At the least, the corporation should prepare a stakeholder map of its stakeholders, like that shown for the Bank of Montreal in Figure 2-1 of Chapter 2.

The corporation can increase its understanding of these stakeholders by answering the following questions that will capture the essential information needed for effective stakeholder management:

1) Who are our stakeholders?

2) What are their stakes?

3) What opportunities and challenges are presented to our firm?

4) What responsibilities (economic, legal, ethical, philanthropic) does our firm have to all its stakeholders?

5) What strategies or actions should our firm take to best deal with stakeholder challenges and opportunities? (Carroll, 1989, p. 62)

A similar approach is to complete a stakeholder analysis worksheet for each stakeholder, like the one in Table 9-1. Note that two parts exist in the lower portion of the worksheet for stakeholders that influence the organization and for those that are influenced by the organization. Some stakeholders are one or the other, while others may be both. There are more comprehensive approaches to stakeholder management and three are described below.

Freeman's Stakeholder Management Capability

According to Freeman (1984), there are three levels in the process an organization uses to manage relationships with its stakeholder groups: (1) identifying stakeholders in the organization and their perceived stakes according to the rational perspective; (2) determining the organizational processes used to manage relationships with stakeholders and fitting these processes with the stakeholder map of the organization; and (3) understanding the set of transactions or bargains between the organization and its stakeholders and deciding whether these negotiations fit the map and the processes. Freeman states that organizations develop a "Stakeholder Management Capability" defined in terms of their ability to conduct these three levels of analysis together (1984, p. 53).

Table 9-1 Stakeholder Analysis Worksheet

Definition

Stakeholder—An individual or group who can influence, or is influenced by, the operations (or activities) of an organization.

Stakeholder Identification

Stakeholder _____

Sub-categories _____

Stakeholder Analysis

Influences the Organization _____

   How? _____

   Organization's response _____

   How satisfactory is the response? _____

Influenced by the Organization _____

   How? _____

   Stakeholder's response _____

   How successful is this influence? _____

The rational level involves preparing a stakeholder map that identifies specific stakeholders. For example, the stakeholder map should include the names of interest groups influencing the corporation or the government agencies with which the corporation is involved. Stakeholder maps at the "generic" level vary little among corporations: thus a more detailed list is necessary. A problem arises in that membership among groups may overlap, for example, someone can be an employee but also a shareholder through stock purchase plans. It is important to consider the role of stakeholders when identifying them. There may also be networks or coalitions among stakeholders, and these should be indicated somehow. An attempt must be made to ascertain the "stake" of each group and the power they have, keeping in mind that different perceptions of stake and power exist (1984, pp. 54–64).

The second level, "process," identifies the procedures used to assess stakeholders. Freeman mentions some possibile procedures, including portfolio analysis, which he believes applies to some stakeholders but is too financially oriented, and strategic management, which applies if stakeholder questions are included in each component (1984, pp. 64–69).

The "transactional" level deals with the actual interaction with stakeholders. It is important to employ managers with the appropriate value set to deal with particular stakeholders if the relationship is to be an effective one. An obvious example is dealing with the media. Some executives are not comfortable dealing with the media, and such contact should be assigned to someone with skills in that area (1984, pp. 69–73).

A stakeholder management capability emerges that is a function of stakeholder map analysis, organizational process, and stakeholder transactions. There must be a "fit" among the three elements, that is, an understanding of the stakeholders, the processes for dealing with them, and the transactions used to carry out relationships with stakeholders. Freeman believes that managers should place less blame on particular stakeholders and voluntarily undertake to satisfy the corporation's key stakeholders. Failure to do so can even bring government involvement (1984, pp. 73–74). Some other aspects of Freeman's approach to managing stakeholder groups include the following:

- stakeholder behaviour should be analyzed to distinguish between actual and observed behaviours, and to identify cooperative-potential behaviour (changes in actual behaviours that would be more helpful to the corporation) and competitive-threatening behaviours (those that might harm the corporation) (pp. 131–132)

- managers should attempt to explain stakeholder behaviour by placing themselves in the position of the stakeholder—stating the stakeholder's objectives and examining their beliefs about the corporation (pp. 133–134)

- consideration should be given to the possibility of stakeholder coalitions forming between stakeholders with common interests which may lead to joint behaviour (pp. 135–136)

- some approaches to dealing with stakeholders can be identified: swing, the approach to those groups with relatively high cooperative potential and relatively high competitive threat; defensive, the approach to those groups with relatively low cooperative potential and relatively high competitive threat; offensive, the approach to those groups with relatively high cooperative potential and relatively low competitive threat; and hold, the approach to those groups with relatively low comparative potential and relatively low competitive threat. Each of these groups should be treated differently, with specific stakeholder programs; for example, the relationship with a swing stakeholder may be changed through lobbying for government legislation; a defensive stakeholder may be handled by linking issues to others that the stakeholder views more favourably; an offensive stakeholder may be convinced to change objectives; and a hold stakeholder would have the existing relationship with the corporation reinforced (pp. 139–152).

Freeman's work is the basis upon which the diagnostic typology of organizational stakeholders is formulated.

The Diagnostic Typology of Organizational Stakeholders

One methodology for assessing and managing stakeholders is outlined by Savage, Nix, Whitehead, and Blair (1991) and appears to be based on Freeman's generic stakeholder strategies (Freeman, 1984, pp. 142–144). The authors, Savage et al., claim that stakeholders' significance or influence depends on the situation and the issues involved, and as a result, managers must use the appropriate methods to deal with various stakeholders. Two assessments are considered critical: the assessments of stakeholders' potential to threaten the organization, and of their potential to cooperate with it.

Diagnosing the potential for threat involves ascertaining the stakeholder's power to disrupt the organization's accomplishment of its objectives. Diagnosing the potential for cooperation allows the organization to move beyond defensive and offensive strategies against a threat to a situation in which cooperation with stakeholders allows the organization to accomplish its objectives. Several factors affect a stakeholder's potential for threat or cooperation. These are outlined in Table 9-2, along with an indication of whether the factor increases or decreases the stakeholder's potential for threat or cooperation.

The stakeholder's potential for threat or cooperation becomes the basis for categorizing, on a matrix, the types of stakeholders. Figure 9-3 indicates that stakeholders can be classified into four types—supportive, marginal, nonsupportive, and mixed blessing—and that different strategies exist for responding to each type. The following is a brief description of each stakeholder type and corresponding strategy.

Type 1—Supportive Stakeholder and Strategy   This is the ideal stakeholder as it provides support by being a low threat and high on potential for cooperation. Examples are Boards of Directors, managers, employees, parent companies and possibly suppliers and service providers. The strategy for managing this type of stakeholder is encouraging the cooperative potential and not ignoring them or taking them for granted.

Type 2—The Marginal Stakeholder and Strategy   These stakeholders are neither highly threatening nor especially cooperative. They potentially have a stake but it varies by issue or is limited to particular issues. Examples are consumer groups, shareholders, and professional associations for employees. The strategy for managing stakeholders of this type is to monitor them closely while recognizing that their interests are narrow and issue specific.

Table 9-2 Factors Affecting Stakeholder's Potential for Threat and Cooperation

	Increases or Decreases Stakeholder's Potential for Threat?	Increases or Decreases Stakeholder's Potential for Cooperation?
Stakeholder controls key resources (needed by organization)	Increases	Increases
Stakeholder does not control key resources	Decreases	Either
Stakeholder more powerful than organization	Increases	Either
Stakeholder as powerful as organization	Either	Either
Stakeholder less powerful than organization	Decreases	Increases
Stakeholder likely to take action (supportive of the organization)	Decreases	Increases
Stakeholder likely to take nonsupportive action	Increases	Decreases
Stakeholder unlikely to take any action	Decreases	Decreases
Stakeholder likely to form coalition with other stakeholders	Increases	Either
Stakeholder likely to form coalition with organization	Decreases	Increases
Stakeholder unlikely to form any coalition	Decreases	Decreases

SOURCE: Grant T. Savage et al. (1991). Strategies for assessing and managing organizational stakeholders. *Academy of Managmenet Executive*, (5)2, p. 64.

Figure 9-3 Diagnostic Typology of Organizational Stakeholders

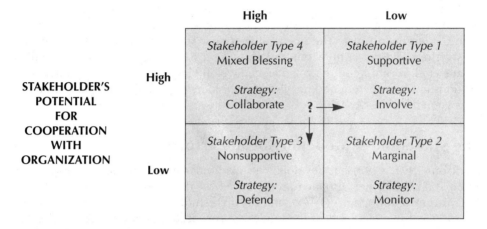

STAKEHOLDER'S
POTENTIAL FOR THREAT TO ORGANIZATION

SOURCE: Grant T. Savage *et al.* (1991). Strategies for assessing and managing organizational stakeholders. *Academy of Management Executives,* 5(2), p. 65.

Type 3—The Nonsupportive Stakeholder and Strategy   These stakeholders have a high threat potential, but low cooperation potential. Because of this, they are the most challenging to manage. Examples, for a manufacturing firm, are competing firms, employee unions, government, and perhaps the media. The strategy to follow with this type of stakeholder is defensive, attempting to reduce the organization's dependence on the stakeholder.

Type 4—The Mixed Blessing Stakeholder and Strategy   These stakeholders play a major role in the organization as their threat and cooperation potential are high. Examples are employees who are in short supply, important clients, and organizations with complementary products or services. The two arrows in Figure 9-3 represent the two possibilities for such stakeholders, to become supportive or nonsupportive. The strategy to deal with this type of stakeholder is collaboration of some sort, for example, joint ventures, alliances, or mergers.

Savage et al. outline a stakeholder management process based on this typology. The first step is to identify the key organizational stakeholders by considering factors such as relative power, the specific context and history of the relationship, and specific issues that may be salient. Next, managers diagnose stakeholders according to critical dimensions of potential for threat or cooperation. Following this step, appropriate strategies are formulated to enhance or change current relationships with the key stakeholders. Finally, the strategies must be effectively implemented, including the possibility of transforming the stakeholder relationship from a less favourable to a more favourable one if appropriate. Strategies should attempt to satisfy the needs of marginal stakeholders minimally and to satisfy the needs of supportive and mixed blessing stakeholders maximally. Savage et al. recommend that managers develop objectives for the organization's relationship with current and possible stakeholders as part of an ongoing strategic management process.

The Stakeholder Model of Social Performance

Clarkson (1991, 1992) has developed a stakeholder model of social performance and a stakeholder performance profile based on the research of Carroll (1979) and Wartick and Cochran (1985), and his own studies of corporate social performance. The three elements of the model are corporate stakeholder responsibility, responsiveness, and management of stakeholder issues. Corporate stakeholder responsibilities are focused on five principal stakeholder groups: customers, employees, shareholders, suppliers, and the public. The responsiveness of the corporation to these stakeholders is referred to as a posture or strategy, which is an evaluation or measurement of the level of responsibility demonstrated by the corporation in its management of stakeholder relationships. According to this evaluation, the posture or strategy is categorized as being reactive, defensive, accommodative, or proactive, with the former two being considered unsatisfactory and the latter two, satisfactory. The third element of the model involves the management of stakeholder issues, or the performance of the corporation with regard to issues identification, issues analysis, response development, and response implementation. Clarkson's model (shown in Figure 9-4) indicates that the corporation must identify its primary stakeholder groups, define the issues that concern these stakeholders in their dealings with the corporation, and determine the corporation's strategy of responsiveness for dealing with the issues (Clarkson, 1992, p. 13).

One methodology used by Clarkson to capture data on the corporation's performance on various social and stakeholder issues is the Stakeholder Performance Profile (1992, pp. 15–17). The Stakeholder Performance Profile (SPP)—shown in Figure 9-5—is defined as the graphic presentation of the evaluation of a corporation's management of issues concerning its primary stakeholders.

The SPP contains 42 issues of concern to the primary stakeholder groups of a typical corporation, as identified by Clarkson in previous case studies of social

Figure 9-4 Clarkson's Model

Corporate Stakeholder Responsibilities	Corporate Stakeholder Responsiveness	Management of Stakeholder Issues
Principal Stakeholder Groups	Evaluation of Strategy or Posture	Performance
1) Customers	1) Reactive	1) Issues Identification
2) Employees	2) Defensive	2) Issues Analysis
3) Shareholders	3) Accommodative	3) Response Development
4) Suppliers	4) Proactive	4) Implementation
5) Public		

SOURCE: Max Clarkson. (1992). *A Stakeholder Theory of the Firm: Building on Preston, Carroll, Wartick and Chochran, and Wood.* Working paper, University of Toronto, p. 12.

performance. In addition, the SPP contains eight issues concerning the corporation's history, economic performance, industry, and organization. When corporation case studies are carried out, evaluations or scores are assigned, according to a rating key, to indicate the corporation's performance on the issues.

According to Clarkson, the Stakeholder Performance Profile makes it possible to display systematic evaluations of social and stakeholder performance in a concise graphic form for the first time. The Stakeholder Management Model and the SPP methodology provide the basis for a systematic, empirical analysis and evaluation of a corporation's practices and performance in managing its relationships with stakeholders (1992, p. 15).

Drawbacks to Stakeholder Management

Stakeholder management is now widely referred to by managers in discussions of business's role in society. But, the concept has not been universally accepted and is not without drawbacks. Terence Corcoran, columnist for *The Globe and Mail*, laments the prevalence of the word "stakeholders" in media stories:

> If this year marks the beginning of a trend, the concept of stakeholders could become the corporate flummox of the 1990s, a populist substitute for "maximizing shareholder value," the presumably harsh dominant corporate ethic of the 1980s.
>
> But the rise of "stakeholders" is more than the deployment of a word to gloss over corporate management activities. Using stakeholders in the context of

corporations represents a profound distortion that should be of arresting concern to one segment of the economy in particular: shareholders. (Corcoran, 1990, p. B4)

Corocan's concern is that shareholders, the preeminent group in corporations, have been overshadowed by other groups. The point in mentioning this is to remind readers that not everyone has accepted the stakeholder concept and that many still believe in a traditional, or theoretical, definition of capitalism.

Even Freeman (1984) warns of the pitfalls of using the stakeholder approach as it advocates greater accountability, or openness, to the business system. Some managers, or corporations, may not appreciate the exposure necessary with the concept. Like other management approaches, the support and involvement of top management is critical. However, getting top management's endorsement of the concept without taking actions to involve managers and staff at lower levels in the organization will not enhance the beneficial way of thinking that emerges from the concept.

Figure 9-5 Clarkson's Stakeholders Performance Profile

Company:					
1 The Company	**1**	**2**	**3**	**4**	**NR**
1.1. Company History	•	•	•	•	•
1.2. Industry Background	•	•	•	•	•
1.3. Organization Structure	•	•	•	•	•
1.4. Economic Performance					
1.5. Competitive Environment					
1.6. Mission or Purpose					
1.7. Corporate Codes					
1.8. Stakeholder & Social Issues Mgt. Systems					

Figure 9-5 Clarkson's Stakeholders Performance Profile (continued)

Company:

2 Employees	1	2	3	4	NR
2.1. General Policy					
2.2. Benefits					
2.3. Compensation and Rewards					
2.4. Training and Development					
2.5. Career Planning and Development					
2.6. Employee Assistance Program					
2.7. Health Promotion					
2.8. Absenteeism and Turnover					
2.9. Leaves of Absence					
2.10. Relationships with Unions					
2.11. Dismissal and Dismissal Appeal					
2.12. Termination, Layoff and Redundancy					
2.13. Retirement and Termination Counselling					
2.14. Employment Equity and Discrimination					
2.15. Women in Management and on the Board					
2.16. Daycare and Family Accommodation					
2.17. Employee Communication					
2.18. Occupational Health and Safety					
2.19. Part-time, Temp or Contract Employees					
2.20. Other Employee or H.R. Issues					

3 Shareholders	1	2	3	4	NR
3.1. General Policy					
3.2. Shareholder Comm. and Complaints					
3.3. Shareholder Advocacy					
3.4. Shareholder Rights					
3.5. Other Shareholder Issues					

Figure 9-5 Clarkson's Stakeholders Performance Profile (continued)

The Stakeholder Performance Profile					
4 Customers	**1**	**2**	**3**	**4**	**NR**
4.1. General Policy					
4.2. Customer Communications					
4.3. Product Safety					
4.4. Customer Complaints					
4.5. Special Customer Services					
4.6. Advertising and Marketing					
4.7. Customer Service and Quality					
4.8. Other Customer Issues					

5 Suppliers	**1**	**2**	**3**	**4**	**NR**
5.1. General Policy					
5.2. Relative Power					
5.3. Other Supplier Issues					

6 Public Stakeholders	**1**	**2**	**3**	**4**	**NR**
6.1. Governments					
6.2. Envir. and Public Health Protection					
6.3. Environmental Assessment					
6.4. Other Environmental Issues					
6.5. Community Relations					
6.6. Social Investment and Donations					

Rating Key		
1	Reactive	Very Unsatisfactory
2	Defensive	Unsatisfactory
3	Accommodative	Satisfactory
4	Proactive	Very Satisfactory
NR	Not Rated	

SOURCE: Max Clarkson. (1992). *A Stakeholder Theory of the Firm: Building on Preston, Carroll, Wartick and Cochran, and Wood.* Working Paper, University of Toronto, p. 16

Managers must avoid overexamination, or analysis paralysis, that can prevent action or initiatives from being taken. There is also a possibility of "The Snail Darter Fallacy," which causes managers to spend excessive amounts of time drawing stakeholder maps and analyzing minute behaviours. Distinctions must be made between important and unimportant stakeholders to narrow the list of stakeholders. The small or too insignificant stakeholder and issue must be left to others. However, management must be careful in making these assessments as the "snail darter" stakeholders can at times hold the balance of power on an issue (Freeman, 1984, pp. 188–191).

SUMMARY

This discussion of managing issues and stakeholders focuses on operationalizing a corporation's response to social responsibility and business ethics. Issues and stakeholders management provide frameworks by which corporations can come to grips with what is, or might be, happening in society.

Issues management is comprised of several components: the identification of issues, the analysis of potential impacts, the development of responses, and the implementation of programs or policies to address issues. The approach to each component is outlined, and although the process appears to be logical and straightforward on paper, it is challenging to implement in practice. It should be remembered that issues are viewed from different perspectives focusing on public policy, corporate strategy, and pressure groups. Each perspective has its advantages, and the actual approach used should ideally blend the three and consider all stakeholders.

Issues exist in society at various times and with varying intensity: one way of viewing this flucuation is as an issue life cycle. As with the product life cycle, managers must respond to issues differently at various stages. Hopefully, an effective issues management process will minimize surprises relating to events or trends in society, and coordinate management's response. There are several benefits to practising issues management, including a bottom-line emphasis, that is, it may provide a competitive advantage over rivals.

The second topic in this chapter is stakeholder management. Issue and stakeholder management overlap and should not be considered mutually exclusive. The outcome from either approach will most likely be the same, but the starting point focused on differs. Stakeholder management involves managing relationships with specific stakeholder groups in an action-oriented way. In other words, managers should not just let things happen. Four approaches to stakeholder management are outlined: basic, a preliminary, straightforward approach; stakeholder management capability; the diagnostic typology; and Clarkson's stakeholder model of social performance. These approaches are not the only ones available, but they do provide some appreciation for the implementation of a stakeholder management process.

This chapter discusses some "how to" considerations of social responsibility. The following chapter examines some attempts to measure or report on corporate social performances.

REFERENCES

Ansoff, I. (1980). Strategic issue management. *Strategic Management Journal,* 1(2), 131–148.

Arrington, Charles B., Jr., and Richard N. Sawaya. (1984). Managing public affairs: Issues management in an uncertain environment. *California Management Review,* 26(4), (Summer) 148–160.

Baetz, Mark C. and Donald H. Thain. (1985). *Canadian Cases in Business–Government Relations.* Toronto: Methuen.

Brander, James A. (1988). *Government Policy Toward Business.* Toronto and Vancouver: Butterworths.

Bryson, John M. (1988). *Strategic Planning for Public and Nonprofit Organizations.* San Francisco: Jossey-Bass Publishers.

Carroll, Archie B. (1979). A three-dimensional conceptual model of corporate performance. *Academy of Management Review,* 4(4), 497–505.

Carroll, Archie B. (1989). *Business and Society: Ethics and Stakeholder Management.* Cincinnati, OH: South-Western Publishing.

Carroll, Archie B. (1991, July/August). The pyramid of corporate social responsibility toward the moral management of organizational stakeholders. *Business Horizons,* 39–48.

Clarkson, M.B.E. (1991). Defining, evaluating, and managing corporate social performance: The stakeholder management model. *Research in Corporate Social Performance and Policy,* 12, JAI Press Inc., pp. 331-58

Clarkson, Max. (1992). *A Stakeholder Theory of the Firm: Building on Preston, Carroll, Wartick and Cochran, and Wood.* Working paper, University of Toronto.

Coates, Joseph F., Vary T. Coates, Jennifer Jarratt, and Lisa Heinz. (1986). *Issues Management: How You Can Plan, Organize and Manage the Future.* Mt. Airy, MD: Lomond Publishers, Inc.

Corcoran, Terence. (1990, December 15). Disclosing the great stakeholder hoax. *The Globe and Mail,* p. B4.

Crookell, Harold. (1991). *Managing Business Relationships with Government.* Scarborough, ON: Prentice Hall Canada.

Dutton, Jane E., Eric J. Walton, and Eric Abrahamson. (1989). Important dimensions of strategic issues: Separating the wheat from the chaff. *Journal of Management Studies,* 26(4), 379–396.

Freeman, R. Edward. (1984). *Strategic Management: A Stakeholder Approach.* Boston: Pitman.

Johnson, Jon. (1983, Fall). Issues management—What are the issues? *Business Quarterly,* 48, p. 22.

Kingdon, J. W. (1984). *Agendas, Alternatives and Public Policies.* Boston: Little, Brown.

Mahon, John F. and Sandra A. Waddock. (1992). Strategic issues management: An integration of issue life cycle perspectives. *Business and Society,* 31(1), 19–32.

Murray, V. V. (ed.). (1985). *Theories of Business–Government Relations.* Toronto: Trans-Canada Press.

Rea, K. J. and Nelson Wiseman (eds.). (1985). *Government and Enterprise in Canada.* Toronto: Methuen.

Savage, Grant T., Timothy W. Nix, Carlton J. Whitehead, and John D. Blair. (1991). Strategies for assessing and managing organizational stakeholders. *Academy of Management Executive,* 5(2), 61–75.

Stanbury, W. T. (1986). *Business–Government Relations in Canada.* Toronto: Methuen.

Wartick, Steven L. and Philip L. Cochran. (1985). The evaluation of the corporate social performance model. *Academy of Management Review,* 10(4), 758–769.

Wartick, Steven L. and Robert E. Rude. (1986). Issues management: Corporate fad or corporate function? *California Management Review,* 29(1), (Fall) 124–140.

Weimer, David L. and Aidan R. Vining. (1992). *Policy Analysis: Concepts and Practice* (2nd ed.). Englewood Cliffs, NJ: Prentice Hall.

CORPORATE SOCIAL PERFORMANCE

INTRODUCTION

The framework of corporate social responsibility outlined at the beginning of Part II comprises three components: responsibility, responsiveness, and performance. Chapters 7, 8, and 9 deal with social responsibility and responsiveness, and this chapter discusses corporate social performance.

THE OUTCOMES OF CORPORATE BEHAVIOUR

Wood's (1991) framework, described in the Introduction to Part II, labels corporate performance as "outcomes" and identifies three: "the social impacts of corporate behaviour, regardless of the motivation for such behaviour or the process by which it occurs; the programs companies use to implement responsibility and/or responsiveness; and the policies developed by companies to handle social issues and stockholder interests" (Wood, 1991, p. 708).

When considering social impacts, all the activities of the corporation are examined. There has been considerable focus on oil spills, unsafe working conditions, and air pollution. These are the types of actions that are observable and open to assessment, the visible aspects of corporate social responsibility. But, everything a corporation does has some social impact, not just the obvious.

Corporations may undertake social programs to meet specific needs. For example, a corporation may fundraise for the Special Olympics. Corporate social policies are formed to address problems or areas of great interest or importance. Thus, a corporate social policy may be developed for the hiring of disabled persons and the accessibility of the workplace. Affirmative action policies and programs to hire women or minorities are another example. Most corporations respond to social impacts and develop social programs and policies on an ad hoc basis. Ideally they should have a comprehensive corporate social policy, but this is seldom the case.

The remainder of this chapter reviews topics relating to corporate social performance including the relationship of social performance to profitability; the correlation of community service goals with various organizational characteristics; corporate performance criteria; the measurement of social performance; and socially responsible investment. These are followed by some assessments of Canadian corporate social performance.

CORPORATE SOCIAL RESPONSIBILITY AND PROFITS

It is generally accepted that the blind pursuit of maximum profits is socially irresponsible. It is also believed that most enterprises have multiple objectives, some of which are social in nature. If these statements are accurate, it is interesting to speculate about the relationship between the extent of an enterprise's socially responsible actions and its level of profitability. There are several positions that can be argued, including the following:

- expenditures on social objectives reduce profits, especially in the short term
- expenditures on social objectives contribute to long-term profits
- the benefits from expenditures on social objectives may diminish after some point

The conclusion from studies is that the relationship between social responsibility and profits is not a very clear one—some studies have found a positive relationship while others have found no relationship. Other researchers have found a curvilinear relationship that might look something like that shown in

Figure 10-1 Social Responsibility and Profits

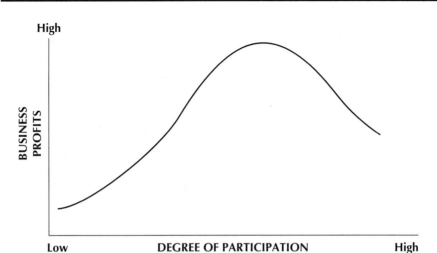

Figure 10-1. Up to a point, increased expenditures on social responsibility are associated with higher profits, but past this point further increases are associated with lower profit levels (Bowman and Haire, 1975; Brooks, 1986, pp. 10–14).

SOCIAL GOALS AND ORGANIZATIONAL CHARACTERISTICS

Corporate social performance varies considerably among corporations, and it is not understood why some commit more resources and effort to it than others. Kraft and Hage (1990) attempt to find out why some corporations place more importance on community service, one form of social performance, than others.

Their study correlates community service goals in 82 corporations, across several industries and over time with organizational characteristics such as goals, niches, structures, context, and performance. They formulate 11 hypotheses, which they test with the following results.

1) *The greater the profitability of the firm within its industrial sector, the greater the emphasis on community service.* (p. 12) This hypothesis is based on the relationships between profits and social responsibility discussed in the previous section), which was found not to be significant.

2) *The greater the emphasis on the prestige of the firm within its industrial sector, the greater the emphasis on community service.* (p. 12) The authors hypothesized

that the prestige of a corporation is important to its emphasis on cummunity service if there is concern for its image in the community. A significant relationship does exist, but the relationship is not clear as the causes of increased emphasis may lie in other areas, for example, the availability of slack resources.

3) *The larger the size of the firm within its industrial sector, the greater the emphasis on community service.* (p. 13)

4) *The greater the emphasis on the assets growth of a firm within its industrial sector, the greater the emphasis on community service.* (p. 13) This hypothesis, along with hypothesis #3, attempts to associate the influence of slack resources by relating community service to total assets and asset growth. The results show that corporations with greater assets and concerned with assets growth did place greater emphasis on community service.

5) *The greater the structural complexity of a firm within its industrial sector, the greater the emphasis on community service.* (p. 13) This hypothesis suggests that corporations with complex structural features place more emphasis on community service. For example, more highly educated employees and employees from a wide variety of occupations may contribute more to community service activities than others. The results show that this correlation is not significant.

6) *The greater a firm's emphasis on product quality of a firm within its industrial sector, the greater the emphasis on community service.* (p. 13)

7) *The greater the technological complexity of a firm within its industrial sector, the greater the emphasis on community service.* (p. 13)

8) *The broader the product line of a firm within its industrial sector, the greater the emphasis on community service.* (p. 13) Hypotheses #6, #7, and #8 suggest that corporations who were more innovative with technology, producing new or improved products of higher quality, are also more community service minded. The results show a significant correlation only for hypothesis #6.

9) *The greater the emphasis on price competition within an industrial sector, the less the emphasis on community service.* (p. 13) This hypothesis states that the existence of competitive pressure, especially price competition, has a negative impact, but the results do not show a significant correlation.

10) *The greater the centralization of a firm's decision-making structure within its industrial sector, the less the emphasis on community service.* (p. 14)

11) *The greater a firm's emphasis on short-term profits within its industrial sector, the less the emphasis on community service.* (p. 14) It was proposed that centralization of decision-making may indicate that corporations are more concerned about profit maximization, regardless of sound costs, and that corporations place more emphasis on short-term profits. The results show

that correlation described in hypothesis #10 is not significant, but significant in hypothesis #11.

Kraft and Hage conclude that there is a performance–causes–community service relationship. The purpose of this brief summary is not to arrive at definite answers about why some corporations perform more socially than others. It has to be recognized that every relationship is very complex, and at this time research has not found clear relationships between corporate social performance, profits, or other organizational characteristics.

CORPORATE SOCIAL REPORTING

Corporate social reporting can take different approaches and is often referred to as social auditing. A social audit is a systematic assessment that identifies, measures, evaluates, reports, and monitors the effects an enterprise has on society that are not covered in the traditional financial reports. The purpose of social auditing is to provide information to management and to various stakeholders about the impact of the enterprise on society, and to provide a basis of accountability for the social consequences of corporate activities. Such audits can be used to assess existing performance, to evaluate the performance of managers in relation to social objectives, to provide an information base for planning, and to serve as a measure for assessing future performance.

There are many social auditing approaches. The main ones are:

- *Inventory*—a listing of social activities without any evaluation.

- *Program Management*—statement describing particular programs or initiatives including an indication of the resources committed.

- *Process*—a more elaborate approach incorporating the inventory and program management approaches. It includes an assessment of how each social program came into being, a statement of each program's objectives and the rationales behind each activity, and a description of what has been accomplished.

- *Cost or Outlay*—a social-economic operating statement that tabulates the expenditures an enterprise makes on social objectives less the negative costs for social objectives not addressed. The approach is to measure the total social impact, positive and negative.

- *Social Responsibility Accounting*—a system of accounting that tabulates social costs and benefits with the objective of the best social return for the social investment made.

- *Social Indicators*—an audit of the community is conducted using social indicators to provide data on the most pressing needs. Corporate social performances are compared or related to community or social indicators.

Although often referred to, there are few true examples of social audits that can be identified in Canadian business. It is not an easy process: the list of social activities may be lengthy, there are problems with standards and measurements, and audits are of limited value if not made public. Social auditing received substantial attention among researchers and practitioners in the 1970's and early 1980's. Buchholz states that the "social audit, through generating some useful and interesting ideas and concepts, never readily produced anything approaching a consensus on ways to measure social performance" (1991, p. 23). On the other hand, Wood suggests that social reporting is an area of research that should be reviewed "to help give substance to the evaluation of corporate social performance" (1991, p. 708).

PERFORMANCE CRITERIA, INCLUDING ETHICAL

Managers have to move toward thinking about all the corporation's performance and ethical criteria, but this has not traditionally been done. Hosmer (1991) claims that in the past corporations had a hierarchy of managerial responsibility that went from operational at the bottom through functional and technical to conceptual at the top. To this hierarchy, Hosmer adds ethical managerial responsibilities and identifies performance criteria for the complete hierarchy, as shown in Figure 10-2.

The operational level is at the bottom of the hierarchy of managerial responsibilities. At this level, goods or services are provided, customers are served, revenues are generated, and bills are paid. The performance criteria at this level include satisfying customers, improving products, and conserving assets. These criteria are listed opposite the appropriate portion of the hierarchy in Figure 10-2.

Functional management involves developing marketing, production, and financial policies, and the performance criteria include maximizing revenues, minimizing costs, and optimizing return. At the third level, improved planning and performance are developed through the activities of the human resource, data processing, and engineering departments with performance criteria being the involvement of people, utilization of information, and the application of technology. Conceptual management involves strategic management-type planning including the development of corporate missions, assessments of the environment, assessment of resource capacity and capability, establishment of objectives, selection of a strategy, and strategy implementation. The performance criteria are objectives, the ability to gain an advantage, and building competencies.

Hosmer states that if these four managerial activities perform well and if their twelve performance criteria are met, then the corporation could be considered as operating with "adequate economic efficiency (converting scarce resources into essential goods and services at minimal costs) and with satisfactory effectiveness (providing returns or achieving "rents" above the mean for all other firms in the industry)" (1991, 52). The question posed, then, is "Is this enough?" Ethicists and social philosophers respond no.

The traditional view of the corporation as represented by the four managerial responsibilities must be broadened in scope. This extended view of the corporation includes its contributions to national communication, transportation, education, and health care systems and the influence of global trade agreements, monetary exchanges, cost factors, and resource constraints. This extended view leads to the ethical level of activities and responsibilities.

Figure 10-2 The Managerial Responsibility Hierarchy and Performance Criteria

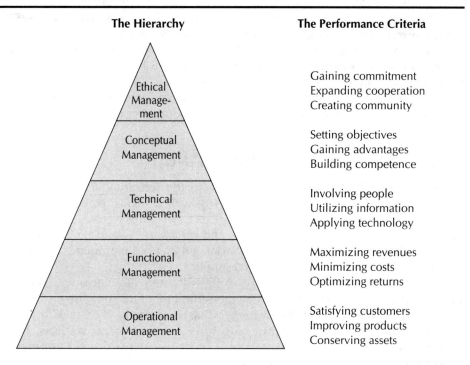

The Hierarchy	The Performance Criteria
Ethical Management	Gaining commitment Expanding cooperation Creating community
Conceptual Management	Setting objectives Gaining advantages Building competence
Technical Management	Involving people Utilizing information Applying technology
Functional Management	Maximizing revenues Minimizing costs Optimizing returns
Operational Management	Satisfying customers Improving products Conserving assets

SOURCE: Adopted from Hosmer, LeRue Tone, Managerial responsibilities on the micro level, *Business Horizons*, July/August, 1991, pp. 49–55.

The distribution of the benefits granted and the allocation of costs or harms imposed by the corporation are activities at this level. Examples of benefits distribution would be increasing salaries, paying bonuses, raising dividends, or the building of plants, while examples of allocating harm would be cutting salaries, eliminating bonuses, reducing dividends, or downsizing or closing plants. These activities are challenging and difficult to do in such a manner that all stakeholders are satisfied. Hosmer argues that stakeholders in an extended organization who believe they have been treated "rightly" or "justly" will be committed to the organization, and more willing to cooperate, and tend to develop a sense of communicating that leads to a total organizational effort. This will lead to a corporation that will perform with economic efficiency, and respond with competitive effectiveness in addition to the commitment to total organizational effort (1991, 54).

Senior executives should make use of ethical principles in distributing benefits and allocating harms rather than economic criteria. The ethical principles and theories discussed in Chapter 8 would be used to determine which criteria are "more right" or "more just" by all stakeholders. Ethical management performance criteria are the most difficult to learn, as they are the least measurable. Managers who are intuitively aware of social responsibilities, ethical formulations, and social responsiveness, are those who are better prepared to stride toward these abstract ethical performance criteria.

The next section of this chapter considers social performance from another perspective: how suppliers of capital evaluate socially responsible performance.

SOCIALLY RESPONSIBLE INVESTING

Socially responsible investment (SRI) refers to the screening of investments in the corporate sector for their social benefits, as well as their financial or economic actions. These investments are usually stocks of publicly traded enterprises, but some funds are comprised of bonds and others are "balanced." This is also referred to as "ethical investment" or "social conscience investment," and in the context of the environment, "green investment."

There is a growing awareness of the possibilities of achieving acceptable rates of return and social objectives at the same time. Individual investors have an appreciation of this, but the awareness has most likely been fuelled by the investment decisions of churches and other religious organizations, trade unions, women's organizations, the cooperative systems, the environmental movement, universities and colleges, and pensions funds.

The Canadian financial community has quickly responded to the growing awareness of and demand for socially responsive investments. Several mutual funds have been established that have "socially responsible" objectives, including:

1) The Ethical Growth Fund, established by Vancouver City Savings Credit Union

2) The Crown Commitment Fund, managed by Crown Life Insurance, Toronto

3) The Summa Fund, managed by Investors Group Inc., of Winnipeg

4) The Environmental Investment Canadian Fund and Environmental Investment Fund, sponsored by Energy Probe, Toronto

5) Clean Environment Equity and Clean Environment Balanced Funds by Acuity Investment Management, Toronto

6) The Dynamic Global Green Fund by Dynamic Funds Management, Toronto

These funds are categorized into two types, "do gooder" or "objectionable." A "do gooder" fund invests in corporations with good environmental records and enlightened industrial and stakeholder relations. The other type, "objectionable" funds, screen out objectionable corporations; those, for example, involved in alcohol, tobacco, weapons, and nuclear power (Trapunski, 1983).

These funds have sensitized managers to the fact that at least some investors make investment decisions based upon how socially responsible the enterprise is. It is not possible to measure the impact on business in any definitive manner, and the total investments in these funds are small in comparison to the total mutual fund market.

The motives of the financial community raise compelling thoughts. Does it really believe in socially responsible investing or is this simply a response to a market demand? Are the funds merely shrewd marketing? The motives of investors can also be questioned. How long would they continue to invest in a socially responsible fund that lost money?

The Investment Criteria or "Screens"

The criteria, or "screens," used in making socially responsible investments vary by fund and provide a method by which a prospective investment is judged to be socially acceptable. The activities that might be considered socially irresponsible or unethical include:

- poor employee/labour relations
- failure to promote racial and sexual equality and affirmative programs
- the manufacture of weapons
- involvement in the nuclear industry
- the manufacture of "sin" products such as alcohol or tobacco
- the conducting of business in apartheid South Africa or other repressive regimes violating human rights
- enterprises that are not environmentally sensitive; for example, those that pollute
- manufacturers or providers of unsafe goods and services; for example, asbestos products involved with questionable marketing practices (for example, misleading advertising) and especially exploitive marketing in Third World countries

- enterprises that use animals in product testing
- involvement in gambling and pornography

It should be noted that not all funds apply all the above criteria. In fact, most are very selective. For example, Exhibit 10-1 lists the criteria used by the Ethical Growth Fund.

Exhibit 10-1

Investment Objectives and Policies for the Ethical Growth Fund

Investment Objectives

The investment objective of this Fund is to maximize long-term capital return by investing in a diversified portfolio consisting primarily of Canadian common stocks, all within the ethical and moral framework of the investment policies. The assets of the Fund may from time to time, however, be placed in different classes of assets such as short-term investments, bonds, debentures, and equities (common or preferred shares).

Investment Policies

In addition to the fundamental investment objective of the Fund, the Declarations of Trust provide certain investment policies. The Fund will be socially responsible, meaning that the Fund will use specified ethical and moral standards in making investments and the monies of the Fund will only be invested in securities of North American corporations which meet the criteria established from time to time by the Trustees. For these purposes the following criteria must be met on any investment in a North American corporation:

1. The corporation must have either its registered or head office located in Canada and its shares and other securities must be either traded or about to be traded on a stock exchange in Canada.
2. The corporation should encourage progressive industrial relations with all members of its staff or employees.
3. The corporation should regularly conduct business in, and with, a country or countries that provide racial equality within its or their political boundaries.
4. The corporation should not derive a significant portion of its income from tobacco.
5. The normal business of the corporation should be the provision of products or services for civilians (non-military).
6. If the corporation is an energy corporation or utility, its major source of revenue should be from non-nuclear forms of energy.
7. The corporation should consistently strive to comply with environmental regulations established by governments and government agencies, and be committed to implementing environmentally conscious practices.

SOURCE: The Family of Ethical Funds, *Consolidated Simplified Prospectus*, dated September 27, 1993, pp. 8–9.

The Social Investment Organization (SI0)

The Social Investment Organization was formed in 1990 to promote ethical and alternative investing in Canada. It is a non-profit organization and maintains an independent information source for those involved in social investment (*The SIO Forum*, 1990).

Investors do not have to purchase mutual funds or belong to the SI0 to make social investments. Individuals can develop their own fund based upon their own values and objectives. Financial newspapers regularly discuss social investing and books on this are available (for example, Kinder, Lydenberg and Domini, 1992; Ellmen, 1990).

Problems of Remaining Socially Responsible

What is a socially responsible investment? Ideally, it is one that does not violate any of the activities on the list above. If the criteria on this list had to be met, few investments would be made. There are some problems with socially responsible investments as suggested by the following situations.

1) What if the company held experiences a violent strike after several years of good labour relations?

2) How does a fund distinguish between good and bad? For example, does military production include trucks and jeeps; or do airlines pollute?

3) What if society's standards change? For example, fast food firms may fall from favour. What does the fund do if it has substantial holdings in those firms?

Apparently, it is not easy to be socially responsible. The Ethical Growth fund found this out when questioned about the ownership of Imasco Ltd. shares, the parent company of Imperial Tobacco. When the fund was originally established, this type of investment was included. Imasco Ltd. is no longer included in the fund.

The Performance of Socially Responsible Investment

The financial performance of socially responsible investment funds has been reasonable. For example, The Ethical Growth and Summa Funds have out performed the average of all Canadian equity funds in the past three and five year periods. Like any other mutual fund, past performance does not guarantee future performance. It is not clear whether or not mixing profits and principles will actually pay investors over the long term.

Another dynamic of social investing is the role of the pension fund. It is possible that the managers of such funds will come under pressure from fund contributors to invest in such a way that reflects their social values. The managers, in turn, might make an investment decision on social criteria which pressures corporation managers to behave in socially responsible ways. The influence of such pressure is not clear at this time. Even so, individuals making direct investments or indirect investments through funds may be prompting decisions that influence managers to improve their corporation's social performance.

CANADIAN CORPORATE SOCIAL PERFORMANCE

There have been three comprehensive research efforts to assess Canadian corporate social performance: the Royal Commission on Corporate Concentration, "Corporate Social Performance in Canada," Study No. 21 (1977) (Canada, 1978), a study undertaken by Brooks (1986) on behalf of the Society of Management Accountants of Canada, and the research of Clarkson (1988) at the University of Toronto.

The Royal Commission's Study of Social Performance

The Royal Commission report in 1978 discussed the social consequences of corporate concentration and arrived at several conclusions (Canada, *Report*, 1978, Chapter 16): society expects business to be humane as well as efficient; the corporation cannot incur unlimited costs that will not be recovered in sales or that restrain profits; all costs of solving social problems cannot be placed on businesses, as corporations operate within a narrower and sometimes ruthless economic framework; Canadian business can only be as responsive to social demands as others outside this country will allow it to be; business managers should not be expected to always to be in the forefront of social change; and society should be careful about the kinds of social obligations it asks business to assume, while business should be equally cautious in accepting them.

The Report stated that society and corporations have agreed that corporations have a social responsibility, but that the challenge is to give meaning to the ambiguousness of this responsibility. It went on to identify techniques of corporate response, codes of behaviour, and social reporting, and commented on the place of law in corporate social responsibility. The Commission saw little reason to encourage the idea that codes of behaviour, whether formed by corporation or by the government, would contribute positively to corporate social responsibility. This, one might venture to say, cynicism was attributed to the nature of social responsibility and to the limitation of codes. Insofar as social reporting such as social accounting and social auditing, the Commission found doubtful that it would be possible to devise systems to measure the social impact of business decisions ever approximating financial accounting systems. However, it believes social reporting may develop in the future. Lastly, legislation will improve social responsibility when government is convinced that social concerns cannot be left to the whims of corporate conscience or when the results of legislative inaction are judged to be intolerable. Since the law, however, as it is constituted may not go far enough to solve a social problem for some, and too far for others, it concluded that traditional legal weapons are often inadequate to deal with corporate social conduct or misconduct.

The Royal Commission also prepared a background paper on corporate social performance in Canada (Mactaggart et al., 1977). This paper presented the results of a mail survey of 1083 Canadian corporations with $10 million or more annual gross revenues and generated 284 usable responses. The corporate social involvement process was viewed as consisting of three stages: (1) a general awareness among corporate management that the firm is a social and political, as well as economic, institution, and a recognition of specific impacts of corporate activity in society, and their consequences; (2) analysis (data gathering and interpretation) and planning related to both general awareness and specific impacts, and (3) direct response, including changes in internal policies and organizational structures as well as modification to external behaviour (1977, 17). A portion of the survey's results are as follows:

1) As the size of the firms increases (either on the basis of annual gross revenues or total number of employees), the levels of awareness/recognition, analysis/planning, and response to corporate social involvement increase.

2) Companies with above average after-tax profits demonstrate higher levels of response at all three stages of social involvement than do those with below average profits.

3) The extent of Canadian ownership appears to have little effect on the responsiveness of the firms to corporate social involvement. Generally, foreign-controlled firms seem to be as responsive at each stage of involvement as the "Canadian" firms.

4) There are significant variations in levels of response to corporate social involvement by type of industry. However, these variations do not reveal any clear pattern from one question to another.

5) Type of organizational structure (centralized or decentralized) does not significantly influence the stage of corporate social involvement.

6) Throughout the analysis, responding firms reported involvement in "analysis and planning" more frequently than in actual response. This is not inconsistent with the "state of the art" in Canada. It suggests that many firms (particularly the larger ones) are thinking and planning relative to their corporate social involvement but moving cautiously into the "response/implementation"

stage of development. There appears to be a growing potential for active corporate social policies, but they have not yet been formalized and implemented.

The above is only a part of the findings, but it does provide a sense of Canadian corporate social performance in the 1970's. More detailed results are available in the paper along with more case studies.

The Society of Management Accountants' Study

A comprehensive study of the social performance of Canadian business was undertaken by Brooks (1986). His study found that the ten most common topics in the social objective statements of Canadian business enterprises were those listed in Table 10-1. This study was completed in the mid 1980's, and explains why topics such as business ethics and concern for the environment were not included. Brooks' (1986) main findings and conclusions are as follows:

1) The effects of corporate decisions on the quality of life should be included in the social performance scale and, as more Canadian executives pursue corporate social performance, an integration of economic and social objective will occur.

2) The management of corporate social performance will be increasingly formalized through such practices as the preparation of statements of corporate social objectives and programs to raise the social awareness of employees.

3) Social Performance Guidelines (SPC) should be developed by industry to provide a basis for comparison of enterprise performance, and management should emphasize managing and disclosing corporate social performance.

4) Canadian society will continue to expect higher levels of social performance and accountability from business enterprises (Brooks, 1986, pp. 263–267).

The University of Toronto Study

Man Clarkson, a professor at the Faculty of Management, University of Toronto, started a research project identifying corporate social performance in 1983, and it has been ongoing since then (refer to Chapter 8 for recent reports of Clarkson's research). Clarkson (1988) based his model on the work of The Royal Commission on Corporate Concentration and the research of Wartick and Cochran (1985) and Carroll (1979), and used students to assess corporate social performances through industry case studies.

The study has resulted in extensive findings, only some of which are reviewed here. Corporations considered to be high social performers were characterized as: (1) having clear, explicit, widely circulated statements of mission or purpose which mentioned social and ethical goals; (2) scanning systems included social and political trends and issues; (3) the output of these scanning systems

Table 10-1 Ten Most Important Topics in Canadian Statements of Social Objectives

1. Corporate citizenship
2. Conduct of personnel
3. Product or service-related commentary
4. Planning
5. Shareholders
6. Trust of the company name and representatives by the public, business community and employees
7. Competence of personnel
8. External communications
9. Customer needs
10. Internal communications

SOURCE: Leonard J. Brooks, Jr. *1986 Canadian Corporate Social Performance,* Chapter 6, Hamilton: The Society of Management Accountants of Canada.

were included in strategic planning; (4) there were linkages between statements of mission or purpose and the process of strategy formulation and implementation; and (5) the corporations were involved in public policy issues in a meaningful way.

Thirty-two corporate case studies were conducted, and the social performance of 17 corporations was described as "satisfactory," as they had above average economic performance and a proactive social orientation. Seven corporations with average economic performance and a proactive or accommodative social orientation were also considered to have satisfactory social performance. In the case of the remaining eight corporations, social performance was unsatisfactory, as their social orientation was accommodative while having below average economic performance. Economic orientation outranked social orientation in the less-profitable corporations, and the study concluded that there was a lower level of awareness and analysis of social and public policy issues in these corporations. Clarkson's research is continuing, and he is refining his model as more data is generated.

The evidence of corporate social performance in Canada is incomplete, but most corporations are sensitive to the issue. More specific discussions of corporate social performance follow in Part III.

SUMMARY

This chapter completes Part II, covering the theoretical and conceptual materials of corporate social responsibility, responsiveness, and performance. The discussions of corporate social performances were not intended to be specific, and concrete, but instead to be conceptual approaches.

Corporate social performance deals with the outcomes of corporate behaviour and whether they are socially beneficial or socially harmful activities. In all situations, profits are a factor. Despite demands on corporations to be socially responsible, they still must be economically responsible and earn profits. But the question becomes "how much profit?" The relationship between social responsibility and profits is not clear, but some researchers have found a curvilinear one to exist.

The next question addressed is "why some corporations place more emphasis on social activities than others." A study clarifying this issue is summarized. Some of the study's results established significant relationships between emphasis on social activity and such various structural features as size, growth, employee characteristics, products quality, price competition, and centralization of decision making. The findings did not evoke a clear portrait, but the study did establish performance-causes-community service relationships. The significant element to remember is that many features or characteristics of corporations impact on their social performance.

As measurement approaches have not yet received attention, more general criteria of social performance are discussed. It is argued that there is a hierarchy of managerial responsibilities—operational, functional, technical, conceptual, and ethical. Performance criteria exist for all levels in the hierarchy. This approach to social performance evaluation suggests that social awareness be incorporated in all decision-making and not left to after-the-fact measurements.

A section of the chapter describes socially responsible investing and the screening of investments in the corporate sector for social benefits. This type of investing is an indirect type of social performance measurement. The influence of social investing on managerial decision-making is difficult to assess, but it has the potential for increasing the awareness of social performance of business corporations.

Some findings of major studies of Canadian corporate social performance are summarized. One author concludes that the measurement of social performance should be formalized in the future. This study is followed by a discussion of corporate social performances. Despite the advocacy for greater measurement of social performances and the availability of a variety of measures, faint and inappreciable progress has been made in the past 10 years.

The theoretical and conceptual discussion of corporate social responsibility, responsiveness, and performance in this part serves as a gneral background portfolio for more focused discussions of corporate social activities in Part III. More specific issues relating to how the corporation responds to challenges will be examined in the following chapters.

REFERENCES

Bowman, E. H. and W. Haire. (1975). A strategic posture towards corporate social responsibility, *California Management Review,* 18, pp. 49–58.

Brooks, Leonard J. Jr. (1986). *Canadian Corporate Social Performance.* Hamilton: The Society of Management Accountants of Canada.

Buchholz, Rogene A. (1991, July/August). Corporate responsibility and the good society: From economics to ecology, *Business Horizons,* pp. 19–32.

Canada. (1978). *Report of the Royal Commission in Corporate Concentration.* Ottawa: Supply and Service Canada, Catalogue No. Z1–1975/1.

Carroll, A. B. (1979). A three dimensional conceptual model of corporate performance, *Academy of Management Review,* 4, pp. 497–505.

Clarkson, Max B. E. (1988). Corporate social performance in Canada, 1976–86, *Research in Corporate Social Performance and Policy,* 10, pp. 241–265.

Ellmen, Eugene. (1990). *The Canadian Guide to Profitable Ethical Investing.* Toronto: James Lorimer & Company.

Hosmer, LaRue Tone. (1991, July/August). Managerial responsibilities on the micro level, *Business Horizons,* pp. 49–55.

Kinder, Peter D., Steven D. Lydenberg, and Amy L. Domain (eds.). (1992). *The Social Investment Almanac: A Comprehensive Guide to Socially Responsible Investing.* Toronto: Fitzhenry and Whiteside.

Kraft, Kenneth L. and Jerald Hage. (1990). Strategy, social responsibility and implementation, *Journal of Business Ethics,* 9, pp. 11–19.

Mactaggart, R. Terrence et al. (1977). *Study No. 21. Corporate Social Performance in Canada: A Background Report* (Royal Commission on Corporate Concentration). Ottawa: Supply and Service Canada. Lot No. Z1-1975/1. pp. 41–21.

The SIO Forum. (1990, Summer). A Publication of The Social Investment Organization.

Trapunski, Edward. (1993, February 18). Ethical funds are targeting members of credit unions, *The Globe and Mail,* p. C5.

Wartick, S. L. and P. L. Cochran. (1985). The evolution of the social performance model, *Academy of Management Review,* 10, pp. 758–769.

Wood, Donna J. (1991). Corporate social performance revisited, *Academy of Management Review,* 16(4), pp. 691–718.

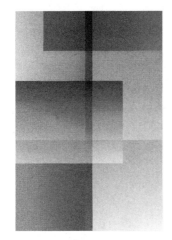

PART III

CHALLENGES IN THE BUSINESS STAKEHOLDER ENVIRONMENT

Chapter

The environment in which business functions is full of challenges that managers must address. In this section, some of the socially related challenges are examined. It is not possible to address all the challenges, and hence nine have been selected.

The nature of corporate ownership has always been challenging for Canadian managers, especially given the predominance of foreign subsidiaries in Canada. Recently, institutional investors, indirect owners such as through mutual and pension funds, are exerting influence that has advantages and drawbacks for managers. This is examined in Chapter 11.

The issue of corporate governance reform has been considered over about 20 years, but has received more prominence recently. This reform has implications for many stakeholders, not just owners, directors, and managers, and is key to the corporation's view of corporate social performance. Chapter 12 examines this issue.

Chapter 13 examines aspects of the role of government in the business enterprise system. Governments are important stakeholders, but it is important to recognize the implications of the changes in their role.

Corporate giving, or philanthropy, is a function considered to be paramount in the social performance of the corporation. Chapter 14 looks at the challenges involved in deciding to give or to not give money away.

A key stakeholder of any corporation is the employee. Chapter 15 discusses issues relating to human resources. Among the topics considered are employee loyalty, the work ethic, and the impact of business on family life.

Competitors and competition are examined in Chapter 16. Competitors are the other corporations competing in the same market, and hence the regulation of competitive behaviour is discussed. Competition also focuses on the recent use of the term "competitiveness" and what the implications are for Canadian business.

Chapter 17 discusses consumers, the most fundamental stakeholder group in the business enterprise system. This chapter illustrates how many corporations have, in the past especially, been driven by production instead of the dynamics of the market. The sovereignty of the consumer is defined and elaborated.

The natural environment has received considerable attention. Chapter 18 summarized the implications of the compelling attention being paid to the physical or natural environment.

The final chapter in this part examines the challenges involved with managing two stakeholder groups, the media and interest groups. Examples illustrate the issues and challenges.

All together, these chapters cover a substantial number of the issues and challenges that managers must cope with in their attempts to improve corporate social performance.

ISSUES OF OWNERSHIP AND CONTROL

Introduction

Changing Ownership Patterns

Who Cares About Ownership and Control of Canadian Business?

Summary

References

INTRODUCTION

The ownership patterns of Canadian business are changing, and owners are in due course recasting their influence on the corporation. This chapter outlines these changing ownership patterns and the consequences of the changes. The roles owners, managers, and governments have are identified in the second section. The impact on another stakeholder, directors, is examined in the next chapter.

CHANGING OWNERSHIP PATTERNS

In Chapter 5, the types of owners of the Canadian business enterprise system were outlined. That discussion focused on ownership and did not refer to control. The relationship between ownership and control is a complex one and is shifting, with implications for owners, directors, and managers. The following outlines some of the issues relating to this shifting relationship.

Widely Held Versus Concentrated Ownership

Most corporations that Canadians invest in are controlled by a dominant shareholder. Only 25 of the corporations in "The Top 500" (1992) listing are considered to be widely held (that is, no one shareholder holding more than 20 percent). The issue of control is critical to owners in both widely held and concentrated ownership situations.

In the situation where the ownership of the enterprise is widely dispersed among thousands of shareholders, it is argued that management actually controls the enterprise (Berle and Means, 1932; Blumberg, 1976; Galbraith, 1967; Monsen and Downs, 1968; Schumpter, 1942). Individual investors lack the means, and perhaps the will, to unite and challenge management's decisions. These investors are often apathetic, or side with the instructions or views of management. Even if shareholders oppose management, they are at a disadvantage in any proxy fight or vote to challenge management.

At the other extreme, investors who are shareholders in corporations dominated by one or a few shareholders who have controlling interest are also virtually powerless. Their few votes make no difference, as sufficient votes are controlled by the dominating shareholder. However, an irony exists here. The well-being of the small shareholder is actually dependent on the decisions of the dominant shareholder. This is not necessarily bad: figures on the performance of such dominated firms has indicated that they often outperform composite stock exchange indexes (Brodie and Siklos, 1988; Spence, 1985).

Wider distribution of ownership is still a desired state. For example, an editorial in *The Financial Post* stated:

> ..., the widest possible ownership of our economic resources is the best guarantee of preserving a competitive enterprise system. Competition within economic sectors reduces the likelihood of government seeing abuses in the system, and therefore lessens the chance of state intervention ("Wider Ownership ...," 1986, 8).

But encouraging Canadians to invest in stocks is still a challenge. The reasons given in a Toronto Stock Exchange study for the relatively low participation in the stock market were: 44 percent of those who do not invest in stocks consider the market too risky; one-third of those who are not shareholders do not have enough confidence in stockbrokers; and three-quarters of the respondents cite lack of money as the reason for not investing in stocks (*Canadian Shareowners*, 1986, 22).

Minority Versus Majority Shareholders

The widely held versus concentrated ownership issue naturally leads to the treatment of minority shareholders by dominating, or majority, shareholders. This has become an issue with the increase in the number of takeovers where the rights of minority holders are being overlooked. It is required by law that all shareholders be offered the same price, but there are other problems involving new issues and non-voting shares.

New issues of shares are made as a tactic to discourage a takeover. The problem is that existing shareholders will likely have their share value diluted, and this may reduce the chance of getting a higher price for their shares in any takeover bids. Sometimes these offers are "bought deals"; that is, the whole issue is sold to one purchaser, like a common share portfolio company. The issue of non-voting shares to raise capital and the implications on control are discussed in the next section.

The recourse available to minority shareholders relates to the matter of control. The obvious recourse is to sell, but this may not be advantageous to the shareholder. Minority shareholders are often widely dispersed, and thus it is difficult to develop an organized dissent. Some jurisdictions require that a "majority" of the minority shareholders must approve a takeover or management proposal, but it is difficult to mobilize even this scale of opposition. Shareholders are often ill informed of the implications of the deal or proposal, and usually side with management or the majority shareholder's position out of ignorance. There is, however, some change in this, in that mutual fund and pension plan managers are beginning to challenge majority shareholders.

Treating all shareholders alike is an issue of ownership and control. The two following sections discuss the problems being experienced by minority shareholders, voting versus non-voting shares, and passive versus active shareholder roles.

Voting Versus Non-Voting Shares

Traditionally, the ownership of one share has meant one vote and, at least in principle, the owners of shares directed the affairs of the corporation by evaluating management's performance and deciding upon the acquisition and disposal of assets. In other words, shareholders had certain rights based upon their voting privileges. This has changed with the introduction, in 1981, of non-voting or restricted shares (sometimes referred to as "uncommon" shares). Non-voting shares are common shares without voting privileges, while restricted shares involve some limit on voting; for example, only one vote for every 10 or 100 shares owned. It is estimated that about 11 percent of the shares traded on Canadian stock exchanges is in these types of shares (Shortell, 1986).

The creation of these types of shares allows management to control the corporation by concentrating voting power in the hands of a few friendly stockholders. Also, existing dominant owners can retain their control while still being able to raise capital. Up to 95 percent of the equity of some corporations is held by non-voting shareholders. The result is ownership (or stake) without control (or influence), and the fundamental tenet that ownership entails control is contradicted. Such a circumstance is believed to represent a threat to economic democracy and might lead to a decay of a central feature of the free market system.

These "uncommon" shares have been used as a defence against takeover, another aspect of control. As mentioned previously, this might not be in the best interests of the existing shareholders. Some jurisdictions require that existing shareholders approve the creation of these share classes, and in some cases, even the approval of the "majority" of the minority shareholders is necessary. Sometimes existing shareholders are protected by coat-tail provisions that require equal treatment of the holders of "uncommon" shares during takeover bids, and in other cases it has been suggested that these shareholders should be allowed to elect representatives to the Board of Directors.

The case can be made that voting shareholders have been unjustly treated. It is quite likely that non-voting shareholders might also be unjustly treated.

Passive Versus Active Shareholders

This section tries to capture the potential influence of several categories of owners who have been inactive, or passive, in the past. The discussion focuses upon: individual investors; the professional money managers who control the pension funds, mutual funds, and trusts; the managers of the common share portfolio companies; venture capitalists; and the institutional owners.

Individual Investors

Owners of small share holdings have not been active participants in controlling the activities of the corporation for the many reasons already mentioned in the previous part of this chapter. Despite having adequate information on the activities of the corporation, many small shareholders simply cast their votes with management without considering alternatives. There may be a feeling of hopelessness, but nevertheless they have some responsibility for at least being informed about the corporation and exercising their voting privileges. A large portion of shareholders are "nonregistered" in corporation records, and instead their holdings are recorded through the Canadian Depository for Securities. Effective March 1, 1988, public companies whose shares were listed on the Toronto and Montreal stock exchanges were required to send annual reports and proxy materials to all shareholders. This new arrangement provided the opportunity for owners of shares to exercise rights as shareholders which previously were not exercised. Although individual investors may not in reality have much power, they should exercise any power that they process through voting rights.

Professional Money Managers

Included in this group are the individuals who manage pension funds, mutual funds, and trusts. In the past, these managers were "passive"; that is, they did not exercise voting rights or otherwise attempt to influence the affairs of the corporation despite owning substantial numbers of shares. It is now argued that these professional money managers should be actively protecting the interests of the indirect owners. This does not mean involvement in the day-to-day decision making, but instead examining acquisitions, takeover bids, anti-takeover tactics, and major expenditures that will impact on the long-term performance of the enterprise. These money managers could not only protect their clients' interests, but also the interests of other minority shareholders by, for example, opposing the issuance of non-voting shares. Also, they have the resources to be "active" with research staff to examine proposals and the finances required for soliciting proxies and initiating legal actions.

There are arguments for and against the "active" role of the professional money managers. The first favorable argument is simply that since they represent owners they have an obligation to be involved. Also, they have the resources and the means to undertake action and coordinate their actions with other professional managers, a course of action that individual investors do not have. Counter-arguments include: the Board of Directors adequately represents owners; too much pressure may be placed on corporate managers to produce results that will reflect in fund performance measures; the personal power of the money managers may distort corporate management decisions; and abiding fear that money managers, as a group, may have too much power in the financial system. The Pension Commission of Ontario was concerned about the money managers having too much power and believed that it was preferable that a "passive" role be maintained. At one time, the Government of Ontario was giving consideration to legislation that would forbid pension fund managers from voting shares held in their funds.

The one type of professional money manager not mentioned is the manager of trusts. The issue of control is not as important in the case of trusts, as those who established the trusts most likely specified rules and procedures to be followed and who was to be making decisions with regard to the investments made.

Common Share Portfolio Company Managers

Several issues have arisen with these types of firms: there is a question as to who has the voting rights for the shares held, the holders of the preferred shares, the holders of the instalment receipts, or the managers of the portfolio companies. There is a possibility of a voting force being created if the managers exercise voting rights, the same argument as with pension and mutual funds managers. Another issue involves who receives shareholder information such as annual reports and proxy statements. Some corporations selling shares to portfolio companies have requested direct access to the shareholders. Finally, there is a possibility of avoiding insider trading regulations. Corporate insiders could own shares through the portfolio company and thus avoid regulations. Securities commissions are presently studying these issues.

Venture Capitalists

The issue with this group has to do with the degree of control. Venture capitalists request different forms of involvement when assisting an entrepreneur, such as participation in decisions on the number of representatives on the board of directors, assumptions of control if the enterprise appears to be failing, and participatory decision-making surrounding certain reporting requirements. It is generally believed that the entrepreneur loses some control when venture capitalists become involved.

Nonprofit Organization Owners

These owners seldom attempt to influence the actions of the enterprises in which they have invested. However, there are exceptions, such as where church groups have challenged enterprises who are involved in apartheid South Africa or in unethical marketing practices in developing nations. Through publicity, they may exert some influence, but they are not a major controller of corporate actions.

The Pros and Cons of Employee Ownership

It is claimed that ownership increases morale and company loyalty, motivating employees to greater effort. Productivity rises and higher profitability results. The term "worker capitalism" is often used to describe employee ownership, as workers are turned into capitalists through stock ownership. If widespread, employee ownership could lead to a deconcentration of wealth. Employee ownership has been shown to be an important variable in reviving the fortunes of enterprises that were not profitable enough to satisfy existing owners. Although not bankrupt, these enterprises, or branch plants, were often abandoned by their owners and rescued by management, entrepreneurs, and employees. In this manner, jobs were saved.

Employee ownership is not without difficulties. Employees who invest in the enterprise for which they work are in effect increasing their stake in the enterprise. Their jobs, and often savings and pensions, depend now upon the fate of one enterprise. Seldom do employees have majority ownership and control of the enterprise. Management may still run the enterprise as they wish, not relinquishing control to employees. By not disclosing financial and operating results, employees are often unaware of how well the enterprise is doing, and in some cases, employees may be manipulated by management as needed information is not available. If employees own shares, their participation in decision making may lead to nothing getting done, with endless meetings, discussions, and votes being very time consuming. In some cases, token democracy is practiced in the workplace despite the employee involvement in ownership, and the prospects for job security are not enhanced.

Employee ownership might provide another opportunity for management to control the enterprise. Some ESOPs (employee share ownership plans) have been labelled MESOPs, management entrenchment or management enrichment stock ownership plans ("ESOPs: Revolution or Ripoff," 1985, p. 94). Often a majority of shares are held by an entrepreneur or manager who orchestrated the employee buyout. In some cases, the entrepreneur, along with outside investors, has been accused of taking too much of the control, that is, ownership. In the case of stock purchase and option plans in large public companies, ESOPs might even help managements insulate themselves from hostile takeovers by increasing stock distribution in a group that would likely side with management.

Management Buyouts and Corporate Buybacks

Management buyouts and corporate buybacks should also be considered in relation to the issue of who controls the enterprise. In the case of management buyouts, the interests of existing shareholders must be considered. The concern is whether or not the shareholders receive a fair price. Only "insider" information can ascertain the true value of the enterprise, and this information may not be available even to the board of directors. Nevertheless, management buyouts often save the enterprise from failing, being dissolved, or being rationalized into the operations of a new owner.

Corporate buybacks involve the repurchasing of the enterprise's own shares. What must be ascertained is whether or not this is good or bad for shareholders, and what the implications are for control. Managers always claim to be making the best use of the shareholders' funds and justify the buyback in several ways. The buyback of shares reduces the dividends that have to be paid out and lessens the dilution of share value caused by stock purchase and option plans. Reducing the number of shares on the market will translate into higher per share value. Stock prices are increased by improved price/earnings ratios and the interest created in the stock by the increased market activity. It is argued that backbuys are logical when an enterprise downsizes or divests of some of its interests.

On the other hand, there are drawbacks. Borrowing to fund the repurchase means swapping debt for equity, increasing interest expense. It is a practice viewed by some as a vote of nonconfidence in the economy as the enterprise is not using available funds to finance operations, research and development, or expansion.

Buybacks are interesting when viewed from the perspective of management. It could be a technique for making controlling shareholders even more powerful by reducing the participation of individuals in the ownership of the enterprise. Management might also use this technique as a defense against hostile takeover, and might refinance at some future time by issuing non-voting shares in place of the voting ones.

Influence of Non-traditional Owners

In the discussion of owners in Chapter 5, several less common categories of ownership were identified; namely, customers, producers, and unions. In the case of consumer cooperatives, membership may be as apathetic as the individual investors, and therefore not necessarily participate in the governance of the enterprise. As cooperative enterprises become larger and the business operations more sophisticated, management gains influence over members, not too different from what happens with individual investors (Stewart-Patterson, 1985). The history of mutual insurance companies has not been good as far as the participation of policyholder owners in corporate governance. Again, managers appear to control the enterprise.

Producer cooperatives suffer from some of the same problems as consumer cooperatives. It is claimed that some large Western Canadian cooperatives have, in effect, been taken over by managers (Clancey, 1979). In the case of union ownership, conflicts of interest might easily arise. Unions might consider the creation or retention of jobs at the expense of profits, which might endanger the economic viability of the investment fund.

The Accountability of Government-owned Enterprises

The accountability, or control, of the enterprises owned by the government has been a major public administration issue for some time. A federal government report in 1977 entitled *Crown Corporations, Direction, Control, Accountability* contained proposals on the management and control of government, owned enterprises (Canada. Privy Council Office. *Crown Corporations . .* , 1977). Most Auditor General's Reports since 1976 have focused on some aspect of Crown corporation accountability. The Royal Commission on Financial Management and Accountability in the federal government concluded that the existing accountability framework was inadequate and recommended that enterprises be appropriately categorized on the basis of mandate, direction, control, and evaluation, and that reporting mechanisms be in place to ensure accountability (Canada. *Royal Commission on Financial Management and Accountability,* 1979). In addition, provincial governments have conducted studies and inquiries into the operation of their government-owned corporations. The Economic Council of Canada conducted an extensive study of public enterprises and reported in 1986 (Canada, Economic Council of Canada. *Minding the Public's Business,* 1986), and published several research studies on these enterprises, including one on *The Organization and Control of Crown Corporations* (Berkowitz and Kotowitz, 1985).

Sexty referred to the control problem being experienced as an "accountability dilemma" (Sexty, 1983). The trend to making Crown corporations operate in a more commercial manner has resulted in several accountability problems, including: (1) the newly defined, commercially oriented objectives of many public enterprises may be in conflict with social objectives in the national interest; (2) the consequences of evaluating performance based on commercial criteria, that is, profits; (3) the tendency for public enterprise managers to expand through diversification in an effort to improve commercial performance; (4) the method of calculating subsidization payments for non-economic activities required by the government; (5) the price at which a public enterprise should be sold to the private sector; (6) the degree of autonomy that should be granted the enterprises and their managements; and (7) the techniques for controlling and evaluating the commercial enterprises (Sexty, 1986).

Even with enterprises owned by governments, control is an issue. It has been suggested that some public enterprises in Canada are not controlled by anyone, but a more serious suggestion might be that managers have been influential. Even when public enterprises are privatized, the issue of ownership and control relationships does not disappear. Governments have to consider carefully who the enterprises are to be sold to—for example, individual investors through public offerings, pension or mutual funds, privately held corporations, or employees (Sexty, 1986). Every sale raises issues of ownership and control, and the public policy implications have to be thought through.

This section has synthesized the issues relating to the ownership and control of Canadian business enterprises. From this discussion, it is recognized that ownership does not necessarily equate with control. Some owners exert considerable control while others have virtually none. Corporate managers who may have no ownership interests often have significant influence over enterprises. Professional money managers who represent owners have not exercised control in the past, but might be a greater influence in the future. The final section of the paper identifies the two key players in the ownership versus control issue and explains why managerial accountability is critical.

WHO CARES ABOUT THE OWNERSHIP AND CONTROL OF CANADIAN BUSINESS?

After reviewing the categories of owners and the issues surrounding control of business enterprises, some observations can be made about who cares about the existing state. Several stakeholders are involved: owners, directors, government, and managers. The status of owners has been discussed in this section and

Chapter 5 and the consequences for directors will be reviewed in the discussion of corporate governance. Governments express their caring in the form of legislation and regulation, and some examples are provided. Managers care because they have the largest stake in the system at this time. In many categories of ownership, managers were identified as having considerable influence. For example, it was argued that managers have significant control in: widely held corporations; enterprises involved in employee ownership plans; and government-owned enterprises. These two groups are discussed in turn.

The Role of Government

Federal and provincial governments have appreciated the significance of the business enterprise system and have encouraged ownership by Canadians in a variety of ways. Some examples of government policies promoting ownership that have been used in recent years include:

1) Government "framework" regulation, such as incorporation legislation and competition policy, influences ownership conditions and control arrangements.

2) The federal government allows individuals investing in shares of Canadian enterprises to receive a tax credit on dividends received. The purpose is to encourage Canadians to participate in the Canadian business enterprise system through stock purchase.

3) Individuals were allowed to claim capital gains from business activities or transactions in shares to a lifetime maximum of $100,000. The capital gains exemption was eliminated in 1994.

4) Some provincial governments have attempted to encourage stock ownership through "stock savings plans." Stocks of companies headquartered and operating within the province were eligible for the plan. Individual investors received tax credits or deductions from taxable income by participating in the plans. For example, under Alberta's plan, taxpayers were allowed to save up to $3000 in taxes by investing in companies listed on the Alberta Stock Exchange. Some other provinces operated similar plans, all intended to promote increased levels of equity investment in corporations within the particular province.

5) A 20 percent tax credit on the cost of shares in national labour-sponsored venture capital corporations is available to individuals.

6) Federal and provincial governments have initiated various programs to encourage and assist small business formation.

7) Employee ownership has been encouraged through taxation policy, and assistance is given through grant, loan, and loan guarantee programs.

8) The securities industry is regulated by the provinces (main provinces being Ontario, Quebec, Alberta, and British Columbia), but some initiatives are being taken to establish a federal commission on securities to standardize laws and regulations and to respond to the development of an international integrated financial market.

Two areas where government action has been mixed is competition and securities laws. The legislation on merger and related matters is now in place. However, it is doubtful that the amendments will appreciably influence the concentration of corporate ownership in, or alter control of, Canadian enterprises. Securities Commissions do not appear to have kept pace with the problems of minority shareholdings and "uncommon" share classes. Existing securities laws do not appear to provide adequate protection for minority shareholders, and regulation will be required to enshrine minority shareholders' rights. Regulation might also be required for Board of Directors representation for minority and non-voting shareholders. The treatment of shareholders in takeovers and buy-outs should be addressed, as should the adequacy of information disclosure.

Government initiatives get a mixed review. This is not surprising given that the issues relating to ownership and control are complicated, with legislated solutions not always readily available. The matter is further complicated by federal and provincial governments both having jurisdiction over aspects of ownership and control.

The Role of Managers

Although government is unwilling or unable to resolve ownership and control issues, the role of managers should not be ignored. Traditionally, managers were to work for the interests of shareholders by maximizing their return. But it can be argued that managers appear to be behaving as if they owned the enterprises instead of merely managing them. Accountability to owners is questionable in many ownership categories. Shareholder democracy is not practised in most enterprises with directors selected by management from a small group, shareholders meetings being ineffective forums to challenge management actions, and proxy votes advantageous to management. Managers have also been accused of focusing on the short-term performances of their enterprises and ignoring the enterprises long-term well-being. Managerial competence is being questioned as performance declines in many sectors of North American business. Thus, the desirability of increasing management dominance is a concern.

Managerial Accountability

However, there is a counter to the above argument. It is claimed that managers have obligations to "stakeholders" other than owners. These other stakeholders include employees, suppliers, customers, creditors, and communities. It is interesting to note that none of these stakeholders have the freedom possessed by shareholders to sell their "stake." Yet, the stakes of these other groups in the business is just as great in relative terms. The result is that the manager must balance a multitude of conflicting claims. Which groups will have the most influence in the future is open to question. In relation to the ownership and control issue, the groups that are having the greatest impact are the professional money managers working on behalf of the indirect owners.

The role played by the professional money managers has altered substantially in recent years from a "passive" to an "active" one. As a result, the influence of corporate managers may be reduced. The managers of the pools of capital held in pension and mutual funds are exerting their influence by challenging takeover or purchase proposals, and simply by voting the shares they control. They are initiating court challenges in addition to lobbying governments and securities exchange commissions for changes to enhance ownership rights. At the present time, it appears that the professional money managers are spearheading a movement for change.

There are indications of positive changes in managers and the investment community. Many corporate managers are aware of, and practice, social responsibility. The stakeholder approach to management is being implemented in many enterprises. Some reform is taking place in corporate governance structures, and possibilities of democratizing the corporation are being considered (discussed in the following chapter). Ethical mutual funds are now offered to investors, and their investment decisions reflect the social responsiveness of enterprises and their managers. Even the increasing employee ownership plans, although not without problems, represent one aspect of an increasing emphasis by management on employee participation. If managers are becoming more socially responsible and are giving more consideration to the stakes or interests of all stakeholders in the business enterprise, the impact of their control might be in the best interests of society.

There are challenges associated with the ownership and control of Canadian business enterprises. But, the situation should not be viewed as one of hopelessness. The composition of ownership is always changing and at the same time there is a shifting influence, or control, by various owners. Given the dynamic nature of the Canadian business enterprise system, there will always be some stakeholders who will care enough to challenge the existing centers of influence.

SUMMARY

The "owner" stakeholder should not be viewed as any stereotype. Chapter 3 clearly establishes that there are several different types. The influence of the various owners shifts over time, and this results in differing views of the social responsibilities of the corporation.

Ownership has become more concentrated mainly due to the increasing role of indirect ownership through pension and mutual funds. In the 1980's, takeovers of one sort or another resulted in minority shareholder groups existing in many corporations and an increased concern that their interests were not be submerged by the majority owner or owners. At the same time, non-voting common shares were being offered with increaseing frequency. Again, the issue of shareholder voice became an issue.

Even though they have the right to participate through voting, many owners are passive investors. The question arises as to the appropriate role of pension and mutual funds managers in the governance process and whether or not their influence is advantageous to the corporation.

Ownership by stakeholders with another role complicates the ownership responsibilities. Employee ownership is an example of this, but there are also examples of customers and producers (suppliers) owning stakes in a corporation. The problem arising is a conflict between these roles.

During the 1980's, management buyouts and corporate buybacks were common. What is in the best interests to the original shareholders is questionable, as financers make deals often financed by debt of questionnable quality. Finally, governments still own many business corporations, and the issue here focuses around the accountability of these enterprises.

Throughout this disussion, the issue has usually been one about control. Ownership seldom equates with control, and as ownership shifts, so does control. Governments have influenced ownership, and to some degree control. But, the role of managers and their accountability is what is important especially for social responsibility activites of the corporation.

The next chapter covers a related topic, corporate governance, which also focuses on the accountability of managers and the director and owner stakeholders.

REFERENCES

Berkowitz, M.K. and Y. Kotowitz. (1985, July). *The Organization and Control of Crown Corporations,* Ottawa: Economic Council of Canada, Discussion Paper No. 285.

Berle, Adolph A. and Gardiner C. Means. (1932). *The Modern Corporation and Private Property.* New York: MacMillan.

Blumberg, Phillip I. (1976). *The Megacorporation in American Society.* Englewood Cliffs, N.J.: Prentice-Hall.

Brodie, Terry and Richard Siklos. (1988, January 18). A revealing ranking of Canada's top tycoons. *Financial Times of Canada,* pp. 18–19.

Canada. Economic Council of Canada. (1986). *Minding the Public's Business.* Ottawa: Supply and Services Canada, Catalogue No. EC22-135/1986E.

Canada. Privy Council Office. (1977). *Crown Corporations: Direction, Control, Accountability.* Ottawa: Supply and Services Canada, Catalogue No. CP32-29/1977.

Canada. Royal Commission on Financial Management and Accountability. (1979, March). *Final Report.* Ottawa: Supply and Services Canada, Catalogue No. 21-1977/1.

Canadian Shareholders: Their Profile and Attitudes. (1986, December). Toronto: The Toronto Stock Exchange.

Clancey, Brian. (1979, January). The awesome clout of the co-ops, *Canadian Business,* pp. 26–31, 61–63.

ESOPs: revolution or ripoff? (1985, April 15). *Business Week,* pp. 94–108.

The Top 500. (1992, Summer). *The Financial Post Magazine,* pp. 88–125.

Galbraith, John Kenneth. (1967). *The New Industrial State.* Boston: Houghton-Mifflin.

Monsen, R.J. and A.B. Downs. (1968, June). "A theory of large managerial firms, *Journal of Political Economy,* 72, pp. 221–236.

Schumpter, Joseph. (1942). *Capitalism, Socialism, and Democracy.* New York: Harper.

Sexty, Robert W. (1983, January-March). The accountability dilemma in Canadian Public enterprises: Social versus commercial responsiveness," *Annals of Public and Co-operative Economy,* 54, (1), pp. 19–33.

Sexty, Robert W. (1986). *Summary of the Issues Involved in the Commercialization and Privatization of Public Enterprise,* Parts 1 & 2. St. John's, Canada: Faculty of Business Administration, Memorial University of Newfoundland, Working Papers 86–14 & 86–15.

Shortell, Ann. (1986, October). Does the small shareholder have any clout? *The Financial Post Moneywise Magazine,* pp. 60–63.

Spence, Richard. (1985, January 28). Rating Canada's business elite, *Financial Times of Canada,* p. 1.

Stewart-Patterson, David. (1985, May 9). Co-ops fighting cynicism, apathy, *The Globe and Mail,* p. B5.

Wide ownership still best policy (1986, April 5). *The Financial Post,* p. 8.

REFORMING CORPORATE GOVERNANCE

INTRODUCTION

The preceding chapter examined the shifts in ownership patterns, the challenges presented for managers, and the role of government. This chapter focuses on the Board of Directors and the challenges that are confronting it. The discussion of this topic goes under the title Reforming Corporate Governance and usually refers to a discussion of changes to the Board and its operation.

Chapter 5 outlined the traditional roles of the Board and directors. This chapter defines corporate governance, identifies the issues relating to governance, and summarizes some of the recent discussions of this topic.

DEFINING CORPORATE GOVERNANCE

A governing system includes the processes, structures, and relationships through which decisions are made. Nations often have formal constitutional documents,

Figure 12-1 Stakeholders in Corporate Governance

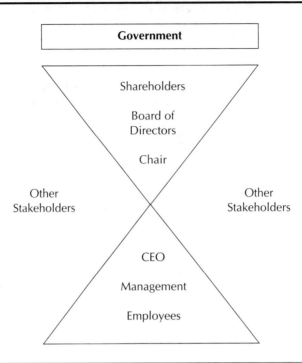

but corporations seldom do. However, there is a governance system in corporations even if not formally constituted. One definition of corporate governance is the processes, structures, and relationships through which the shareholders, as represented by a board of directors, oversees the activities of the business enterprise. A second frequently used definition is from the literature.

> Governance is concerned with the intrinsic nature, purpose, integrity, and identity of the institution, with a primary focus on the entity's relevance, continuity, and fiduciary aspects. Governance involves monitoring and overseeing strategic direction, socioeconomic and cultural context, resources, externalities, and constituencies of the institution (Mueller, 1981, p. 9).

In the first definition, the owners and director stakeholders were mentioned representing a more traditional view. In the second definition, the scope is much greater and the word constituencies is used in recognition of the numerous stakeholders that influence the governance of the corporation. A third definition is a more practical or applied one:

> "Corporate governance" means the process and structure used to direct and manage the business and affairs of the corporation with the objective of enhancing long-term

value for shareholders and the financial viability of the business. The process and structure define the division of power and accountability among shareholders, the board of directors and management and can have an impact on other stakeholders such as employees, customers, suppliers and communities. (Draft Report of The Toronto Stock Exchange Committee on Corporate Government in Canada).

The stakeholders are identified in this definition and the stakeholders are listed. The most important are identified in Figure 12-1 and discussed in the following pages.

STAKEHOLDERS IN CORPORATE GOVERNANCE

The Government's Role

As government regulates the incorporation of a business enterprise, it is included in the figure. The Canada Business Corporations Act (CBCA), the provincial corporations acts, and other legislation and regulation relating to the issuing of securities, competition policy, intellectual and industrial property, industrial relations, consumer protection, and bankruptcy impact upon the behaviour of the business corporation. In other words, this legislation provides the "framework" within which business enterprises form, operate, and cease to exist.

The Shareholders' (Owners') Role

Shareholders are, in theory, the ultimate authority within the corporation. In some corporations, there are hundreds of thousands of individual investors, none of whom own a substantial number of shares. Examples of such companies are Bell Canada, with over 330 000 shareholders, and the Bank of Montreal, with almost 100 000. At the other extreme, the shareholder stakeholders may be comprised of a few individuals (as in the case where a family group owns all the shares, for example, as with Eaton's) or of one or a few other corporations. In between these two extremes are many variations of shareholder makeup. Shareholders usually do not participate directly in the management of a corporation, especially if there are large numbers of them. According to incorporation legislation, they elect individuals to represent them with the Board of Directors (as provided in the CBCA, section 100(3)) and to appoint auditors (CBCA, section 127). But, in reality, the control of the corporation is delegated to the Board, which is mandated to look after their interests.

The Role of the Board

The role of the Board is to monitor and evaluate the corporation's activities and performance (CBCA, section 97(1)). The Board has the power to select, evaluate, and terminate the chief executive officer and top management (CBCA, section 116). The Directors are required to provide shareholders with financial statements and an auditor's statement (CBCA, section 149 (1)), and other financial and operational information required by the articles, by-laws, or a shareholder agreement. This information is usually presented as an Annual Report.

The Board should be planning for the longer term and ensuring for continuity and succession in the management term. Usually major transactions and ventures are evaluated and approved. A role assumed recently by some boards relates to addressing issues of corporate responsibility beyond the immediate interests of shareholders and employers; that is, the corporation's social responsibility.

The Role of the Chairperson

One member of Board is selected to be chairperson. The role of this director is the same as for all chairpersons of any committee: the calling and chairing of meetings, the preparation of meeting agendas, and the distribution of all materials required by the directors. Shareholders, directors, and the chairperson are usually considered to be the "external" component of a corporation's governance system, and the chief executive officer (CEO), top management, and employees the "internal" component.

The Role of Management

The CEO and top management are the main contacts that the "internal" component has with the corporation. In some corporations, the directors and top management are the same persons (referred to as "insiders"), and the chairperson of the Board and the CEO is the same person. However, in the corporate governance system, the roles are different even if the individuals are the same.

The "internal" component of the corporation is represented by the bottom triangle in Figure 12-1. This component is based upon the enterprise's structure, or hierarchical arrangement. The basic functions of an enterprise, marketing, finance, production, and human resource management are carried out within the departmental arrangements at various organizational levels. Management information, budgeting, planning, and control systems are developed to ensure that the business activities of the enterprise are carried out as intended. The focus in this discussion will be on corporate governance aspects of this component.

ISSUES RELATING TO CORPORATE GOVERNANCE

The corporate governance system has not worked perfectly. Exhibit 12-1 summarizes some of the issues. The rights of shareholders are an area of concern and are usually discussed as problems of "shareholder democracy." More attention has been devoted to this recently as takeovers or mergers that were resisted, or engineered, by management have resulted in some shareholders being mistreated. Also, it is questionable whether minority or widely dispersed shareholders have any influence in selecting members of the Board.

The Board has been the object of many suggestions for reform to overcome problems relating to its selection, composition, and organization. The commitment and interest of some members has been questioned. In addition, it is suggested that some members are not adequately informed by management of the activities of the corporation. It is considered undesirable for an individual to hold both the CEO and chairperson's positions. It is argued that the monitoring and evaluative role of the Board is thereby reduced. Even if Chair and CEO are separate individuals, there can still be an imbalance between the Board, and the CEO can, by his or her style, dominate the activities and effectiveness of the Board.

Within the hierarchy of the corporation, there are many complications in managing the organization, including the challenge of communicating down to lower levels, and the dominance of short-term operating results over longer-term policy considerations. Employee participation is also an issue, and for the most part corporations are still not considered democratic organizations.

The Corporation and "Democracy"

There is a conflict between the manner in which a corporation is governed and the broader democratic principles of a nation's government. At the shareholder level, voting rights are based upon share ownership and abuses occur, infringing upon the rights of some shareholders. Most employees have no say in the governance of the enterprise. The general public is removed from any access to the system of corporate government.

This apparent lack of adherence to democratic processes questions the legitimacy of the corporation. However, many reforms have been proposed as a result of some of the issues or problems mentioned in this section. These proposals for reform will be discussed in a later section.

Stakeholders Not Involved

Related to the question of democracy is the lack of participation of many stakeholders in the governance system. Issues casting doubt on whether or not such stakeholders as shareholders actually play an influential role in the governance of the corporation have been raised. However, other stakeholders have little, if any, influence on corporate governance. Such stakeholders include: consumers, public interest groups, society at large, lenders/creditors, and suppliers.

Exhibit 12-1

Issues Relating to Corporate Governance

Stakeholder	Issues
Government	• Disclosure regulations and the philosophy toward incorporation, as expressed in the CBCA and provincial companies acts. • Amount of protection to be provided the public regarding the issuing of securities.

Shareholders	• Shareholder apathy
	• Shareholder democracy including:
	  – Separation of ownership and control
	  – non-voting shares
	  – rights of minority shareholders
	  – disclosure of information
	• Role of institutional investors

The Board of Directors	• Qualifications and duties • Term of office • Nature, composition, size and organization of Board (including committee structure) • Search for appropriate role • Member commitment and interest • Director liability • Compensation • Interlocking directorship conflicts • Limits on number of appointments • Information flow and availability • Role in strategic planning • "Internal" versus "outside"
Chairman of the Board	• Selection process • Independence from management • Duality of Chair and CEO • Imbalance between Board and CEO • Term of office
Management (Chief Executive Officer)	• Conflict in roles if member of Board or Chair • Leadership style
Management (Three levels— top, middle, supervisory)	• Emphasis on short-term profits instead of long-term performance. • Blockage of information to CEO & Board
Employees	• Problems of communications downward in organization • Lack of employee participation in governance • Challenges of motivating employees and receiving commitment • Influence of labour relations legislation

An issue exists as to whether or not these other stakeholders should have significant influence. The primary purpose of the corporation is an economic one, and it is argued that a departure from this focus causes confusion. Mechanisms for involving these other stakeholders have been proposed, but not widely accepted or implemented, and a following section will discuss these mechanisms. It would be interesting to imagine a business enterprise where corporate governance was defined as the processes, structures, and relationships through which the stakeholders (instead of shareholders) oversee the activities of the business enterprise.

Reform of corporate governance has been discussed extensively for two decades, and, in particular, the topic has received considerable attention in recent years. It is not possible to discuss all the issues relating to this topic or to summarize all the literature, but the following sections review some of the literature focusing on Canadian contributions.

DISCUSSIONS OF CORPORATE GOVERNANCE REFORM

Types of Governance Structures

Two issues frequently mentioned in discussions of governance are the balance of "inside" versus "outside" members of the board and board leadership; that is, an independent board chairperson versus a combined CEO and chairperson role. Rechner (1989) combined these two issues to form a corporate governance matrix (Figure 12-2) from which four types of governance structures emerge. Each of these types is briefly described.

Type 1 - Majority Outsiders and Independent Board Leadership   The author considers this the ideal type of structure for effective governance, as it increases the possibility of avoiding the shortcomings associated with the other choices; that is, the lack of independence associated with insiders and the vested interest leadership of the combined CEO/chairperson. This structure is not that common in corporate America, according to the author, a conclusion that is also true in Canada.

Type 2 - Majority Outsiders and CEO Duality   This type was found to be common among large industrial corporations. The advantages of majority outside directors who are independent is offset by allowing the CEO to also function as board chairperson. The CEO duality allows the CEO to exercise too much control over the type and quality of information presented, or in other words, to control the board's agenda.

Figure 12-2 A Corporate Governance

	Independent Board Leaderships	CEO Duality
Majority Outside Directors	Type 1	Type 2
Majority Inside Directors	Type 4	Type 3

SOURCE: Paula L. Rechner. Corporate governance: Fact or fiction? Reprinted from *Business Horizons,* July/August 1989, p. 13. Copyright © 1989 by the Foundation for the School of Business at Indiana University. Used with permission.

Type 3 - Majority Insiders and CEO Duality   This type of Board is virtually under management's control and could be referred to as a "rubber-stamp" board. It is this situation that has led advocates of governance reform to focus on alteration of board composition.

Type 4 - Majority Insiders and Independent Board Leadership   The dominance of insiders is somewhat offset by the independent chair. This situation is the least likely of the four types to exist.

Rechner believes that Type 1, majority outsiders combined with independent board leadership, is likely to be the most effective, but management, and especially CEO's, are reluctant to give up control.

Mintzberg's Democratization of the Corporation

In his book *Power In and Around Organizations,* Mintzberg (1983, Part V) identified eight different views on who controls the corporation ranging from government to neoconservative managers. One of these views Mintzberg labelled "Democratize It" and proposed formal devices to broaden the governance of the corporation. The existing governance structure of the corporation does not allow for political freedom, freedom to publish, freedom of speech, and the right of trial, as no judiciary exists independent of the corporation's management. The law is that shareholders govern through the Board of Directors and managers serve as trustees. In widely held corporations, the shareholders are often unable to exercise their power.

Mintzberg claims that the corporation might be democratized by two means: representative democracy and participative democracy. Two groups have been involved in democratizing the corporation, employees, an internal influence, and interest groups, external influences. The result is four basic forms of corporate democracy:

1) Worker representation—workers have representatives on the Board of Directors. The European "co-determination" would be an example.

2) Pluralistic representative—"public interest" representatives are elected to the Board of Directors.

3) Worker Participation—workers are given some control of decision making; for example, worker councils.

4) Pluralistic participation—external influence groups are somehow included in internal decision making.

The four forms are presented in matrix form in Figure 12-3.

In the United States, there has been some discussion of pluralistic representative democracy by allowing interest groups, such as consumers or environmentalists, to have representatives on the Board of Directors, already a common practice with non-profit institutions. Problems with the idea, such as how to ascertain representation and conflicts of interest, have precluded its use. In Europe, representation of one group, workers, is common. Co-determination, as it is referred to, is considered to have several faults, including the following: it leads to politicization of decision making, it increases bureaucracy, it hampers entrepreneurial drive, it dilutes responsibilities, it delays decision, and it endangers the unity and flexibility of management. Moreover, it is considered to be incompatible with the free market system and existing concept of private property rights.

Mintzberg concludes that worker representation has had a minor impact upon business. It does not automatically increase participation by workers, and actually concentrates power at the top. Only one interest group is involved, labour, and selection of representatives is not easy. The commitment and involvement of representatives presents a dilemma. Part-time representatives are too busy with their jobs to devote much time to their representative role, and therefore are often unable to question management. Full-time representatives may have the time and knowledge but may lose touch with those they are representing. Representatives are often considered remote from their constituents, and many workers have been found to be disinterested in the approach.

Figure 12-3 Four Basic Forms of Corporate Democracy

		Groups Involved	
		Internal Influences (employees)	*External Influences* (interest groups)
Focus of Attention	*Board of Directors*	Worker Representation Democracy (European-style, e.g., "co-determination" or worker ownership)	Pluralistic Representative Democracy (American-style, e.g., "public interest" directors)
	Internal Decision-Making Process	Worker Participatory Democracy (e.g., works councils)	Pluralistic Participatory Democracy (e.g., outsiders on new product committees)

SOURCE: Henry Mintzberg. (1983). Who should control the corporation? *Power In and Around Organizations*. Englewood Cliffs, NJ: Prentice-Hall, p. 546.

On the other hand, representative democracy gives an air of legitimacy to the governance of the corporation. Benefits include: opening the channels of communication, spurring management to pay more attention to the human side and to recognize the needs of workers; and greater access to management information, with some influence being exerted over working conditions, social, and personnel policies. Nevertheless, economic goals are still foremost, and little difference has been made to the distribution of power and how decisions are made.

The approach to participative democracy is more internal to the firm and is referred to as worker participation, or participative management. Workers are involved in decision making, but with little success according to Mintzberg. Representatives are often uninformed and managers do most of the talking and initiate actions. Workers are usually interested in the direct effects on them, and then only in the short term. Mintzberg also states that the need for coordination in an organization precludes the serious use of participative democracy.

Examples of pluralistic participation are consumers being involved in product safety decisions, consumers serving on new product committees, and environmentalists being consulted on new plant locations. Mintzberg claims that there are many approaches to pluralistic participation but that all pose problems: who should serve as representatives?, how many representatives should there be?, how should the representatives be chosen?, and who should choose the representatives? Mintzberg believes that greater efforts should be made to democratize power in an organization.

The Thain and Leighton Study

Two University of Western Ontario School of Business professors, Donald H. Thain and David S. R. Leighton, undertook a study of Canadian corporate governance with the sponsorship of the National Centre for Management Research and Development. Extensive materials have emerged from the study, and only a portion of the results are summarized here.

Directors of Subsidiaries

Leighton and Thain (1990) pointed out that the role of the director varies with ownership patterns and that patterns differ between Canada and the United States. The job of an independent director in Canada differs mainly due to the fact that in Canada most corporations are controlled by a single owner, whereas in the U.S. corporations are more widely held. They claim that independent directors in corporations controlled by a block of shares, or single owner, have less autonomy than directors in widely held corporations. The majority owner has the power to get what he or she wishes, and the best an independent director can do is delay action. The authors conclude that as a result Canadian independent directors should not be evaluated in the same manner as would such directors in widely held U.S. corporations. These comments are particularly relevant to Canadians who serve as directors of subsidiary corporations.

A New Code of Conduct

Thain and Leighton (1992, Spring) described a new code of behaviour for directors as well as an old code (described in Chapter 5). Many pressures are resulting in a new approach to describing the job of a director, or a "new code," outlined as follows:

- manage the business and affairs of the corporation as they are legally required to do

- function as a trustee to represent the interests of stakeholders such as employees, customers, suppliers, local communities, and the public and as a consultant to size up the performance of management

- take the job seriously and do it well

- do what is right including the pursuit of excellence in professional conduct and ethical principles
- support those who are worthy instead of basing support on tradition or political consideration, and continually question the status quo
- use the board routines and infrastructure such as communications, meetings, documents, committees, routines, and relationships to make sure problems and challenges are dealt with
- get the information needed rather then relying on that provided by management
- build good relationships in the board and its organization network
- work on getting the culture right in board operations by encouraging informality, dialogue, openness, humility, and good attitudes
- if necessary, rock the boat

According to the authors, making the new code work will be challenging requiring commitment from directors and will largely depend upon the chairperson.

The Role of the Chair

Thain and Leighton (1992, Summer) identified the board chair's role as key to reforming corporate governance, as the chair has the ultimate formal authority and responsibility for the management of any corporation. They feel that it is the chair that will determine whether directors behave according to the old or new code of conduct, and that the job of the chair is to manage the board so that it performs effectively. The chair's job varies from one corporation to another depending upon how adequately the responsibilities of the board are fulfilled and ownership.

The responsibilities of the board are represented by five basic tasks identified as: appointing and supervising the CEO and other officers; directing and evaluating strategy; representing shareholders and maintaining shareholder relations; protecting and enhancing the corporation's assets; and fulfilling fiduciary and legal requirements. Those basic tasks are performed differently depending upon whether the corporation was privately owned, controlled by one owner, or widely held. For example, corporations that are controlled by a single owner usually use boards mainly in an advisory capacity. Where minority shareholders exist, the interests of these owners must be represented. In widely held corporations where management tends to dominate, the interests of shareholders must be kept in focus.

Stated briefly, Thain and Leighton identified the following points that an effective chair should consider:

- understand the job and its importance

- learn to perform the roles of a chair, such as discussion leader, spokesperson, referee, politician, decision maker, leader, follower, motivator, teacher, cheerleader, disciplinarian, moralist, confidant, coach, and so on.
- handle tough and sometimes nasty problems with skill
- push for top corporate performance
- work with other key managers individually and collectively
- develop and manage the corporation's strategic agenda
- manage the board which includes managing board meetings, preparing for meetings, staying in touch with board members, working with board committees, managing board performance through evaluation, and developing the board through recruitment, retirement, and improving operating effectiveness.

It was also concluded that board performance should be measured regularly, that changing the culture of a board is relentlessly demanding, that the chair must behave as a leader, and that chairs will need to get tougher with their CEOs. The question, "Should the Chair be CEO?" is addressed in a concluding section. The authors believe that the CEO and chair positions should be separate, as there is a fundamental conflict of interest involved. The CEO has responsibility for the general management of the , where the chair is responsible for management of the trusteeship function of the board. They anticipate little hope for improvement in board performance unless the positions are split.

The Evaluation of Director Performance

The evaluation of director performance has not been done in the past despite the performance appraisal process being widely used in other levels of the corporation. Thain and Leighton (1992, Autumn) address this issue and conclude that the board chair must initiate the process. A set of objective criteria must be in place before a performance appraisal system can work. The authors presented a sample position description for directors which identified directors' responsibilities and listed six categories of duties: selection of the management; monitoring and acting; strategy determination; policies and procedures; reporting to shareholders; and legal requirements. They also proposed some standards of performance of directors that will attempt to establish a measurable target against which directors can be rated on how well they are performing their job. Quantitative and qualitative measures are necessary, with examples of the former being attendance at meetings and preparation for meetings, and of the latter overall good judgment in addressing issues and compatibility with the group.

In response to the question, "Who should do the evaluation?", Thain and Leighton say that the chair should be a central player with assistance sought from few long-time and respected outside directors. They consider the evaluation of members essential if the board is to be better managed, but they also caution that there are many obstacles to the process.

Board Renaissance

Gillies (1992, April; and 1992) also examines past board practices and discusses their transition to something better. He argues that the globalization of markets is the most important factor forcing change in the boardroom. Canadian corporations must become more competitive, and two priorities for directors are: (1) to work with governments to ensure policies are in place that do not place corporations at a disadvantage and (2) to ensure that their corporations are managed strategically in the context of the global marketplace. Other factors that Gillies claims are causing board reform include: anxiety over the environment and the challenges of dealing with environmental problems; responding to stakeholders' demands including ethical considerations as a part of management decision making; and fiduciary responsibilities relating to such things as interlocking directorships, conflicts of interest, and sufficient disclosure of information to shareholders.

According to Gillies, boards will be in transition in the 1990's moving from Thain and Leighton's old code to a new code. Directors will have to be involved in a continuing learning process about management processes, markets, and their responsibilities to the corporation and all stakeholders. The survival of Canadian enterprises depends on a rapid transition to corporate governance practices suitable for the 21st century.

FINANCIAL INDUSTRY REACTIONS

Academics have not been the only group advocating changes to corporate governance. In fact, the discussions within the academic community have most likely spurred initiatives in the financial industry. Three such initiatives are summarized.

The Pension Investment Association of Canada

The Pension Investment Association of Canada (PIAC) represents 120 public and private pension funds from all provinces except Prince Edward Island. PIAC's mission is to promote the financial security of pension fund beneficiaries through sound investment policy and practices. In 1994, it developed a document called "Corporate Governance Standards" which addressed four areas: obligations of boards of directors, executive compensation, takeover protection, and shareholder rights.

Exhibit 12-2 lists the PIAC corporate governance standards in two areas: obligations of boards of directors and shareholders rights. PIAC believes that corporate management is accountable to the Board of Directors and in turn the Board reports to shareholders. The Board of Directors has a responsibility for maximizing long-term growth of shareholder values. The Association states that separate roles be defined for board members and management. Directors are to represent all shareholders and shareholders should not interfere with management. This is accomplished by ensuring Boards are capable of independent thought and action so that directors can effectively discharge their responsibility of overseeing corporate performance. Shareholder ownership rights must also be recognized in order to preserve the full integrity and value of the ownership characteristics of common stock. The PIAC document also established standards for incentive compensation and takeover protection which are not discussed here.

The Fairvest Rating

Fairvest Securities Corp. developed a corporate governance rating system based upon the standards developed by PIAC. The company is a Toronto-based international stock brokerage having a reputation as a shareholder rights advocate. Fairvest rates the governance of big companies by quantifying the way they handle board obligations, shareholder rights, takeover protection, and incentive compensation. Fairvest sells its ratings to pension funds and investment managers.

The rating allows for a maximum of 100 points broken down as follows:

1) Board obligations are worth a maximum of 50 points broken down into five items: independent directors (10 points); average length of board service over seven years (3 points); separate chairman and CEO (10 points); existence of audit, compensation, and nomination all with majority of independent directors (21 points); and Board size of 15 or less (6 points).

2) Shareholder rights are worth 30 points and are distributed as follows: equal voting shares (18 points) and confidential voting (12 points).

3) The absence of takeover protection provisions or restrictions is assigned 10 points.

4) Executive compensation is assigned 10 points broken down as 4 points if the compensation plan reserves fewer than 5 percent of shares; 3 points if stock incentive plans have fixed term; and 3 points if options are not given at a discount.

It is not evident yet what impact such a rating has. Fairvest released its ratings for the major banks, with the Royal Bank of Canada receiving the highest at 81 points and the National Bank of Canada receiving the lowest at 55 points (Blackwell, 1994).

Exhibit 12-2

PIAC Corporate Governance Standards

Obligations of Boards of Directors

The following points are essential for Boards of Directors to function effectively.

1. The majority of the Board of Directors is independent of management and has no financial interest in the affairs or the property of the company, other than as a shareholder.

2. The role of Chairman of the Board is different from that of Chief Executive Officer and it follows that one person cannot fulfil both roles without conflict. Therefore, the Chief Executive Officer runs the company with the Chairman ensuring that the Board effectively judges management's performance.

3. Committees have become accepted mechanisms of corporate governance. Corporations of sufficient size include at a minimum:

   • a Nominating Committee
   • an Audit Committee
   • a Compensation Committee

   The majority of members of each of these committees are independent of management, as is the committee Chairman.

4. The Board consists of fewer than 12 or at most 15 members, which is small enough to be cohesive and effective. Since directors have to take responsibility and be accountable, they need to be remunerated accordingly and they must limit the number of their other directorships in order to devote adequate time to each board.

Shareholder rights

The following standards are necessary to protect shareholder rights.

1. Effective shareholders will keep themselves informed about corporate governance issues, not shrink from an activist role and manage their proxy votes in order to protect stock ownership rights from erosion.

2. Effective shareholders will not allow a preoccupation with the short term to interfere with management's ability to concentrate on long-run returns, productivity, and competitiveness.

3. The proxy voting system must ensure that neither management nor shareholders are able to dominate the system or exercise undue influence.

4. All shareholders should be treated equally, with the same rights per share, with the exception of stock purchased as a part of a senior class with separate, explicitly defined rights. Any issuance of new stock with rights beyond those in the shares outstanding should be offered on a pro-rata basis to existing shareholders before it is sold to outsiders.

SOURCE: Corporate Governance Standards of the Pension Investment Association of Canada. (1994). Toronto: Pension Investment Association of Canada. Reprinted with permission.

The Toronto Stock Exchange

In May, 1994, the Toronto Stock Exchange Committee on Corporate Governance in Canada released a draft report titled *Where Were the Directors?: Guidelines for Improved Corporate Governance in Canada* (1994). The main points of the report are summarized in Exhibit 12-3. Concern had been expressed that directors had not been sufficiently involved in overseeing corporate performance, and that if they had been more effective, some of the serious difficulties and failures experienced by corporations could have been avoided. A committee of the Exchange prepared a draft report for discussion and invited comments. It is planned that corporations be required to disclose their governance practices in 1995. The committee suggests that listed companies be required to disclose compliance or non-compliance, but the corporate guidelines would not be a requirement of being listed on the Exchange.

Exhibit 12-3

Guidelines for Improved Corporate Governance — The Toronto Stock Exchange

The following have been proposed for effective corporate governance:

1. The board of directors of every corporation should explicitly assume responsibility for the stewardship of the corporation and, as part of the overall stewardship responsibility, should assume responsibility for the following matters:

    (i)   adoption of a corporate strategy;

    (ii) succession planning, including appointing, training and monitoring senior management;

    (iii) a communications program for the corporation; and

    (iv) the integrity of the corporation's internal control and management information systems.

2. Unrelated directors should be in the majority on the board.

3. A committee should be appointed, composed exclusively of outside (non-management) directors which will have the responsibility for proposing new nominees to the board and for assessing directors.

4. An orientation and education program should be provided to new members.

5. The size of boards should be reduced to a number which facilitates more effective decision-making.

6. The board of directors should review the adequacy and form of the compensation of directors.

7. Committees of the board of directors should generally be composed of outside directors, a majority of whom are unrelated directors.

8. Every board of directors should have in place appropriate structures and procedures to ensure that the board can function independently of management.

9. Position descriptions should be developed for the board and for the CEO.

10. The Chair of the board should not be a member of management.

11. The audit committee of every board of directors should be composed only of outside directors.

SOURCE: *Where Were the Directors?: Guidelines for Improved Corporate Governance in Canada.* (1994). Toronto: The Toronto Stock Exchange.

The guidelines are considered important for the interests of shareholders, directors, and management. Shareholder value should be enhanced but the financial viability of the corporation must also be ensured. Improved corporate performance is likely from improved corporate governance and benefits to shareholders will also occur. The committee states that this is not only in the best interests of shareholders but also serves the public interest generally. Effective governance is necessary for the credibility of the corporate sector, and this credibility is essential if business is to make a full contribution to Canadian economic and social life.

This review of corporate governance indicates that most of the issues identified in Exhibit 12-1 have been examined and proposals have been made to address them. Corporate governance has become important to understanding the relationships between the owners of a corporation and society.

SUMMARY

For the business enterprise to respond to economic, social, technological, and political challenges, it must address problems with the way a corporation is governed. This chapter has described the governing process as it focuses on the Board of Directors.

The role of directors in change is considered key. If there is no change at the top of the governance structure, there is unlikely to be effective and enduring change at lower levels in the organization. There are dozens of issues relating to the reform of corporate governance, and it is not possible to address them in detail. However, the studies and comments of some studies of this issue are summarized to give an appreciation of current thinking. This academic discussion has not gone unnoticed by the financial industry. Several initiatives are being undertaken by the private sector to address the issues surrounding corporate governance. Addressing these issues will enhance the credibility of the business system in society.

The reform of corporate governance focuses on the owner, director, government, and management stakeholders, and is one of the several changes in the business environment. Reforming corporate governance is one aspect of improving society's understanding of the business system and corporate behaviour.

REFERENCES

Blackwell, Richard. (1994, May 26). "Big banks seen as soundly governed, *The Financial Post*, p. 7.

Corporate governance standards of the pension investment association of Canada. (1994). Toronto: Pension Investment Association of Canada.

Draft Report of The Toronto Stock Exchange, Committee on Corporate Governance in Canada. (1993). Toronto: The Toronto Stock Exchange.

Gillies, James. (1992). *Boardroom Renaissance: Power, Morality and Performance in the Modern Corporation*. Toronto: McGraw-Hill Ryerson.

Gillies, James. (1992, April). The new, improved board game. *Canadian Business*, pp. 74–78.

Leighton, David S. R. and Donald H. Thain. (1990, Autumn). The role of the corporate director, *Business Quarterly*, pp. 20–24.

Mintzberg, Henry. (1983). *Power In and Around Organizations*. Englewood Cliffs, N.J.: Prentice-Hall.

Mueller, Robert K. (1981). Changes in the wind in corporate governance," *Journal of Business Strategy*, 1(4), pp. 8–14.

Rechner, Paula L. (1989, July-August). Corporate governance: Fact or fiction?, *Business Horizons*, pp. 1–15.

Thain, Donald H. and David S. R. Leighton. (1992, Spring). The director's dilemma: What's my job?, *Business Quarterly*, pp. 75–87.

Thain, Donald H. and David S. R. Leighton. (1992, Summer). Improving board effectiveness, *Business Quarterly*, pp. 19–33.

Thain, Donald H. and David S. R. Leighton. (1992, Autumn). Improving board effectiveness by evaluating director performance, *Business Quarterly*, pp. 23–32.

Where Were the Directors?: Guidelines for Improved Corporate Governance in Canada. (1994). Toronto: The Toronto Stock Exchange.

THE GOVERNMENT: INFLUENCING AND BEING INFLUENCED

INTRODUCTION

Understanding the role of government requires review of a wider spectrum of topics. The first topics in this chapter identify the scope of government involvement in the business system in general terms. But it is important to recognize that the scope of changes and the trends in government involvement are discussed. One trend in particular, privatization, is elaborated upon; it is a significant development for business as it provides many opportunities.

One area of governmental influence in business that does not receive much attention derives from the impact of the Canadian Constitution. Canada is governed by federal and provincial jurisdictions, and barriers exist to conducting business across provincial borders. During the constitutional debates of the late

1980's and early 1990's, the "economic union" issue was addressed but not resolved, and business continues to face the barriers to trade within Canada. A following section discusses how business might or does influence government. Three possibilities for influence are discussed, involvement in politics, lobbying, and corporate public affairs departments. A final section reviews some of the business–government relationships in Canada.

THE SCOPE OF GOVERNMENT INVOLVEMENT IN THE BUSINESS SYSTEM

The influence and involvement of government in the business enterprise is substantial and has been documented well elsewhere; for example, in: *Business-Government Relations in Canada* (Stanbury, 1986), *Policy Analysis: Concepts and Practice* (Weimer and Vining, 1992), *Government Policy Toward Business* (Brander, 1988, and *Breaking The Shackles: Deregulating Canadian Industry* (Block and Lermer, 1991). This section is a brief summary of the impact of government on business and emphazes the substantial interactions between the two.

The following is an abbreviated listing of the main dimensions of government involvement in the business system.

Government Expenditures

The expenditures of all governments, federal, provincial, and municipal, amount to over 40 percent of GNP. Included in such expenditures are all salaries, the procurement of goods and services, and grants. Business enterprises supply a large portion of the goods and services sought by government.

Taxation

Business enterprises are involved in collecting taxes for governments, the most obvious being the retail sales tax and the payroll deduction of personal income tax. They also pay taxes on profits, but the total amount they contribute is substantially less than that raised by personal income taxation.

Tax Expenditures

Tax expenditures are potential revenues the government chooses not to collect and are any form of incentive or relief granted through the tax system rather than through government expenditures (Stanbury, 1986, p. 54). Examples of such tax expenditures are: accelerated depreciation, inventory valuation adjustment, capital gains exemptions, and several business deductions. Figure 13-1 illustrates the magnitude of these tax expenditures and their relationship to corporate size.

Figure 13-1 Relationship between Corporate Income Taxation Paid and Tax Expenditures

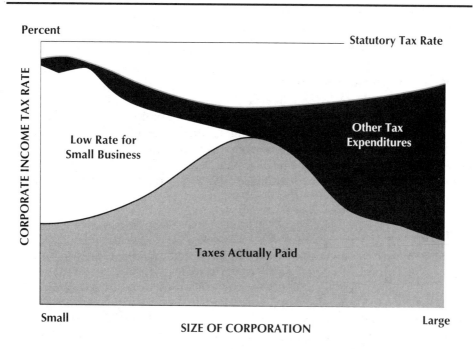

Corporations do not pay the statutory tax rate but, instead the taxes actually paid are less (represented by the grey area). Smaller businesses avoid taxes through the lower rate available to them and the tax expenditures involved are shown by the white area. Other tax expenditures are represented by the black area and are available more to larger businesses. Government influences business through tax expenditures, either by granting or withdrawing them. It should be noted that tax expenditures are also available to individuals—for example, through registered retirement saving plans, child tax credit, basic personal exemption, tax credit for donation to charities and political parties, and the age exemption.

Protective Measures

These measures are tariff and non-tariff barriers that exist to protect Canadian industry. Since 1879 Canadian manufacturing has been protected by tariffs and other barriers such as quotas and regulations. Industries receiving substantial protection in the past have been textiles and shoes, furniture, and appliances. It is argued that this has caused some Canadian industries to be less efficient than they might have been. Freer trade is reducing the influence of these protective measures; for example, through the General Agreement in Tariffs and Trade (GATT), the U.S.–Canada Free Trade Agreement, and the North American Free Trade Agreement. Protective measures also exist between provinces, a topic that will be discussed later.

Loans and Loan Guarantees

Governments are suppliers of debt capital to many business enterprises. The federal and all provincial governments operate financial institutions or development agencies that lend to businesses. For example, the federal government operates the Federal Business Development and the Export Development banks, and provincial governments operate development agencies lending to business enterprises. Loan guarantees are also available, and they are a substantial assistance to business enterprises as they reduce the debt load.

Bailouts

Canadian governments have a long history of coming to the assistance of failing business enterprises. Bailouts occur to varying degrees and can take different forms. The bailout may involve a one-time capital infusion to overcome a crisis, or the complete takeover of the corporation. Bailouts may involve loans, loan guarantees, and equity positions, or combinations of all. In the 1980's, bailouts were common as, for example, with Dome Petroleum, Chrysler Canada, Massey-Ferguson, and Maislin Industries. In the 1990's, governments are less willing to provide complete bailouts but instead provide assistance to a bailout arrangement that might also include assistance from shareholders, creditors, and employees. The 1992 bailout of Algoma Steel of Sault Ste. Marie is an example where the Ontario government provided loan guarantees, employees took wage concessions and an ownership position, and the banks also became owners.

Regulation

An Economic Council of Canada report defined economic regulation as "the imposition of constraints, backed by the authority of a government, that are intended to modify economic behaviour in the private sector significantly" (*Reforming Regulation*, 1991, xi).

Theoretically, the regulation of the economy and the business enterprise system should be done by the forces or influences of the marketplace. But, in practice, this is not the way it works, and a mechanism is required to control monopoly and oligopoly powers, to control the transfer of income from producers to consumers, and to increase efficiency in production. Regulatory organizations do a variety of things, including establishing prices and levels of service, mediation between enterprises, advising governments on policy, controlling expenditures, administering acts or regulations (such as licensing), and operating as quasi-judicial bodies. Table 13-1 is a listing indicating the extensiveness of regulation in Canada.

Table 13-1 The Scope of Regulation in Canada

- **Communications**
  Broadcasting
   Radio (AM, FM)
   Television
  Telecommunications
   Telephone
   Telegraph
   Satellite
   Cable TV

- **Consumer Protection/Information**
  Disclosure (product content labelling, terms of sale, etc.)
  False and misleading advertising
  Sales Techniques (merchandising)
  Packaging and Labelling
  Prohibited Transactions, e.g., pyramid sales, referral sales
  Weights and Measures

- **Cultural/Recreational**
  Residency requirements
  Language (bilingualism)
  Canadian content in broadcasting
  Horse racing
  Gambling (lotteries/casinos)
  Sports
  Film, Theatre, Literature, Music, e.g. Canadian content

- **Energy**
  Nuclear
  Natural Gas
  Petroleum
  Hydro-electric
  Coal

- **Environmental Management**
  (a) Pollution Control

  air
  water
  solid waste disposal
(b) Resource Development
  minerals
  forestry
  water
(c) Wildlife Protection
  hunting
  fishing
  parks/reserves
  endangered species
(d) Land Use
  planning/zoning
  development approval
  sub-division
  strata-title
(e) Weather Modification
(f) Environmentally Friendly Products

- **Financial Markets and Institutions**
  Banks
  Non-banks
   Trust Companies
   Management Companies
   Finance Companies
   Credit Unions/Caisse Populaire
  Pension Plans
  Securities/Commodities
  Transactions
  Insurance

- **Food Production and Distribution**
  (a) Agricultural Products Marketing
    pricing
    grading
    storage
    distribution
    entry

Table 13-1 The Scope of Regulation in Canada (continued)

supply
(b) Fisheries (marine, freshwater)
   price
   entry
   quotas
   gear

• *Framework*
Competition Policy
Anti-dumping laws
Foreign investment
Bankruptcy laws
Corporation laws
Intellectual and Industrial Property
   copyright
   industrial design
   patents
   trade marks
Election laws
   contributors
   spending
   reporting
lobbying

• *Health and Safety*
(a) Occupational Health and Safety
(b) Products - Use
   explosives
   firearms
   chemicals
(c) Product-Characteristics
   purity
   wholesomeness
   efficacy
   accident risk
(d) Building Codes
(e) Health Services
   nursing homes
   private hospitals

emergency services
(f) Animal Health
(g) Plant Health

• *Human Rights*
Anti-discrimination legislation in respect
   to hiring, sale of goods or services etc.
Protection of privacy, personal
   information reporting

• *Labour*
Collective bargaining
Minimum wage laws
Hours of work, terms of employment

• *Liquor*
Characteristics, e.g. alcoholic content
Distribution and sales

• *Professions/Occupational Licensure*
Certification/Licensure
Registration
Apprenticeship

• *Transportation*
Airlines (domestic, international)
Marine (domestic, international)
Railways
Inter-city Buses
Taxis
Pipelines
Trucking
Urban public transit
Postal Express
Courier services

• *Other*
Rent control
Metrication
General wage and price controls

SOURCE: Adapted from *Responsible Regulation: An Interim Report by the Economic Council of Canada.* (1979). Ottawa: Supply and Services Canada, Catalogue No. EC22-70/1979, p.11. Note that some of the above areas may have been deregulated since the list was compiled.

Various governments regulate the operation of business enterprises through commissions, tribunals, agencies, and boards. The following are examples of industries regulated by government-sponsored regulatory agencies: petroleum, insurance, pipelines, some agricultural products including dairy and poultry products, utilities (electric, telephone), transportation (trucking, rail, airline, bus, taxi), communications (radio, television, cable TV) and securities. Government, in one form or another, directly regulates about one-third of the economy through more than 600 organizations. Examples of such regulatory organizations are the Canadian Radio–Television Commission, Canadian Transportation Commission, the National Energy Board, and public utilities boards in most provinces.

Regulation impacts every business enterprise, and every Canadian. Deregulation has reduced some regulation in selected areas as, for example, with airline and truck transportation. Not all regulation is imposed by government, as business has initiated a lot of it.

Government-Owned Enterprises

Governments at all levels own and operate businesses that provide goods and services that could also be supplied by private sector enterprises. Government-owned enterprises, often referred to as Crown corporations, were formed or acquired for a variety of reasons, including to maintain employment (e.g., the Cape Breton Development Corporation), to fill a gap in the private sector's provision of goods or services (e.g., the Canadian Broadcasting Corporation), to promote economic activity (e.g., the Manitoba Development Board), to provide services the public is compelled to purchase (e.g., automobile insurance in B.C., Saskatchewan, and Manitoba), to enhance incomes (e.g., The Canadian Wheat Board), to ensure adequate and stable supplies of important goods and services (e.g., Petro Canada), and to control the distribution of goods and services (e.g., liquor corporations or control boards).

Many goods and services are provided Canadians by government owned enterprises that operate much like commercial enterprises and, in some cases, compete with privately owned enterprises. During the past decade, many government-owned enterprises have been sold or dissolved as governments became disillusioned with their operation or concluded that the private sector could operate such corporations more effectively.

Mixed Enterprises

Mixed enterprises are those in which a government owns equity in a private sector enterprise. Governments or their agents have an equity interest in a substantial number of privately named enterprises that ranges from small numbers of voting shares to effective control through a substantial but minority interest, to more than one-half the voting shares, which provides legal control. The influence of the government varies from a hands-off approach to explicit direction, which challenges private sector managers and may adversely affect the performance of the enterprise.

Chosen Instruments

"Chosen instruments" have become another mechanism used to implement government policy, whereby a business enterprise within a particular industry receives some form of special attention from government through grants, purchasing policy, or tax incentives. The support from government usually goes to a technological leader, an enterprise that is positioned in the industry as a "lead" or "core" company. The intention is to pick a "winner" which will be supported, or preferred, by government for the purposes of developing new technology, or penetrating an export market. The enterprise is asked to concentrate on a particular technology, product, or process, and certain "understandings" surround the designation of the particular enterprise including: that other firms will stay out of that particular commercial activity, and that banks will support the enterprise because of the government favouritism. The government may also support the chosen instrument through a domestic purchasing policy, and some have speculated that such enterprises will be exempt from competition policy restrictions.

The "chosen instrument" is most common in the aerospace, electronic, communication, and energy industries. Examples include the Alberta Gas Trunk Line Co. (natural gas transmission), Interprovincial Steel and Pipe Co. Ltd. (pipe and other steel products), Spar Aerospace Ltd. (space technology), and Lumonics Ltd. (laser technology)

Use of the chosen instrument is, in effect, another form of protectionism. Tariffs might be lowered, but other ways to protect domestic industry are being devised. Another issue concerns whether or not the government would actually keep its hands off the enterprise. Management would, at least implicitly, be attempting to "cater" to government civil servants and be being careful not to upset the "favoured status" bestowed upon the enterprise.

If there are several enterprises in the industry, which one to choose becomes a problem. If one, or more, enterprises are successful, it can be questioned whether there is any need to choose. Furthermore, the shareholders of the "chosen" enterprise will most likely benefit while those of other industry enterprises will not, raising the equity question.

Some other issues that would have to be resolved by government include the problem of 11 Canadian governments designating chosen instruments; whether another instrument in the wide array of government involvement is necessary; and the anti-competition nature of the arrangements. Canada has no national plan to back up the chosen instruments at the present time, and thus, the approach used appears carried out on an ad hoc basis.

The chosen instrument might be compared to the Crown corporation in implementing government policy. Crown corporations usually do not change their mandate to reflect changing environments, or do not have a "sunset clause." Chosen instruments must continue to adapt to the environment, especially those involving government. An advantage of the chosen instrument is the ability to get support from the private sector, as sources of capital are more willing to lend to chosen instruments that have firm government contracts. It is argued that as the chosen instruments are not government-owned, they have greater flexibility than Crown corporations.

The use of chosen instruments may be considered a form of "corporatism." However, private initiative is involved and may be one way of restoring some function to the private sector, for example, in research and development and export trade, or preventing further government ownership in the business system. Chosen instruments are considered to be a permanent institution in the Canadian business enterprise system and may be one approach used by governments to develop an industrial strategy.

Suasion

This type of involvement is the least obvious. The government attempts to persuade business to change its behaviour in a particular direction that it considers preferable. Stanbury outlined several ways this is accomplished (1986, pp. 73–75), but only two examples are provided here. The government may hold intensive discussions with business enterprises or industry associations about a particular topic; for example, on work safety or environmental solutions. Through these talks, business agrees to particular actions that will satisfy governments needs. A second example relates to the pressure applied to business through the process of having a parliamentary committee investigate a particular topic. At various times, a committee has studied the rates charged on credit card balances. Legislation or regulation has not resulted from these committee investigations but the companies become more sensitive to the issue and at least make token adjustments to their rates.

The purpose of this section has merely been to acquaint readers with the extent of government involvement in the business system. But the degree of involvement changes over time. Since about 1980, there has been a reduction of government involvement, and this change is discussed in the next section.

TRENDS IN GOVERNMENT INVOLVEMENT IN THE BUSINESS SYSTEM

Since World War II, most nations with a business enterprise system have experienced increasing government involvement, requested by various stakeholders and also by business. The Depression in the 1930's and government participation in the economy during World War II led to an expectation, and acceptance of, government involvement by most citizens. Government incentives, subsidies, and tariff protection made involvement quite acceptable even to business interests. This intensive government involvement in the business system has been summarized by Lermer (1984), and Bird and Green (1985). Stanbury (1986) highlighted the myriad of regulations, and reports of the 1985 Ministerial Task Force on Program Review documented the role of government (especially three reports, *Regulatory Programs, Regulatory Agencies,* and *Services and Subsidies to Business*).

The first signs that the trend was reversing appeared about 1980. The counter trend was represented by such things as deregulation, deficit reduction, and privatization. Some terminology used to describe aspects of the trend were user pay, contracting out, market-sensitive pricing, full-cost recovery, self-regulation, and government withdrawal. In addition, there were indications that governments wanted a return to a "market" environment in the business system, something advocated by business leaders but not always in reality welcomed. Manifestations of this trend were the Economic Council of Canada's report on regulation (*Reforming Regulation,* 1981), the reports of the *Royal Commission on the Economic Union and Development Prospects for Canada* (1985), the Department of Transportation's paper *Freedom to Move — A Framework for Transportation Reform* (1985), and the Quebec Government's Task Force on Deregulation report *Regulate Less: Regulate Better* (1986).

The Trend to Government Involvement

Table 13-2 is used to explain the trends that lead to intensive government involvement; that is, the situation prior to the 1980's. Two variables are used to explain the government involvement trend:

1) the market structure, divided into three categories, "non-market," "quasi-market," and "market"; and

2) the sector of economic activity which is classified as "private," "joint private/public," and "public."

A "non-market" structure is a monopoly, or near monopoly, situation where no, or very little, competition exists. Governments would regulate this market environment. The "quasi-market" structure is similar to an oligopoly where few firms compete. There would be some government involvement usually to regulate the less than perfectly competitive environment. The "market" structure is the closest to the perfect competition model, as many firms compete with one another with a minimum of government regulation.

The "private" sector of economic activity is owned by individuals or corporations, whereas the "public" sector indicates government ownership or operation.

The "joint private/public" sector represents some partnership between the private and public sectors. The government participation takes several forms, including ownership, loans and loan guarantees, endorsement of orderly marketing arrangements, and administrative tribunal regulation. Government might spend large sums for goods and services in particular industries, and may be the major or only customer.

The two variables result in nine possibilities of government involvement as indicated by the boxes in the matrix in Table 13-2. Examples of each possibility are provided on the matrix and represent the circumstances existing in about 1980. Each of the government involvement possibilities is defined on the following page:

Table 13-2 Examples of Government Involvement*

Sector of Economic Activity	Market Structure		
	Non-Market	*Quasi-Market*	*Market*
Private	Privately owned utilities, e.g., Bell Canada, Cdn. Utilities. Airlines that operate routes with no, or little, competition. Geographical monopolies e.g., a bank serving an isolated community.	Brewery industry with high regulation. Auto manufacture. Trucking industry. Intercity buses. Banking. Rent-controlled housing.	Least government. Small scale printing firms. Most retailing, especially independent, small stores. Fast food outlets. Many service industries.
Joint Private/ Public	Marketing boards. Brewers Retail (Ontario)	Chosen instruments. Professional licensures. U.S. defence industry. Radio/TV licensing. Aerospace industry. Petroleum industry. Airport rental car outlets. Taxis. Uranium and potash orderly marketing arrangements.	Mixed enterprises. Joint ventures. Government preferential purchasing policies. Government regulation of occupations, e.g., insurance agents, undertakers.
Public	Gov't owned utilities, e.g., Ontario and Saskatchewan hydro, Alberta Telephone. Gov't owned transportation enterprises e.g., Air Canada, B.C. Rail.	Government ownership of two steel mills, Sidbec & Sydney Steel. Government owned parks.	Public enterprises competing with private sector firms. Government departments operating commercial services, e.g., printing or computer services.

* Examples are of about 1980 and may not reflect the present situation.

Private Non-market A monopoly or near monopoly exists where there is no, or little, direct competition, and enterprises are privately owned. A high level of government regulation most likely exists.

Private Quasi-Market The degree of competition is less and firms may even operate cooperatively or in unison. Not all aspects of competition are operative; for example, there may be an absence of price competition or some restriction in distribution. Usually high barriers to entry exist. There is a moderately high amount of government regulation or involvement. Some highly protected industries would be included in this classification.

Private Market Business enterprises are privately owned, many firms comprise an industry, and firms compete with respect to product design, innovation, pricing, distribution, and advertising. There are low barriers to entry, and the industry is fragmented with no one firm dominating the market.

Joint Private/Public Non-Market A monopoly is jointly owned, or the government endorses a market arrangement that in effect stifles competition.

Joint Private/Public Quasi-Market Much the same as the "market," but the government mandates the condition of less than perfect competition by placing restraints on how individuals or enterprises compete. Government subsidies may exist.

Joint Private/Public Market Joint ventures exist between the government and private sector. They might be shared ownership or government support through loans or loan guarantees, and preferential purchasing.

Public Non-Market The sole supplier of a good or service is government-owned. The operation of government departments that supply goods or services would also be in this category.

Public Quasi-Market Government owns a firm in an industry comprised of few firms. Similar circumstances to Private Quasi-Market except that government dominates.

Public Market Government owns business enterprises that compete with ones privately owned. Also included would be a service or product provided by any agency of government that is also available from the private sector.

A word of caution is necessary for the assignment of examples to the matrix. Examples can be assigned most easily to the four corner boxes. Distinctions amongst examples for the boxes in the "Quasi-Market" column and "Joint

Private/Public" row are often less clearcut. Nevertheless, positioning of examples on the matrix assists in understanding the extent and type of government involvement.

The Reversal of the Trend

The examples provided in Table 13-2 represent government involvement up to about 1980. Examples of the trend toward decreasing government involvement in the business system are provided in Figure 13-2. Each of the numbered lines represents an instance of this trend and each is explained below. Note some of the examples mentioned have occurred while others are proposed and being considered.

Figure 13-2 Trend Toward Decreasing Government Involvement in the Business System

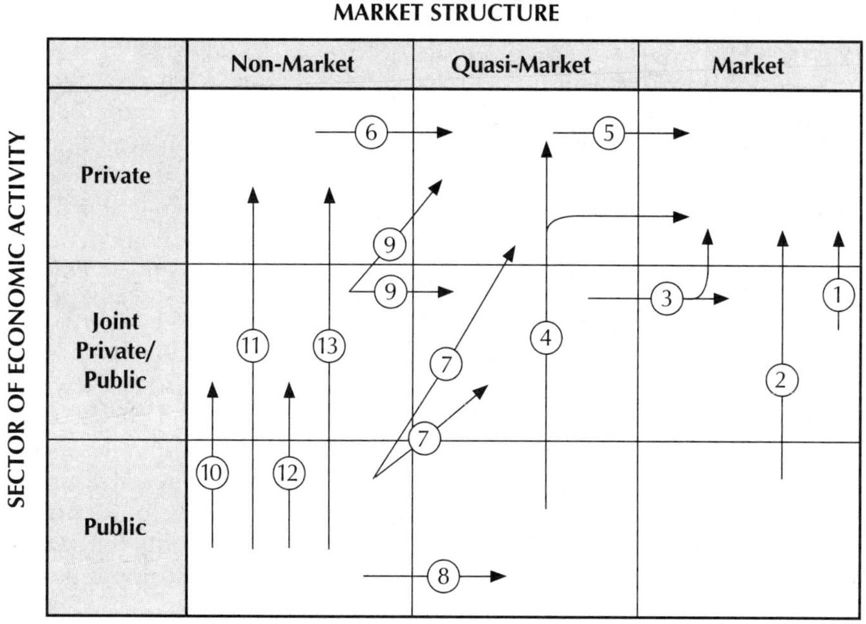

1) Government reduces its regulation or ownership; for example, the federal government's sale of its remaining shares in Air Canada. The introduction of industry self-regulation would also be an illustration; for example, Saskatchewan independent insurance agents and brokers are allowed to regulate themselves instead of being regulated by a government agency (as also in Ontario, Quebec, and B.C.).

2) Privatization of government-owned enterprises (partial privatization would end in "joint private/public," module). An additional example is requiring that government services such as printing and computer services be performed by private enterprises.

3) Government regulation, or self-regulated industry mandated by government, is reduced. Examples: the deregulation of professional organizations, the increasing number of outlets available for car rentals at airports, and the removal of restrictions on number of taxicabs allowed to operate in an area. Deregulation of the petroleum industry is a further example depending upon the control (or portion of ownership) the government retains.

4) Privatization of public enterprises to "quasi-market" or "market" environments. Examples: sale of de Havilland Aircraft and Canadair, and the operation of government-owned institutions by private enterprises.

5) Efforts to lower trade barriers such as tariffs and quotas are occurring through GATT and FTA. This reduces government involvement and exposes an industry to greater competition, that is, to market forces. Examples: the removal of quotas on shoes. This is also illustrated by the removal of barriers to entry, whether created by government or other means. Examples: the proposal to allow the four pillars of the financial industry, banks, life insurance, stock brokers, and trust companies, to provide services presently restricted to one or the other; allowing of foreign banks to operate in Canada; and allowing the operation of "brewpubs" and the establishment of small, local breweries. The deregulation of trucking has made that industry more competitive.

6) Government deregulation in the privately owned airline and telecommunications industries. Examples: the allowing of charter airlines to operate scheduled airline service in Canada; the competition in long distance telephone service; the competition existing in data transmission; and the increasing number of cablevision channels available, including pay TV and specialty channels, and the emerging delivery of television via satellites. Even natural monopolies are open to competition. Technological developments have resulted in inventions such as cellular radio telephones, multipoint (TV) distribution systems, and fuel cells making competition for telecommunications, cable TV, and electric utilities feasible.

7) The introduction of competition in the provision of some goods and services provided by government is proposed. Example: proposals to use voucher systems to provide education and medical services which may lead to totally private systems or joint efforts. Governments might delegate some aspects of consumer protection regulation such as maintenance of weights and measures, inspections, and grading to business enterprises.

8) Attempts by government to operate public enterprises or supply government services on a "commercial" basis, that is, to make a profit or to break even. Example: Canada Post. Also, making government-owned public utilities or transportation firms commercially viable. Examples: Canadian National and Marine Atlantic. A further example is the requirement of government agencies to operate on a full cost recovery basis, as might be the situation with printing and computer services (profit centre concept). Another possibility is the establishment of independent local airport authorities.

9) The restructuring of government regulation to make the operations of government-owned or mandated agencies more responsive to market forces. Example: the revision of marketing board regulation to introduce more effective methods to reflect market demands, or the elimination of the boards. An additional example is provided by Brewers Retail, owned jointly by the breweries, which controls the sale and distribution of beer in Ontario. This monopoly arrangement is allowed by the government. Recently, it has been proposed that grocery stores be allowed to sell beer. Such a development would change the market structure from a Non-market to a Quasi-Market one (and may be even a Market structure!).

10) Partial privatization of a government-owned monopoly; for example, the partial sale of Petro Canada. A different example would be government-owned hydro corporations diversifying their sources by purchasing electricity from entrepreneurs who operate privately owned generators, municipalities that generate power by burning waste, and large industrial plants that supply themselves and sell the excess. Electricity distribution would remain a monopoly.

11) Complete privatization of a government-owned monopoly. Example: the sale of Teleglobe Canada.

12) Contracting of services previously performed by public servants. Example: private management of hospitals or other health care institutions.

13) Contracting of, or withdrawal from, services formerly performed by public servants; for example, private sector firms providing garbage collection, street cleaning, and maintenance and security contracts for public buildings. If more than one firm allowed, directional arrow would also be to the Quasi-Market column.

Figure 13-2 indicates a movement from regulation to deregulation, restricted competition to market competition, concentration to deconcentration, and public (government) to private ownership. This movement or trend is represented by a shifting of economic activity upward and to the right on the matrix; that is, from a Non-Market environment, and Public Sector toward a Market environment and the Private Sector.

It is difficult to predict how long this trend will continue. The trend toward increasing government involvement spanned about 50 years, and the reversal has occurred only in the last few years. As with most trends, exceptions exist and are discussed in the next section.

Exceptions to the Current Trend

Although there is a trend to less government involvement in the business system as expressed by deregulation, privatization, contracting out, self-regulation, and government withdrawal, there are exceptions that indicate a continuing and even increasing role by government.

In the mid-1980's, some examples of these exceptions were:
- The bailout of two banks in western Canada.
- Continuing subsidies to Via Rail and the operation of the unprofitable Mirabel airport.
- The Federal Government granted the multinational pharmaceutical companies a 20-year monopoly on the production of drugs they develop, extending a previous four-year monopoly.
- Governments were considering equal pay for work of equal value legislation.
- Federal and provincial governments continue to provide a variety of tax breaks, subsidies, loans, or grants to business; for example, the loans to General Motors of Canada to modernize a plant and to Ford New Holland Inc. to purchase Versatile Farm Equipment.

Nevertheless, the overall trend seems to be away from government involvement.

The Impact of Decreasing Government Involvement

The trend toward less government involvement is a complicated process. Substantial changes are required in how government regulates business, ensures competition, permits industrial concentration, allows foreign ownership, and protects industries considered key, infant, or labour-intensive.

The trend should include the formulation and enforcement of a more viable competition policy so that a market system operates. Little would be accomplished if government domination of some industries is replaced by private domination. Privatization of government-owned monopoly enterprises is of doubtful benefit, as a private monopoly may not differ that much from a public one. Regulatory mechanisms might even increase in order to monitor performance of the private monopoly to protect the public interest.

One way to view the reversal of the government involvement trend is to examine it from the perspective of the stakeholders in the business system. Exhibit 13-1 summarizes the impact on selected stakeholders. There is little

---

Exhibit 13-1

Impact of Decreasing Government Involvement on Selected Stakeholders

It is difficult to generalize about the impact of all aspects of the trend toward decreasing government involvement in the business system. The following provides some possibilities for selected stakeholders.

Business Corporations

Decreasing government involvement provides many opportunities for business enterprises, including: reducing costs as a result of increased competition among supplies of telecommunications and transportation; increasing demand for some products; for example, deregulation of the airline industry has increased demand for passenger airplanes; and allowing an enterprise to diversify and compete in previously restricted areas. The trend will also place more demands upon business enterprises. Competition might increase, requiring new products, more innovative marketing and improved production methods. Increasing competition may lead to bankruptcies or forced reorganizations for those firms which cannot compete, and may result in fewer firms operating in an industry. Business is expected to assume more responsibility for "self-regulation" of its activities.

Consumers

In many areas, consumers may be paying lower prices for many goods and services and have a greater selection available. The trend toward privatization and withdrawal of government services such as inspections might expose the consumer to greater risk in the marketplace. Full cost recovery and user pay may raise the prices of some services.

Employees

Increased competition for business enterprises might lead them to demand that employees accept lower wages. Increased productivity reduces the need for workers, leading to layoffs or reduced hiring. Some forms of government regulation have allowed higher costs to be passed on to consumers, and with increased competition this is less likely to occur. On the other hand, the formation of new businesses may increase employment opportunities, as they provide goods and services formerly supplied by governments.

Government

The trend might lead to the reduction or elimination of some government departments or regulatory agencies. This might lead to less employees being required in the civil service. Government's influence over the economy is reduced and the private sector is expected to generate economic activity. This latter point is one that might be overlooked by government and business stakeholders. Governments may ignore competition issues in their haste to privatize or contract out. Business stakeholders are not above taking advantage by restricting or eliminating market forces.

---

doubt that a change in government involvement constitutes a dynamic element in the Canadian business system. It could be argued that uncertainty may be introduced for business; that is, what business loses as government involvement is reduced must also be considered. Some direct benefits (grants, tax incentives) may be lost, as will protection of monopolies by regulation or tariffs. It is predicted that Canadian business will be faced with a more competitive environment, both domestically and internationally, and that monopolies, which are almost always produced and sustained by governments, will be fewer and shorter. Some consequences of the trend toward less government involvement might be the transfer of jobs from the public to the private sector, the possible widening of share ownership in Canada, and hopefully, increased competition.

Government involvement is a dynamic aspect of the Canadian business system. Whether the trend portrayed in Figure 13-2 endures is a matter of speculation and some doubt. Government involvement has had a long history and is well entrenched in the system. Already, doubts about the commitment of Canadians to reduced government are being expressed. For example, one businessperson has suggested that Canadians are in a more "interventionist mood" after "flirting with more power to the private sector" and that they are "losing their nerve about instituting conservative market-style policies" (Mittelstaedt, 1986).

Some caution is necessary in interrupting this trend. One might conclude one trend from selected highly visible cases when the overall trend might be the opposite. Also, some time lags might exist between when, for example, changes in public policy are announced and/or implemented and when these changes have a meaningful impact upon business. Whether or not the boundaries between the public and private sectors will be altered is not yet clear. Neither is it certain that decreasing the role of the government and increasing the role of the private sector business enterprises will fundamentally alter the values or attitudes Canadians have toward the business system.

Privatization, one manifestation of lessened government involvement is discussed in more detail. It has substantial implications for business enterprises.

THE PRIVATIZATION OF GOVERNMENT

There are many definitions of privatization. The one selected for use here is attributed to David Heald and says that privatization can be viewed as a "strengthening of the market at the expense of the state" (1984, p. 36). After reviewing several definitions of privatization, Goodrich concluded that they had four things in common: privatization is defined as the provision of public service by the private sector; there are degrees of privatization, complete or partial; there are many techniques or forms of privatization (for example, diversitive, contracting out); and difficult terms are used that have overlapping meanings (for example, "contact public agencies" and "contracting out service delivery,") (1988, p. 13).

Privatization is often considered as the sale of government-owned business enterprises to the private sector. It should be clear from the above discussion that this is not the case. There are several privatization possibilities, several of which are summarized below:

1) Privatization of the financing of services which continue to be produced by the public sector. In effect, public services are financed through user fees or other charges. An example would be charging sufficient rates to cover all costs for ferry services. The funding for the Canada Pension Plan is based upon payroll deduction contributions by recipients.

2) Privatization of the provision of a service which continues to be financed by the public sector out of government revenues. This involves contracting out of the provision of services to the private sector and is a common practice. Services that are being contracted out include garbage collection, street cleaning, and road construction. Many public institutions have had food, laundry, janitorial services, housekeeping, data processing, and security services provided by private sector corporations. Management contracts are another form of contracting out where corporations operate hospitals and correctional institutions. The closure of postal stations and the franchising of postal services in retail outlets is another example.

3) Load-shredding, or the transfer of state functions to the private sector. This involves contractual agreements where private corporations build and operate facilities such as airport terminals or hospitals. Governments might allow private operators, or may rent the facilities back.

4) Sale of government-owned enterprises. Such enterprises are sold to private sector owners completely or in part. This is a worldwide phenomenon, and in Canada the federal and provincial governments have sold in whole or in part, or have otherwise disposed of, dozens of corporations. Examples of corporations sold or being considered for sale include: Nova Scotia Power, CN Hotels, Sydney Steel, Asbestos Corp, Sky Dome, Alberta Government Telephones (Telus Corp), Canadair, PWA Corp, Saskatchewan Oil and Gas Corp., Air Canada, Potash Corp. of Saskatchewan, and Petro Canada. An issue arises as to the types of owners to which the corporations should be sold. A summary of the advantages and disadvantages of selling to various owners is given in Table 13-3.

5) The liberalization of public policy. This means the relaxation of any statutory monopolies or licensing arrangements which prevent private sector firms from entering markets which, in the past, were exclusively supplied by the public sector. An example would be the permitting of liquor or wine to be sold through privately owned outlets. Another possibility is allowing the operation of schools or nursing homes where previously they were only government-operated.

Thus, there are several ways that private sector businesses can provide services formerly delivered by government; namely, participation in conventional markets where buyers and sellers compete for projects, contracts to perform work, monopoly franchises where the private company provides services at specified standards, management contracts and acquiring ownership of the corporation. The purpose

Table 13-3 Summary of Advantages and Disadvantages of Selling to Various Types of Owners.

	Advantages	Disadvantages
Small Investors (Individuals where ownership is widely dispersed)	• Increases share ownership by public • Makes more difficult to renationalize • Minority holding retained allows government to control (might also be considered a disadvantage)	• Possibility of takeover by large institution later • May expect government bailout if problems arise • Cost involved of making offering too attractive and misleading public • Limit to amount of share offerings that can be absorbed • Counter argument about why a citizen should purchase something already owned • May have to legislate to prevent takeover
Institution-Owned (e.g., pension & mutual funds)	• Financial capability	• Secrecy surrounding who actual owners are
Private Corporations (sold to one corporation)	• Usually have financial capability • Most likely to maximize sale amount	• Might result in increased concentration • Possibility of selling out too cheaply to large, private corporate interests • Some sales only transfer monopolies from a public to a private one • Excluding foreigners lowers price
Employees	• Avoids concentration of ownership by big financial institution • Popular action for employees to be given stake • Employees motivated to improve productivity	• If fails in the future, the owners may be back to the government for a bailout • Any future share offering dilutes control of the original employee purchases • Fear that they will sell and be purchased by big institutions (ownership becomes concentrated) • Questionable if employees should obtain ownership rather than general public • Vulnerability of investing in same enterprise where one works (and possible loss of employment and savings) • Employee ownership scheme might be perceived as a union-busting tactic • Powerful groups of employees may benefit at expense of others • If management, have an advantage over others
Customers	• Users have control over operations • May be more responsive to needs of customers.	• May not have managerial capability • May not be able to finance purchase • If fails, government may be forced to operate again.

of this section is not to discuss the pros and cons of privatization, but instead to identify the implications for business enterprises. There is an extensive literature on the concept and its appropriations. For example, Hardin (1989) opposes government-owned corporations, or the Fraser Institute publication *Privatization, Tactics and Techniques*, in which (Walker, 1988) advocates all forms of privatization.

The privatization trend provides numerous opportunities for business. The challenges for entrepreneurs and managers are to make sure they are aware of the possibilities by monitoring government initiatives. This is accomplished by getting on mailing lists of government agencies of interest (to become aware of tender and proposal calls), develop personal contacts with public officials, seek advice from successful government contractors, subscribe to relevant government publications, and monitor local newspapers for published information on government needs and contracts out for bid (Goodrich, 1988, p. 17). In addition, proposals might be undertaken at the entrepreneur's own initiative that might stimulate interest by government officials.

The final aspect to be considered is whether or not the privatization trend will continue. In the near future, it appears that governments are in increasing need to raise funds, or reduce costs. Governments are relying more upon business to introduce advanced technology for the many services they provide, and there is a desire to reduce government bureaucracy and foster more private sector involvement in public sector services. Privatization should be viewed as a normal outgrowth of the free enterprise system. As long as it provides society with goods and services in a satisfactory manner, the opportunities for business providing these goods and services will increase.

THE IMPACT OF THE CANADIAN CONSTITUTIONAL DEBATE ON THE BUSINESS SYSTEM

The constitutional debate preoccupied Canadians and governments in the later 1980's and early 1990's. Canada is governed by the federal, ten provincial, and two territorial governments, and this has an economic impact. The division of powers in the existing Constitution decentralizes authority over business, delegating matters to the provinces. Such delegation results in interprovincial barriers to trade. Some proposals in the constitution debate attempted to address the economic consequences, but, of course, no changes were agreed to. The following sections discuss these two topics.

Interprovincial Barriers to Trade

Canada's constitutional arrangement lends itself to barriers to trade being created between provinces, and, indeed, some of them create barriers to trade between Canada and other nations. The following are some examples of barriers that have existed.

- Agricultural supply management marketing boards control the production of commodities by province.
- Out of province (and country) wine is discriminated against by provincial control regulations.
- The Quebec government will pay urban transit commissions a subsidy on new vehicles only if they are produced within the province.
- Technical regulations prevent trucking companies from operating in all provinces.
- Professionals, such as accountants, architects, lawyers, and doctors are licensed provincially.
- Labourers, such as carpenters, are not allowed to work on Quebec projects unless they are residents.
- Moosehead beer, produced in Saint John, N.B., is available to Americans but could not be purchased in Ontario or Quebec until recently.
- Preferential procurement policies still exist in most provinces.

These are but a few of the interprovincial barriers to trade that prevent Canada from becoming a common market. The implications for business are clear: some enterprises are precluded from doing business in particular provinces, or costs are increased by having to meet provincial requirements.

Constitutional Proposals

The decentralization of authority proposed in the constitutional discussions would not have enhanced the situation. The federal government recognizes the need to reduce the interprovincial barriers, and the package proposed in September 1991 contained several economic or business-related issues.

1) Section 121 stated that "Canada is an economic union within which persons, goods, services, and capital may move freely without barriers or restrictions based on provincial or territorial barriers, (referred to as the common market clause).

2) The Government of Canada would have the power to manage the economic union, but federal laws in this regard have no effect unless approved by two-thirds of the provinces with at least 50 percent of the population. Provinces would be allowed to opt out.

3) The Government of Canada and the provinces would harmonize their economic policies, including the scheduling of budget and the harmonization of fiscal policies, with Canada's monetary policy.

4) There would be closer cooperation on regulation of the securities industries, bankruptcy law, and unfair trade practices; consultation on the issuing of broadcast licenses; giving provincial governments sole responsibility for tourism, forestry, mining, and housing.

The proposal did not succeed, and Canadian business remains in the same situation it was in prior to the constitutional discussions. However, other initiatives are being undertaken by the federal government and some provincial governments to reduce interprovincial barriers. The economic situation remains where free trade exists between nations, particularly Canada and U.S. and possibly within North America, yet business cannot operate in an open or free market within Canada itself.

To this point, the discussion has been of how government influences business. The second part of the chapter focuses on the approaches used by business to influence governments.

INFLUENCING GOVERNMENT

Business cannot leave to chance the relationship that may exist between it and the government. Thus, corporations and business associations make efforts to achieve what they consider desirable. This section discusses two efforts in this regard, business involvement in politics and lobbying activities. The operation of corporate affairs departments is also discussed.

Business Involvement in Politics

There are many issues associated with the business's involvement in politics either as business enterprises or businesspersons, and there are pros and cons to such involvement. It is a pluralistic right for business to be involved, as enterprises are an institution in society and thus have a moral responsibility to take part in the political system. Business influences society and, in addition, corporations pay taxes. Businesspersons are very knowledgable of economics and finances, and have the information and skills to make a contribution to the political process. Participation by business is necessary to counter-balance the anti-business activity of other groups; for example, of unions.

On the other hand, there are some downsides to business involvement. It is argued that politics should be left to politicians, and business should be publicly neutral. Politicians have to address issues across a wide spectrum, and businesspersons are not necessarily qualified to deal with many of the social issues the government must address. Business is already accused of exerting too much power in society, and the involvement of businesspersons in politics could upset the pluralistic balance in society. Business involvement might also be interpreted as being biased, thus having an adverse affect on customers or shareholders. There is a risk of alienating a particular government that could result in legislation or regulation not desirable to business. It is difficult to "win" on many of the emotional and highly political issues such as abortion, gun control, and human rights.

Nevertheless, business is involved in politics in several ways. The following is a discussion of this involvement.

The Financing of Political Parties

Corporations are a major source of funds for parties other than the NDP. When deciding whether or not to make political donations, the executive and/or Board is faced with these possibilities: to donate to no party; to donate to one party only; or to donate to all parties equally or disproportionately. Depending upon their decision, a corporation could find itself out of favour as it backed the wrong party. Thus, many larger corporations tend to support more than one party even if the amounts are token to the second and third parties.

There are other ways that corporations contribute to party financing other than through direct dollar contributions. A corporation can provide a party with free office space or legal and other services to politicians during an election campaign. Some corporate executives operate as political "bagmen" by soliciting financial support for a particular party on company time. Also, corporations contribute to political leadership campaigns where the money involved can be as great as an election campaign.

Most financial support received from corporations is not justified or even widely known. Some larger corporations justify their financial contribution as supporting democracy in Canada. The following is a comment in Imasco's Annual Report about the $120 500 the company donated to political parties in 1991!

> Imasco makes donations to political parties and other organizations that support the principles of a strong private business sector and democratic government.
>
> Imasco has never sought, expected or received any consideration for political donations other than the satisfaction of having contributed to the proper functioning of the democratic political process. (Imasco Annual Report, 1992, p. 19.)

Business does contribute substantial funds to many political parties in Canada and the implications of this financing are constantly being discussed.

Publicly Expressed Support for a Candidate or Party

Support for a candidate or party can be expressed in several ways. A corporation can invite campaigning politicians to address employees or company property. If this is done, a decision must be made as to whether to invite candidates from one, some, or all parties. Corporate executives might allow the circulation of political materials to employees, and, again, the question arises as to which party or parties should be allowed. A company executive might endorse a candidate in a newspaper advertisement with his/her affiliation mentioned, or executives may be allowed time off to work for a particular candidate. In the latter case, the issue arises as to whether or not other employees should be granted a similar privilege.

Publicly Expressed Views on Political Issues

Business expresses views on political issues by purchasing advertisements, usually via contributions to industry or trade associations which support or oppose some political issue. Company newsletters might carry articles favouring or opposing current political issues, and corporate executives make speeches in which they comment on important political issues.

Some businesspersons argue that in expressing views on political issues business is not being partisan (Taylor, 1991). The positions, they say, do not have anything to do with political parties, but merely with economic self-interest. Business is merely favouring one policy over another, not one party over another. Taylor examined business involvement in political issues such as the Canada-U.S. Free Trade Agreement, support of the GST, support for a major administrative reform program in the federal public service, and support for the policies of the Bank of Canada. Despite Taylor's argument, some Canadians believe that the views of business are too persuasive and have received too much consideration.

Executives Running for Public Office

Does a person who becomes an executive of a major corporation have a responsibility or obligation to participate in the political process beyond the usual requirements of good citizenship? The response could be "yes," but...! Most executives are not cut out for political life, and conflicts of interest make it more difficult. Executives have management skills to bring to government, presumably as much as the occupational groups that are most common in elected positions now; namely, lawyers, teachers, university professors, journalists, and engineers.

Macfarlane (1988, p. 38) in a *Financial Times Of Canada* article lamented the absence in the House of Commons if anyone who "would qualify as a leader in Canadian business." He went on to say:

> Not that the captains of industry and finance wouldn't be welcome in politics. It's obvious they have much to offer. Why, then, do so few become politically engaged, other than as party fundraisers and backroom functionaries? Because electoral politics isn't nearly as rewarding as business. It certainly doesn't pay as well. The hours are dreadful. The working conditions—relentless media scrutiny, a severely diminished private life—leave a great deal to be desired. The rhetorical

question, 'Why would anyone want to go into politics?' has been uttered a thousand times in the private clubs where the country's business leaders confide in one another over a scotch.

Macfarlane pointed out that "politics is the highest form of community service and should not be viewed as a job but as a mission." He concluded by stating: "If more of our business leaders were prepared to make the sacrifice it requires, our political life would be richer, our continued welfare as a country more certain." Not everyone is this convinced of the desirability of businesspersons entering politics.

Management's Position on Employee Participation

Management must formulate policies relating to employee participation in the political process. Policies should address such issues as:

- Will an employee be allowed to campaign for any party or candidate on site?
- Will the company grant an employee time off to campaign for public office?
- Should the company encourage employees to join a political party?
- Should the company encourage employees to contribute to a political party?
- Should employees be encouraged to campaign for a manager and/or owner who is running for public office?
- Should the company encourage employees to write letters supporting the company's position in a political issue?
- Should employees be encouraged to join organizations designed to make the political climate more favourable to business (e.g., the National Citizens Coalition)?
- Should the company allow employees to be active and visible in political organizations even on their own time?

It is argued that Canadian business is very involved and influential in politics. Coleman portrayed Canadian business as having powerful influences on public policy without much accountability (1988). Businesspersons must concern themselves with how they are perceived as influencing government policy and whether or not their positions are in the best interests of not only the corporation but of other stakeholders, including owners and society at large as well.

The types of involvement in politics by business and businesspersons are one way to influence politics, and thus public policy. An even more direct approach to influencing government is through lobbying activities.

Business Lobbying

Lobbying is defined as all attempts to influence directly or indirectly any government activity, and includes any attempt to influence legislators, their staffs, civil servants, and members of regulatory agencies. Specifically, the act of lobbying government can be defined as to include:

1) attempting to influence the making or amending of legislation and regulations;

2) attempting to influence the making or changing of government policies or programs;

3) attempting to influence government decisions in the awarding of grants, contracts, contributions, or any similar benefits; and

4) attempting to influence government appointments to boards, commissions, and any other public office (Carson, 1988, p. 8)

Business Lobbyists

There are several types of business lobbyists. Business enterprises attempt to influence government through lobbying performed by business interest groups or associations. Examples of business interest groups that act as lobbies include the Business Council on National Issues (an organization comprised of the chief executives of the largest corporations); the Canadian Federation of Independent Business; the Canadian Bankers' Association; the Electrical Association; and the Automobile Parts Manufacturers Association. Table 13-4 lists the types of business interest groups as identified by Stanbury (1986, pp. 308–310) and provides examples of each. It is estimated that there are hundreds of such associations that regularly lobby government by distributing literature and information, appearing before parliamentary committees, royal commissions, inquiries, and other bodies, and interviewing politicians and civil servants.

The second type of lobbyist is the consultant who specializes in government–business relations and is paid by a business enterprise, a group of enterprises, or a business association to make contact with government, or to tell business how to influence government. Someone has estimated this type of lobbying to cost hundreds of millions of dollars a year, involving hundreds of consulting firms usually located in Ottawa and provincial capitals.

Frank (1988) referred to lobbyists of this type as "government relations consultants," further identifying such categories as independent consultants, management consulting firms, public relations/communications firms, and lawyers. Government relations consultants monitor government activities for clients and help them develop strategy and actively lobby for their clients. Independent consultants are often former politicians, civil servants, and political staff, sometimes with industry experience, who operate as individuals or in small partnerships. Such lobbyists usually specialize in one or a few areas and do not provide the array of services offered by government relations consultants. Management consulting firms monitor government initiatives on behalf of clients, but usually are more interested in providing management consulting.

Public relations/communications firms sell their ability to provide a total marketing package, including government relations, public relations, and advertising. Many lawyers lobby for clients and help them understand the legislative process and the legal implications of legislation or proposal regulation.

A third type of business lobbyist exists where corporations develop lobbying capability "in-house," often referred to as government relations or public affairs staff. Such departments usually report to top management and constantly monitor the political environment for developments that will impact the corporation and industry. They prepare positions for management and may be involved directly in lobbying, or in making presentations to government departments or agencies and civil servants.

Table 13-4 Business Interest Groups

Type	Examples
Umbrella Associations (also referred to as peak organizations)	Business Council of National Issues Canadian Chamber of Commerce Canadian Federation of Independent Business
Sectoral Associations	Canadian Manufacturers Association Grocery Products Manufacturers of Canada Canadian Real Estate Association Retail Council of Canada Fisheries Council of Canada
Activity-Specific Associations	Canadian Direct Marketing Association Canadian Export Association Packaging Association of Canada
Industry-Specific Associations	Canada Bankers' Association Canada Pulp and Paper Association Bakery Council of Canada Mining Association of Canada Canadian Textile Institute
Product-Specific Associations	Canada Portland Cement Association Canadian Toy Importers Association Soap and Detergent Association of Canada Automotive Parts Manufacturing Association of Canada Canadian Paper Box Manufacturers Association

Pros and Cons of Business Lobbying

There are pros and cons to business lobbying. It is argued that business must lobby to offset the influence of other groups. It should be pointed out that business groups are not the only lobbyists. Consumers, farmers, labour organizations, environmentalists, and religious groups, to name a few, all lobby governments. In fact, such interest group lobbying is part of Canadian society. It is believed that with each group presenting its point of view, government is better prepared to formulate public policies satisfactory to Canadians. Business argues that its opinion or perspective must be made known to governments if informed decisions are to be made about public policies affecting business.

Lobbying is criticized for several reasons. In the past, some of the practices of lobbying groups were unethical, as seen, for example, by use of bribes, the offering of gifts, the making of improper political contributions, and even blackmail. As a result, many view lobbying as a distasteful, undesirable activity. It is also argued that the business lobby is far too powerful and presents a view that is too one-sided. Other groups in society claim there is unequal access to government and that business is over-represented, while others are under-represented. The cost of business lobbying can be passed on to consumers through the prices paid for goods and services, while other groups, such as consumers and environmentalists, do not have the financial and human resources to lobby effectively.

Increased Lobbying and its Regulation

Business lobbying activities have grown. One reason for this is the increased involvement of government in the business enterprise system. This has necessitated greater lobbying to ensure that business interests are protected. Also, once one enterprise or group starts to lobby, others follow out of necessity. It should be remembered that business groups often lobby against one another in an attempt to influence a government decision. For example, Canadian shoe manufactures might lobby for increased tariff protection, but business enterprises that import shoes might lobby for lower tariffs. This point illustrates that business lobbying is not just business against other groups in society.

Nevertheless, increasing concern was being expressed about business lobbying, and the Federal Government passed an act respecting the registration of lobbyists in 1988. In this act, the definition of lobbyist referred to "paid lobbyists" and included those who lobby on behalf of clients and employees of enterprises and organizations that function as lobbyists. According to the government, the purpose of the legislation is not to regulate lobbying, but to make the lobbying process better understood by identifying who is doing it and on what issues.

Paid lobbyists are required to register under a two-tiered system. Tier-one lobbyists are professional third-party paid lobbyists who often represent more than one client at a time. Tier-two lobbyists are employees who, as a significant part of their duties, lobby on behalf of their employer. Employees of corporation trade unions or professional associations fall into this category. It was expected that about 15 000 would register under the law, but by 1993 the registry listed 800 tier-one lobbyists and 2300 tier-two lobbyists. It is estimated that there are about 225 lobbying firms in downtown Ottawa, and more in provincial capitals who are not required to register. During 1992–1993, a parliamentary committee reviewed the legislation and heard from witnesses who either claimed the registration process was sufficient or that the legislation was ineffective.

The government is a major stakeholder in the business system influencing business operations, and as discussed in this section, business influences government policies, legislation, and regulation through involvement in politics and lobbying.

Corporate Public Affairs Departments

Public affairs or government relations departments were established in many large corporations with the responsibility to manage the interactions between business and government. Managers of such departments should have knowledge of governmental decision-making processes, and of accountability to and credibility with relevant government officials.

Although public affairs initially focused on the relationship between business and government, its role in some corporations has been expanded to include community relations, media relations, environmental monitoring issues management, and public relations. Baetz (1993) found that the roles of government relations (GR) unit managers are more diverse than observed previously; the responsibilities of the GR unit have broadened, for example, serving more than one division, and one finds more in-house consulting to various line departments. The study found that GR unit managers were generally satisfied with the impact and effectiveness of their unit both within and outside the firm (1992, p. 522).

Public affairs or government relation units continue to play a role when the corporation is attempting to influence government and in interpreting government's influence upon the corporation.

Through these three approaches, involvement in politics, lobbying, and public affairs departments, business does influence government policy making and regulation. A final section outlines approaches to understanding the business-government relationship.

EXPLANATION OF THE BUSINESS–GOVERNMENT RELATIONSHIP

Substantial literature exists on the relationship between business and government in Canada. In this section, some concepts, frameworks, and theories that have attempted to explain this relationship are presented. This is not a comprehensive overview, as the materials selected represent only some of the research available. References have been provided for those interested in further reading.

Conceptual Map of Business–Government Relations in Canada

Murray and McMillan (1983) defined and summarized contemporary business–government relations in Canada from a review of the literature. They defined business–government relations as having two component parts: issues and relations. The issues are policy matters decided by government that have an impact upon business; for example, monetary and fiscal policies, government ownership of corporations, or regulation such as consumer or environmental protection. The matter of concern with any issue is the degree of congruence or conflict between the two parties, which can range from none to substantial conflict. The relations component refers mainly to the degree of influence each party exerts over the other in the process of making decisions on the issues in question. Again, there is a range of influence from co-opting governments to domination of business.

The authors generated six basic types of business–government relations, as outlined in Table 13-5 and summarized as:

Type I High congruence and business interests prevail over those of others, producing a "pro-business" climate.

Type II The situation where the interests of others are preferred by government, but because of its power, business is able to force its views to prevail producing an "anti-government" relationship.

Types III and IV Government dominates the relationship, but when there is high congruence on issues the relationship is pro-government, while high conflict is anti-business.

Types V–VI A relative balance of influence exists in the relationship. Placid relationships exist when there is high congruence on issues, while turbulent relationships exist when there is a high degree of conflict.

Table 13-5 Basic Types of Business–Government Relations

Relations: Relative influence in decision-making	Parties' positions on issues	
	High Congruence	High Conflict
Business-dominated	Type I Pro-business	Type II Anti-government
Government-dominated	Type III Pro-government	Type IV Anti-business
Relatively balanced	Type V Placid-stable	Type VI Turbulent-changing

SOURCE: V.V. Murray and C.J. McMillan. (1983). Business-government relations in Canada: A conceptual map. *Canadian Public Administration*, 26(4), p. 597.

Murray and McMillan concluded that pure situations of each type seldom exist, and that in the real world relationships vary depending upon the issues and specific parties involved.

The authors identified five major schools of thought that explained business–government relations: the macro perspective (social content schools), interpretive school, the failure of business school, the failure of government school, and mechanisms of interaction school. The macro perspective school held that the "state of business-government relations is merely a by-product of the ideologies and structures of the prevailing social, economic and political institutions of society" (1983, p. 597). There are several groups that analyze the relationships from this perspective, including Marxists, corporatists, and pluralists.

The interpretive school concentrates on a number of basic values, attitudes, and beliefs, which influence the way the parties interact and their positions on issues. This approach "concentrates on attempting to document in a detailed and sophisticated way the mutually incompatible viewpoint of business, politicians and senior civil servants" (1983, p. 600).

The "failure of business" school explains government involvement in the business system as occurring because business has allowed it to happen. The explanations for this situation are that business has not devoted sufficient effort to the business–government relationship, that what it has done is based on insufficient knowledge of the issue and the process involved, and that there is a general task of skill in dealing with government (1983, p. 602). The opposite position is represented by the "failure of government" school, which blames politicians and civil servants. Reasons for this include the way democratic politics is practised—for example, politicians' promises to voters; and the complexity of the policy-making structure; that is, the organizational arrangements of government.

The final school of thought explaining business–government relations is referred to as a "mechanism of interactions." The position here is that the focus has been in structures and processes with each party (as represented by the two previous schools) while ignoring the existence of other stakeholders who might or could influence relations between government and business. The total process of inaction relating to a particular policy might be influenced by such stakeholders as organized labour, consumer groups, environmental protection groups, and by other levels of government and the media. The exclusion of these other stakeholders requires far greater sophistication on the part of business, which it has failed in most of the time (1983, p. 606).

Murray and McMillan summarize the subject of business–government through developing types of relations and identifying schools of thought, and other researchers have built on their research, or added to the body of knowledge. The following is a selected list of studies with brief summaries that are illustrative of the extensive research performed in the business–government relations area.

Problems in Business–Government Relations

Bartha (1985) claimed that business does not approach its socio-political environment in a systematic way and that it fails to integrate an awareness of the external environment with internal planning and decision making. He identified the impediments to the internalization of external considerations as factors that reflect insufficient understanding of the political system, inherent weaknesses or the socio-political data base, non-operational concepts of social responsibility, and a narrowly defined mandate for the public affairs function in a corporation.

An Interpretative Understanding of Business–Government Relations

The authors, Taylor and Murray (1987), presented the results of a study that supported the "interpretative school of thought" to business–government relations. This school of thought emphasizes the underlying values, attitudes, perceptions, and beliefs that business and government hold about each other, their relationships, and the specific policy issue(s) under discussion and identified by Murray and McMillan (1983). The resulting subjective interpretations interfere with the actions taken by the parties, making accurate communication and collaborative decision-making very difficult.

A study was conducted to measure some of these beliefs and values held by the two parties empirically. It was found that in 1984 there were massive differences of opinions between business and government on the general state of the business–government relationship. Leaders of larger businesses believed that their relationships with government had deteriorated and that government had become too interventionist. Government leader respondents did not agree to the same extent. Predictably, business respondents blamed the roles of politicians and senior civil servants and government respondents blamed certain characteristics built into the business leaders' role in society. But both groups agreed that previous structures and processes governing their interaction were inadequate and that the place to begin the improvement of relations would be in reform of the mechanism of interaction.

Taylor (1992) replicated the Taylor and Murray (1987) study on business–government relations. The results indicated that both business and government respondents saw a marked improvement in the relationship during the 1984–88 period. In particular, business leaders were much more positive about the relationship. Taylor stated that an obvious explanation of the change was the shift to the right in the political ideology of the Progressive Conservative federal government elected in 1984. But he also found significant shifts in attitudes with perception bring less role-specific. This meant that each party had a clearer understanding of the role of and constraints placed upon the other side. Business was found to be communicating better with government through consultants, lobbyists, trade association, and other experts. The Business Council on National Issues (BCNI) and the Canadian Federation of Independent Business (CFIB) were identified as the two most successful business associations. Respondents thought there were "not enough regular face-to-face interactions between CEOs and senior politicians and public servants" and that "the news media did more harm than good to business-government relations" (1992, p. 256). Additional background on Taylor's research can be obtained by reading Taylor (1989) and (1991).

SUMMARY

Government intervenes in the Canadian business system in a multitude of ways which are identified as government expenditures on goods and services, taxation of business enterprises, the granting of exemptions from taxation (tax expenditures), various protective devices used to shield Canadian business from foreign competition, the granting of loans and loan guarantees, the bailing out of failing enterprises, the ownership of business enterprises in whole or part, the granting of special status to some enterprises, and through suasion. The purpose in identifying these 11 involvements is not to itemize the magnitude of each, but instead to gain an appreciation of the broad scope of government involvement in the business system.

The status of government involvement is not static but changes over time. The trend toward increased involvement after World War II appears to have been reversed in about 1980. The argument is made that government is now less involved in the business system as a result of a shift toward a preference for a private market system. This shift is manifested in several ways: contracting out, user pay, deregulation, and privatization.

Privatization is discussed in detail for two reasons: it is necessary to clarify that privatization involves any transfer from government to the private sector (not only the sale of government-owned corporations) and because the trend to less government involvement; that is, privatization, has a major implication for business, as it provides opportunities for the private sector to perform operations formerly done by the state. It should be realized that changes in government involvement are just trends, and should not be interpreted as being absolute. Exceptions to the trends exist, and although less government appears to be the case, it does not mean that there will be no government. Thus, businesspersons must still be sensitive to the role of government.

Business operations in Canada are impacted by the nature of the country's Constitution, which decentralizes authority over many aspects of government to the provinces. This decentralization of authority over economic matters has resulted in the erection of barriers to business, or trade, across provincial borders when free trade is taking place between nations in North America. This problem is being addressed by the governments, but a resolution of the problem seems distant. The "Economic Union" proposed in the constitutional debate did not survive. In fact, most of the constitutional proposals would have resulted in greater decentralization. Thus business is left to be conducted within a nation where barriers to trade exist.

The discussion to this point in the chapter focused in the influence government had on business. The emphasis now switches to examining how business influences government. In this chapter, three main approaches were examined: involvement in politics, lobbying, and corporate public affairs departments. Business does influence government, but does not always get its way. Some claim that the influence is too persuasive, which is not desirable for society. Businesspersons consider their influence to be insufficient. This issue is explored in more detail in the final section which reviews selected explanations of the government–business relationship in Canada. Types of business–government relations are identified as well as five major schools of thought. One, the interpretive school, is discussed further, and studies are reviewed that show how business–government relations have changed during the 1980's.

The government is a major stakeholder, and this chapter has only begun to explore some of its influence and how it is influenced.

REFERENCES

Baetz, Mark C. (1992). Rethinking the government relations unit, *Canadian Journal of Administrative Sciences*, 9(4), pp. 310–323.

Bartha, Peter F. (1985). Organizational competence in business-government relations: A managerial perspective, *Canadian Public Administration*, 28(2), pp. 202–220

Bird, Richard and Christopher Green. (1985). *Government Intervention in the Canadian Economy*. Toronto: Institute for Policy Analysis/University of Toronto Press.

Block, Walter, and George Lermer (Eds.). (1991). *Breaking the Shackles: Deregulating Canadian Industry*, Vancouver: The Fraser Institute.

Brander, James A. (1988). *Government Policy Towards Business*. Toronto: Butterworths.

Carson, Bruce. (1988). *Registration of Lobbyists*. Library of Parliament Current Issue Review. Ottawa: Supply and Services Canada. Cat. No. YM32-1/86-18-1988-05E.

Coleman, William D. (1988). *Business and Politics: A Study of Collective Action*. Montreal: McGill-Queens University Press.

Drohan, Madelaine. (1991, April 17). "CMA assails trade barriers," *The Globe and Mail*, p. B3.

Frank, Tema A. (1988, Summer). "The Lobbyists," *Canadian Business Review*, pp. 36–38.

Freedom to Move: A Framework for Transportation Reform (1985), Ottawa: Supply and Services Canada, Cat. No. T22-69/1985E.

Goodrich, Jonathan N. (1988, January-February). Privatization in America, *Business Horizons*, pp. 11–17.

Hardin, Herschel. (1989). *The Privatization Putsch*. Halifax: Institute for Research in Public Policy.

Heald, David. (1984). Privatization, analysing its appeal and limitations, *Fiscal Studies*, 5(1), pp. 36-46.

Imasco Annual Report 1991. (1992). Montreal: Imasco Limited.

Lermer, George (Ed.). (1984). *Probing Leviathan: An Investigation of Government in the Economy*. Vancouver: The Fraser Institute.

Macfarlane, John. (1988, April 4). Do businessmen have a duty to run for public office?, *Financial Times of Canada*, p. 38.

Mittelstaedt, Martin. (1986, December 18). Interventionist mood among Canadians detected by Cohen, *The Globe and Mail*, p. B16.

Murray, V. V. and C. J. McMillan. (1983). Business-government relations in Canada: A conceptual map, *Canadian Public Administration*, 26(4), pp. 591–609.

Reforming Regulation. (1981). Ottawa: Supply and Services Canada, Economic Council of Canada, Cat. No. EC22–93/1981E.

Regulate Less: Regulate Better. (1986). The Final Report of the Task Force on Deregulation. Quebec: Government of Quebec.

Regulatory Agencies. (1985). A study team report to the task force on program review. Ottawa: Supply and Services Canada, Cat. No. CP32–50/21–1985E.

Regulatory Programs (1985). A study team report to the task force on program review. Ottawa: Supply and Services Canada, Cat. No. CP32–50/20–1985E.

Regulatory Reform Strategy. (1986). Ottawa: Privy Council Office.

Responsible Regulation: An Interim Report by the Economic Council of Canada. (1979), Ottawa: Supply and Services Canada, Cat. No. EC22–70/1979.

Royal Commission on the Economic Union and Development Prospects for Canada-Report. (1985). Ottawa: Supply and Services Canada, Cat. No. 21–1983-1E.

Services and Subsidies to Business. (1985). A Study Team Report to the Task Force on Program Review. Ottawa: Supply and Services Canada, Cat. No. CCP32–50/2–1985E.

Stanbury, W. T. (1986). *Business-Government Relations in Canada*. Toronto: Methuen.

Taylor, Allan R. (1991, Spring). Business politics and politicians, *Business Quarterly*, pp. 11–17.

Taylor, D. Wayne. (1991). *Business and Government Relations: Partners in the 1990's.* Toronto: Gage.

Taylor, D. Wayne. (1987). An interpretative approach to understanding and improving business-government relations, *Canadian Journal of Administrative Sciences,* 4(4), pp. 353–366.

Taylor, D. Wayne. (1992). An interpretive understanding of the improvement in business–government relations, *Canadian Public Administration,* 35(2), pp. 250–257.

Taylor D. Wayne and Victor V. Murray. (1987). An interpretive understanding of the non-fulfilment of business-government relations, *Canadian Public Administration,* 30(3), pp. 421–431.

Walker, Michael A. (Ed.). (1988). *Privatization, Tactics and Techniques.* Vancouver: The Fraser Institute.

Weimer, David L. and Aidan R. Vining. (1992). *Policy Analysis: Concepts and Practice,* Second Edition. Eaglewood Cliffs, NJ: Prentice-Hall.

CORPORATE PHILANTHROPY: DONATIONS, VOLUNTARISM, AND SPONSORSHIP

INTRODUCTION

Corporate philanthropy is described as the effort of business to contribute socially to society and is manifested by donations of money or goods and services in kind, voluntarism where corporate employees work for social causes, and sponsorship of events that will in some way contribute to society. Alan Taylor, chairman and CEO of the Royal Bank of Canada, describes philanthropy as the active effort to help others and to be constructively involved in community life (1991). He suggested that philanthropy takes many forms. This chapter focuses on three: corporate giving or the making of donations, support for employee voluntarism, and sponsorship of social events and causes.

CORPORATE DONATIONS

There are many examples in a long list of corporate philanthropy, some of which follow.

- A responsible drinking campaign sponsored by The Distillers of Canada.
- "Share the Light," an energy assistance program sponsored by Newfoundland Power Limited and administered by the Salvation Army, designed to help families in need to pay their energy bills.
- The Royal Bank Award, giving $100 000 to a Canadian or Canadians whose outstanding accomplishments have made an important contribution to human welfare and the common good.
- Ronald McDonald houses, sponsored by McDonald's Restaurants of Canada, where the parents of seriously ill youngsters can stay while their children are treated in hospital.
- An outdoor gallery of contemporary Alberta art, supported by Hook Outdoor Advertising of Calgary.
- Pledges by The Canadian Business Task Force on Literacy, formed by 32 corporations to combat illiteracy.`
- Pledges by Alexanian & Sons, a small, family-owned carpet business, of almost $75 000 to Opera Hamilton, and sponsorship and support of Theatre Aquarius and the Hamilton Philharmonic Orchestra.

There is no shortage of organizations or causes: there are now 70 000 charities registered for taxation purposes.

Canadian business enterprises donate to a variety of causes and organizations, including health and welfare agencies, educational institutions, community services, service clubs, civic projects, arts and culture groups, athletic organizations, and environmental groups. Some enterprises spread contributions across a variety of causes, while others are more focused in their giving. In addition to the donation of money, corporate giving or philanthropy can involve the donation of goods and services. Statistics on corporate giving are provided in Table 14-1. The statistics do not indicate that business is particularly generous.

Society expects business to direct some of its profits to social causes and organizations. In 1986, a Decima Research survey found that 8 out of 10 Canadians believed corporations have a responsibility to provide support to charities and non-profit organizations. This section provides arguments for and against corporate giving, examines how the decision to donate is made, and indicates trends in corporate giving.

The Arguments for Corporate Giving

The following are the main arguments in support of business giving:

Table 14-1 Statistics On Corporate Giving in Canada

- In 1991, 85 percent of the $4.9 billion donated to charities came from individuals. It is estimated that about 10 percent was given by business enterprises.

- The amount donated by business represents about 0.45 percent of pre-tax profits. In the late 1960's, donations equalled about 0.8 to 1.0 percent. A comparable recent American figure is 1.9 percent.

- Corporate donations are made by 10 percent of all corporations. Half of Canada's large corporations and 85 percent of medium-sized ones give nothing.

- The following are the percentages of corporations in various industries who give nothing:

Manufacturing	26%
Retailing	29%
Agriculture, forestry & fishing	40%
Transportation, communication and other utilities	41%
Mining	56%
Services	66%
Financial services	74%

- Corporations share their giving among charities approximately as follows:

Health & Welfare	45%
Education	25%
Culture	14%
Civic	7%
Athletics	1%
Other	8%

SOURCE: Tom Kierans. (1990, June). Charity begins at work. *Report on Business Magazine,* pp. 23, 25; Michael Valpy. (1989, August 17). Business community slow on the draw. *The Globe and Mail,* p. A8; Michael Valpy. (1989, August 23). Why are Canadians such stingy donors? *The Globe and Mail,* p. A8; Anne Kingston. (1992, December 19). Choosing a charity, *The Globe and Mail,* p. B20.

1) Corporate giving is one way to express social responsibility to the community and to show that business is not just concerned with society as a market.

2) It promotes an image of good citizenship and creates goodwill, important as business must be accepted by society.

3) Most business persons recognize that the volunteer sector provides some services very efficiently, and that even business enterprises benefit from such services as, for example, employees belonging to Alcoholics Anonymous.

4) There are direct benefits to the enterprise; for example, through promotions or advertising, tax breaks, or public recognition for good deeds.

One of the strongest cases made for corporate philanthropy was made by Allan Taylor, a Royal Bank chairman. He stated that there are three major reasons why a profit-seeking business enterprise should provide financial support to charitable and non-profit organizations: (1) corporate giving is one of the facets of responsible corporate citizenship; (2) the company's success is tightly linked with economic health and social conditions in the community in which it operates, and thus a company should invest in the organizations that underpin community vitality; and (3) there are significant benefits to be derived from a corporate community investment program in terms of employee commitment, corporate reputation, marketing visibility, and relationships with customers, suppliers, neighbours, and governments (Raymond, 1991).

The Arguments Against Corporate Giving

The following summarizes the arguments against corporate giving:

- The funds given actually belong to shareholders, and it is presumptuous for management to make the decision to give the funds in the first place, and then secondly to choose particular recipients.
- Business enterprises should not become involved with social welfare as that is the job of governments. If business did support social causes, it could give business more power in society when many feel that it has too much already.
- By supporting any cause or organization, the enterprise might become accountable for the actions taken by the charity, or adverse publicity could damage the enterprise's image or reputation.
- Usually there are no guidelines, no standards to measure against, and no evaluation process for making decisions and monitoring corporate giving. The benefits of corporate giving are seldom measurable or directly related to the enterprise.

Making Corporate Giving Decisions

In earlier times, corporate giving decisions were made by individual executives who were often members of the family in such corporations as Eatons, Woodwards, Burtons, Molsons, and Labatts. Today, the one-man dominance has, in most cases, yielded to a committee consensus, and the process is more complicated.

In the more formalized processes, the decisions relating to corporate giving are made in head offices by chief executives and the Board of Directors with assistance from a committee. The first decision relates to the donations budget. According to Martin (1985, p. 240), budgets are set as a percentage of expected pre-tax profit, increased an arbitrary amount from the previous year, and set in relation to industry norms or in comparison to peers, or upon a formula based upon number of employees.

Some corporations carefully establish the objectives for giving so that some guidelines are available to ascertain how much money is given and to whom. Criteria for evaluating requests are formulated and used by in-house staff or consultants in making decisions. Some givers perform cost-benefit analyses of the grant, while others require that social performance programs must be proactive. Grants given in one year are evaluated prior to another grant being made. Some corporate givers, such as Imperial Oil Ltd. and John Labatts Ltd., have managers of contributions to supervise the process.

Despite the formalization suggested above, the single most important influence in the decision-making process is still the Chair of the Board or the CEO.

Organizations Influencing Corporate Giving

Organizations outside the corporation that influence the process include:

- *The Canadian Centre for Philanthropy*   Established in 1980, the centre's mission is to promote the generous application of charitable time and funds, and to strengthen the philanthropic community of Canada through research and training. The centre initiated the IMAGINE program, a Canada-wide corporate and individual awareness program to increase support for charitable non-profit organizations.

- *The Council for Business and the Arts in Canada (CBAC)*   This is a central resource for business involvement in the arts and with the CCA sponsors annual awards to enterprises involved in supporting the arts.

- *The Canadian Conference for the Arts (CCA)*   A national, non-profit organization based in Ottawa and supported by government that encourages the development of arts in Canada.

- *The Institution of Donations and Public Affairs Research (IDPAR)*   A non-profit organization formed in 1975–76 to provide members, primarily large corporations, which information and research on the corporate giving practices and trends in Canada.

- *The Philanthropic Advisory Service of the Canadian Council of Better Business Bureaus* An organization that ascertains which charities are financially responsible.

Charitable Foundations

There are about 1000 charitable foundations in Canada that donate to a wide variety of causes including education, health, environment, community development, and arts and culture. According to the Income Tax Act, a charitable foundation is defined as "a corporation or trust constituted and operated exclusively for charitable purposes." Several families and corporations have chosen to establish foundations to support charities. These foundations are established by wealthy individuals or families and support a wide variety of social activities or causes. The largest private foundation in Canada is the J.W. McConnell Foundation with assets of about $310 million (McConnell was a former publisher of the *Montreal Star*). In his will, Harold Ballard, owner of the Toronto Maple Leafs, directed that a large part of his estate be used to endow a foundation in his name (Downey, 1990). The Canadian Centre for Philanthropy publishes *The Canadian Directory to Foundations*, a comprehensive directory of donation givers in Canada.

It is important to distinguish among the different types of foundations. These are as follows.

Family: These foundations are established by the families who own various business enterprises. They are the best known and account for 80 to 85 percent of all foundations. Often the family retains an interest in their operation. Examples are the Samuel and Saidye Bronfman, R. Samuel McLaughlin (G.M. Canada), and Molson foundations.

Community: Community foundations normally have the following characteristics: funds are derived from the contributions of many donors, usually through bequests; grant programs are designed to benefit the particular city or region served; activities are regularly reported to the public; the governing body represents broad segments of the community; and the use of funds may be altered if purposes designed by the donors become impracticable. There are over 20 active community foundations in Canada with Vancouver and Winnipeg having the largest. Corporations may have made donations to such foundations.

Corporate: Corporate foundations are legally independent of corporations but are closely associated through their boards. Some have been established so that the level of donations is stabilized and less likely to fluctuate with profit levels. This enables the corporation to maintain a consistent level of support which sustains the operation of charitable organizations. There are about 23 corporate foundations in Canada.

Special Interest: Some health organizations and hospitals have formed foundations that often serve as fund-raising units. The funds raised are allocated directly to the hospital with which they are affiliated. An exception is The Hospital for Sick Children Foundation, which allocates funds across Canada. These foundations seek funds from corporations as well as from individuals.

Government: Foundations have been formed in some provinces to allocate funds raised through lotteries. The Ontario Trillium Foundation is an example.

The largest 50 foundations in Canada manage 80 percent of the assets of all foundations and provide 65 percent of grants (Arlett and van Rotterdam, 1987).

Foundations are being swamped by demands for funds as other sources of corporate philanthropy decline. Corporate involvement in foundations is substantial, and most are associated with some business enterprise or family.

Rejecting Requests

Either through formal or ad hoc processes, decisions are made to fund, but also to reject requests. A request is typically rejected when: policy excludes a particular type of project or charity; there are not enough funds; a donation has already been made to an organization with parallel services; the organization is located outside of the corporation's community; there is no Revenue Canada registration number; there are inadequate financial statements; no new approaches are being accepted; the size of the request is too large; or the corporation receives too many requests (Martin, 1985, p. 240).

Another form of rejection is the decision to cease giving to a particular organization. Such a decision may have serious consequences, including the failure of the organization. Many causes are rejected because they are somehow controversial. For example, many corporations are reluctant to support Planned Parenthood organizations because of possible backlash from anti-abortion groups. There is without doubt a tendency to seek out safe causes on the part of those who make the donating decision.

Some Trends in Corporate Giving

A number of trends have occurred that have impacted upon corporate giving. Large requests from universities and hospitals have resulted in a higher portion of the donation budget being committed to five-year programs. This doesn't leave much opportunity to fund new causes or groups.

The economic recession has also resulted in a decline of corporate giving. According to a Conference Board of Canada survey, Canadian corporations planned to give less in donations during 1993. Thirty-three percent of respondents expected to cut charitable donations, while 19 percent expected to give more. Donations to education, the environment, and the United Way were to remain the same, but cutbacks were planned for donation to arts and culture, civic causes, hospitals, and sports (Vardy, 1993).

The Canadian Centre for Philanthropy initiated the IMAGINE corporate program to increase awareness of charitable giving and volunteering. The program is striving to persuade companies to commit to a policy of donating at least one per unit of domestic pre-tax profit (based on the average of the three preceding years) to the charities and non-profits of their choice. The impact of the IMAGINE program is not known yet. Business enterprises in Canada are supporting a wide variety of charities in Canada, and this support has become much more important as government grants have declined. For those corporations that donate on a regular basis, philanthropy is a responsibility, a part of the cost of doing business. For other corporations, it is a frill. It appears that some enterprises are willing to give, but are becoming more selective and will have to be convinced to part with their money.

One area of corporate philanthropy will be discussed in detail — support for arts organizations. Similar treatments could have been given to such other areas of major support as health and welfare, education, and athletics. The arts, however, illustrate challenges confronting both corporate givers and non-profit receivers.

BUSINESS AND THE ARTS

Traditionally, supporting the arts has been the duty of federal, provincial, and municipal governments. Because of financial constraints, governments are no longer as willing to hand out enormous amounts of money to keep the arts community in Canada thriving. As a result, arts and cultural organizations are turning to business for support.

The Variety and Types of Support

Good examples of corporate support for the arts can be found from the list of recipients in *The Financial Post*'s Business in the Arts Awards. The 1992 and 1993 recipients, by category, are:

Sustained Support:

Molson Breweries of Canada Ltd.
>   Nominated by Toronto's Harborfront Corp. for support and cultural activities.

James Richardson & Sons, Winnipeg
>   Nominated by the Winnipeg Symphony Orchestra for three decades of support including sponsorship of special concerts, encouraging employee volunteer work, and offering substantial financial gifts.

Innovative Support:

Standard Life Assurance Co.
>   Nominated by the Ottawa Ballet for the company's support for the renovating one of its properties on Ottawa's Bank Street.

Loblaw Co. Ltd.
>   Nominated by Canadian Stage Company for Loblaw's support of the free outdoor Shakespearean theatre in High Park, Toronto.

Community Support

Quebec and Ontario Paper Company Ltd.

   Nominated by Carousel Players, St. Catharines, Ontario, for the company's financial support of professional children's theatre.

Calgary Copier Ltd.

   Nominated by Alberta Theatre. Project included "adopting" the non-profit group and volunteering its time and services to solicit donations from other companies.

   These examples are illustrative of the wide spectrum of arts and cultural activities supported, including those of museums, art galleries, symphonies, opera and ballet, and theatrical troops. The current level of funding is in the range of $25 to $30 million and has been static at that level for over 10 years. Only about 10 percent of businesses give to the arts. Within this 10 percent, support is concentrated, with 10 percent of the enterprises involved providing 90 percent of the support.

   Business support can take many forms including direct cash donations; the purchase of seats, memberships or advertising space; the subsidization of employee subscriptions to arts-related activities; the purchase of works of art; donations in kind of products and services; the support of scholarships and residencies; and event sponsorship. Business also becomes involved in special support and/or promotional campaigns where it donates certain funds to an arts organization every time a consumer purchases a particular product or service. Donations may also be in the form of staff support or expertise, in areas such as planning, promotion, and marketing, or through other more general services.

   The arts and culture industries cannot be ignored. It is estimated that they generate $9.2 billion in annual revenues and provide 235 000 jobs. The relationship between the arts and business communities is receiving considerable attention, as it is realized that benefits can accrue to both parties from healthy and active arts and cultural industries.

Corporate Art Collection—An Example of Support for the Arts

The walls of corporate offices across the country are often covered with the artistic efforts of Canadians. The purchase of art by business enterprises is one way of supporting the arts in this country. For example, the Toronto-Dominion Bank has a collection of 6000 Canadian paintings, work on paper, sculptures, and Inuit objects. The reasons given for such activity include good corporate citizenship, social and cultural responsibility, and improvement of the working environment.

   Art is often collected because of a personal interest by an executive. Purchasing is usually focused on Canadian artists with the intent of helping them to survive, and is viewed as one way that the corporation can meet its social responsibility to the community. The status of the collection sometimes depends on an individual executive's involvement in the corporation, and collections may be disposed of when he or she leaves. An example is provided at Norcen Energy Resources Ltd., which had acquired a collection of 400 works as a result of the personal interest of a former chairman. After his retirement, Norcen donated the collection to art galleries.

Selection of art is a problem for business enterprises. Some corporations, including the Toronto-Dominion Bank, Teleglobe Canada, the Bank of Nova Scotia, and the Royal Bank of Canada, have established curatorial departments that supervise the acquisition and maintenance of the collection. A policy is developed that leads to greater continuity in the collection. Art consultants assist in making decisions, and the Canada Council's Art Bank will assist in the search for such consultants. More businesses appear to be moving toward formalizing their art collection and collecting, and relying less on the whims of one executive.

Critics of corporate art collection say that often the best contemporary artists are ignored as works have been chosen that are "safe" and that match office decor. Art collecting can become merely an aspect of interior decoration rather than a commitment to supporting the best Canadian art. What corporations expect to achieve by collecting art and what the Canadian art community wants may differ. It's not clear how much help corporate purchases of art has been.

Benefits Accruing to the Arts Community

Funding from business means that higher quality productions are possible, leading to a higher profile in the community, and perhaps nationally. Support for an arts organization could allow it to reach the point where it could start giving back to the community through taxes, expenditures on materials and staff, and support of other smaller groups.

Business involvement often leads to a more effectively managed organization as the purpose, or "raison d'être," is more clearly defined, better planning is implemented, and financial administration enhanced.

Benefits Accruing to the Business Community

There are many benefits to business from some involvement in the arts and cultural industries. These benefits include:

- improved community relations
- increased public awareness of the business enterprise
- demonstration of a commitment to the community

- a well-run and supported arts community, especially in smaller centres, assists in attracting and retaining high-level executive talent
- a well-supported cultural sector means that Canadian culture is better known and respected, creating national pride
- associate consumption is involved with arts events, and business provides most of these; for example, the dinner before the concert. In towns like Stratford, Ontario, home of an annual Shakespeare Festival, there are spin-offs for hotel, restaurant, and retail enterprises.
- business enterprises wish to identify with successful arts and ventures, as it strengthens their image as innovative and creative people

However, while these benefits may be part of enterprise's objectives, there is evidence to suggest that many business enterprises are taking another view of their support. No longer are donations and patronage enough; many business enterprises are expecting something more.

Many businesses now expect a partnership where something more in return is received than "small print" recognition. In some cases, corporate sponsorship is considered a calculated investment from which a return is expected. Both parties believe this to be satisfactory as long as all obligations and expectations are specified and agreed to at the beginning of the arrangement.

However, the trend is away from donations and toward making sponsorship a part of the marketing package. This approach brings greater visibility and recognition to the business. Sponsorship is analyzed so that a message is delivered to a "target" group. There may even be possibilities of merchandise sales tied to the sponsored event. Other benefits to business can be in the form of better employee morale or through the provision of an impressive platform for entertaining customers.

In other words, support for the arts is now being viewed from a marketing perspective with plans to ensure that the "right" people in sufficient numbers are reached at a reasonable cost to achieve some objective. For example, Canadian Pacific's support for TV Ontario's "Visions" was an effort to overcome its mundane image of an enterprise involved in staple industries. The aim was to create the image of a lively, positive corporation on the "leading edge" of innovative, educational techniques and creativity. In a survey conducted by the Council for Business and the Arts in Canada, over half of the corporations use the marketing budget to determine if there is a measurable rate of return on any particular donation or sponsorship.

Concerns About Corporate Support

The trend to a "marketing" orientation to supporting the arts has raised concern. Marketing can be viewed as being too "commercial," as products or services are being directly promoted. Also, conditions can be placed on support which are considered a threat to artistic freedom. Support may be given to activities and events where a marketing tie-in is possible, while other activities are neglected. There is a fear that some artistic cultural groups could become very successful at promoting themselves from the marketing perspective expected of business, leaving other less aggressive groups without support.

Some of strongest supporters of the arts and culture in Canada produce products that may not be considered socially desirable; for example tobacco, beer, and liquor. The issue is one of whether a group should be associated with the consumption of these products. Society might even find such support unacceptable. For example, in 1987 the federal government proposed legislation to prohibit the advertising and promotion of tobacco products. Yet enterprises in the tobacco industry have been innovative and imaginative in their support of the arts. Groups now receiving support from the tobacco industry may find it difficult to accept such support in the future, or if the legislation is implemented, may find this source of funds eliminated.

Suggested Ways for Improving Business Support of the Arts

The federal government's Task Force on Funding of the Arts that reported in July of 1986 recommended the use of a tax incentive in the form of a 125 percent tax credit similar to that given for political contributions. Such an incentive would mean that the government would be foregoing some tax revenue, and with high deficits, the initiative appears unlikely.

About 150 business enterprises belong to the Council for Business and the Arts in Canada. Established in 1974, the Council encourages and stimulates business support of the arts. It is a co-sponsor of *The Financial Post* Awards for Business in the Arts presented annually to Canadian business enterprises involved in sustained and innovative support for the arts.

Supporting the arts is not a one-sided affair with business taking the initiative. If arts organizations are more business-like—that is, market-oriented, with consistent and orderly appeals—they might be more successful in obtaining business support. In particular, more business-like budgeting and financial management in arts organizations would give business greater confidence that its money is being appropriately spent. Business dollars are being increasedly sought, and the arts organizations more likely to succeed are those with a blend of first-rate fundraising techniques, well-managed non-profit budgeting systems, and excellent artistic and social programs.

The implication for arts organizations is that they will have to start paying more attention to the business side of their affairs. However, this presents a dilemma. It means that some organizational effort will be directed away from artistic pursuits, which might adversely affect the quality of productions. Also, well-established, sophisticated, well-run, and high-profile organizations will get the largest share of business support. Small organizations needing business support to develop may be bypassed.

A Different View of Support for the Arts

A neoconservative view of support for the arts questions the benefits of subsidized art, either by government or business. Walker (1986) opposes all subsidization as he claims that it has authoritarian and elitist implications. He argues that the subsidization of the arts is a thinly disguised redistribution of income to higher income citizens. Handouts to the arts prevent the consumer (or taxpayer) from influencing the product to be provided; that is, the market is not choosing the productions to be staged. The granting of funds from government agencies also limits the extent of support for experimental artistic endeavours. Walker feels that support should be linked to the audience that can be attracted, and proposes that consumers would be provided with vouchers and allowed to spend them on what they prefer.

The Current Situation

Despite neoconservative views on the matter, many business enterprises appear willing to provide support to the "arts and culture" stakeholder. Apparently, most business enterprises believe that the market is unable to provide arts productions without some type of support. However, the nature of the support is changing, and it appears that business enterprises are influencing the behaviour of this stakeholder more than in the past. Corporations are demanding more in terms of sponsorship and attempting to match corporate advertising agendas to the needs of the arts groups threatened with loss of independence. Corporate supporters are less tolerant of the casual management practices of arts groups and are demanding more business-like systems and accountability.

Support for the arts is declining from government sources at a time when demands are increasing. Corporations are swamped with requests for funding, and the competition for corporate funds is greater. In the economic recession of the 1980's and 1990's, total corporate funding is down, and at the same time business support for the arts is shifting toward marketing-oriented sponsorship. Taken together, business and the arts is a major and dynamic area.

CORPORATE VOLUNTARISM

Corporate voluntarism refers to the time and talent employees commit to community organizations. Corporations view voluntarism as giving something back to the community and society, and as an expression of good corporate citizenship.

The principle of voluntarism is well established in society, and there is a continuing need to recruit and motivate members of society to support the many voluntary organizations. Employee voluntarism has become more important for two reasons: the decline of the professional volunteer of the past, the homemaker who did not work outside the home; and the increasing need for volunteers to serve (Hart, 1987). The former point results from more women working, and the latter refers to the increasing load on volunteers during cutbacks in government support and greater demand from an aging population.

The Benefits and Drawbacks

There are benefits to employers, employees, and, of course, the non-profit organizations involved. But, there can also be drawbacks, especially for employers and employees. Many of these benefits and drawbacks for the parties are summarized in Exhibit 14-1.

The general benefits for employers include the creation of a better community environment, opportunities for employee team-building, and corporate image-building. For employees, general benefits are that the personal involvement improves the quality of life in the community, contracts are made with community members, especially helpful to new employees in an area, and that an educational and broadening experience is received.

Organizations Supported and Forms of Support

A Conference Board of Canada study in 1986, although some of the data are dated, provides a considerable background to the concept of employee voluntarism. The study found that a large majority of the 926 corporations responding were in favour of and supported employee voluntarism. Voluntary activities encouraged involved organizations such as the United Way, professional associations, business and trade associations, the Chamber of Commerce, service clubs, Junior Achievement, and community athletic groups. But several voluntary activities were sometimes excluded from employer support, and these were trade unions (not in collective agreement), political parties, religious groups, and special interest advocacy groups.

The forms of support identified in the study were the provision of facilities, time off, schedule adjustment, support through donations or sponsorships, assistance with personal expenses incurred while undertaking voluntary activities, extending special recognition to employees exhibiting outstanding performances, and issuing letters of thanks. Most corporations did not consider support and recognition for volunteer work to be an element in the regular performance review process. A slight majority of respondents considered voluntary experience when assessing a candidate for employment (Hart, 1986).

Exhibit 14-1 Employee Voluntarism: Advantages and Disadvantages

Advantages:

- Benefits employee morale by enhancing professional skill development, providing a learning experience, and providing a personal experience.
- Good for the community.
- Good for the organizations supported.
- Improves the company's local and national image or profile.
- Good for the overall environment in which employees, customers, and the company must operate.
- Can contribute to corporate team-building, employee involvement initiatives.
- Sets a good example.
- Helps employees integrate with the community, provides a source of contacts or a network, and encourages a sense of community commitment.

Disadvantages:

- Possible employee resentment at perceived coercion to participate.
- Possible distractions from the job, corporate objectives.
- Cost in dollars and time.
- Implication of picking "winners" or "losers" from among community organizations—that is, deciding which to support.
- Possibility of controversy over objectives of some voluntary organization reflecting adversely on the company.
- Some employees may over-commit themselves, impacting upon job performance.
- A controversy involving the efforts of an employee volunteer may reflect unfavourably on the company.

SOURCE: Adapted from Peter M. Brophey. (1987, Spring). Corporate voluntarism: Putting something back. *Canadian Business Review.*

Corporate Policies Regarding Voluntarism

Many corporations do not just allow employee voluntarism to exist without some policies being formulated to serve as guidelines in the activity. A study by the Toronto Board of Trade highlighted some corporate actions that would encourage involvement in the voluntary section:

- providing information for new employees on available volunteer organizations and opportunities;
- establishing employee programs to involve pre-retirees in volunteering their time;
- providing recognition or awards to employees who volunteer to spur additional employee involvement;

- encouraging employees to volunteer via corporate-sponsored loaned executive and paid leave programs; and,

- forming a Corporate Volunteer Council with neighbouring businesses and firms, to achieve greater company involvement in the voluntary sector. ("Corporate Volunteering," 1986)

The Conference Board of Canada study summarized policies on voluntarism into three categories: encouraging, enabling, and promoting. Encouraging policy statements set the tone or position of the corporation relating to employee voluntarism, and are positive statements about the value of volunteer activities. Enabling policies provide guidelines to managers and employees regarding the implementation of the positive policy. They often set the boundaries and establish procedures relating to voluntarism; for example, the policy relating to a leave of absence to work for a voluntary organization. Overall, enabling policies facilitate the participation of employees in voluntary activity. The third policy category promotes participation in voluntary activity. These promoting policies recognize and reward employee achievement in voluntary activities. Taken together, these types of policies encourage employee voluntarism in Canada (Hart, 1986).

Employee voluntarism is most successful where top management, especially the Chief Executive Officer, indicate that it is a worthy and commendable activity. Top management support is vital for the corporate volunteer program to succeed.

Challenges and Opportunities

Employee voluntarism faces some challenges and opportunities, according to the Conference Board of Canada. The first challenge is for all parties involved, employers, employees, and the voluntary organizations, to recognize and account for the human resource contribution made by corporations in support of voluntarism. Volunteer efforts might well take away from the corporation's bottom line, adversely affecting its performance. Working out arrangements in the situation where the employee's time is billable is viewed as a major challenge. Developing policies for employee volunteers covered by collective agreements is another challenge, and one that most corporations have not addressed. A related challenge involves union concern that volunteers may do jobs that might well be done by members of other unions. Corporations should also consider liability issues that may arise from the use of company facilities. There is the potential for a conflict between the goals of the corporation and the wishes of the employees. Employee voluntary activities should not erode the company's ability to accomplish its mission while, on the other hand, corporate involvement in voluntarism may be perceived by some as an invasion of an employee's privacy.

The Conference Board of Canada identified three opportunities for such involvement: retired employee participation, partnership with government, and employer-volunteer co-operation. Retired employers are a potential source of assistance and their involvement should be encouraged. It is doubtful that volunteer activities can meet all community needs and activities that coordinate private sector voluntary organization efforts, and hence government programs should also be considered. Finally, corporations or business organizations could serve as clearing houses which would facilitate employee voluntarism by matching skills and competence with needs (Hart, 1986).

Employee voluntarism has endured even though the difficulties created by the economic downturn of the 1990's have seriously impacted some corporations. Employee voluntarism is one form of corporate philanthropy and another example of socially responsible behaviour.

CORPORATE SPONSORSHIP

One definition of corporate sponsorship is that of "a partnership which has been established for mutual benefit between a business sponsor and an event or a non-profit" (Bihl, 1992). A distinction should be made between corporate donations and sponsorship. A donation is a gift that goes one way, from a corporation to an arts group, while a sponsorship, if a single event or if a series of events, confers benefits on both parties. Although the above quotation refers to an arts group, sponsorship is now a widespread phenomenon, as illustrated in the following:

1) Petro-Canada's "Share the Flame" sponsorship as part of its support for the 1988 Calgary Winter Olympic Games. This is one of the most successful corporate sponsorships carried out in Canada.

2) Proctor and Gamble Inc. developed the "Always Changing Program" in which a feminine-protection product was tied to an educational effort aimed at teachers, parents, and young girls. Teachers' kits, booklets, samples, exhibits, and a workshop at an educator's conference were involved.

3) Air Canada and John Labatt sponsored Toronto's 1991 Festival of Festivals International film program.

4) The Thomson Family contributed $4.5 million (11 percent of the total cost) to Roy Thomson Hall in Toronto. Companies such as Chrysler Canada Ltd. and the Royal Bank of Canada sponsor programs at the Hall.

5) Trimark Investment Management Inc. is sponsoring an exhibit of Canadian artist David Milne's work.

6) Imperial Tobacco Ltd. sponsors the Player's International Tennis Tournament.

7) Reebok sponsored Amnesty International's "Human Rights Now!" tour starring Bruce Springsteen, Sting, and Tracy Chapman at a cost of $12 million.

As can be seen from these examples, sponsorship covers a wide range of sports, cultural, and educational events. There are also examples of extending corporate sponsorship programs to such social concerns as literacy, race relations, drug abuse, and environmental issues. Sponsorship provides a definite link between business and social issues.

Charity or Marketing?

Some acknowledge that corporate sponsorship has little to do with charity, donations, or philanthropy but instead is a business or marketing arrangement. Yet, companies often mention sponsorship in "Involvement in, or Contribution to, the Community," sections of annual reports. The trend toward sponsorships has been found to be attractive for a variety of reasons:

- favourable media exposure, or publicity
- opportunity to entertain clients
- building company/product presence
- reaching select market segments
- business-to-business networking
  (Bihl, 1992)

Sponsorship is one way to increase corporate awareness, as broad exposure of a name or logo increases recognition and may result in a purchase decision. It is considered a positive and low-cost image-building approach and allows targeting; that is, the sponsorship can be directed at specific audiences or potential customers.

The corporate sponsor looks for a charitable situation that satisfies the company's marketing ambitions and that coincides with the needs of the charity group. There needs to be some common ground so that both parties benefit. To accomplish this, the sponsorship agreement should define clearly the role and needs of each partner. For the corporation, the sponsorship must fit into the marketing scheme, while the charity's integrity must not be threatened. A well-defined plan is necessary to avoid failure and disagreements. Many now consider corporate sponsorship to be a form of advertising.

Challenges and Dangers to Sponsorship

The objectives of the sponsorship program must be clearly identified, and as pointed out above there must be a proper fit. Sponsorship is now so common that it has lost its novelty, and thus its capability to attract attention. The public may be cynical about the cause-related sponsorship, or simply not understand the linkage. Many question the appropriateness of the support given by tobacco and alcohol companies to arts. The government might question whether or not some sponsorship violates advertising regulations, especially in the case of tobacco promotion.

Corporations may find it difficult to keep their hands off the event after the initial agreement is reached, and the relationship may turn "sour." The return from a sponsorship is seldom precisely known, and it might be difficult to withdraw support without attracting attention. For example, the sponsorship of the Canadian equestrian team became awkward for some corporate sponsors when the sport experienced problems with drugs and dishonesty. But the withdrawal of support becomes a problem, as without corporate sponsorship, many programs fail.

As a form of corporate philanthropy, sponsorship has advantages and drawbacks, even though it has become quite popular in the last 10 years. The final section of this chapter reviews some of the issues surrounding all types of corporate philanthropy.

CURRENT CORPORATE PHILANTHROPY ISSUES

Throughout this chapter, references have been made to various challenges, difficulties, or changes in the area of corporate philanthropy. This section will identify and briefly explain these issues.

Three of the five issues relate to the trend toward sponsorship and the association of philanthropy with marketing—namely, charitable investment, strategic giving, and cause-related marketing. Two other issues are examined: the demands placed by business on the receivers of support to operate more efficiently, and the implications of "sin" industry philanthropy.

The Charitable Investments Approach

It is becoming increasingly difficult to find a clear distinction between philanthropy and sponsorship. Dienhart (1988) discussed the compatibility between philanthropy as an altruistic art and corporate self-interest that prevents true philanthropy. The business environment is tougher now and corporations must be more organized about philanthropy policies. Corporate giving can create friends, but it can also alienate those who did not receive support. Managers must plan how to preserve the virtue of the provider and the dignity of the receiver. Thus a method, or strategy, of charitable investments should be formulated. One such approach is referred to as charitable investing, an attempt to align donations with corporate products and objectives.

Dienhart classifies concepts of charity as strict or broad. The strict notion of charity would classify "an art as charitable only if the giver had no expectations of receiving any benefit from the art," while a broad notion of charity would "allow the giver to expect some benefit from the art, but of course, would not require it." The author believes that the broad notion of charity should be accepted, but then "the question arises as to whether there would be a limit to the self benefit that a giver could expect from an act of charity" (1988, p. 65). It is difficult to determine how much self-interest is allowable before it discredits an act of charity.

There are many meanings to the word "investments," but the author concludes that in the context of charity the term prudence is most suitable. Corporations can benefit or suffer from treating charities like investments, that is, as prudent expenditures. Thus, the concepts of charity and investments are complimentary. The author concludes that the moral status of the giver and the receiver are intact. Donations guided by charitable investment do not result in the donors losing moral credit for their arts, and they not degrade those who receive the charity.

The implementation of the charitable investment approach is important if the intentions are misinterpreted; for example, corporate giving is considered as just another marketing tool or as merely a tax write-off. In particular, actions can be taken to avoid this problem. An independent committee or foundation can be given authority for making the decisions. It is important for a manager to understand the management challenges confronted by non-profit organizations, and it is helpful to set long-term budgets.

Given the tough economic times, and the increasing demands for corporate donations, managers must develop a charitable investments strategy and not leave the process to ad hoc decision making.

Strategic Giving

A similar approach to charitable investment is strategic giving, an attempt to rationalize the shareholder interest with corporate philanthropy. Some believe that it is really shareholders' money that is being given away. In order to avoid complaints from shareholders, management should act in enlightened self-interest as a counter argument to the profit maximization position of shareholders. Thus, strategic giving is donating with an eye to the company's eventual best interests (Zetlin, 1990, p. 10).

Strategic giving leads companies to make contributions within their own areas of interest. For example, funding of educational programs would be considered appropriate, or support for a park facility that could be used by employees and their families. This enlightened self-interest, however, may not lead to support for women's shelters or housing for the poor where the benefits to the company are not as evident. Although strategic giving is a way of justifying philanthropy consistent with shareholder interests, it would require managers walking an ethical tightrope when rationalizing their proposals for support of particular charities.

Cause-Related Marketing

Another trend is toward cause-related marketing, or tying donations to the purchase of a particular product. For example, the purchase of a particular brand of frozen vegetables results in a contribution to a food bank or the purchase of cake mix helps to fund a health cause. There are several criticisms of this approach, as it pushes philanthropy past even the marketing aspect of sponsorship.

Cause-related marketing is considered another way of making a profit, and there are fears that it will replace philanthropy by reducing the amount of no-strings corporate giving. The selection of causes is problematic. Safe, non-controversial causes are selected that will sell, and some companies base their selection of charities on opinion polls conducted to ascertain the most popular causes.

This approach to corporate giving is likely to continue as government funding declines, making commercial tie-ins inviting to non-profit organization managers. For business, it makes their product "stand out," and if they can associate with the correct "hot" causes, sales performance improves. Target audiences are chosen and promotional strategies are selected making corporate giving "like selling soaps suds" according to some critics. These critics question whether self-interest charitable investment or strategic giving is not becoming self-serving commercial activity.

Demands for Efficiency in Non-profit Organizations

Accompanying the trends to charitable investment/strategic giving is the demand from business that non-profit organizations must be more efficient. The argument is that since corporations are tightening their belts, charitable organizations must also become more efficient. Included in this request for efficiency are demands that organizations share resources, avoid duplication, and reduce administrative costs. Charities must develop strategic plans, information and control systems, and generally improve administrative systems.

With the trend to sponsorship and cause-related marketing, pressure is on charities to produce returns, to be more accountable, and to ensure high visibility for their corporate supporters. Managers of charities argue that this restricts their activities and might prevent them from achieving their objectives. Corporations are also focusing their support on particular programs, projects, or events and are reluctant to provide support for basic operating expenses, placing even more pressure on the charitable organizations. In addition to the reduction of corporation giving, there is also a decline in the amount of support available.

Implications of "Sin" Industry Philanthropy

A controversy has arisen about the support received by arts and sports organizations from industries such as tobacco and alcohol. There is some irony—even in the recession these corporations remained profitable and had funds available as other companies cut back.

An article in *The Globe and Mail* by Stephen Godfrey illuminated the issue well (1992). Godfrey discussed the campaign by arts and sports groups for continued paid sponsorship of their events by tobacco and alcohol companies. These organizations claimed that freedom of expression and choice were not threatened; Godfrey wrote that this was simply the need for money by desperate organizations.

The 1989 Tobacco Products Control Act banned tobacco advertising on television, newspapers, and magazines but allowed sponsorship. Godfrey questioned whether the immediate public good achieved by the survival of arts groups was sufficient to offset the long-term damage done by allowing sponsorships that enhanced "product recognition." He claimed it is only a matter of time before public pressure curtails tobacco and alcohol company sponsorship, and that it is sad to see the financial interests of the groups override ethics.

There are implications for funders and receivers. For the tobacco and alcohol companies legally allowed to operate, it poses the problem of how they can demonstrate corporate citizenry except by making donations with the expectation of nothing in return, not even company identification. For the receiving organizations, they are derived of a reliable and major source of funds.

SUMMARY

This chapter has attempted to address the challenges of managing a corporation's corporate philanthropy initiatives. Three types of philanthropy were examined: donations, voluntarism, and sponsorship. In addition, one section dealt with corporate giving as it relates to the arts, and a concluding section identified current corporate philanthropy issues.

The arguments for and against corporate donations, or giving, were reviewed, and the issue of whether or not such activity is in the best interests of the corporation and its shareholders, in particular has not been resolved. Once the corporation decides to become involved in corporate giving, another challenge emerges—how to manage the process. A decision-making process involving committees or foundations should be established if the corporation wants to be consistent and perceived to be treating all requests fairly. Although something positive can be gained from donations, there is the possibility of negative outcomes when requests are rejected. Rejections must be handled as professionally as successful requests. Philanthropic decision-making is even more challenging given the increasing demands for corporate support and the limited amount of funds available. In addition, there is a trend toward tying giving to economic gains, an issue that re-emerges throughout the chapter.

The arts sector was selected as an example of the influence of corporate donations. Business supports a wide spectrum of arts sector activities in a variety of ways. There are benefits to both parties, but several concerns are associated with corporate support, including the trend to a "marketing" orientation. Some still question the appropriateness of corporate donations in the arts, but there remains strong involvement in this area by business despite the economic downturns.

Volunteers have not received much attention in the discussion of corporate philanthropy. Employees of corporations make contributions to charitable organizations often with the encouragement of managers. Many corporations have well-defined policies relating to employee volunteer activities so that conflicts with work obligations are avoided or to protect the reputation of the corporation. Although voluntarism is usually encouraged, it is not without challenges for management.

Since 1980, sponsorship has grown as a form of philanthropy. Discussion continues as to whether such an activity is support of a charity or an aspect of marketing. Corporations are pressured for greater return on donation funds, and tying support to sponsorship of projects or events appears to result. The discussion of sponsorship is a logical lead into the examination of the trend toward corporations seeking to satisfy economic as well as social objectives with corporate philanthropic initiatives. Two approaches to this trend, charitable investment and strategic giving, are described, as is cause-related marketing. In addition to these issues, corporate management is demanding more efficiency and accountability from non-profit charities, and receivers of support from "sin" industries corporations are being challenged for accepting it.

Corporate philanthropy appears to be a relatively straightforward matter. But in practice, this is not the case, and managers must plan and establish policies to implement initiatives to support charitable endeavors.

REFERENCES

Arlett, Allan and Ingrid van Rotterdam. (1987, March 9). The power of giving. *The Financial Post*, pp. 13, 15.

Bihl, Elizabeth. (1992). Sponsorship makes good business sense. *Canada Export*, 10(11), pp. 2, 7.

Corporate volunteering (1986, Spring). *Voluntary Section Program Newsletter*, Faculty of Administrative Studies, York University, p. 1.

Dienhart, John W. (1988). Charitable investments: A strategy for improving the business environment, *Journal of Business Ethics*, 7(1&2), pp. 63–72.

Downey, Donn. (1990, April 28). Ballard's generosity surpasses that of several billionaires, *The Globe and Mail*, p. A1.

Godfrey, Stephen. (1992, March 14). "Smoke gets in their eyes, or how artists justify tobacco sponsorship," *The Globe and Mail*, p. C1.

Hart, Kenneth D. (1987, Spring). Emerging patterns of volunteerism, *Canadian Business Review*, pp. 13–15.

Hart, Kenneth D. (1986, October). *Employee Volunteerism: Employer Practices and Policies.* Ottawa: Conference Board of Canada. Report 14-86-E.

Kingston, Anne. (1992, December 19). Choosing a charity, *The Globe and Mail*, p. B20.

Martin, Samuel A. (1985). *An Essential Grace: Funding Canada's Health Care, Education, Welfare, Religion and Culture.* Toronto: McClelland and Stewart.

Raymond, John. (1991, July 18). Worth repeating. *The Globe and Mail*, p. B6.

Taylor, Allan R. (1991, Spring). Chairman's message, *Royal Bank Reporter*, p. 3.

Vardy, Jill. (1992, December 2). Companies to be less charitable, *The Financial Post*, p. 6.

Walker, Michael. (1986, June 14). Let's base arts aid on demand, not supply, *The Financial Post*, p. 9.

Zetlin, Minda. (1990, December). Companies find profit in corporate giving, *Management Review*, pp. 10-15.

EMPLOYEES AND THE CHANGING WORKPLACE

INTRODUCTION

Employees are almost always identified by corporations as critical or key stake-holders. The management of this stakeholder group has always been a challenge, and given the downsizing, retrenchment, and technological changes of the 1990's it will be even more so. This chapter will not review the employee in terms of human resource management but instead establishes the present-day employment setting by discussing the current interpretation of the work ethic, including the status of employee or corporate loyalty. The changes in the workplace do have an impact on unions and result in changes for these organizations. At the same time, the rights or freedoms expected by employees are increasing, in some cases by government initiative. This discussion provides the employment setting, and the final section of the chapter identifies and briefly examines several issues relating to the employee stakeholder.

THE WORK ETHIC

The work ethic is a set of values which holds that work is important to members of society insofar as work influences the qualities or character of individuals; that work is a purposeful activity requiring an expenditure of energy with some sacrifice of leisure; that some gain, usually monetary, is involved; and that through work a person not only contributes to society but becomes a better individual. The work ethic as a concept had its beginnings in religion, and when people refer to it they are usually talking about something called the "Protestant Ethic," equating religion with labour. Work was believed to be the worthy way to serve God, a calling through which one proved one's worthiness of redemption.

Working hard and accumulating wealth were seen as outward signs of a person's morality. They also provided some assurance of a good life on earth as well as a good afterlife. The basis for the work ethic is not clear; for while religion is involved so is economics. It is even argued that Luther's doctrine of the work ethic was based upon economics, rather than religion. There were three trends occurring in Germany in the 1500's that substantiate this view: population increases, price inflation, and unemployment (Bernstein,1988).

Although under the Protestant ethic work was considered as divine dignity, the concept lost some of its piety because the accumulation of wealth countered the religious basis of the ethic, and consumption, much of it conspicuous, made possible by the earnings of work, was inconsistent with saving and investment, or frugality.

Today there are often calls for a return to the work ethic of the past. Arguments can be made for both positions.

The Work Ethic—A Thing of the Past or Alive and Well?

Many people consider work as only a part of life and instead want time to spend with family, satisfaction from what they do, and a sense of purpose from their job and life. This phenomenon is also described as backing off the fast track and focusing more on the quality of life. Work, by itself, is no longer as sufficiently fulfilling as it was in the past. This is manifested in several ways, as for example:

- opting out of the labour force—for example, early retirement
- collecting unemployment or welfare payments rather than accepting low-paying or unattractive jobs
- taking up second or third careers
- refusing to perform overtime work
- questioning traditional authority
- downsizing and the resulting layoffs
- two-career householders less dependent upon one salary

One counter argument for this is that employees are working harder than ever and that more is expected of them in terms of productivity and improved quality, with comparisons made to Japanese workers. Evidence of the work ethic includes the long hours management and professional persons spend at their jobs or places of business. Work has become an obsession to many, as workers have to run harder to keep up with inflation or to make ends meet, and more work is expected from the same number of employees and often from fewer employees. Workers fear job loss, and fewer people are available for backup.

Do Canadians still believe in the work ethic? The answer is generally "yes." The federal government conducted a twofold survey to explore Canadian attitudes toward work in general, to better understand their behaviour in the labour market, and to examine the attitudes of workers to their current jobs and whether or not they found satisfaction in them. The study found several indications that the work ethic is in good health.

- Canadians are, in principle, committed to work.
- Canadians choose work over most leisure activities when they have to make that kind of choice.
- Canadians would rather work than be on unemployment insurance.

Other studies have found that Canadians are both strongly motivated to work and that most express overall satisfaction with their jobs.

Despite expressions of support for work, many employees are alienated by the pressures of the work environment and the threat of job loss. This situation and what needs to be done is expressed in the following quotation:

> Today, our competitive and secular society requires a high level of productivity for survival. Current research and experience strongly suggest that we redefine the traditional concept of the work ethic to stress employee involvement, responsibility, and autonomy. Beyond this, we should also understand that a modern work force based on brains rather than brawn requires a corporate culture whose positive and participative values serve as milestones for the future. It is these work values, plus the personal talents supporting creative productivity, that form the twentieth century equivalent of the old work ethic. (Bernstein, 1988, p. 11).[1]

A New Employment Contract

The work ethic assumed an individual would work hard and be committed to a particular job over a long period. Many persons have been employed by the same employer for decades, and often for their whole career. But it appears that this situation will change in the future and will have implications for how we view the work ethic. A new, unwritten employment contract may be operating

---

[1] Reprinted from *Business Horizons*, May/June 1988. Copyright © 1988 by the Foundation for the School of Business at Indiana University. Used with permission.

in the workplace that has the following features: few guarantees of job security, pay based upon job performance, de-emphasis on loyalty, and no regular or logical career promotions. Worldwide economic, competition, technological, and social changes are altering employment prospects for people, and management is viewing and treating employees differently.

Possible changes in attitudes toward work and the existence of a new employment contract both impact upon the loyalty of the employee to the employer and vice-versa.

Employee Loyalty

Loyalty creates that extra effort and extra drive in employees to perform. It encourages self-motivated behaviour, and reflects employees' confidence in management, their vision, and the enterprise's purpose. Loyalty means commitment by employees to the organization they work for. In turn, employers are loyal to employees by providing career-long employment, good salaries, and other benefits. But has this relationship changed with the new employment environment?

Most managers probably believe that employees should be loyal. Signs of a lack of commitment are easy to detect (turnover, early retirements), but measuring loyalty is much more difficult. Low turnover is not necessarily a sign of loyalty, but instead may mean that employees are tied through benefit plans (particularly pensions), or that no other job opportunities exist. Managers should also be cautious of extreme loyalty; over-zealous behaviour by an employee does not necessarily mean that the employee is performing in the best interests of the enterprise. But, given the pressures of change, it may not be possible for management to provide some of the things that in the past encouraged loyalty, for example, job security and good compensation packages.

Employees in today's society often want to be entities unto themselves and are seeking challenging opportunities. Many consider loyalty to "self" more important than to the enterprise. Such employees might be seen to have loyalty and dedication to the job itself, rather than to the enterprise they are employed by to do that job. On the other hand, many employees wonder why they should be loyal when organizations may lay them off. It is management's responsibility to provide the environment that engenders loyalty. Intelligent human resource management goes a long way toward doing this. Employees must first be trusted and managers must be loyal to employees. It is critical for managers to give trust and loyalty before expecting it. Managers often assume that they cannot expect loyalty, but loyalty and the commitment it involves can be generated by management initiatives.

In order to improve loyalty, managers must communicate a persuasive corporate image to employees. Employees who demonstrate loyalty must be appropriately rewarded (not only by monetary compensation). In pursuit of loyalty, management should bear in mind the following: loyalty must be a corporate priority and it must start at the top with the CEO; persons at all levels in the organization must be involved; the process takes a long time; and token, one-shot, efforts must be avoided. Managers must be careful to distinguish between employee loyalty to individuals and to the organization (enterprise). Loyalty to individuals represents personal loyalty and is not as beneficial as loyalty to the organization, which is more enduring.

The blind loyalty of employees that may have existed in the past is unlikely today. On the other hand, managers are finding it more difficult to demonstrate that employees owe them loyalty. The situation is summarized in the following quotation:

> For management in North America, postmodernism means having to deal with workers whose commitment to an employer can never be taken for granted. This does not, however, mean that they have no emotional investment in their employment. According to attitudinal research, they feel angry and guilty when the organization they work for violates their personal values. They are no longer willing to let management unilaterally dictate policy on external issues such as ecology. If they feel strongly about their employer's negative actions, they feel just as strongly when it shows things which they perceive as positive. Thus a company that makes its people feel they are engaged in doing something socially worthwhile can be the beneficiary of a degree of motivation money can't buy. But unquestioning loyalty to the firm is history, and nowhere more so than in corporations that have had to trim their payrolls in the interests of productivity or simple survival. The assumption behind old-fashioned dedication was that there was a more or less permanent pact between employees and employers. They would throw themselves body and soul into their jobs in return for (nearly) life-long employment. In the present atmosphere of intense competition and financial stringency, no North American company is in a position to make that sort of guarantee. ("What's Become of Loyalty?",1991)

Apparently corporate loyalty needs to be redefined in the context of the current situation, where jobs are less secure. It is unreasonable to expect dedicated efforts from employees whose future is insecure. But employees still basically want to think well of the company they work for, as it means thinking well about themselves. Employers will have to honestly explain the need for retrenchment, technological change, and heavier individual workloads. The meaning of loyalty may be a difficult concept to come to grips with in the 1990's.

It must be recognized that what happens as a stakeholder group is not at the discretion of management. Unions exist in some sections of the economy, but their traditional role toward protecting employees is under challenge and changing. Meanwhile, employees are gaining rights and freedoms through shifts in society's thinking and government initiatives.

CHALLENGES TO UNIONS

Unions have influenced the relationships between corporations and their employees, and the framework for industrial relations in this country is widely known. This section does not seek to review this material but focuses instead on how this relationship is being, or might be, altered by many challenges confronting unions.

Union membership has been relatively stable at about 30 percent of the civilian labour force. This percentage has been maintained by the strength of the unions in the public sector. The following is a sample of the challenges confronting unions in the 1990's:

Increasingly Competitive Environment Like business enterprises, unions are influenced by the increasing demands for competitiveness. Competition from foreign corporations places pressure on business and unions. However, it should not be assumed that unionized workforces are an obstacle to competitiveness, but it does change the expectations of employees and unions. In the public sector, competitiveness is reflected in more demands for employee productivity and government's intransigence regarding wages and other benefits.

Changing Characteristics of the Workforce There has been a decline in employment in the traditionally unionized sectors and increasing importance in sectors that traditionally have been non-unionized. Thus, unions are losing "blue-collar" members, and are not picking up new members in the "white" and "pink" collar occupations. Professional, technical, and white-collar employment predominates, and potential members are difficult to recruit and, if recruited, they are more demanding. There is increasing immigration into Canada from countries with less of a union tradition than those of previous sources of immigrants. More women have entered the workforce, and it is alleged that they are not as interested in supporting unions.

Anti-Union Tactics Many in society dislike the "bigness" of union organization, the union movement's association with socialism, and the alleged undemocratic nature of union governance. Some business enterprises deliberately engage in anti-union activities such as union avoidance and union trusting. Union avoidance prevents a union from being formed and examples of tactics to prevent this may be the firing of non-productive or dissatisfied employees, as they are most likely to initiate the forming of a union or be susceptible to approaches by a union organization; the firing of "trouble makers," often defined by alleged union activity; the stalling tactics after a union is formed; and the issuing of warnings of consequences from forming a union. Different tactics might be followed if a union is already in existence. Management could decide to escape unions by moving operations to union-free areas. It might also decide to contract out work; that is, use outside workers to perform tasks previously performed by its own employees. This means that fewer employees would be hired, and thereby the influence of the union is reduced. Sometimes unionized enterprises set up affiliated companies that are non-unionized to perform some operations, a common practice in the construction industry.

Changing Work Rules Job tasks are changing with more demand for a multi-skilled workforce. Also, the patterns of working times has changed with more part-time employment. More flexibility is required in work rules, and this creates problems for union management.

Deregulation and Privatization The deregulation of many industries puts more pressure on business and in turn affects employment practices. Some business enterprises are forced to become much more efficient, and this might involve employing fewer persons. The selling off of government-owned corporations might also threaten unions as these corporations are dissolved or scaled down to respond to competition.

Decertification This is the procedure for removing a union's recognition as the exclusive bargaining representative. There have been instances where employees have sought to leave a union. In the United States, right-to-work laws prohibit collective bargaining contracts from requiring union membership as a condition of employment.

Concession Bargaining This occurs where a business enterprise requests "concessions" from a union when negotiating an agreement. A common form of a concession is reduced wages, but concessions also might involve changed work rules. The following stories illustrate what may happen in this area:

> "Domtar workers agree to concessions to save jobs" (*The Globe and Mail,* March 22, 1993, p. B9).
>> Unionized workers at Domtar Inc. plants have agreed to workplace changes, more flexible hours of work (allowing plants to operate 24 hours), and more flexibility in the tasks performed by various trades (allowing a workplace to perform various tasks).

> "Concessions approved" (*The Globe and Mail,* March 18, 1993, p. B2).
>> Workers at Canada Safeway Ltd. in Alberta have agreed to working longer hours for less money.

> "Air Canada pilots agree to 5% pay cut" (*The Globe and Mail,* July 16, 1993, p. B1).
>> Air Canada pilots tentatively agreed to a 5% cut in salaries to avoid layoffs and to assist the company to reduce its losses.

These concessions are not without some quid pro quo from management, for example, bonus payments or job security.

Competing for Members Occasionally, unions fight amongst themselves to represent a group of employees, and may even "steal" members from each other. For example, the United Food and Commercial Workers lost 23 000 members when the Canadian Auto Workers convinced Atlantic Canada fishery workers to switch to them. Unions also compete when recruiting new members in occupations not previously unionized.

Technology Advancing technology changes how jobs are performed and the types of qualifications required. Automation often replaces workers. Unions often resist technological change as many of their members are displaced.

Public Sector Downsizing Employment with government has provided good compensation with job security in the past. But, this is changing with early retirement, stable salaries, and rollbacks and layoffs.

Whether or not all these challenges have diminished the influence of unions is debatable. Workers usually join unions out of a sence of powerlessness, the need for solidarity, and to have a voice that will be heard. Poor treatment of workers by management often leads to demands for participation in decisions influencing their jobs, and thus their lives. They must believe that they are receiving their "fair share" of their rewards (wages) and that justice exists (fair treatment).

These challenges mean that unions are also re-inventing themselves, as business enterprises have done as they, too, face the same crisis management encounters from global competition. Unions are developing new strategies such as rationalizing their organizations for efficiency, targeting new markets, competing for members, and developing policies relating to childcare, pay and employment equity, and better benefits for part-time workers.

As a result, the relationship among unions and other business stakeholders is impacted. For example, unions are entering into partnership arrangements with governments and corporations relating to training and investment programs, job evaluation systems, pay equity, and corporate rescue plans. Unions are sensitive to these new or altered relationships, not wanting to be pushed into them nor left out.

The new employment contract way of thinking instead of the traditional work ethic arrangement combined with the challenges identified places demands on unions. While this is happening, employers are seeking, and in some cases being granted, new rights or freedoms often without the initiative coming from unions.

EMPLOYEE RIGHTS

Many employees are seeking greater participation in decisions affecting the work environment. Moreover, many businesspeople are also committed to greater employee involvement as an approach to improving working conditions and performance. Many aspects of how employees are treated is legislated by governments but the status of employees is influenced by voluntary actions of employers or advocated by employees seeking greater participation. The result might be viewed as employee claims to certain conditions in the workplace, or employee rights. One way of expressing these rights is as "freedoms" as outlined in Table 15-1. A review of these freedoms will reveal that some rights or freedoms have been secured while the status of other freedoms is still doubtful. However, the trend toward some form of contemporary human resource management will lead to a greater fulfilment of these freedoms.

Some experts refer to this as the employee rights movement, and indicate that these rights are becoming more important in protecting the interests of employees than union organizations are. These rights are being "legalized" by government. Some examples are:

1. *Right-to-know laws*   These laws require enterprises to disclose information that employees should have; for example, the presence of hazardous substances in the workplace.

2. *Mandatory retirement*   Laws are being considered to ascertain whether or not employees should be required to retire at particular ages.

3. *Shutdown notice and severance pay*   These laws relate to the length of notice that must be given in the event of a shutdown and amounts of severance pay that must be paid to laid-off employees.

4. *Employee privacy*   Laws are clarifying rights to privacy and the use of polygraph tests.

5. *Access to employee files*   Employees are being allowed access to their employment files to ascertain appropriateness of documents and to respond to adverse enclosures.

6. *Marital status and sexual orientation*   Laws will prevent discrimination on these bases.

7. *Equal pay*   Legislation is being designed to not only ensure equal pay for work but also to ensure equal pay for work of equal value.

8. *Unjust dismissal laws*   In the future, there may be laws to control arbitrary and unjust dismissal of employees.

Another way that employee rights are being enhanced is through the practice of human resources management. An enterprise that practices good employee relations pays competitive salaries and benefits, provides amenities to

Table 15-1 Fourteen Freedoms in the Workplace

1) *Freedom to be hired fairly and openly*   Everyone will have an equal opportunity to be hired and not discriminated against because of race, religion, creed, sex, or national origin.

2) *Freedom to be trusted*   Employees should be trusted and misunderstandings investigated in such a manner that the employee's side of the story is fairly obtained and objectively stated.

3) *Freedom of Speech*   An employee's views on matters not work-related should not be restricted as long as expressed off the job. Freedom of speech on the job is more difficult to define, but enlightened management should provide some mechanism for employees to express views they might hold.

4) *Freedom from intrusions*   This relates mainly to matters of privacy. Examples of intrusions are mandatory drug and AIDS testing and lie detector tests. Any form of surveillance of off the job lifestyle is unacceptable and on the job surveillance is only performed with employee awareness.

5) *Freedom of safety and health*   Employees should be able to work in a safe environment.

6) *Freedom from stress*   The workplace should not be so stressful that it affects the health of employees. Employers should attempt to reduce stress in those occupations where it is greatest; for example, in employment as servers, nurses, computer programmers, telephone operators, and sales representatives. Employees should not be penalized for refusing to carry out directions that violate laws or norms of morality.

7) *Freedom in off-hours*   There should be some separation of work from non-work-related activities. Personal life styles in off-hours should not be restricted.

8) *Freedom from sexual harassment*   Employees should not be harassed or discriminated against for sexual reasons.

9) *Freedom of information*   Information about the enterprise's operations that will affect the employee's welfare should be communicated accurately and promptly. Information filed about individuals should be available to them.

10) *Freedom from propaganda*   Employees should not be subjected to unreasonable expressions of views or opinions held by management on any issue. For example, pressure to encourage employees to contribute to specific charities is unacceptable.

11) *Freedom to participate* Worker involvement in management is desirable and many approaches are possible.

12) *Freedom in fringe benefits*   Fringe benefits should be available to employees with some flexibility possible to suit individual needs.

13) *Freedom of due process*   Employees are entitled to a fair hearing before an impartial official, board, or arbitrator when disagreements occur. Employees should not be arbitrarily penalized, intimidated, demoted, or transferred without an adequate explanation.

14) *Freedom from unfair firing*   Dismissal should be for just reasons and not arbitrary.

SOURCE: The fourteen freedoms are as listed by Robert Ellis Smith in his book *Workrights* (1983). New York: E. P. Dutton, Inc. The descriptions were prepared by the author

employees such as recreational facilities and day-care centres, has a system for handling grievances or complaints, and involves employees in decision making is less likely to be unionized.

The decline of the influence of unions does not mean that management will be allowed a free hand. New legal requirements imposed by government and fair treatment of employees through human resource management will ensure that employees are receiving their fair share in the business enterprise system. Unions will continue to exist, and indeed, will be necessary for many industries. Understanding them and their operation is essential for anyone associated with business.

The concept of the work ethic has been used to establish the different positions employees and employers find themselves in the 1990's. Work has changed, and so has the approach to employees. Although employees may be still considered a critical resource, many issues confront human resource management. The format of this chapter departs somewhat from others in that what follows is a listing of several issues with a brief discussion. The purpose of this chapter is not to provide readers with a comprehensive examination of each issue, but instead to provide an appreciation of a wide range, multiplicity, and complexity of issues existing in this area.

ISSUES IN THE WORKPLACE

This section of the chapter identifies and briefly describes some issues that have emerged or that continue to persist in the workplace, placing demands on employers and employees. Social and ethical considerations exist in all these issues, and management must deal with them in a sensitive manner.

Six issues have been selected for consideration from the hundreds of possibilities. These are work force reduction, managing part-time employees, occupational health and safety, political correctness, privacy, and balancing work and family. The issues were selected for their timeliness; for example, as with political correctness, or to illustrate the continuing need to address old problems; for example, occupational health and safety. Also included is a listing of other issues prominent at this time.

Work Force Reduction

Permanent shutdowns and large layoffs create serious personal and social problems for workers and communities. Workers are, of course, without income and benefit plans, and the social consequences might include marital discord, health problems, and even suicides. Communities are expected to meet the demand for their services, including social welfare and lost taxation revenue, and face declines in the viability of other enterprises operating in the area. In Canada, shutdowns and layoffs are serious, as such a large portion of our industry operates as branch plants which are always susceptible to closure and because of the prevalence of one-industry communities, where alternative employment opportunities may be limited.

Plants close or enterprises go out of business for a variety of reasons. Enterprises may be industries with declining markets for their products. Other enterprises may seek to establish in non-union, low-wage areas, or at locations closer to new markets. Other reasons for closure may include: automation, rising energy costs, inadequate capital investment, transportation difficulties, foreign competition, costly government regulations, and depressed demand for products. Some enterprises may change their corporate strategy, which when implemented means a rationalization of operations.

The Employer's Initiative

It seems unfair that the heavy burden of job loss be shouldered by employees alone, and alleviating measures might be necessary on the part of business enterprises or government. More specifically, business enterprises, governments, and workers themselves can take some initiatives to alleviate the problems caused by shutdowns and layoffs. To avoid layoffs enterprises can:

- seek a product mandate for the branch plant from the parent company
- sub-contract work out at peak times to avoid layoffs when downturns occur
- employ part-time or temporary workers for peak periods who would be laid off instead of full-time employees
- reduce overtime to preserve regular jobs
- curtail or freeze new hiring

After the decision to shut down or lay off becomes inevitable, management can initiate a variety of actions to reduce the work force. In terms of what is most favourable to employees, the first possibility would be to reduce the work force through natural attrition, including hiring freezes. The next possibility is induced redeployment; for example, transfer-out incentives, early retirement incentives, severance pay incentives, compensation freeze or reduction and optional part-time or short-work schedules, work sharing, or leave without pay. These actions are followed by those that are referred to as involuntary redeployment; that is, involuntary transfer-out within the plant or firm, demotion or down-grading, and involuntary part-time or short-work schedules. If these actions are insufficient to reduce the work force, layoffs will be necessary. Two possibilities exist, layoffs with or without outplacement assistance. Outplacement assistance includes such things as retraining, job search counselling, severance pay, continuation of medical benefits, and advance notice of layoff (Greenhalgh et al., 1988).

The social and ethical implications of the above possibilities for management are complex and serious. It is argued that management shows its real level of competence and concern for employees when they face up to workforce reduction and plan for it with the interests of employees in mind. In the possibilities identified above, management concern for employee well-being is greatest when work force reduction occurs through natural attrition and least with layoffs without outplacement assistance. In the past four years, the integrity of management with regard to treatment of employees has been seriously tested on many occasions.

Government Involvement

There is another stakeholder who is almost always involved when the workforce is reduced—the government. Governments, including local ones, can do the following to lessen the impact: reduce or wave property taxation; provide tax credits or incentives to continue operating; bail out the enterprise either with financial assistance or by taking them over; provide subsidies for employing workers; ease pollution standards to reduce operating costs; and provide supportive infrastructure through downtown revitalization or community development.

In addition, there is another policy initiative that government could take—legislating advance notice of shutdown or layoffs. The existing requirements vary by province and the number of employees involved. Business usually argues for short notices or none at all while labour unions have argued for notices of up to one year. Although the issue appears straightforward, close examination reveals many pros and cons.

Arguments based upon natural justice and social compassion are often used to advocate long advance notices. This would provide workers with the opportunity to seek alternative employment or otherwise plan for the future. A long advance notice provides the opportunity for employees or governments to initiate actions to prevent the shutdown or layoff. Advance notices also reduce the immediate costs to the government and local community.

There is concern that requiring long advance notice interferes with management rights to make business decisions, and reduces the enterprise's flexibility to take actions in its best interests. Enterprises are concerned that various stakeholders will initiate actions harmful to the interests of enterprise. For example:

- employees might leave
- customers might disappear
- creditors might lose interest in lending money

All this leads to decline in productivity and reduces profitability, and might even hasten closing or endanger the economic wellbeing of the enterprise. It is also argued that jobs are only saved for a short time, and that the advance notice requirement in itself does little to solve the problems that gave rise to the shutdown or layoff. Business also believes that advance notice requirements might discourage new industry and might actually encourage plants to open elsewhere. As advance notices are not required in most foreign countries, or some provinces, their existence in one location could be a drawback to those enterprises subjected to it. Finally, some closings and layoffs cannot be anticipated very far in advance. This is particularly true for small businesses, where last-minute decisions are more likely. Advance notice requirements have different implications for business enterprises, the business system, governments, and, of course, employees. Imposing such a requirement must be eventually considered in light of the possible consequences for all involved.

Workforce reduction is an employee stakeholder issue that managers have had to cope with for several years, and may have to cope with for several more. It is one of the most socially and ethically sensitive issues where the economic and social objectives of an enterprise come into contradiction.

Managing Part-time Employees

About 17 percent of the labour force is comprised of part-time employees. This figure has increased in recent years as managers attempt to increase productivity by hiring part-timers during peak periods and as the growing service sector provides employment suitable to part-time employment.

The treatment of part-time employees has become an issue especially as it relates to compensation and fringe benefits. Business enterprises are not required to extend many benefits to part-timers, although some do so voluntarily. The difference in benefit coverage between full and part-time employees is substantial. For example, whereas 96 percent of full-time employees have supplemental medical coverage, only 19 percent of part-time employees do. Similar figures for life insurance coverage are 99 versus 22 percent and for pension plans, 94 versus 18 percent

Pressure is increasing on business enterprises to beef up benefits to part-time employees, and to pay them better. The response from business is that any improvement in wages or benefits involves substantial costs. It is argued that benefits should at least be prorated according to the portion of hours worked per week. Businesspeople point out that this would be costly, as substantial paperwork would be necessary. Business also points out that there are different types of part-time workers:

- regular part-time who are attached to the work force on an ongoing basis,
- temporary help hired through employment agencies for short durations,
- casual part-time workers who are in and out of the work force,
- seasonal workers who work only during particular times of the year.

Different types of part-time workers want different benefits. For this reason, all part-timers should not be treated the same. Regular part-timers may wish to participate in benefit plans. Indeed, in some types of businesses, such as retailing, managers rely substantially on this type of employee. In this case, treatment comparable to full-time employees might be appropriate. Temporary help should seek benefits from their employment agency which might retain them on a continuing basis. Casual and seasonal part-timers are less committed to regular employment, and it is not appropriate to provide them with full benefits.

Governments might require business enterprises to provide better benefits. But business says that it is not justified and will reduce part-time employment opportunities. The treatment of part-time employees is an issue that employees themselves, unions, managers, and governments will be examining more closely in coming years. Some of the problems are the lack of security in the jobs, as part-time employees are the first to be laid off during a downturn. Part-time jobs seldom offer any career opportunities and there are few chances for employees to upgrade themselves.

Despite the disadvantages, only one in five part-timers wants to work full-time. The flexibility provides individuals with the opportunity to travel, to pursue personal interests, and to achieve a more harmonious balance between work, personal life, leisure time, and community involvement—all compelling attractions.

Lastly, the use of part-time employees presents another challenge for management—namely, how to motivate them. The level of commitment to the corporation may be less, given the temporary nature of the job. Some fast-food operations have managed to motivate young part-time and poorly paid employees successfully. However, it may be more difficult to motivate such employees in other occupations.

Occupational Health and Safety

At first glance, it appears that this topic is not timely or appropriate for the 1990's. Despite attention by management and legislation and regulation by governments, occupational health and safety remains an issue. At a 1991 conference on the topic, speakers lamented the lack of public concern about occupational health and safety. Until the public regards unsafe working conditions to be as socially unacceptable as smoking, impaired driving, or pollution, not much will be done about it (Galt, 1991).

The cost of workplace accidents and occupational-related illness is estimated at $4-billion in direct costs and more than $8-billion in indirect costs. The costs might be even higher if absenteeism resulting from work-related accidents and illness was fully reported. Often workplace accidents and illness are associated with injuries received in plants or mining operations. But today there are numerous other causes of occupational health and safety problems; for example, key board injury suffered by computer operators, illness related to sick building syndrome, the possibility of danger from VDT/computer terminals, the implications of shift work, and the increasing incidence of melanoma skin cancer with indoor professionals. The reference to the "public's lack of concern" is interesting and suggests that there must be widespread support for action from Canadians before the issue will be addressed more seriously. Logically the stakeholders more directly involved, that is managers, employers, unions, and government, should be initiating actions rather than relying upon public pressure.

Political Correctness

Many managers are finding it a challenge to behave in a "politically correct" manner. Today, managers must accommodate differing religious observances, maternity leaves, differences among employers of various nationalities, and appropriate references for mature women, minorities, and the disabled workers. Table 15-2 identifies some of the appropriate and inappropriate language in range of management areas.

Managers must put in place policies to encourage politically correct language but also to appreciate the importance of cultural diversity in the workplace and to avoid the stereotyping of workers. There are logical reasons for such policies. Canadian business might be helped in competing globally by this country's multiculturalism, which may even give a corporation a competitive advantage. Likewise, the attitude toward mature employees should not be negative. Recent research has shown that the job performance of older employees only declines slightly.

Privacy in the Workplace

Employers require information on prospective and present employees. The collection of this information may lead to an invasion of employee privacy. In turn, citizens have rights of privacy, and the extension of these rights to employees of corporations is at issue, with a dilemma existing between the needs of the company versus the employee's privilege of dignity and worth.

There are several reasons why employers need information on employees: to prevent the hiring of unsuitable persons; to monitor for theft; to ascertain employee productivity; to ensure safety of services and products; and to protect other employees and consumers of the company's products. Privacy is an issue for employees at all levels in the organizations as well as for managers. The following are areas where employee privacy may be invaded:

Drug Testing New and existing employees may be required to take tests for drug usage. There are issues as to when and how this should be done. For example,

Table 15-2 Politically Correct Communications

Changing social patterns and increased awareness require greater sensitivity in language and word usage. The following are some examples from various areas of operations.

Area	Use	Avoid
Job Position Titles	Business Executive Manager	Businessmen or businesswomen
	Supervisor Tradesperson	Foreman Tradesman
Sex-Role Stereotyping	Informal agreement or contract Conference delegates and their guests	Gentlemen's agreement Conference delegates and their wives
Use of Word "Man"	Artificial, constructed, manufactured, of human origin, synthetic.	Man-made
	Men and women in society Environmental studies	Man and society Man and his Environment
Demeaning words	Women Feminist Women	Girls (for adults) Women's libber Broad, chick
Reference to Disabilities	Person with an intellectual disability	Mentally retarded
	Person with disability Seniors	Physically challenged Aged, elderly
	Person with disability since birth	Birth defect
	Person who has arthritis Person who has a spinal cord injury	Cripple, lame

should employees be required to submit to tests without cause? Who is selected for testing and how is it performed? Is the testing accurate? Should employees be dismissed on the basis of test results only? Many employers now only require testing where employee or public safety is an issue, as for example, with airline pilots.

Polygraph Testing   The use of lie detectors is a sensitive matter for employees. The reliability of such tests is questioned, as in the need for the procedure. Honesty tests, banks of questions that probe individual intentions, are sometimes used in place of polygraphs. Their use is also questioned, as employees are embarrassed by the personal nature of many questions.

Employee Surveillance   Employees might be monitored in several ways such as electronic and telephone eavesdropping, bugging and taping of conversations, camera recording of activities, and the searching of office desks, lockers and mail. Despite the need to prevent theft and to provide security, most forms of surveillance are resisted by employees.

Defamation and Negligent Hiring   The obtaining of information about job applicants from former employees is a problematic area. Employers need some information so that applicants can be appropriately screened. But former employers have problems in releasing information that is privileged to another employer, and they can be taken to court for defamation of character. The prospective employer may be charged with negligent hiring, that is, the manager is liable for a worker's crimes or negligence on the job if the employer fails to screen for personality quirks or past misdeeds. A major objection to the monitoring of performance is its secretiveness. Employees often do not know when it is done, or how it is done, and are not informed of the results.

Confidentiality of Employee Records   With computer-generated data banks common, there is increasing concern about the confidentiality of personal data. These data banks exist in governments and businesses, for example, in credit bureau records, and can often be linked by common identification numbers such as the social insurance number (SIN). Errors can exist in the data that the individual may not be aware of. Yet companies must obtain and store information for personnel records and for government requirements.

Monitoring of Social Life   An example of this is questioning one employee's relationship with another, whether dating, married, or living common law. Employees associating with employees of competitors may also present a problem, as might alternative lifestyle relationships.

Genetic Screening   Genetic screening to identify health problems has been considered by some employers. The reasons given are to ascertain the appropriateness of an individual for some occupations that have a higher health risk, and to identify employees who would burden a health plan. The former may be considered a legitimate reason and the latter intended to hold down costs. The *Annual Report 1991–92* of The Privacy Commission reviewed this matter and made several recommendations. Recommendations most applicable to the workplace were:

1) Every person should have a reasonable expectation of genetic privacy.

2) Neither government nor the private sector should compel persons to learn their genetic traits or disorders.

3) Employers should not require genetic testing for employment, whether to identify undesirable genetic traits in employees or applicants, or to identify

genetic changes due to workplace exposures; only true voluntary testing would be allowed (Privacy Commission, 1992, p. 25).

These examples of privacy in the workplace illustrate the ethical and legal dilemmas associated with how privacy should be maintained, what should not be done, and what should be allowed. Governments are involved and may be forced into legislation and regulation of this area, and it is considered desirable for corporations to be proactive and divulge voluntary responses to the issues. The changing rules governing the workplace complicates the task of managers and the lives of employees. It is difficult to identify when the reasonable expectation of privacy outweighs the company's need for information, and a balance needs to be struck between personal freedom and the common good.

Balancing Work and Family

Several social and economic trends have impacted the workplace: increasing numbers of mothers are working; the number of single parent families is on the rise; dual-income households are more common; more fathers are involved in childcare and home chores; the workplace is aging; the service sector is growing; and there are pressures from unemployment. These trends influence employers and employees. For managers and the organization, there are problems associated with job commitment and employee loyalty, turnover, job satisfaction, work competence, and absenteeism. For employees, problems include work-family conflict, perceived stress, possible mental health difficulties, and decreased life satisfaction. Managers must anticipate, plan, and prepare for the resulting new workplace dynamics, in particular, the balancing of work and family responsibilities. Two recent studies have addressed this issue: a Government of Canada study, "Balancing Work and Family: a Study of the Canadian Work Force" (1992), and a Conference Board of Canada Report (Paris, 1989).

Several findings emerged from the government study, which was conducted by several researchers. Higgins et al. (1992) concluded that there is a greater need for work-time and work-location flexibility, that is, an alternate to the five-day, 9 to 5 office schedule. Despite the need for flexibility, most employers maintained traditional work arrangements which caused conflicts with family demands such as:

- excessive work hours limiting time with one's family,
- the work day either starting too early or ending too late, restricting quality time with the family; and
- work schedules often not mixing with child-care arrangements and other family activities.

The authors stated that sensitivity to family concerns by employers lagged behind the emergence of those concerns as an issue with employees (1992, pp. 36–37).

Another study addressed the question "Why is it that so many employees are spending so much of their time in paid employment?" (Duxbury et al., 1992). The author found that the data provided no absolute answer but suggested the following possibilities: long work hours were necessary to accomplish more material things employers desired; employees had not mastered the skills of managing, especially delegating or prioritizing; the economic consumer climate made employees more concerned about the security of their jobs; employees obtained personal satisfaction from doing their jobs well; employees enjoyed the recognition bestowed on them for a job well done; and work loads increased due to decreasing numbers of employees in many work units. The authors included "that employers of the '90's will have to make significant changes to work place policies, through provision of work-time and work-location flexibility, in order to minimize the potential negative effects involved with balancing work and family demands" (1992, p. 45).

The Conference Board study discussed the demographic and social developments and their implications on the workforce. It also surveyed Canadian employers to assess their family-supportive benefits, policies, and practices. Family-related supports were more likely to be found in larger organizations and public-sector companies. Programs such as child care, alternate work arrangements, leaves, employee assistance programs, and relocation assistance were considered by employers offering them to improve human resource management. The respondents found such programs effective in recruiting and retraining employees, in reducing employee stress, in maintaining employee morale, and in reducing the rates of absenteeism.

The study found that the majority of employers surveyed did not offer benefits for the care of children or elderly or disabled relatives. The reasons given were that it was costly, that no such need had been expressed by employees, and that such benefits had never been considered. Respondents felt that employees had the primary responsibilities for finding solutions to work and family conflicts. According to the study, future family-related support programs depend upon how the corporation assesses its employees' needs; the impact of these supports on recruitment, retention, and productivity, and the cost effectiveness of these supports.

Both studies indicate the need for programs to assist employees in balancing the demands of work and family. The need is established in the government study while the Conference Board report provides evidence of what corporations are doing and likely to do in the future. It appears that any future programs will be economically driven despite the demands created by changing social and economic demands.

Other Workplace Issues

In addition to the challenges presented by the six issues discussed above, there are numerous others. The following is a selected list to illustrate the scope and complexity of workplace issues confronting managers.

Pay Based Upon Performance The trend to pay based on performance, that is, bonus and incentive plans, gain sharing, profit sharing, and stock purchase, is not without its problems. Although they have many advantages, complications arise with these plans.

Pay Equity There are several forms of pay inequity in Canada, and two are of particular concern: the pay gap that has traditionally existed between men and women, and unequal pay for the same work. Pay equity is a component of employment equity and focuses on equal pay for equal work. In recent years, the issue has taken on a new dimension: equal pay for work of equal value. This is a step beyond equal pay for equal work, which advocated that individuals doing the same work with the same competence should be paid the same regardless of age, sex, or any other factor. Equal pay for work of equal value means that it must be decided what the value is for two entirely different types of work. For example, a secretary may be performing work of equal value to a janitor. There are several implications of equal pay for equal work that provide challenges for management.

Sexual and Personal Harassment Sexual harassment is a sexual solicitation or advance made by an employer or other person who is in a position to confer, grant, or deny a benefit or advancement when the person making the solicitation or advance knows or ought reasonably to know that it is unwelcome. Personal harassment is any sort of unwelcome, offensive, or objectionable comment, gesture, or other behaviour that threatens a person's job, chances of advancement or promotion, or general well-being. Harassment of any type is not acceptable in the workplace.

Responding to Increasing Demands for Fringe Benefits Employers are being required to provide more fringe benefits for employees such as employee assistance programs, fitness or wellness programs, childcare, and eldercare.

Accessability for Those Disabled Employees must give consideration to making the workplace accessible to those disabled. Legislation requires some initiatives, but many employers make special efforts to employ those disabled (Smith, 1992; McKay, 1991).

Substance Abuse in the Workplace The abuse of drugs or alcohol is an increasing problem for managers. There are high costs involved in terms of absenteeism, benefits, and lost production (Gibb-Clark, 1990; "Special Report: Substance Abuse in the Workplace," 1992).

Training Everyone recognizes the need for training, but employees, unions, employers, or governments, appear unwilling to pay for it. There is also some question as to what type of training should be conducted (Gherson, 1993). There is some irony to this issue as many are predicting a shortage of skilled labour in the near future (Stoffman, 1991; Fowlie, 1992).

Lack of Traditional Promotional Opportunities   In the past, employees expected promotion up the ranks of the corporation. Many of these opportunities are now gone with downsizing and delaying. Corporations must now motivate employees in circumstances where traditional promotion patterns are no longer available.

Whistle Blowing   The treatment of persons who disclose undesirable and illegal practices of their employers is still a problem. Most corporations fail to accommodate dissent, and most employees who do "blow the whistle" on their employer suffer unfavourable consequences of some sort (Saxe, 1989).

Appointment of Women to Boards of Directors   Very few women are appointed to the Boards of Directors of Canadian corporations. It is estimated that less than 10 percent of directors are women (McKenna, 1992).

Promotion of Women in Management Positions   Women are faced with invisible ceilings and walls, and thus few are promoted to top management positions. The invisible ceilings exist to prevent women from being promoted beyond a particular level, and invisible walls prevent lateral moves within the organization necessary to obtain the experience for top positions (Lopez, 1992; "Women in Management," 1990).

Pension Plan Management   The treatment of employee pension plans has become controversial for several reasons, including the use of funds to encourage early retirements; employer withdrawal of surplus funds; the financial viability of the funds; and the cost of administering the plans.

Telecommuting or Working at Home   Some employees work at home and communicate with their place of employment through computer connections to telecommunication networks. There are implications for this, good and bad, for employers and employees (Galt, 1992).

SUMMARY

The workplace is changing, and the employee stakeholder and corporation managers are facing a new reality. The old concept of the Protestant work ethic is gone and a different ethic has emerged. Employers will be treating employees differently than in the past. Some refer to this as the new employment contract.

The question is whether or not employees and employers fully realize the complications of this new working arrangement.

Associated with the changing work ethic and work arrangement is loyalty—both of the employee to the corporation and vice versa. The concept of employee loyalty is being seriously challenged under the circumstances, and implications for employers and employees if they haven't already will have to change. If employers and employees are impacted by the changing workplace, so are unions, a employee stakeholder voice in unionized workplaces. Unions are faced with many challenges, but they too are responding with changes. While unions represent or protect employee interests of about one-third of the workforce, non-unionized employer relationships with employees are being influenced by an increasing number of employee rights. Some of these rights are legislated, while others are being granted as corporations recognize their appropriateness.

There are numerous issues related to the employee and the workplace. Six were discussed in the second section of the chapter: workforce reduction, managing part-time employees, occupational health and safety, political correctness, privacy, and balancing work and family. These issues are examples of the issues that managers must come to grips with when dealing with the human resource management area. They illustrate the dynamic nature of the employer-employee relationship.

The employee and the changing workplace presents an array of social, ethical, legal, and managerial problems for business. Employees are a critical stakeholder group, and their circumstances are alternating faster than ever. Treating the challenges presented in a socially responsible manner requires enlightened management.

REFERENCES

Balancing work and family: A study of the Canadian work force. (1992). *Optimum: The Journal of Public Sector Management,* 23(2) pp. 25-69.

Bernstein, Paul. (1988, May/June). The work ethic: Economics, not religion, *Business Horizons,* pp. 8–11.

Duxbury, Linda, Catherine Lee, Christopher Higgins, and Shirly Mills. (1992). Time spent in paid employment, *Optimum: The Journal of Public Sector Management,* 23(2) pp. 38–45.

Fowlie, Laura. (1992, September 7). Skilled labour crisis ahead. *The Financial Post,* p. 4.

Galt, Virginia. (1992, September 19). Oh, give me a home. . . *The Globe and Mail,* pp. A1, A4.

Galt, Virginia. (1991, March 14). Workplace accident tab reaches $4-billion. *The Globe and Mail,* p. A3.

Gherson, Giles. (1993, March 13). Building better workers. *Financial Times of Canada,* pp. 10–12.

Gibb-Clark, Margot. (1990, October 17). CEOs say drug, alcohol abuse rising. *The Globe and Mail,* p. B3.

Greenhalgh, Leonard, Anne T. Lawrence, and Robert I. Sutton. (1988). Determination of work force reduction strategies in declining organizations. *Academy of Management Review,* 13(2) pp. 241–254.

Higgins, Christopher, Linda Duxbury, Catherine Lee and Shirly Mills. (1992). An examination of work time and work-location flexibility. *Optimum: The Journal of Public Sector Management,* 23(2) pp. 29–37.

Lopez, J.A. (1992, March 4). Women also found with invisible walls. *The Globe and Mail,* pp. B1, B4.

McKay, Shona. (1991, October). Willing and able. *Report on Business Magazine,* pp. 58–63.

McKenna, Barrie. (1992, June 30). Women face closed door to boardrooms. *The Globe and Mail,* pp. B1, B14.

Paris, Hélène. (1989). *The Corporate Response to Workers With Family Responsibilities.* Report 43-89, Ottawa: Conference Board of Canada.

Privacy Commissioner. (1992). *Annual Report.* (1991–92). Ottawa: Supply and Services Canada. Cat.No. IP30-/1992.

Saxe, Dianne. (1989, January 5). The right to blow the whistle. *The Globe and Mail,* p. A7.

Smith, Vivian. (1992, November 17). Breaking down the barriers. *The Globe and Mail,* p. B24.

Special Report: Substance Abuse in the Workplace. (1992). *Canadian Business Review,* 19(2) pp. 14–28.

Stoffman, Daniel. (1991, September). Brave New Work. *Report on Business Magazine,* pp. 33–41.

What's become of loyalty? (1991, March/April). *Royal Bank Letter.* 72(2).

Women in management. (1990). *Journal of Business Ethics,* 9(4–5) pp. 243–454.

CHAPTER 16

COMPETITORS AND COMPETITIVENESS

INTRODUCTION

Competition is necessary, even crucial, for an effective market economy. It encourages innovation, productivity, entrepreneurship, and efficiency. The principle beneficiary when competitive forces exist is the consumer, who is provided with quality products, choice, and the best possible price.

Competition, as one of the fundamentals of the business system, is discussed in Chapter 3. In the context of business, competition is a struggle or rivalry for supremacy, often expressed as market share, amongst corporations. Two or more corporations offer the same or similar product or service to consumers whose patronage they attempt to attract in many ways, for example, by offering a better product, through use of advertising, or by superior distribution or service. Competition might result in the defeat or destruction of one of the corporations. Business failures do result from competition, and if only one corporate structure survives, a monopoly situation exists. Although competition does result in the failure of some business enterprises, the usual result is that some survive and new businesses enter the industry. Thus, competitors are a stakeholder group that most managers must recognize and respond to in some way.

Table 16-2   Industrial Concentration (Measured by Sales)

Ranking of Major Industries	Concentration Ratio Percentage of Industry Sales Controlled by Largest Firm	
	Top 4	*Top 8*
1 Storage	90.8	93.5
2 Tobacco products	90.7	99.9
3 Transport equipment	70.4	76.1
4 Petroleum and coal products	67.9	91.1
5 Communications	67.6	78.0
6 Rubber products	60.8	83.3
7 Primary metals	60.4	75.0
8 Public utilities	51.9	71.7
9 Transportation	47.1	52.4
10 Beverages	46.8	65.5
11 Metal mining	46.1	66.0
12 Textile mills	38.6	46.9
13 Mineral fuels	36.0	56.9
14 Paper and allied industries	33.8	47.6
15 Electrical products	33.8	44.5
16 Non-metallic mineral products	27.0	45.4
17 Printing, publishing, and allied industries	25.2	36.7
18 Chemicals and chemical products	23.3	35.1
19 Other mining	20.6	30.8
20 Knitting mills	18.8	28.6
21 Wood industries	18.4	25.0
22 Food	17.7	27.2
23 Leather products	17.6	28.2
24 Machinery	16.1	24.7
25 Metal fabricating	13.7	22.4
26 Miscellaneous manufacturing	12.6	17.9
27 Retail trade	11.1	18.0
28 Furniture industries	10.1	17.2
29 Services	9.8	13.4
30 Wholesale trade	9.5	14.4
31 Clothing industries	6.1	9.5
32 Agriculture, forestry, and fishing	4.3	6.4
33 Construction	4.1	6.3

SOURCE: Reproduced by authority of the Minister of Industry, 1994, Statistics Canada. *Corporations and Labour Unions Returns Act Report, Part I—Corporations.* Ottawa: Supply and Services Canada. Catalogue No. 61-210, p.28.

There are two concerns about industrial concentration, the possibilities for collaboration and higher profitability. Managers in more highly concentrated industries must plan quite differently than managers in industries where there are many competitors. In highly concentrated industries, firms behave in a similar fashion. For example, packaging changes are copied and prices matched. In less concentrated industries, it is much more difficult to keep track of all competitors and to predict their behaviour. Economists have been concerned that firms in highly concentrated industries tend to be more profitable. Although there is some evidence to support this concern, it has not been definitively proven to be the case.

The dimensions of corporate power have been identified, and the next selection summarizes why it is of concern.

Concerns Over Corporate Concentration

The extent of corporate and industry concentration is significant, as economists hold that it affects industry conduct and performance. Economic theory and actual experience suggest that the smaller the number of firms accounting for a large proportion of an industry's output, the more likely it is for anti-competitive practices to prevail. In highly concentrated industries with five rivals or competitors, a firm would have more latitude regarding price, output, and product development than firms in the industry acting interdependently. Less discretionary power exists when industry concentration is low, as the existence of many rivals forces firms to behave independently. In this case, prices, output levels, and new product developments are more likely to be determined by market forces than by the decisions of the leading, or largest, firms.

The high degree of market concentration in some industries plus the high degree of concentrated ownership constitutes a centre of power in society. When this concentration is combined with a capability to influence other stakeholders, especially governments, a controlling power structure is set in place. Many Canadians are fearful of this bigness. The discussion in this chapter has focused on corporate power and influence at a national level, but it should also be remembered that concentration in corporate power increases on a regional basis. The example often cited is the influence of the Irving family in New Brunswick, but there are thousands of communities whose economic well-being is controlled by one corporation or the business holdings of one family.

Corporate power which comes through a collective action common in concentrations of ownership has been referred to as supracorporate centralization. Such centralization takes several possible forms: informal cooperation and coordination to formal linkages through interlocking directors; joint ventures; membership in trade and industry associations, public affairs groups, and government advisory groups; and in personal association through clubs and other social contacts. It is argued that the concern with such increased corporate power is not with the influence over resource control or market behaviour, but rather with the impact on public policy making. Business organizations are perceived to be in a privileged position with easier access to government. Business's points of view are also promoted by several public affairs research groups such as the Conference Board of Canada, the C.D. Howe Institute, the Niagara Institute, and the Fraser Institute. These groups have influence. They are perceived as being independent and expert, but for the most part they are offsprings of corporate sponsorship and reflect a conservative bias (Beck, 1983).

Government's Concern

Over the years, the Federal Government has conducted studies and held royal commissions on the influence of large corporations. In April 1975, Prime Minister Pierre Trudeau appointed the Royal Commission on Corporate Concentration. It was given a broad term of reference to inquire into, report upon, and make recommendations concerning:

1) the nature and role of major concentrations of corporate power in Canada;

2) the economic and social implications for the public interest of such concentrations; and

3) whether safeguards exist or may be required to protect the public interest in the presence of such concentration.

In March 1978, the Commission presented its report to the government. Some of its conclusions were:

- Those corporations that can be considered large in Canada are in general small in comparison with large corporations elsewhere in the world.

- Corporate concentration is higher in Canada than it is elsewhere, but concentration in Canada has changed little since the mid-1960's.

- Diversification of conglomerate corporations has probably not increased concentration within industries and may even have increased competition.

- Foreign direct investment may have helped to sustain the level of concentration in some industries by making it more difficult for domestic firms to enter and survive in them.

- No further concentration should be allowed in banking.

- Large corporations should take steps to overcome a deep-rooted and widespread public suspicion about their motives and there is an increasing public impatience with their bureaucratic insensitivity.

- There should be further and better disclosure of business information.

- There is little evidence that large corporations have power to influence official decisions and public opinion.

- The social implications of business are inherent in an industrial system and, in general, have little to do with corporate concentration.

The Royal Commission concluded its report by stating:

> In summary, the influences that have shaped the Canadian economy have made a high degree of concentration inevitable. If changes occur they are likely to be in the direction of more rather than less concentration, chiefly because of international competitive influences. Public responses to concentration should recognize that profound and far-reaching changes are not practicable. The best mix of benefits and burdens should be sought through vigilance and the selective use of the appropriate instruments of public policy. While we have recommended a number of improvements, we conclude that no radical changes in the laws governing corporate activity are necessary at this time to protect the public interest (p. 413).

Since the Royal Commission on Corporate Concentration Report, two other Federal Government reports have found difficulties with big business ownership in the petroleum and newspaper industries.

A report by the Director of Investigation and Research of the Bureau of Competition Policy entitled *The State of Competition in the Canadian Petroleum Industry*, released in 1981, found that the major oil companies, Imperial, Texaco, Shell, and Gulf, acted jointly to entrench their market position through the use of anti-competitive practices at the expense of other enterprises in the industry and of the Canadian consumer. The report made recommendations on how unfair competition by the major oil companies might be reduced. In 1986, another inquiry into the petroleum industry rejected the accusation that firms in the industry were overcharging customers.

The Royal Commission on Newspapers conducted in 1981 found that corporate concentration was too high in the newspaper industry. It recommended that new laws be enacted to limit the number of newspapers owned by one chain and to restrict a chain's involvement in areas other than newspapers. Competition in the newspaper industry has increased with the establishment of new dailies in several cities, but has declined in other areas with the takeover of some newspapers and the cessation of publication of others.

None of these reports have provided clear answers to the problem of corporate power. Answers are sometimes not clear because large size does not always mean less competition. Policy choices will have to be made by Canadians through their government. Even the government is very careful in its policy toward competition in the business system.

The reason for lack of government action may stem from the fact that the benefits and drawbacks of corporate concentration are not clear, as outlined in the following section.

Arguments for Bigness

There are arguments that favour corporate bigness. Size is necessary in order to achieve economies of scale, to support aggressive marketing, and to finance research and development. These are traditional arguments and are often accompanied by the claim that Canadian firms are small by world standards, where size is necessary for survival. Such an argument is relevant to firms competing on a global scale, but may be less appropriate for companies operating within Canada's domestic market.

If a successful company is prevented from taking over an ailing company, the benefits from the existence of the former firm may be lost; for example, jobs may be maintained in a particular locale. Oligopolies do not automatically mean higher prices and reduced choice, especially if alternatives are available through substitution or foreign competition.

It is argued that conglomerate-type corporate structures have benefits. A major shareholder makes management more accountable for the capital resource it controls than would be the case in widely held corporations. The conglomerate usually has the ability to nurse an ailing or underperforming business back to health. Further, conglomerate ownership seldom contributes to concentration within an industry.

Corporate power is also offset by the power exerted by labour and government in the economic system. New, small enterprises are always forming to compete with large corporations. Some claim that bigness eventually leads to disintegration in some form. As an illustration, the recent trend to restructuring into smaller, more efficient units and the divestment of non-core business supports this claim.

The Dilemma of Corporate Power

Corporate power is associated with the legitimacy of business issues. How corporate power is used is a concern to many Canadians because there are three ways the stakeholders in the business system are influenced: economically, politically, and socially.

The economic power of corporations is of concern to smaller business competitors, consumers, and suppliers, for example. Smaller competitors do not want to be driven out of business by large, dominant firms. Consumers want the choice of goods and services that result from vigorous competition among many sellers. Suppliers do not want to lose all their bargaining power when negotiating with large business. Similar points could be made for other stakeholders.

Corporate power might be exercised in the political or public policy formulation area. Canadians, and even other sectors of the business community, fear the influence of a few large corporations, families, or groups of businesses. For example, the Business Council on National Issues, an organization comprising the executives of the 150 largest corporations, commands attention with governments and has been influential in forming public policy during the 1980's. Corporate political power must be used wisely so as not to upset the pluralistic balance of power among all stakeholders, especially interest groups.

Lastly, corporate social power is important and is usually discussed as social responsibility and business ethics. Despite the power of corporations, managers and owners must respect the integrity and dignity of other stakeholders.

ENVIRONMENTAL INFLUENCES ON COMPETITIVE RIVALRY

When competition is discussed as a fundamental of the business system, the desirability of a rigorous rivalry among firms is depicted. In some cases, competition is portrayed as a "dog-eat-dog, survival of the fittest, win or die philosophy." Some argue that such a philosophy is dangerous to many stakeholders, including consumers, employees, creditors, and suppliers, as well as the "defeated" competitors.

So far in this chapter, the state of competition in Canada has been represented quite differently, with concentrations of corporate power in the hands of few corporations. The real state of competition is somewhere in between the "survival of the fittest" and the "concentrated" scenarios. The degree of competition varies over time, across industries and even within industry segments, and by location. Competitive rivalry and the number of competitors is always shifting, as they are influenced by many environmental forces, some of which are encouraging greater competition and others that are decreasing competition. These two possibilities are discussed, with the influences encouraging competition divided into two sections, "Government Influence to Encourage Competition" and "Other Factors Increasing Competition."

Government Influence to Encourage Competition

Competitive behaviour or the conduct of business in Canada is regulated by the *Competition Act* (R.S.C. 1985, c. C-34). Government regulation often reduces competition in the economy—for example, through zoning laws, the licensing of professions and business, tariff protection, enforcement of entry standards, and laws to protect Canadian culture. This Act establishes the basic principles for the conduct of business in Canada so that competition is encouraged and maintained. The purpose of the Act is to:

1) promote the efficiency and adaptability of the Canadian economy;

2) expand opportunities for Canadian participation in world markets, while at the same time recognizing the role of foreign competition in Canada;

3) ensure that small and medium-sized enterprises have an equitable opportunity to participate in the Canadian economy; and

4) provide consumers with competitive prices and product choices (Section 1.1).

If they could be accomplished, these four purposes would result in an ideal marketplace. Competition would spur efficiency and adaptability, encourage Canadian companies to be competitive enough to compete in foreign markets, allow foreign competitors to serve Canadian customers, ensure smaller businesses were able to establish and operate, and provide consumers with a choice of products at reasonable prices.

Passed in 1986, the *Competition Act* works differently than earlier legislation. It divides offences into criminal and non-criminal and provides for remedies other than legal action. The criminal offences are listed in Table 16-3. These result in prosecutions in the criminal courts, where strict rules of evidence apply and cases must be proven beyond a reasonable doubt. The remedies or penalties include fines and/or imprisonment, and individuals as well as companies can be charged. Prohibition orders (court orders forbidding certain activities) and interim injunctions (temporary court orders forbidding certain activities) may also be sought.

Non-criminal reviewable matters (listed in Table 16-3) are reviewed by a Competition Tribunal, then referred to the Director of Investigation and Research. Interim injunctions or orders can be issued by the Tribunal, or cases can be resolved by written undertakings to remedy an anti-competitive activity without having a full inquiry or judicial proceeding. The Director can also be approached for his or her opinion on whether a particular business activity will raise competition concerns.

The offences listed in Table 16-3 must be recognized for what they really are; that is, methods or activities used by businesses to reduce or eliminate competition. This provides the rationale for regulating such activities. An area of particular interest to competition is that involving acquisition or mergers.

The term "merger" in the *Competition Act* is intended to cover a broad range of acquisition or takeover activity and defines "merger" in terms of ". . . the acquisition or establishment, direct or indirect, by one or more persons, whether by purchase or lease of shares or assets, by amalgamation or by combination or otherwise, of control over or significant interest in the whole or a part of a business of a competitor, supplier, customer or other person" (Section 91).

The Director of Investigation of Research and the Competition Tribunal examines a merger according to several factors, including:

- the market share obtained and a merger will generally not be challenged where: (i) the post-merger share of the market accounted for by the four largest firms in the market would be less than 65 percent, or (ii) the post-merger market share of the merged entry would be less than 10 percent;
- the effectiveness of foreign competition;
- whether the business of a party to the merger has failed or likely is to fail;
- the availability of acceptable substitutes;

Table 16-3   Summary of Business Conduct Covered by the *Competition Act*

Criminal Offences

Conspiracy   Any agreement, arrangements, or combinations designed to lessen competition unduly in relation to the supply, manufacture or production of a product. Examples are: fixing prices or preventing new competitors from entering the market (Section 45).

Bid-rigging   An arrangement between two or more persons or corporations where one party will refrain from bidding in a call for tenders, or where there was collusion in the submission of bids (Section 47).

Price discrimination   Price discrimination exists when a supplier charges different prices to competitors who purchase similar volumes of an article (Paragraph 50(1)(a)).

Predatory Pricing   There are two types of predatory pricing: (i) selling products in one region of Canada at prices lower than in another region for the purpose of lessening competition (Paragraph 50(1)(b)); and (ii) selling products at unreasonably low prices where the intent is to lesson competition (Paragraph 50(1)(c)).

Price Maintenance   This involves attempts to influence upward or to discourage the reduction of price at which another person supplies or advertises a product, or refusing to supply anyone because of that person's low pricing policy (Section 61(11)).

Misleading advertising or descriptive marketing practices   Examples include: unsubstantiated performance and durability claims, misleading warranties, mispresentations as to regular price, failure to disclose adequate information in promotional contests, double ticketing, pyramid selling, sale above advertised price, and bait and switch selling (when a product is advertised at a bargain price, but a reasonable supply of it is not available) (Sections 52, 54, 57, 58, 59).

Non-Criminal Reviewable Matters

Mergers   All mergers are reviewable by the Competition Tribunal chaired by a judge and includes large members to ensure a business perspective during proceedings (Sections 91 through 125).

Abuse of dominant position   The Act provides remedies where dominant firms engage in anti-competitive behaviour such as: acquisition of a customer who would otherwise be available to a competitor to impede a competitor's entry into the market; purchase of products to prevent the reduction of existing price levels; and selling articles at a price lower than the acquisition cost to discipline or eliminate a competitor (Sections 78 and 79).

Other reviewable matters
Refusal to deal (Section 75)
Consignment selling (Section 76)
Exclusive dealing (Section 77)
Tied selling (Section 77)
Market restriction (Section 77)
Delivered pricing (Sections 80 and 81)
Specialization agreements (Sections 86 through 90)

SOURCE: Compiled from Consumers and Corporate Affairs Canada, (1990, November). *An Overview of Canada's Competition Act*. Director of Investigation and Research, Information Bulletin No. 4; *Annual Report for the year ended March 31, 1992*. Director of Investigation and Research, Competition Act, Catalogue No. RG 51–1992.

- the presence of barriers to entry that prevent potential competitors from entering the market;

- the extent to which effective competition remains in a market affected by the merger;

- the likelihood that the merger would remove a vigorous or effective competitor;

- the extent of change and innovation in the market;

- a vertical merger is of concern when it increases barriers to entry or when upstream interdependence is facilitated by forward integration into retail; and

- conglomerate mergers, that is, a merger between parties that do not compete in the same relevant market or in relevant markets that are vertically related, are only examined where it can be demonstrated that, in absence of the merger, one of the merging parties would likely have entered the market *de novo* (Consumer and Corporate Affairs Canada (1991). *Merger Enforcement Guidelines*).

Other Factors Increasing Competition

Although the role of government in encouraging competition in the Canadian economy is important, it is only one of several factors determining competitive behaviour. The following is a selected list of such factors.

Entrepreneurship It should be remembered that the business system involves a life cycle process in which enterprises are formed, grow, and dissolve. There is a constant supply (or birth) of new, small businesses many of which grow in stature and provide competition for large, well-established firms. The startup of new business is essential and has been the focus of considerable attention in the past decade. Entrepreneurship is also occurring within large corporations, where it is referred to as intrepreneurship, and involves units of large organizations being operated as independent businesses.

Deregulation Government initiative to deregulate has influenced the growth of businesses, as discussed in Chapter 13. For example, the deregulation of the trucking industry has allowed small firms to complete. The removal of the ban on Sunday shopping has increased competition in the retail industry.

Privatization Government efforts to sell off the business enterprises it owns have increased opportunities for entrepreneurs. Also, functions previously carried out within government departments are now being provided by outside enterprises. Chapter 13 discussed the implications of the wide spectrum of initiatives possible under privatization.

Technology   A multitude of technological developments have encouraged competitive rivalry. New technology has led to new business enterprises, for example, in electronics and various computer-related industries, and has changed how other industries operate. An example of the latter is that the feasibility of small production runs are now possible with new high-technology processes.

Decline of Natural Monopoly   Utility-type companies often operated as natural monopolies; for example, in telephone and cable television. With deregulation and new technologies, neither of these industries can now be considered a natural monopoly. Competition exists in the telephone industry, although presently only in long distance, and cable television will likely lose its protected status in the future.

Global Trends in Trade   The reduction of some barriers to trade is increasing competition in Canada. GATT arguments encourage international trade as has the US–Canada Free Trade Agreement. Many corporations now operate on a global scale producing products where it is most advantageous to do so.

Influences Reducing Competition

The following is a list of influences, or environmental forces, that are reducing competitive rivalry in the Canadian business system.

Intellectual Property   Intellectual property is an umbrella term for patents, copyrights, industrial designs, and trademarks. Although there is no foolproof protection of such property, government does provide the mechanism to prevent the wholesale copying of inventions and written materials. This is done to promote the orderly conduct of business where the originator of innovations retains rights but others are made aware of the new discoveries. Without this mechanism, there would be less incentive to create and disseminate new ideas.

Although an intellectual property protective system is needed, it does have a downside. In effect, it creates a monopoly for what many feel is an extended period of keeping prices higher and limiting choices. Some industries have used this to effectively reduce competition for extended periods. The drug industry has convinced government it needs protection from generic competition for periods of 20 years and more, a period some consider more than adequate to recover research and development costs. In Canada, life forms have not been patentable, but the government is under increasing pressure from global enterprises to extend patent legislation to life-form developments. Even though necessary, intellectual property protection should also be viewed as reducing competitive rivalry, with disadvantages to other businesses and consumers.

Government Legislation/Ownership   As outlined in Chapter 13, there has been a trend to private ownership and markets in the past decade. But, there still are restrictions on competition; for example, through marketing boards, professional licensure, and zoning regulations, to name a few. Interprovincial trade barriers imposed by provincial governments continue to restrict competition in Canada.

International Trade Barriers   Despite free trade agreements, many barriers to trade exist, especially non-tariff barriers.

Mergers/Takeovers   Mergers or takeovers tend to occur in cycles with the later 1970's and 1980's being two periods of high acquisition activity. Such acquisitions can reduce competition, especially if they are horizontal acquisitions in the same industry.

Business Collaboration   Corporations are collaborating with one another in various ways; for example, through joint ventures, strategic alliances, or partnerships. There are a variety of motives for such collaboration. One motivation is to reduce what is considered wasteful or duplication of efforts. For example, the American automobile industry is collaborating to develop a pollution-free electric vehicle and the pharmaceutical industry to fund a cure for AIDS. There is no doubt that the pooling of resources has appeal especially to counter foreign competition. But there is always the temptation to collude to boost profits by restraining production, raising prices, and squelching threatening technologies. It is also argued that collaboration reduces inventiveness and the zeal to win. Many still believe that a better way to generate new ideas is through competition, and that collaborative activities need to be monitored carefully.

From this discussion of environmental influences it is clear that at any time there are forces at work to increase or decrease competitively rivalry. Governments play a definite role in maintaining the balance among the forces. But the balance is always shifting and is impacting on stakeholders in various ways. The next section examines another dimension in competition, the recent phenomenon referred to as "competitiveness."

NATIONAL COMPETITIVENESS

The competitive nature of business in Canada is one dimension, and the competitiveness of Canadian business on world markets is another. The success of Canada's business enterprises is important to trade, and thus, to the country's economic well-being. Obviously, managers can influence the competitiveness of Canadian corporations. This section will review some measures of Canadian business competitiveness in world markets.

The World Competitiveness Report

One measure of national competitiveness in industrialized countries is completed annually by the World Economic Forum and the International Institute for Management Development. Overall, Canada's rank was fifth out of 24 industrialized countries in 1990, but dropped to eleventh place out of 26 in 1992.

The *World Competitiveness Report 1990* defines business competitiveness as the ability to design, produce and market goods and services, the price and non-price qualities of which form a more attractive package of benefits than those of competitors. The assessment of national competitiveness is based upon responses to questionnaires to executives in all the countries included in the report (Gibb-Clark, 1990). The ranking is based on eight factors of competitiveness.

1) *Domestic economic strength*   The size of the economy, investment, inflation, and economic growth are evaluated. Canada's ranking: 15.

2) *Internationalization*   The measures involved include the extent of participation in international trade, investment flows, protectionism, international links, and export diversity. Ranking: 17.

3) *Government*   This is a measure of the type of government interventions that are detrimental to the international competitiveness of business. Included are consideration of debt and reserves, tax rates and revenues, and the legislative and regulatory environment. Ranking: 11.

4) *Finance*   The size of banks, the capitalization of stock markets, the availability of venture capital, interest rates and financial alternatives are used to assess the performance of capital markets and financial services. Ranking: 7.

5) *Infrastructure*   The presence of the necessary resources and systems needed by business is assessed by examining: oil imports, resource self-sufficiency, and adequacy of communications and transportation systems. Ranking: 3.

6) *Management*   This factor considers the extent to which enterprises are managed in an innovative, profitable, and responsible manner. This is measured by looking at product quality and pricing, productivity, compensation, use of technology, employee turnover, corporate financial performance, and managerial behaviour. Ranking: 15.

7) *Science and Technology*   The success in basic and applied research is assessed by considering business expenditures in R&D, the number of scientists in industry and patents and protection of intellectual property. Ranking: 17.

8) *People*   This is a measure of the workers in the economy including age distribution, unemployment rates, educational levels, and motivation and skills. Ranking: 8.

Of particular concern is the low ranking of Canadian business in the "management" factor. The reasons identified for this low ranking included:

implementation of strategies falls short of set goals, managerial rewards encourage short-term orientation, senior management is rarely experienced in international business, the price/quality ratio of domestic products is seen to be inferior to foreign competitors, time to innovate or to market a new product is longer, total quality control is neglected, and corporate profits are expected to be low (Enchin, 1992). Overall, the report raises concerns about the effectiveness of Canadian government policies and the efficiencies of the business enterprise system.

Porter's Assessment of Canadian Competitiveness

Michael Porter of the Harvard Business School has assessed the competitiveness of nations in his book *The Competitive Advantage of Nations* (1990). He identified the following four elements of competitive advantage that reinforce each other:

1) *Firm Strategy, Structure, and Rivalry*   The conditions under which companies are created, organized, and arranged, the number of companies in an industry, the intensity of competition, and the extent of public versus private ownership.

2) *Factor Conditions*   The nation's position in factors of production such as skilled labour, natural resources, education, and wage rates.

3) *Demand Conditions*   The nature of home-market demand for the industry's product or service, and the sophistication of consumers and the media exposure of products.

4) *Related and Supporting Industries*   The presence or absence of supplier industries and other related industries that are internationally competitive.

The four elements and their interrelatedness are shown in Figure 16-1. Porter did not study Canada's competitiveness, although he was later hired by the Canadian Government and the Business Council on National Issues to carry out such an assessment. The report, *Canada at the Crossroads: The Reality of a New Competitive Environment* (Porter, 1991) was released in October 1991. It is difficult to summarize the report, but an overview is provided by Enchin (1991). Brief mention will be made of Porter's assessment of Canadian competitiveness according to his four determinants.

With regard to "Firm Strategy, Structure and Rivalry," the Report stated that surveys of Canadian attitudes toward competition and risk reflect a greater emphasis on security, and that static, cost-based strategies are used in many industries because of factor (resource) abundance. Strategies in many industries were inward-looking, with 70 percent of Canadian manufacturers not serving export markets. This insular orientation could be traced to a number of characteristics of the Canadian market: traditionally high tariffs that sheltered Canadian firms; weak domestic rivalry; high levels of corporate concentration;

Figure 16-1   The Determinants of National Competitive Advantage

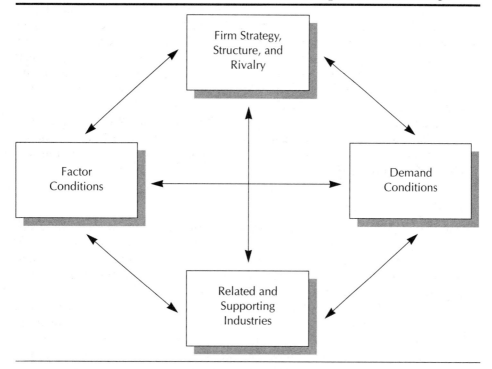

historically weak competition laws, and interprovincial trade barriers (Porter, 1991, pp. 55–56).

Canada ranked quite well in basic factors such as natural resources, climate, and unskilled and semi-skilled labour. In particular, Canada's physical resources are a significant source of international competitive advantage. Advanced factors developed through sustained and sophisticated investment in both human and physical capital are much weaker. There are problems with Canada's educational system, shortages of skilled labour in some occupations, and declining enrolment in the science and engineering disciplines. Canada's capital market and financial system are adequate but the cost of capital has been a problem (Porter, 1991, pp. 49–51).

In his studies of competitive advantage in various countries, Porter found that if companies are to gain competitive advantage it is important to have demanding buyers for their products or sources in the domestic market. In Canada, he found that demand conditions have not put strong pressure on companies to innovate, upgrade, or anticipate international needs. Apparently Canadian consumers are rarely at the leading edge in demanding innovative consumer goods and are reluctant to voice complaints or to use advocacy agencies to pressure companies to improve (Porter, 1991, pp. 51–52).

Lastly, Canada's industry clusters are usually narrow and shallow, reflecting a limited presence of indigenous related and supporting industries. Such key inputs as machinery and equipment are purchased from foreign suppliers. The reasons for this include the tendency for foreign-owned firms to source firms abroad; a high degree of internal integration and the desire to obtain their own supply capabilities; government policies that spread industrial development across the country rather than concentrating it; and underdeveloped linkages among the other determinants of competitive advantage (Porter, 1991, pp. 53–54).

Overall, Porter concluded that Canadian business was ill-equipped for the future, that the comfortable insularity of the old order would have to change, that systemic barriers to change must be removed, and that a new vision for the Canadian economy is needed.

The Kodak Canada Studies

Kodak Canada Inc. commissioned three studies on Canadian business and economy, *New Visions for Canadian Business* (Rugman and D'Cruz, 1990), *Fast Forward* (Rugman and D'Cruz, 1991), and *New Compacts for Canadian Competitiveness* (D'Cruz and Rugman, 1992). Although all are relevant to the discussion of competitiveness, only the most recent study is discussed.

D'Cruz and Rugman (1992) believe that despite increasing awareness of Canada's lack of international competitiveness, little progress is being made to solve the problem. They introduce a new framework designed to bring together the key actors in Canada's business community to address the competitiveness challenge. Ten strategic clusters are identified, that is, groups of firms within a geographical area in the same or related industries, along with a list of likely flagship firms. A flagship firm would be responsible for developing links or networks with suppliers, customers, competitors and the non-business infrastructure within each cluster, including unions, universities, and government. The 10 clusters and flagship companies are listed in Table 16-4.

The development of these business networks and non-business linkages would support the clusters as they develop global strategies and perform at international standards. In addition to the recommendations in the two previous studies, the authors make four new recommendations for making Canada internationally competitive using strategic clusters and flagship companies:

Leadership The private sector chief executive officers must provide leadership to improve Canada's international competitiveness in making certain that the business links within each cluster and with the non-business infrastructure are developed.

Desire All Canadians must perform at international standards, and activities in each cluster must be measured against international benchmarks rather than against domestic standards that Canadians are too willing to accept.

Table 16-4   The Largest Companies in Canada's Ten Key Strategic Customers

Firm Name (Ranking in 500)	Total ($m)	US (%)	Offshore (%)	Foreign (%)	Ownership
1. The Western Canadian Forest Products Cluster					
1 MacMillan Bloedel (–)*	3,003	48	33	81	Canada
2 Fletcher Challenge (101)	1,060	n/a	n/a	n/a	New Zealand
3 Crown Forest (113)	1,061	n/a	n/a	n/a	New Zealand
Average	**1,741**			**81**	
Total	**5,224**				
2. The Alberta Energy Cluster					
1 Imperial Oil (6)	10,223	7	n/a	5	U.S.
2 Shell Canada (16)	5,508	20	n/a	20	Netherlands
3 Petro-Canada (17)	5,317	n/a	n/a	n/a	Canada
4 Nova (19)	4,736	12	7	19	Canada
5 Amoco Canada (24)	4,444	n/a	n/a	n/a	U.S.
6 Total Petroleum (31)	3,180	n/a	n/a	n/a	France
7 TransCanada Piplines (41)	3,033	28	0	28	Canada
8 Mobil Oil Canada Ltd. (64)	1,870	n/a	0	n/a	U.S.
9 ATCO (82)	1,442	n/a	n/a	n/a	Canada
10 Suncor (89)	1,374	8	2	10	Canada
11 Alberta & Southern Gas (110)	1,076	n/a	n/a	n/a	U.S.
12 TransAlta Utilities (112)	1,064	n/a	n/a	n/a	Canada
13 Chevron Canada Resources (114)	1,058	n/a	n/a	n/a	U.S.
14 Norcen Energy Resorces (115)	1,052	7	7	14	Canada
Average	**3,241**			**16**	
Total	**45,377**				
3. The Prairie Farming Cluster					
1 Canadian Wheat Board (27)	4,111	n/a	87	87	Canada
2 Saskatchewan Wheat Pool (61)	1,943	n/a	n/a	n/a	Canada
3 Cargill (74)	1,612	n/a	n/a	n/a	U.S.
4 Alberta Wheat Pool (98)	1,223	n/a	n/a	n/a	Canada
5 United Grain Growers (104)	1,125	n/a	n/a	n/a	Canada
Average	**2,003**			**87**	
Total	**10,014**				
4. The Eastern Canadian Forest Products Cluster					
1 Noranda Forest (–)*	4,555	n/a	n/a	n/a	Canada
2 Moore (36)	3,231	60	31	91	Canada
3 Abitibi-Price (39)	3,088	27	0	27	Canada
4 Domtar (51)	2,314	11	0	11	Canada

Table 16-4   The Largest Companies in Canada's Ten Key Strategic Customers (continued)

	Sales				
	Total	**US**	**Offshore**	**Foreign**	
Firm Name (Ranking in 500)	**($m)**	**(%)**	**(%)**	**(%)**	**Ownership**
4. The Eastern Canadian Forest Products Cluster (continued)					
5 CP Forest Products (–)*	2,313	n/a	n/a	n/a	Canada
6 Repap Enterprises (97)	1,227	41	0	41	Canada
Average	**2,788**			**43**	
Total	**16,728**				
5. The Base Metal Mining Cluster					
1 Alcan Aluminium (7)	10,217	33	54	87	Canada
2 Inco (31)	3,627	31	58	89	Canada
3 Horsham (34)	3,253	100	0	100	Canada
4 Noranda Minerals (–)*	2,671	n/a	n/a	n/a	Canada
5 Falconbridge (60)	2,032	39	48	87	Canada
6 Cominco (86)	1,403	39	43	82	Canada
7 Rio Algom (91)	1,343	31	13	44	Britain
8 Placer Dome (107)	1,093	9	58	67	Canada
Average	**3,205**			**79**	
Total	**25,639**				
6. The Southwest Ontario Automotive Cluster					
1 General Motors of Canada (1)	18,458	64	n/a	64	U.S.
2 Ford Motor of Canada (3)	13,706	n/a	n/a	n/a	U.S.
3 Chrysler Canada (10)	7,067	71	n/a	71	U.S.
4 Varity (26)	4,155	38	57	95	Canada
5 Honda Canada (46)	2,454	n/a	n/a	n/a	Japan
6 Magna International (62)	1,927	86	2	88	Canada
7 Toyota Canada (81)	1,505	n/a	n/a	n/a	Japan
Average	**7,039**			**80**	
Total	**49,272**				
7. The Ontario Advanced Manufacturing Cluster					
1 Northern Telecom (–)*	7,899	58	6	64	Canada
2 Bell Canada (–)*	7,655	n/a	n/a	n/a	Canada
3 IBM Canada (22)	4,578	0	n/a	n/a	U.S.
4 Dofasco (35)	3,250	16	10	26	Canada
5 Stelco (57)	2,101	n/a	n/a	n/a	Canada
6 Dow Chemical of Canada (73)	1,630	15	12	27	U.S.
7 General Electric Canada (77)	1,581	17	5	22	U.S.
8 Du Pont Canada (85)	1,411	n/a	n/a	n/a	U.S.
Average	**3,763**			**35**	
Total	**30,105**				

Table 16-4   The Largest Companies in Canada's Ten Key Strategic Customers (continued)

| Firm Name (Ranking in 500) | Sales | | | | Ownership |
	Total ($m)	US (%)	Offshore (%)	Foreign (%)	
8. The Toronto Financial Services Cluster					
1 Royal Bank of Canada (1)	125,938				Canada
2 CIBC (2)	114,196				Canada
3 Bank of Montreal (3)	87,369				Canada
4 Bank of Nova Scotia (4)	87,230				Canada
5 Toronto Dominion Bank (5)	66,900				Canada
6 Trilon Financial Corp. (6)	45,192				Canada
7 Royal Trusco (–)*	40,946				Canada
8 CT Financial Services (10)	35,087				Canada
9 Sun Life Assurance (–)	31,920				Canada
10 National Trustco (12)	15,653				Canada
Average	**65,043**				
Total	**650,431**				
9. The Montreal Aerospace and Manufacturing Cluster					
1 Bombardier (58)*	2,093	11	79	90	Canada
2 Pratt & Whitney Canada (76)	1,584	45	39	84	U.S.
3 CAE Industries (105)	1,120	51	28	79	Canada
4 Asea Brown Boveri (111)	1,065	n/a	n/a	n/a	Switzerland
Average	**1,466**			**84**	
Total	**5,862**				
10. The Atlantic Seafood Cluster					
1 McCain Foods (49)	2,396	n/a	n/a	n/a	Canada
2 National Sea Products (162)	608	45	31	76	Canada
3 FPI (183)	535	n/a	n/a	n/a	Canada
Average	**1,180**			**76**	
Total	**3,539**				

Notes *Where marked, data are from the 1991 corporate annual reports.
For cluster no. 8, size is measured by assets, rankings are from "The Top 100 Financial Institutions."

Sources Except where noted, all data are adapted from the *The Financial Post*, Summer 1991.
(Data on ratios of foreign to total sales are from *Canadian Business*, June 1991.)

SOURCE: Joseph R. D'Cruz and Alan M. Rugman. (1992). *New Compacts for Canadian Competitiveness*. Toronto: Kodak Canada Inc., pp. 56–57.

Figure 16-2   The Attract Model of National Competitive Advantage

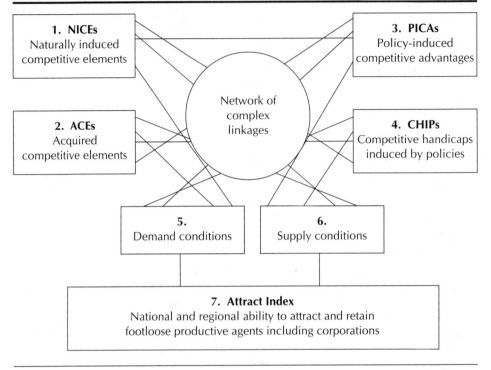

SOURCE: Kimon Valaskakis. (1992, October 31). A prescription for Canada Inc. *The Globe and Mail,* p. B4.

Recognition   Competitiveness audits are necessary for all government programs and expenditures, as they impact on the performance of the 10 strategic clusters.

Involvement   Every Canadian must be involved in the process of making Canada competitive again. Everyone must be informed about competitiveness issues, upgrade their skills, and participate in improving institutions to which they belong or which they influence (1992, p. 60).

The Attract Model of National Competitive Advantage

Kimon Valaskakis, an economist at the University of Montreal, conceptualizes competitive advantage in terms of the increasing transnational mobility of the factors of production (natural resources, labour, capital, and technology) and of the emergence in terms of the stateless corporation. He has developed the Attract Model (Figure 16-2) to describe the new factors that make nations competitive. Six variables comprise an Attract Index of national competitive advantage:

1) *Naturally induced competitive elements (NICEs)*   This is the natural endowment of a country—climate, geography, and natural resources.

2) *Acquired competitive elements (ACEs)*   This describes the acquired elements such as infrastructure, private capital formation, and human resources.

3) *Policy induced competitive advantages (PICAs)*   These are public policy initiatives that induce competitive advantage in a region or nation.

4) *Competitive handicaps induced by policies (CHIPs)*   These are public policy initiatives that induce competitive handicaps which are unanticipated negative efforts on competitiveness resulting from misguided public policies.

5) and 6) *Demand and supply conditions*   The conditions through which competitive advantages and handicaps filter down.

The model results in the Attract Index describing the final capability of that particular region to attract and retain mobile transnational factors of production. The six variables interrelate in a network, with one variable offsetting or complementing another. Thus, tradeoffs are possible, with a weakness in one variable being offset by strength in others.

Valaskakis believes that the situation in Canada today is one where national-level PICAs (that is, national industrial policy) has been rejected in favour of competitive provincial and municipal-level PICAs, which tend to increase taxation and cancel each other out. Also, there is a proliferation of CHIPs as a result of adversarial provincial public policies, and this leads to a serious loss of national competitiveness. Several solutions are presented and rejected, and instead the following should be attempted: the development of a clear and consensual national purpose; elimination of CHIPs that impede progress by greater harmonization of policies among governments; and the development of national PICAs. Through these types of initiatives, a national competitive advantage can be achieved in Canada.

An Overview of Competitiveness

Four assessments of Canada's national competitiveness have been presented. In addition, the National Advisory Board on Science and Technology, the Economic Council of Canada, the C.D. Howe Institute, the Canadian Manufacturers' Association, and the Conference Board of Canada have all released studies on competitiveness. There is no shortage of assessments and recommendations on Canada's competitiveness problem. The four presented in this chapter are not fully discussed, and are more comprehensive than discussed here.

Some observations can be made from this discussion of competitiveness. All the studies make it clear that it is a problem which must be addressed by Canada as a country and by the business enterprise system and its stakeholders, in particular employees, government, Boards of Directors, and suppliers. The World Competitiveness Report identifies the key variables in competition and, in particular, highlights serious problems with Canadian management and R&D. But it does not provide recommendations, as do other studies. Porter's (1990, 1991) approach identifies four key elements and indicates where Canada is weak. His solutions depend upon a vigorous private sector, and he clearly identifies the importance of competitive rivalry in the domestic market. Porter also is aware of the role of government and proposes a type of industrial policy for the country.

The Kodak study relies upon collaboration among business corporations and other sectors to achieve competitiveness. Such collaboration is discussed in a earlier section and poses some difficulties. The Attract Model emphasizes the complex network of linkages between competitive elements, public-policy-induced advantages and handicaps, and demand and supply conditions, an approach somewhat similar to Porter's. The abundance of analysis and advice has not lead to a consensus of what should be done. The next few years will be key to Canadian competitiveness, and it will be interesting to see what private and public sector initiatives will be undertaken.

COMPETITORS, COMPETITIVENESS, AND CORPORATE SOCIAL RESPONSIBILITY

There are implications for social responsibility associated with the degree of competitively rivalry existing in a business system. One position is that increased competition and pressure to be competitive has resulted in an increase in unethical or questionable practices. Industrial spying, espionage, and sabotage are now of such concern that industrial or economic security has replaced national security as a major national issue. Practices range from eavesdropping to theft of R&D technology to hiring the competitor's key employees. It is argued that the practices are much more widespread than reported and that many remain undisclosed either because companies are unaware of them or are too embarrassed to report them.

Several causes of this trend have been identified, including the cutthroat global economy; the lack of corporate loyalty as a result of layoffs, buy-outs, and downsizings; and shorter product cycles necessitating faster responses to competitor initiatives. The copying or counterfeiting of products appears more common and increasingly difficult to control, as there appears little reluctance to steal ideas from others.

Ethical behaviour is complicated by the different standards existing in different countries. Corporations engaging in global business now need a worldwide codes of ethics to accommodate these differences. Some fear that the pressures for national competitiveness will result in adverse affects on Canadians. The workforce may be reduced in Canada as employers move to cheap labour market areas despite the lower labour productivity that is likely. There is also fear for Canadian social programs, such as Medicare and unemployment insurance, and of threats to Canadian cultural sovereignty.

One manager's view of ethics and competitiveness is presented in the following quotation:

> Ethics and competitiveness are inseparable. We compete as a society. No society anywhere will compete very long or successfully with people stabbing each other in the back; with people trying to steal from each other; with everything requiring notarized confirmation because you can't trust the other fellow; with every little squabble ending in litigation; and with government writing reams of regulatory legislation, tying business hand and foot to keep it honest. (Akers, 1989, p. 69)[2]

Akers makes three suggestions to maintain a common moral sense: fortify ethical standards through role models, institute codes of conduct and an honour system; teach ethics in schools; and keep priorities straight by considering the moral order of the world to transcend any single nation-state—that is, understand the place of business in the greater scheme of things.

Business ethics play a prominent role in competition, and it can be argued that without some ethical standards there is no fair competition. There must be some implicit understanding of ethics by competitors in the marketplace. Without this, competition cannot exist, as undesirable behaviour would seriously damage the business system. Despite the aggressive behaviour of competitive rivalry, competition implies fairness to all—competitors and other stakeholders.

SUMMARY

Competition, the rivalry among business enterprises, is a fundamental component of the business system. It is usually enhanced by the number of firms competing in the marketplace. Unfortunately, in Canada the number of competitors is undesirably low.

The concentration of corporate power not only occurs as a result of too few competitors in an industry, but also because a few large corporations, families, or groups of firms own large portions of economic activity. The concern for concentrating economic power in the hands of a few is accompanied by concerns for product and service selection, treatment of suppliers, and prices to consumers. The government, in its role as a regulator of economic activity, is concerned and attempts to encourage and maintain competitive behaviour.

---

[2] Reprinted from "Ethics and Competitiveness—Putting First Things First" by John Akers, *Sloan Management Review*, Winter 1989, pp.69-71, by permission of the publisher. Copyright © 1989 by the Sloan Management Review Association. All rights reserved.

The process of regulating competition and concentration of corporate power is complicated because there are arguments for bigness which have validity. The result is a dilemma over the issue of corporate power. It should be remembered that the corporate power issue must be viewed from three perspectives: economic, political, and social. To consider it an economic issue would be too narrow.

A multitude of influences impact upon the degree of competitive rivalry. The government is a major force with its *Competition Act*, which attempts to enhance competition. But there are other forces operating at all times that tend to increase and decrease competition. The result is a continuous shifting of the status of competition over time and across regions and industries.

The discussion of national competitiveness extends the discussion of competition to a world or global scale. Apparently, Canadian firms have traditionally not been exposed to sufficient competition in the domestic market. This may be one reason for Canada's weakening international competitive advantage as established by the four studies reviewed. Numerous recommendations are made to resolve the problem, but there does not appear to be a consensus forming about which to follow.

Lastly, the implications for social responsibility and ethics are reviewed. Although there appears to be an increase in socially irresponsible and unethical behaviour, ethics are implicitly influencing most of the competitive rivalry among firms. Without this implicit influence, there would be a far different, and most likely, a less desirable business enterprise system operating in Canada.

REFERENCES

Akers, John F. (1989, Winter). Ethics and competitiveness—putting first things first. *Sloan Management Review*, pp. 69–71.

Beck, Stanley. (1983). Corporate power and public policy, in *Consumer Protection, Environmental Law, and Corporate Power*. Ottawa: Royal Commission on Economic Union and Development Prospects for Canada. Cat. No. Z1-1983/1-41-50.

Canada's Largest Corporations. (Annual, May issue). *The Financial Post*.

Consumer and Corporate Affairs Canada. (1991, March). *Merger Enforcement Guidelines*. Director of Investigation and Research. Competition Act. Information Bulletin No. 5. Catalogue No. RG 54-2/5-1991E.

The Corporate 500. (Annual, June issue). *Canadian Business*.

D'Cruz, Joseph R. and Alan M. Rugman. (1992). *New Compacts for Canadian Competitiveness*. Toronto: Kodak Canada Inc.

Enchin, Harvey. (1992, June 22). Canada downgraded in competitiveness report. *The Globe and Mail*, pp. B1–B2.

Enchin, Harvey. (1991, October 25). Canada urged to stop living off fat of the land. *The Globe and Mail*, pp. B1–B2, B6.

Eyton, J. Trevor, O.C. (1986, September 29). Thoughts on the subject of corporate concentration. Speech to the International Trust Executive Forum on the Management of Change, Toronto.

Foreign ownership up slightly. (1992, May 22). *The Globe and Mail*, p. B12.

Gibb-Clark, Margot. (1990). Canada's competitiveness slips. *The Globe and Mail*, June 20, p. B3.

Inter-Corporate Ownership. (Annual). Ottawa: Publications Jobs and Services, Statistics Canada. Cat. No. 61–517.

Palda, Filip. (1993, June). An industrial strategy for airlines. *Fraser Forum*, p. 26.

Porter, Michael. (1991). *Canada At the Crossroads: The Reality of a Competitive Environment*. Ottawa: Business Council on National Issues and Minister of Supply and Services.

Porter, Michael. (1990). *The Competitive Advantage of Nations*. New York: Free Press.

Rugman, Alan M. and Joseph R. D'Cruz. (1990). *New Visions for Canadian Business: Strategies for Competing in the Global Economy*. Toronto: Kodak Canada Inc.

Rugman, Alan M. and Joseph R. D'Cruz. (1991). *Fast Forward: Improving Canada's International Competitiveness*. Toronto: Kodak Canada Inc.

The Top 1000. (Annual, July issue). T*he Globe and Mail Report on Business Magazine*.

Valaskakis, Kimon. (1992, October 31). "A prescription for Canada Inc." *The Globe and Mail*, p. B4.

CONSUMERS
AND THEIR SOVEREIGNTY

INTRODUCTION

The purpose of this chapter is to examine an overlooked and misunderstood concept, consumer sovereignty, and a neglected stakeholder group, consumers. The point is made that a closer approximation to consumer sovereignty should be sought and that there are threats to the concept from public policies and the actions of corporations. Groups of producers preventing the free movement of resources, large corporations dominating markets, and pricing and selection of many products being determined by government are examples of where the sovereignty of the consumer is being threatened. Yet, these threats are created or tolerated by governments. What are referred to as "contrived scarcities" (Hutt, 1936, p. 261) are created by corporations and governments, and any expression of consumer sovereignty in such an environment is distorted, as barriers have been created to frustrate consumer preferences. Contrary to what is claimed, the involvement of governments in the consumer affairs area has not provided the countervailing power to protect consumers from large corporations, producers, and certainly not from governments themselves. The concept of consumer sovereignty seems a weak force to counter the powers of these vested interests, yet alone the powers of large governments, but it is one that should be considered as providing an approach to viewing the neglected role of the consumer in the economic system.

In the following sections, the concept of consumer sovereignty is reviewed first by considering a definition and then examining its role and importance in the economic system. The perspective is not restricted to that of the economist, although economic literature is relied upon extensively. The reasons that the concept has been downplayed in examining how an economic system should function are reviewed. While the concept of consumer sovereignty is not perfect, it is useful for examining the lack of consumer input into the economic system. Several illustrations of government actions and policies are presented to emphasize how consumer interests are ignored, or subordinated to those of others, by the government through its involvement in the market system. A concluding section provides some observations on what is being done to counter the damage inflicted by government, and what can be done to strike a better balance in the economic system whereby consumer interests are represented. Throughout the paper, it is conceded that while the consumer should be sovereign, the extent of this sovereignty and the means of obtaining it are unlikely to be easily resolved.

DEFINING CONSUMER SOVEREIGNTY

A review of the literature does not disclose a definitive definition of "consumer sovereignty." Hutt, who has been credited with coining the term made the distinction between consumers and producers. He clearly stated that consumers direct or command the producers, and that producers obey these instructions (1936, p. 257). Under consumer sovereignty, consumers make their own choices and are free to follow their personal tastes and inclinations independently of the tastes and inclinations of other consumers (Scitovsky, 1976, p. 7). Rothenberg viewed consumer sovereignty as existing in two senses: descriptive and normative (1962, p. 269). In the descriptive sense, a usual definition centred around the idea that consumers dictate the type, quality, and quantity of goods and services to be provided by an economic system. Consumers are the ultimate rulers of economic life through their control of the market. It is the performance of consumers, as shown by the ways in which they spend their money, that determines what goods and services are supplied, and which firms will be successful.

In a normative sense, the efficiency of an economy would be evaluated in terms of the extent to which markets respond to consumer demand and fulfil the wants of the consumers. According to Lerner, consumer sovereignty is the "ideal output" and is associated with democracy, freedom, and efficiency (1972, p. 258). Rothenberg says that the optimality of performance consists of maximizing consumer utilities subject to constraints of available resources and techniques (1962, p. 270).

Consumer sovereignty as an ideal is often discussed in conjunction with words such as democracy, freedom, and efficiency. Pommerehne defined consumer sovereignty as a process of choice in which the choice is free, informed so that the act of choice is meaningful, personal in that it is made by and not for people, and responsible in that the choosers must be aware of the consequences of their choice (1980, p. 539). Rothenberg discussed freedom of choice as a procedure of allowing consumers to use their purchasing power to make whatever voluntary trades they wished on a market. But he pointed out that freedom of choice could exist without consumer sovereignty. A central authority might provide and distribute commodities on the basis of what it discovered consumer tastes to be. The commodities would be distributed by means of market choice. He concluded that optimal, pure competition requires both consumer sovereignty and freedom of choice (1962, p. 271).

Hutt compared the ideal of consumer sovereignty to the ideal of representative government, or democracy. He stated that "at least the same measure of social validity could be claimed for consumers' sovereignty . . ., as could be claimed for a decision by ballot on the assumption of similar rationality on the part of voters in an election and consumers in the market place" (1936, p. 262).

Furstenberg and Spulber (1973, pp. 369–371) tied the terms "democracy, freedom, and efficiency" together by proposing a list of the least restrictive political and economic prerequisites that must be met for a system to be based on consumer sovereignty. There must be a constitutional provision that allows for the maximum freedom of choice consistent with the distributional preferences of a majority of the citizenry, and that makes possible pure competition in the political markets. That is, the entry into politics and political advocacy must be free, but citizenry need not be perfectly informed. The economic prerequisites were: every buyer and seller must be free to contract as he or she chooses for those commodities that can be marketed efficiently; all private markets must be purely competitive; and while the government must be organized to provide for the satisfaction of some wants, it must realize that when it errs, it must be willing to change its scope and methods if its activities are to remain in accordance with consumer sovereignty.

The essential characteristics of a definition are, therefore:

1) Consumers, not producers or governments, dictate the type, quality, and quantity of goods and services to be provided.

2) Elements of democracy are present, including the idea of voting through purchase decisions and that these decisions are made based upon the preferences of a majority.

3) Consumers are free to make their own choices and are not unduly influenced by producers or governments.

4) An economic system operates more efficiently when consumers determine production.

As can be seen, the concept is imperfectly defined as its objective could be considered impossible and its realization in the market far from perfect. Government, or the state, has become involved and is making many decisions that should be made by consumers. As Baumol said, consumers should be protected from those who are convinced that they know better than consumers what is really the best for them (1962, pp. 288–290). The following section on the role and importance of consumer sovereignty reinforces this discussion of a definition.

THE ROLE AND IMPORTANCE OF THE CONSUMER SOVEREIGNTY CONCEPT

Consumer sovereignty is a fundamental element of any market system as it is a manifestation of economic freedom. The concept that the consumer dominates was mentioned by Adam Smith.

> Consumption is the sole end and purpose of all production; and the interest of the producer ought to be attended to, only so far as it may be necessary for promoting that of the consumer. The maxim is so perfectly self-evident, that it would be absurd to attempt to prove it. But in the mercantile system, the interest of the consumer is almost constantly sacrificed to that of the producer; and it seems to consider production, and not consumption, as the ultimate end and object of all industry and commerce (1910, 4(8), p. 660).

Von Mises also emphasizes this point:

> The direction of all economic affairs is in the market society a task of the entrepreneurs. Theirs is the control of production. They are at the helm and steer the ship. A superficial observer would believe that they are supreme. But they are not. They are bound to obey unconditionally the captain's orders. The captain is the consumer. Neither the entrepreneurs nor the farmers nor the capitalists determine what has to be produced. The consumers do that. If a businessman does not strictly obey the orders of the public as they are conveyed to him by the structure of market prices, he suffers losses, he goes bankrupt, and is thus removed from his eminent position at the helm. Other men who did better in satisfying the demand of the consumers replace him (1949, p. 270).

The idea that the consumer is sovereign is mentioned by Drucker:

> It is the customer who determines what a business is. For it is the customer, and he alone, who through being willing to pay for a good or for a service, converts economic resources into wealth, things into goods. What the business thinks it produces is not of first importance—especially not to the future of the business and to its success. What the customer thinks he is buying, what he considers `value', is decisive—it determines what a business is, what it produces and whether it will prosper.
>
> The customer is the foundation of a business and keeps it in existence. He alone gives employment. And it is to supply the customer that society entrusts wealth-producing resources to the business enterprises (1968, pp. 52–53).

Despite the strength of these expressions on the importance of the consumer, the role of the consumer in the marketplace appears to be secondary. Hutt claims that some writers have endeavoured to represent consumers' interests as subsidiary. Modern economics has taught that citizens are first of all producers and only secondarily consumers. Following that reasoning, the progress in consumption depends upon the advance in production, and it is incorrect to subordinate the welfare of the producer to the alleged interests of the consumer. Hutt opposed this teaching and stated that he believed "that the achievements of the productive system can be measured only in terms of the extent to which they represent a response to consumers' will" (1936, p. 258).

The distinction between consumer and producer (any business enterprise, e.g., a manufacturer, and also farmers) mentioned in the definition is an important one to make. It is argued that consumers have relinquished their sovereignty to producers. Producers and consumers may have conflicting interests and the producers' notions of what satisfies consumers may be influenced by what satisfies them as producers. As a result, consumers become impotent as influencers in the economic system (Scitovsky, 1976, p. 273).

It is important in today's economy to make the distinction, as it places a perspective on the performance of the business system that has been ignored. Naturally, evaluating economic performance from a consumer perspective will be disturbing to the established producer interests and to established government policies and programs. But to impede consumer interests is to put short-run, sectional interests before the long-run, general interest (Fulop, 1967, p. 12). This expression of consumerism should not be viewed as adversarial, nor be avoided. It should be encouraged and welcomed by business and governments as restoring a balance in how the economic system is evaluated. It may even be doing business and the government a good turn by forcing both to be more responsive to changing marketplaces.

The principle of consumer sovereignty is unlikely to be observed unless consumers have a freedom of choice and are actually allowed to register their preferences in a market. In this respect, consumer sovereignty is really a front for the individualistic ethic which holds that freedom is valuable in itself. If this ethic is accepted, one must accept the freedom to offer choices as well as the freedom to choose. Businesspersons often argue the former, but forget the latter. It might be argued that governments forget that consumers should have the freedom to choose.

In the 1980's, business spokespersons, and a number of government representatives, advocated a lessening of regulation and a return of market discipline to the economy. They argued for less government involvement and greater economic freedom for business corporations. Little, if any, mention was made of consumer sovereignty as a fundamental element in any competitive market based system. If business, and governments, are advocating greater economic freedom for business, it is only logical that consumers should also be exposed to greater economic freedom and the advantages of a competitive marketplace.

Before discussing how consumers have been deprived of their sovereignty by governments, it is necessary to understand why the concept has not received prominent attention in examining how an economic system should function.

REASONS THE CONCEPT IS DOWNPLAYED

Much of the discussion of consumer sovereignty in the economic literature examines why it is no longer an appropriate concept, or why it doesn't work. Not all the literature has focused on drawbacks, and the counterarguments are presented. The main reason for this review is to indicate how the concept has been downplayed because of the tone of the literature. Hopefully readers will be convinced that even though the concept is not perfect, it still has some validity as an approach to understanding how the economic system might operate more effectively if governments are willing to enable consumers to be more adequately represented.

Possible Manipulation of Consumers

It is claimed that consumers are manipulated by persuasive, at times misleading, advertising. Rothenberg asked whether some taste changes were being induced by producer investment, how much tastes were affected, and whether the changes were important or not (1962, p. 279). Vance Packard (1957) in *The Hidden Persuaders* wrote about consumers being manipulated to purchase goods appealing to some latent needs of which they were unaware: advertisers persuaded consumers, who remained helpless to resist. Scitovsky said that since beliefs could be controlled, consumer sovereignty was not a good standard by which to judge economic performance (1962, p. 264).

It is also argued that as a small number of large firms dominate the market for some goods and services, consumers are being forced to purchase what producers provide. Consumer preferences are manipulated by large corporations in which market power has become concentrated (Baran, 1972; Galbraith, 1971). The theme, explicit or implicit, of Galbraith's *The Affluent Society* (1969) and *The New Industrial State* (1971) is the surrender of the sovereignty of the individual to the producer; in other words, consumer sovereignty has been superseded by producer sovereignty (1970). Mass production requires that consumers purchase the same products, reducing choice for differing or individual tastes—that is, output determines wants when it should be the other way round. Due to large investments, producers cannot take the chance of being wrong, and therefore control the consumer to reduce risk. Consumers become the managed element in the economic system, with purchases planned by those who supply goods and services, and by the government.

It is generally agreed that if consumers are so ignorant, if their preferences so fickle that they can be swayed easily through advertising and, if there is no way to validate advertising claims, then consumer sovereignty lacks a foundation and loses its normative significance (Furstenberg and Spulber, 1973, p. 372, footnote). There are counterarguments, however, to this. Lerner claims that the degree to which consumers are being manipulated by advertising is exaggerated and that there have been unreasonable claims of consumers being "duped, manipulated, and brainwashed into buying what industry wants to sell" (1972, p. 260). According to Bauer, as advertisers became more skilful in the techniques of persuasion, so did consumers in their ability too resist. He claimed that consumers could not be manipulated unconsciously by such persuasive techniques as subliminal advertising (1958, pp. 105–110).

Problems of Evaluation

In product development, there may be a difference between what consumers think the alternatives are and what producers think they are, meaning that the actual market choices may not reveal what consumers really want (Rothenberg, 1962, p. 278). Competing brands are introduced with negligible differences, leading to wasteful market segmentation. The introduction of superfluous differences merely encourages planned obsolescence (Fulop, 1967, p. 62). Fulop also claimed that it would be easier to accept the concept of consumer sovereignty if all goods were produced to order, but that this is more difficult when most goods are produced in anticipation of consumers' demands. She countered by saying that producers whose anticipations are correct earn more, and if wrong, they have to change their plans. Fulop therefore argued that production is still controlled by demand, or anticipated demand (1967, p. 11). It could also be argued that consumers do express their choices through marketing research in which such techniques as attitude studies, test markets, focus groups, and advisory panels assist producers to ascertain what consumers want. Further proof that the consumer still has some voice, and sovereignty, is provided by product failures in the marketplace.

Because of the complexity of products, it is difficult for consumers to choose with certainty and competence—in other words, consumers may not be competent to decide what is best. Fulop claimed that the marketplace contains not only a wide variety of goods, but that the technological complexity of many goods and services make it impossible for consumers to exercise rational judgment or choice (1967, p. 12).

In addition, there is no market to evaluate goods provided by the public sector, such as education, health, roads, clean air, and recreation areas. The provision of free goods or goods at subsidized prices does not relate to market supply and demand. In fact, the free market cannot produce the range of commodities that are socially desirable (Harris, 1978, pp. 300–303). This latter point relates to the main thesis of the chapter, which argues that government involvement has been damaging to consumer interests.

Consumerism and Values

Lerner claims that some of the criticism of consumer sovereignty relates to the antagonism to materialism, selfishness, greed, and the destruction of mankind's natural virtue (1972, p. 260). It is an expression of individualism as opposed to collectivism. There is no doubt that the concept concentrates on the individual instead of society as a whole and largely ignores the higher purposes to which the narrow interest of individual should be subservient (1972, p. 263). But this is true of any economic system based upon individualism and competitive markets. The assumption is that individual decision making is preferable to centralized, unitary decision making. If individualism and self-interest are acceptable as motivators in a business system, it seems logical that they should also be motivators for consumers.

Other related issues are consumer tastes, inequity of income, and the impact of values. Harris asked, "Which wants are to be satisfied?, that is, are all consumers to be treated equally?" A problem posed by these questions is defining the relevancy of tastes. That is, are all tastes correct, or should more preference be given to some? (1978, p. 300). According to Rothenberg, it is not obvious which tastes are the relevant ones to consult as it is difficult to ascertain true preferences (1962, pp. 270–276).

Another issue confusing consumer sovereignty is that of inequality of income. Lerner says that some economists are concerned that the unimportant desires of the rich will have priority over the essential needs of the poor (1972, p. 261). Harris points out that in the voting process the rich have greater power as a result of inequalities in the distribution of income (1978, p. 300). Lerner's counter arguments are that it should be important to low income groups that the goods they require are being provided in an efficient way to satisfy their wants. He believes the problem of inequality of incomes is not the issue, and economists should be more concerned with the growth of productivity and full employment than with the redistribution of income (1972, p. 263).

Finally, the issue of values is of concern to many economists, who according to Lerner, want scholars to limit themselves to propositions completely free from any moral or ethical content (1972, p. 263). Rothenberg claimed that consumer sovereignty was a patchwork of values and therefore meant different things to different people (1962, p. 276). There is no doubt value judgments are involved, but some such judgments are involved when producers or governments make decisions relating to the availability and pricing of goods on the market. Value judgments cannot be avoided.

Imperfect Concept

Admittedly there are drawbacks to the concept of consumer sovereignty, as there are to other economic concepts such as perfect competition and economic freedom. Two quotations are appropriate conclusions to this section. Lerner admits that there may be reasons to downplay consumer sovereignty, but that we should, however, repair it.

> The most legitimate reason for playing down the importance of consumer sovereignty is to be found in the actual deviations of prices from marginal costs where, for political, sentimental, or bureaucratic reasons, the market mechanism is not being applied, or where appropriate technology or legal arrangements have not been worked out. Here the motto must be to try and try again to correct the distortions and to develop the technical and legal mechanisms required (1972, p. 260).

Baumol's summary of several papers on consumer sovereignty is also appropriate here:

> To summarize, there is no question that the notion of consumers' sovereignty is crude and imperfect. It is equally clear that if a group of consumers is left to fend for itself in a completely unregulated market and the government avoids intervention at all costs, those consumers are likely to very poorly served. But these caveats are insufficient grounds for us to give up the very important, if a bit charmingly old-fashioned, value judgement that the purpose of the economy is to serve the individuals who compose it, and that it is they (and not just the highbrows) who are often the best judges of their own ultimate desires. (1962, p. 290).

The conditions of consumer sovereignty are seldom fulfilled in the marketplace, as buyers face high information costs, offensive and often misleading advertising, and shoddy and unsafe goods. Despite its drawbacks, the concept of consumer sovereignty should be used as an approach to better understanding an economic system that is supposedly largely based on a market.

ONE VIEW OF THE CONSUMER'S ROLE

The role of the consumer in the marketplace has not been sufficiently emphasized. A reason for this is that consumers have been blocked out of the market system by business practices and government initiatives. Both business and government have prevented a market economy from functioning in the interests of consumers.

This phenomenon can be illustrated by using Danielsson's social-economic political model. This model (Figure 17-1, Diagram #1) provides some insight into the role of consumers in the system in which the corporation interrelates with its environment. The elements represented in the model are grouped into four subsystems: consumers, the users of goods and services; capitalists, those who control the means of production; labourers, the workers; and the state or government, the bureaucracy entrusted with the legislative, executive, and judicial functions. Danielsson uses the model to illustrate significant confrontations and alliances to the interrelationships between business and society.

In the early period of industrialism, capitalists had supremacy and dominated the means of production and the state, as indicated in Diagram #2. Ownership entitled the owner to leadership, the right to direct and dismiss employees, and allowed for the maximizing of profit while minimizing the remuneration of employees. An alternative for this configuration was provided by Marxist socialism (Diagram #3), which maintained that workers or labour should be protected against the owners' despotism and that workers have some rights to influence working conditions and to execute some control over their superiors and leaders. This configuration never was operationalized at a national level but did lead to the controlled market economy configuration (Diagram #4).

In Danielsson's controlled market economy configuration, government derived its power from the majority of the governed, that is, the workers. Legislation was passed protecting the rights of workers, legalizing unions, controlling working conditions, and specifying minimum wages. The market economy system allowed for buyers, that is, consumers' preferences, to be supreme as long as few market imperfections existed and reasonably free competition prevailed. Consumers accepted this symbiosis with capitalists as it served them well, improving the choice and availability of goods and services.

From a consumer perspective, the controlled market economy configuration had some drawbacks. The market imperfections became greater and competition was reduced. Persuasive, and maybe misleading, advertising manipulated consumers. Mass production required that consumers purchase the same products, reducing choice for differing or individual tastes. Product safety and quality became issues, and business was accused of promoting planned obsolescence. Increasing numbers of markets became dominated by one, or a few, large business corporations. The outcome was the consumerism movement of the 1960's and the consumer legislation passed in the 1970's.

Instead of being aligned with capitalists, consumers, in effect, aligned themselves with government, or the state (Diagram #5). At the same time, Danielsson argued that labourers were aligning themselves with capitalists through various forms of industrial democracy and participative management. From the perspective of consumer sovereignty, Danielsson's models illustrates two problems. Consumer sovereignty was diminished in the capitalist/consumer alliance, and it was also being diminished in the state/consumer alliance intended to protect the consumer from the imperfections of the market system. Each of problems will be discussed.

Consumers yielded their dominance over the market system first to merchants and then to manufacturers. Merchants took the initiative by placing orders and specifying the nature and types of products. Manufacturers decided themselves what would be produced. The consumer's loss of sovereignty would not have been a problem as long as there was an adequate range of alternatives to choose from and if the consumer was able to distinguish good quality from bad. This condition became less fulfilled the more the economy and technology progressed, as illustrated by persuasive advertising and salesmanship, planned obsolescence, and mass marketing.

In the 1960's, the consumerism movement emerged. Governments passed a variety of consumer legislation more strictly regulating such things as conditions of sale, weights and measures, contents and labelling, truth in lending, and warranties and product liability. The emphasis in this type of legislation has been to maintain the operationality of the consumer sovereignty concept by ensuring an information flow to consumers so that they can make rational purchase decisions (Murray, 1973, p. 53). This trend is often mentioned at length in business and society textbooks, but there are several other dimensions of government activity prior to and since 1960 which have not been in the consumer's best interests, and which are discussed in the following section.

GOVERNMENT INVOLVEMENT AND CONSUMER SOVEREIGNTY

The prerequisites of consumer sovereignty are seldom if ever met in the marketplace. The natural recourse is to some form of government involvement as an alternative where governments would exercise varying degrees of influence not legitimated by consumer sovereignty. In other words, the problem has been the neglect of consumer interests by governments, despite some legislative initiatives.

Figure 17-1 Danielsson's "Social-Economic Political Model"

Diagram #1 *A Complete Social-Economic Political Model*

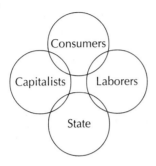

Diagram #2 *The Classical Owner-Dominated Configuration*

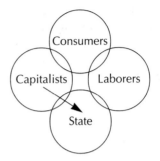

Diagram #3 *The Marxist Configuration*

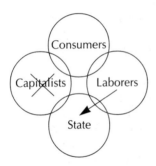

Diagram #4 *The Controlled Market Economy Configuration*

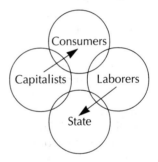

Diagram #5 *A New Scenario?*

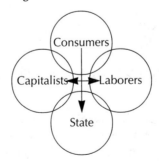

SOURCE: Danielsson, Christer. Business and Politics: Toward a theory beyond capitalism, Plato, and Marx. Copyright © 1979 by The Regents of the University of California. Reprinted from the *California Management Review*, Vol. 21, No. 3. By permission of the Regents.

The consumerism movement emerged in 1960. Since then, governments have passed a variety of consumer legislation more strictly regulating such things as conditions of sale, weights and measures, contents and labelling, truth in lending, and warranties and product liability. It is important to recognize the emphasis in this legislation:

> The overall emphasis of the federal legislation has been to maintain the operationality of the consumer sovereignty assumption by maintaining information flows to the consumer. The thrust of the legislation has been to require disclosure of accurate and truthful information to the consumer so that he can make rational purchase decisions (Murray, 1973, p.55)

However, this type of legislation has not done enough to promote the application of consumer sovereignty, or to offset the damage done by several anti-consumer programs and policies that have been implemented where the impact on consumer welfare has been a secondary consideration. The following are examples of public policies and initiations that have not been in the best interests of consumers.

Producer Oriented Programs   Producers have had substantial influence with governments. Manufacturers have been able to obtain tariff or import quota protection for whole industries; for example, for textiles and shoes in Canada. The agricultural sector in many countries has been able to obtain protection and subsidization from governments. In Canada, as elsewhere, producer or supply marketing boards with control over some agricultural products have been mandated by government and are costly to consumers. This point has been summarized by Stanbury, Thompson, and Zumeta: ". . . much regulation is aimed at protecting and enhancing the position of producer groups at the expense of the unorganized, diffuse consumer groups" (1981, p. 88).

Regulation by Administrative Tribunals   Regulation of monopolies, such as utilities, has not been completely satisfactory from a consumer perspective. Although such tribunals are mandated by governments to protect the public interest, the consumer is often not involved to any extent. The formal hearing process and the cost of preparing and appearing before such tribunals discourages consumer input. Seldom are tribunal members appointed to represent consumer interests nor are mechanisms put in place to encourage consumer input.

Consumer Representation   Governments neglect, or do not appear to be sensitive to, consumer representation on governmental agencies, boards, or public enterprises. The trend in consultation often takes the form of corporatism, or tripartitism, with consumer interests seldom represented (Newman, 1981; Panitch, 1979; Rea and McLeod, 1976; Sexty, 1984, pp. 14–18). Business is often consulted extensively regarding legislation, but consumer input is token at best (Stanbury, 1977). In the United States and Canada, business interests have far more resources and can easily out-lobby underfunded and diffuse consumer interests.

Occupational Licensure and Professional Self-Regulation   Occupational licensure (Friedman, 1962, pp. 137–160) and professional self-regulation (Garvin, 1983; Gupta and Lad, 1983) has often been detrimental to consumer interests. Government regulates licensure and endorses or mandates the self-regulation of many occupations and professions, from undertakers to lawyers, a process which inevitably protects the interest of the regulated group more so than it protects consumer interests, despite claims that consumers are being protected. The boards are seldom required to disclose their operations and are not publicly accountable.

Government Consumer Agencies   Despite the move to protect the consumer, governments themselves behave in ways not necessarily in the consumer's interests. In Canada and several of its provinces, the consumer ministry is often a junior one headed by inexperienced ministers who change frequently. Other ministers representing special groups, for example, agriculture, are more forceful in support of their constituencies. It appears that consumer ministers do not aggressively represent consumer views within government. In Canada, an added complication is the split jurisdiction over consumer matters between federal and provincial governments. Other difficulties include the lack of enforcement of legislation and inadequate penalties for offenders; reluctance to disclose product tests and warn of hazardous products; and civil servants who are isolated from the consumer perspective.

One should not be misled into thinking that consumer sovereignty has been substantially preserved by the numerous legislative initiatives on behalf of consumers. The existence of consumer legislation may have distracted consumers and policy makers from the real threats to consumer sovereignty. These include enhancement of producers at the expense of consumers; inadequate regulatory mechanisms; lack of consumer representation; self-regulating occupations; and ineffective government consumer agencies.

RESTORING CONSUMER SOVEREIGNTY

The question now is how to restore consumer sovereignty. Governments have restricted the choices available to consumers by forcing all consumers to buy products merely to benefit a particular industry or group of producers. A natural reaction would be to force some response from the private sector. Private business could establish consumer affairs departments, employ consumer ombudsmen, or appoint consumer representation on Boards of Directors and internal committees. In the private sector, consumers can take some comfort that business will respond as competition increases or as the importance of the consumer is recognized. Many of the recently implemented management approaches, like total quality management or the learning organization, place some emphasis on consumer satisfaction. But since public policy is a main hindrance to restoring consumer sovereignty, consumers will, unfortunately, have to call on governments to initiate changes and to take actions to ensure appropriate consideration of consumer interest.

Another question is how to get governments to be sensitive to consumer interests while at the same time taking into consideration other public interests. The issue might be viewed as one of restoring the balance, reducing past policies that favoured producers and business and focusing more on consumers' interests. In advocating this balance, it is not necessary to do everything to the sole benefit of consumers; national interest may require some anti-consumer policies (as government has what are perceived to be anti-business policies at times).

A start would be to ensure that there is a consumer presence throughout all government departments and agencies where matters affecting consumers are being considered. This calls for a stronger role for consumer affairs departments, including their active involvement in decision making in such departments as agriculture, finance, and industry and trade. Independent and well-financed consumer councils or research organizations should be established and sponsored by governments, as alternative sources of funding would be doubtful. Such councils should be mandated to watch over consumer interests and to speak up for consumers to government, to public enterprises, and to independent industry and commerce. Consumer representation throughout government agencies and boards would be called for and accomplished by the appointment of individuals who are knowledgeable of consumer interests or have been involved in some facet of consumerism.

A second possibility is to require government to provide estimates of the costs to consumers of all programs. This should be done especially where the costs are not a part of public accounts; for example, the costs to consumers of quotas on automobiles and the cost to consumers of marketing boards. The true cost of government intervention must be disclosed so that consumers, or taxpayers, will be more conscious of them. Some work is being done in this area by research agencies and academics; for example, through the many calculations of the cost of marketing boards to Canadian consumers. An example of the cost to consumers is provided by U.S. policy to limit automobile imports between 1981 and 1985. It is estimated that the quotas transferred the equivalent of a subsidy worth $750 million a year from American consumers to Japanese car makers and $100 million a year to American car makers. A Federal Trade Commission study estimated that the quotas saved about 4600 jobs in the United States, each job annually costing $241 235. Knowing this type of information may encourage more citizens to question the desirability of such a policy and to force the government to consider alternative policies.

This form of accountability is now required of governments in order for consumers to appreciate the costs of governments interfering with consumer sovereignty. Techniques such as benefit-cost analysis are already available to perform this function. But it will take a very forthcoming government to admit openly what its policies cost consumers.

There have been some steps toward greater consumer sovereignty, as, for example, in the deregulation of the air transport industry. There is increasing questioning about the desirability of massive protection and subsidization of the agricultural sectors in many countries. However, more efforts to establish the legitimate position of consumers in the economy must be made and alternatives to existing policies and programs considered. Some aspects of free trade agreements also benefit consumers.

SUMMARY

In a market system, it is logical that consumers would be a stakeholder group of major influence. While other values associated with free enterprise, private property, individualism, competition, and profits have been emphasized, the value associated with consumer influence in the system receives little attention. This value should also be a driving force of the market system.

The chapter defines consumer sovereignty and concludes that a definition includes characteristics as follows: consumers dictate the goods and services to be provided; democracy is involved, as consumers vote with dollars; there should be freedom of choice; and an economic system operates more efficiently when consumers determine production. Some economists, for example, Smith, Von Mises and Drucker, have recognized consumer sovereignty, but for the most part the concept is downplayed or ignored. The reasons for this are varied but include the alleged manipulation of consumers that reduces sovereignty, the difficulty consumers have in evaluating goods and services, and an association of some undesirable values—greed, materialism, and selfishness—with the concept.

The role of consumers in various social-economic systems was discussed. Consumers had a disadvantaged role, and the alliance with government has not been to their benefit. In part, it is argued that governments have been the main reason for the neglect of the consumer and the concept of consumer sovereignty.

Many business enterprises appear committed to restoring consumers to the prominent stakeholder position they should have in a business enterprise system. Unfortunately, another stakeholder, government, continues to hamper the process.

REFERENCES

Baran, Paul. (1957). *The Political Economy of Growth*. New York: Monthly Review Press (Foreward to 1962 printing, xii-xviii), and in Elzinga, Kenneth G. (1972). *Economics: A Reader*. New York: Harper and Row, pp. 42–45.

Bauer, Raymond. (1958, September-October). Limits of persuasion. *Harvard Business Review*, 36, pp. 105–110.

Baumol, William J. (1962). The doctrine of consumer sovereignty—Discussion. *The American Economic Review*, 52(2), pp. 288–290.

Danielsson, Christer. (1979). Business and politics: Toward a theory beyond capitalism, Plato, and Marx. *California Management Review*, 21(3), pp. 17–25.

Drucker, Peter F. (1968). *The Practice of Management* (paperback edition). London: Pan Books.

Friedman, Milton. (1962) *Capitalism and Freedom*. Chicago: The University of Chicago Press.

Fulop, Christina. (1967). *Consumers in the Market: A Study in Choice, Competition and Sovereignty*. London: The Institute of Economic Affairs.

Furstenberg, George M. and Nicolas Spulber. (1973). Is there an economic system based on sovereignty of each consumer? *Zeitscrift Fur nationalokonomie*, 33 (3–4), pp. 361–374.

Galbraith, John Kenneth. (1969). *The Affluent Society*, 2nd. edition revised. Boston: Houghton Mifflin Company.

Galbraith, John Kenneth. (1970, May). Economics as a system of belief. *American Economic Review* (papers and proceedings), pp. 469–484.

Galbraith, John Kenneth. (1971 & 1967). *The New Industrial State* (2nd edition, revised). Boston: Houghton Mifflin Company.

Garvin, David A. (1983). Can industry self-regulation work? *California Management Review*, 25(4), pp. 37–51.

Gupta, Anil K. and Lawrence J. Lad. (1983). Industry self-regulation: An economic, organizational, and political analysis. *Academy of Management Review*, 8(3), pp. 416–425.

Harris, C.P. (1978). What Price Consumerism? *European Journal of Marketing*, 12(4), pp. 299–305.

Hutt, W.H. (1936). *Economists and the Public: A Study of Competition and Opinion*. London: Jonathan Cape.

Lerner, Abba P. (1972, May). The economics and politics of consumer sovereignty. *American Economic Review*, 62(2), pp. 258–266.

Murray, Barbara B. (Ed.) pp: (1973). *Consumerism: The Eternal Triangle—Business, Government, and Consumers*. Pacific Palisades, California: Goodyear Publishing Company.

Newman, Otto. (1981). *The Challenge of Corporatism*. London: MacMillan.

Packard, Vance. (1957). *The Hidden Persuaders*. New York: David McKay.

Panitch, Leo. (1979, Spring). Corporatism in Canada. *Studies in Political Economy*, pp. 43–92.

Pommerehne, Werner W. (1980, October). Fiscal illusion and consumer sovereignty: An exploratory study. *Advances in Consumer Research Proceedings*, Eleventh Annual Conference, 8, pp. 539–544.

Rea, K.J. and J.T. McLeod, (Eds.). (1976). *Business and Government in Canada: Selected Readings*, 2nd edition. Toronto: Methuen.

Rothenberg, Jerome. (1962). Consumer's sovereignty revisited and the hospitability of freedom of choice. *American Economic Review*, 52(2), pp. 269–283.

Scitovsky, Tibor. (1962). On the principle of consumers' sovereignty. *American Economic Review*, 52(2), pp. 262–268.

Scitovsky, Tibor. (1976). *The Joyless Society*. New York: Oxford University Press.

Sexty, Robert W. (1984, June 4). The ideology of Canadian business and the prevalence of public enterprise. Paper presented to the Canadian American Business Development Forum "Business in the Canadian Environment," Michigan State University, East Lansing, Michigan.

Smith, Adam. (1910 printing). *The Wealth of Nations*. Edinburgh: J.M. Dent and Son Ltd.

Stanbury, W.T. (1977). *Business Interests and the Reform of Canadian Competition Policy*, 1971–1975. Toronto: Carswell/Methuen.

Stanbury, W.T., Fred Thompson, and William M. Zumeta. (1981). Regulatory reform: American experience and Canadian prospects. *Journal of Contemporary Business*, 10(4), pp. 81–96.

Von Mises, Ludwig. (1949). *Human Action: A Treatise on Economics*. New Haven: Yale University Press, pp. 270–273.

THE NATURAL ENVIRONMENT

INTRODUCTION

There is increasing concern for the natural environment in Canada. The need for preserving and protecting the environment is now so compelling that there is no question of its relevance for business — the natural environment is an issue that must be addressed.

Concern for the environment has been intensified by disasters such as Chernobyl, Three Mile Island, the Love Canal, and the *Exxon Valdez*, but the depletion of the ozone layer, the greenhouse effect, acid rain, deforestation, pollution, energy depletion, and waste management are steadfast reminders of how compelling an issue our natural environment is.

The word "green" is used extensively in the context of environmental issues relating to business. For example, there is green marketing, green accounting, and there are even green audits. However, as Exhibit 18-1 points out, the term may now be overused and not particularly meaningful.

Many believe that capitalism, or the market system, and environmentalism are incompatible; others do not see a conflict (Block, 1990). A beginning section

Exhibit 18-1

It's a "Green" World

The Globe and Mail (Kesterton, 1991) identified the following environmentally oriented books that used "green" in their titles:

- *Our Green and Living World*
- *Green Goals and Greenbacks*
- *Seeing Green* (politics)
- *Green Rage* (radical environmentalism)
- *Green Justice: The Environment and the Courts*
- *Green Business: Hope or Hoax*
- *Going Green* (for children)
- *Tuning the Green Machine*
- *Keep Earth Clean, Blue and Green*
- *The Green Consumer*
- *Green Lifestyle Guide*
- *Green Parenting*

What does the use of "green" mean? Obviously, it refers to issues related to the environment, and it is used as a noun, adjective, or verb. No one has defined the term clearly, but some criteria should be considered prior to using it. These criteria include the health of humans or animals; not damaging the biophysical environment; not consuming disappropriate amounts of energy or resources; not causing excessive amounts of unusable wastes; and not endangering plant or animal species.

It is doubtful that most uses of "green" strictly meet these criteria. The word appears to be used rather casually.

---

of this chapter establishes what environmental issues are for the corporation and its stakeholders and discusses how business enterprises approach the issue, and how they might in the future. The remainder of the chapter covers key considerations relating to the functioning of business as it relates to the environment.

BUSINESS, ITS STAKEHOLDERS, AND THE NATURAL ENVIRONMENT

The concern for the environment is a growing but not entirely recent is phenomenon. Over 20 years ago, Peter Drucker stated:

> Everybody today is 'for the environment.' Laws and agencies designed to protect it multiply at all levels of government. Big corporations take full-colour ads to explain how they're cleaning up, or at least trying to. Even you as a private citizen probably make some conscientious effort to curb pollution (1972).

EXHIBIT 18-2

Principal Stakeholders and Issues Involved in Business's Response to the Environment

Stakeholder	*Issues from Management's Perspective*
Shareholders	• Investment decisions influenced by the handling of the environment • Risk associated with environment problems or disasters • Establishment of "green" investment criteria
Directors	• Liability for environmental contamination • Challenge of motivating management to address the issue
Employees	• Workplace exposures to environmental problems, e.g., indoor air pollution • Refusal to perform tasks causing environmental problems • Whistle-blowing on employer
Customers/Consumers	• Inconsistencies between environmentalism and consumption (save the planet verses "shop 'till we drop") • Use of environmentally unfriendly products, e.g., paper verses cloth diapers • Waste management • Willingness to accept less "convenient" goods • Willingness to pay higher prices for environmentally friendly products if necessary • The viability of "green" products
Lenders/Creditors	• Need to assess increased financial risk
Suppliers	• Must respond to demands for more environmentally friendly products • Assessing most appropriate transportation and packaging of supplies
Service Professionals	• Familiarity with laws and regulations • Design of appropriate audits • Identification of full environmental cost accounting methods
Competitors	• Consequence of competitive edge being obtained by making products more environmentally friendly
Interest Groups	• How to respond to groups based upon environmental concerns
Media	• How to respond to media coverage of environmental problems
Government	• Complying with laws and regulations • Influencing public policy

---

He predicted the crusade would likely run off the tracks. The 1990's appear to confirm his view.

Environmental issues confront virtually all aspects of the corporation, from the input of resources to the manufacturing process and the workplace conditions through to the way products are packaged and sold. Another approach to the pervasiveness of the environmental issue is given in Exhibit 18-2.

Managers must cope with planning, organizing, leading, and controlling all the aspects of the environmental issue. The issues identified in Exhibit 18-2 are diverse, thus a comprehensive environmental management approach is necessary. The following section identifies how business enterprises deal with the environment.

STRATEGIES FOR THE ENVIRONMENT AND SUSTAINABLE DEVELOPMENT

Business takes a variety of approaches to address the environment. Before examining potential and actual strategies, two concepts need to be defined—the environmental ethic and sustainable development.

The Environmental Ethic

As mentioned, concern for the environment has existed for some time, and an environmental ethic is evolving from this focus on ecology. It is a set of values or principles about practices relating to the environment. Society and many businesspersons now have some sense of obligation or moral responsibility to the environment which is expressed in different ways. For a business enterprise, the values or principles include: new business development needs to take account of the environment from the design stage through to ultimate disposal; environmental management should be the responsibility of staff at all levels as an integral part of their job; environmental performance should be built into the reward structure of the organization; product and process responsibility should be from cradle to the grave; and agreed upon values and beliefs should be used as the guiding principles for conducting all business (Hutchinson, 1992, p. 58).

Some Canadians and many business enterprises are committed to the three "Rs" of environmental protection—reducing, reusing, and recycling. There are two more "Rs"—refuse and reject—they suggest that society should refuse to use products or engage in activities harmful to the ecology and reject the products that do not respect the environment.

Sustainable Development

The concept of "sustainable development" has received attention from governments, international agencies, and some business quarters. Sustainable development is defined as development ensuring that the use of resources and the impact on the environment today does not damage prospects for the use of resources or the environment by future generations. This was a theme in the United Nations World Commission on Environment and Development (1987) report which concluded that not only is continued economic growth possible, it is necessary to reduce poverty and to sustain future generations. Sustainable development has been endorsed by many businesspersons as an approach that allows environmental and economic concerns to coincide and makes economic progress possible.

For business, sustainable development means "adopting business strategies and activities that meet the needs of the enterprise and its stakeholders today while protecting, sustaining, and enhancing the human and natural resources that will be needed in the future" (*Business Strategy for Sustainable Development*, 1992, p. 11). This definition was developed by the International Institute for Sustainable Development (IISD), a non-profit private corporation established and supported by the governments of Canada and Manitoba to promote sustainable development in government, business, and individual decision making. This definition captures the sense of the concept as presented in the World Commission's report, but focuses on areas of specific interest and concern to business. It recognizes that economic development must meet the needs of the business enterprise and its stakeholders. The definition also highlights the dependence of the enterprise's economic activities on human and natural resources as well as to physical and financial capital.

The IISD also conducts research on environment and sustainable development strategies adopted by business enterprises.

Environment and Sustainable Development Strategies

The IISD identifies four business enterprise strategies, fixing problems, compliance with laws and regulations, comprehensive environmental management, and sustainable development. The following four sections are reproduced from the IISD publication *Business Strategy for Sustainable Development*, (1992, pp. 21–24).

Fixing Problems

This strategy entails management's awareness of the potential effect that the enterprise's activities have on the environment, and a decision (voluntary or otherwise) to do something about it. Management concerns focus on resolving environmental problems and implementing "damage control" strategies as problems occur. Problems might involve non-compliance with regulations and/or corporate policies, and addressing significant issues raised by stakeholders or environmental groups.

Business enterprises develop contingency plans to deal with potential environmental problems. The strategy focuses on products and problems. Corporate reporting, if any, is primarily financial in nature, dealing only with disclosing the costs of resolving environmental problems and any related liabilities, where they are probable and can be estimated.

Research suggests that many business enterprises in the industrialized world have adopted this strategy. Increasing recognition of the competitive advantages, as well as growing pressure from regulators, consumers, environmental groups, and others will likely force a significant number of these entities to adopt more comprehensive strategies within the next few years.

Compliance with Laws and Regulations

Concern about exposure to lawsuits and prosecution has motivated many directors and senior executives to adopt strategies of compliance. This is particularly common in countries with a considerable body of environmental legislation and regulation. However, the existence of the legislation does not necessarily lead to this strategy. Some enterprises continue to ignore legislative and regulatory requirements and the effect their activities have on the environment. Those companies that do follow policies of compliance establish programs and organizational structures to implement and monitor their compliance with the legislation and regulations. More progressive companies establish their own environmental policies, which may go beyond the requirements imposed by governments.

These companies also address the organizational issues that arise when ensuring compliance with laws and regulations. Many companies establish separate departments with corporate executives to coordinate and direct their compliance activity. Following a strategy of compliance usually produces significantly improved reporting activities compared to those found under a strategy of fixing problems. Corporate executives responsible for monitoring compliance establish internal newsletters and other forms of internal communication to heighten their employees' awareness of environmental legislation and regulation. These companies prepare and distribute compliance policies and manuals. Increasing numbers of them commission environmental audits to help monitor their compliance. Their external communication programs provide information on how the enterprise is complying with legislative requirements.

Many companies in the industrialized world follow this strategy. Most find it a considerable challenge to co-ordinate and direct all the activities necessary to ensure that the enterprise complies with the burgeoning environmental legislation and regulation. However, in many countries, the cost of not complying with environmental legislation is severe, and can result in civil liability and criminal prosecution.

Comprehensive Environmental Management

Under this strategy, management seeks to gain a competitive advantage by taking an active stance on environmental issues. The focus on processes and systems-simple compliance with legislation and regulation is not sufficient. In these companies, everyone becomes involved in environmental management. Environmental issues are integrated into all aspects of corporate management. Environmental objectives are set for key operating activities; they are not left to just the "environmental services department."

These companies greatly expand their corporate reporting both internally and externally. They establish environmental policies and codes of conduct and distribute them to their various stakeholders. Unlike many public relations-oriented documents issued by companies that follow a strategy of compliance, these statements are more substantive in nature. They provide meaningful and measurable targets for corporate performance. Management also develops the monitoring and reporting systems necessary to determine whether the company's actual performance achieves the intended results. The scope of environmental assessments and audits is frequently expanded.

This strategy has been widely adopted within certain industries in some industrialized countries. The companies that have embraced this approach tend to be ones whose operations have a significant effect on the environment, such as in chemical or mining industries in some countries. Often, these companies have been subject to criticism and/or penalties in the past for poor environmental performance. However, public pressure on these companies often continues, and government and special interest groups enhance their monitoring of the industry. This perceived need for continued scrutiny and monitoring may indicate that companies in these industries have not fully implemented a comprehensive environmental strategy. An example of this strategy is suggested in Exhibit 18-3.

Sustainable Development

Businesses that follow this strategy integrate the concepts of sustainable development into their business strategies and environmental policies. Sustainable development is a natural extension of many corporate environmental policies. It requires that management consider the effect of its activities on the environment and on the long-term interests and needs of the stakeholders. Exhibit 18-4 presents a framework for integrating sustainable development in corporate management and reporting systems, a major component of this strategy.

These enterprises engage in a different type of dialogue and consultation with their various stakeholder groups. Their business strategies and activities are designed to balance the needs for financial returns with the needs of the environment and various stakeholder groups. Mechanisms such as advisory panels and committees are established to facilitate communication with stakeholders.

Exhibit 18-3

Developing an Environmental Business Strategy

The Canadian Chamber of Commerce studied several corporations reaping the benefits of environmental action (*Achieving Environmental Excellence*, 1990), and concluded that there were 10 steps to developing an environmental business strategy:

- *Develop an environmental policy* Environmental goals and objectives are identified in a brief policy document.
- *Appointment of an environmental champion and supporting team* An objective program requires support from the top level of the organization.
- *Conduct an environmental performance review* The review could be considered an audit and the exercise provides information on the status of the environment in the enterprise.
- *Prepare an environmental action plan* This plan outlines the specific tasks that must be completed and will indicate costs, time frames, and responsibilities to ensure completion.
- *Train and motivate staff* The staff must be informed about the environmental policy and action plan, and should be consulted in developing and updating them.
- *Allocate sufficient funds* There must be assurance that sufficient financial resources are available to implement the changes recommended in the action plan.
- *Conduct ongoing market research* Because environmental issues are constantly changing, it is necessary to conduct ongoing research to keep aware of developments.
- *Communicate endeavours and results* Other stakeholders should be informed of the enterprise's efforts in the environment.
- *Adopt a spirit of cooperation between interest groups* There should be spirit of cooperation among business, government, labour, non-profit organizations (including environmental groups), the public, and the academic community.
- *Take a long-term view* A long-term outlook is necessary in developing an environmental business strategy, as some investments do not produce immediate returns.

Another example of integrated environmental planing is provided in *Toward Proactive Corporate Management* (Howatson, 1990).

SOURCE: *Achieving Environmental Excellence: A Handbook for Canadian Business.* (1990). Ottawa: Canadian Chamber of Commerce, pp. 11–17.

Corporate reporting expands in relation to the needs of the various stakeholders. Companies that follow this strategy may prepare and distribute special reports to these groups, or may prepare general purpose reports for wider distribution. They may also engage independent auditors to attest to their report's accuracy and reliability.

The sustainable development strategy is an ideal one to work toward, and one that few business enterprises practice at this time. The remainder of the chapter examines a wide range of considerations that confront managers in their efforts to manage the environmental issue.

Exhibit 18-4

Framework on Managing for Sustainable Development

STAKEHOLDER ANALYSIS

- Have all parties been identified who are, or may be, affected environmentally by the business?
- Has a process been established to regularly consult with stakeholders? Is it operational?
- Is senior management in direct contact with key stakeholders? Does management receive regular reports on other stakeholder relations activities?
- Are the directors informed of the important issues?

POLICIES AND OBJECTIVES

- Is there a written policy on sustainable development?
- Has the policy been formally approved by the board of directors?
- Has senior management established measurable objectives based on the policies?
- Is there a formal process in place to monitor external developments?

OPERATIONAL PLANS

- Is there an operational plan, covering all locations and divisions of the business, designed to bring about the realization of the objectives?
- Does the plan provide for appropriate action for each of the following business functions:
  - strategic and business planning
  - marketing and sales
  - production
  - design, engineering, research and development?
- Are responsibilities clearly spelled out in the organization documentation and individual job descriptions?

CORPORATE CULTURE

- Has a comprehensive training programme on sustainable development/environmental management been designed and implemented for all levels of management and all employees?
- Is there an effective communications programme to reinforce the corporate commitment and training programme?
- Is there a programme in place to encourage employee support and initiatives with respect to sustainable development/environmental improvement?
- Do the recognition, reward, promotion and compensation systems support the firm's commitment to sustainable development and the environment?

MEASURES AND STANDARDS OF PERFORMANCE

- Have sustainable development or environmental criteria been developed, using external and internal measures, to monitor the firm's performance?

- Are the management information systems generating the necessary data to monitor environmental performance?

MANAGEMENT REPORTS

- Do senior management and board of directors receive regular reports on the firm's environmental performance?
- Are external reports on environmental/sustainable development performance provided to the firm's stakeholders?

MONITORING

- Are there processes and procedures to monitor progress internally, including an environmental audit programme?

SOURCE: *Business Strategy for Sustainable Development: Leadership and Accountability in the 90's.* (1992). Winnipeg, Manitoba: International Institute for Sustainable Development, p. 47.

CONSIDERATIONS IN MANAGING THE ENVIRONMENTAL ISSUE

In responding to concern for the natural environment, business enterprises and managers are confronted with several considerations or aspects of managing the issue, or in forming and implementing an appropriate strategy. This section explores these considerations separately. In reality, they are interrelated. The topics discussed also refer back to the environmental and sustainable development strategies previously identified. Considerations fall into different types of strategies but together represent items that managers must consider if they seek to operate with comprehensive environmental management or sustainable development strategies.

Organizational Structural Arrangements

According to Hooper and Roca, management positions and committees should be created to deal with the environment issue. Starting at the top with the Board of Directors, structural arrangements are put in place ensuring environmental matters are addressed, with some boards having environmental committees. It is key to have top management commitment so that there are practical principles to guide the firm's environmental efforts, to integrate environmental affairs with operations, and to encourage environmental professionals to meet mounting environmental requirements (Hooper and Rocca, 1991).

Some business enterprises are hiring senior managers and other staff to focus on environmental matters. Senior managers' positions carry titles such as vice-president, environment; environmental director; corporate manager of environmental affairs; and environmental coordinator. It is still not clear what impact these managers have in the enterprise (Lush, 1990). The cartoon "Back Bench" (The Globe and Mail) questioned the role of these managers when it suggested the following definitions:

- Environment Director: You get to water some of the plants.
- Senior Environment Director: You get to water all of the plants.
- Environment Specialist: You get to talk to the plants.

In addition to senior managers, there are numerous titles for staff with various specialities in the environment—for example, vegetation management biologist, hydrogeologist, and site remediation engineer. One of the challenges is to find persons with the appropriate environmental expertise and knowledge and adequate managerial capabilities, as a combination of managerial and technical expertise is necessary.

The issue of centralization versus decentralization of authority is also a challenge. In large, diversified corporations, it is necessary to have top management commitment, but at the same time environmental matters are usually addressed at the unit or divisional levels. Often committees are formed to provide interlocks between the top and bottom of the organization, and to coordinate efforts across functions or divisions. Such a coordinating environmental group forms policies, establishes standards, and carries out planning strategies.

Business enterprises can also hire environmental experts as consultants. Consulting firms are available to advise on matters such as the following: engineering, equipment design, legal matters, measurement instruments, auditing, risk, and waste disposal. No matter how it is accomplished, business enterprises must address environmental matters with some structural arrangement.

Stakeholder Consultation

Exhibit 18-2 emphasizes the extensive involvement of several stakeholders in the environment issue within the business enterprise. The following briefly outlines some aspects of stakeholder consultation.

Government   Business enterprises should engage in a dialogue with government agencies so that their interests are protected and to contribute to the resolution of environmental problems. Governments may directly regulate activities of the corporation or introduce policy changes through taxation rates, the elimination or establishment of subsidies, international trade agreements, or the creation of markets in tradeable pollution permits. Business enterprises must establish mechanisms so that they can "listen" to what government is considering, and mechanisms so that they can "talk" to government. Listening mechanisms include participation in trade associations; maintenance of public affairs or legal departments; or delegation of responsibility to corporate environmental staff or managers. The talking mechanisms include executive speech making; presentations to government hearings, commissions, or agencies; involvement in trade associations; membership in broad-based advocacy groups; and by hiring public affairs consulting firms (Howatson, 1990, p. 11).

Employees Employees must be kept informed of the enterprise's environmental policies, requirements, problems, and successes, and management should be listening to employees' concerns and ideas. A variety of mechanisms can be used to accomplish this, including articles in newsletters; seminars and discussion groups; internal distribution of annual reports, CEO speeches, and publications on the environment; and inclusion of discussion of environment-related topics at regular workplace meetings and in training sessions (Howatson, 1990, p. 12).

Investors Some shareholders have strong views on the environment and may be active in presenting them. There may be different motivations involved. Some shareholders are concerned with financial matters and expect a gain from their investment, while others base their views on moral or ethical grounds. Some fund managers and individual investors base decisions on "green screens"; that is, a set of criteria to factor the effects of environmental issues and a corporation's environmental stance into the valuation of the firm. According to a Conference Board of Canada study, "other things being equal, a corporation's proactive environmental management practices, communicated to the investment community, are likely to have a favourable effect on the corporation's value" (Howatson, 1990, p. 12).

Local Communities Communities where plants or facilities are located have a substantial stake in the corporation's actions or decisions. This is particularly the case in single-industry communities where employment, economic activity, and municipal taxation revenue are dependent on the corporation. In other communities, local citizens may fear company activities that may damage their health or local environment. It is important to maintain a dialogue between the company and the community to promote understanding and alleviate unwarranted fears. Examples of mechanisms that can be used to accomplish this dialogue include advisory panels, guided tours, and information in local newspapers (Howatson, 1990, pp. 12–13).

Consumers Consumers are pressuring business enterprises to consider environment matters in the production of goods and the provision of services. This influence is discussed in detail in the section titled "Green Marketing." Intermediate or industrial customers are also demanding that a firm's product meet set minimum environmental standards. Foreign customers, especially in the U.S. and Europe, demand certain requirements, like, for example, the removal of chlorine from pulp/bleached paper. Managers must monitor all customers to ascertain their views on the environment.

Environmental Interest Groups   Consultation may appear to be an inappropriate term to use with environmental interest groups. But business must establish contact with such groups and gain an understanding of their purpose and tactics. Dozens of these groups exist in Canada, such as, for example, Greenpeace Canada, Pollution Probe, Earth Day, Energy Probe, The Canadian Coalition on Acid Rain, World Wildlife Fund Canada, the Western Canada Wilderness Committee, and the Canadian Nature Federation. The activities, policies, and initiatives of these groups should be monitored to assess the potential impact on the enterprise. This monitoring function may be performed by the environmental affairs department, the managers responsible for environmental matters, or by consultants.

Environment groups are not always easy to deal with. They can be involved in protests, blockades, boycotts, and sometimes make use of annual shareholders' meetings as platforms for protest. Religious groups participate at meetings as representatives of church-held shares; for example, the Taskforce on Churches and Corporate Responsibility has demanded better environmental reporting from Noranda Forest Inc. Canadian environmental groups are also often a part of a global network of organizations. Protests about logging the Clayoquot Sound forests in British Columbia, as an example, are an allianced effort and have received impressive international attention. Interest groups will be discussed in more detail in Chapter 19.

Society at Large   Individuals in society are involved in the environmental management process: attitudes widely held in society influence a corporation's well-being. Perceptions formed through the media or through participation in environment groups raise public consciousness. Positive public perceptions about corporate environmental interactions are achieved through industry and corporate promotion of environment activities and philosophies through television and print advertising; inclusion of environmental sections in annual reports; the issuing of environmental progress reports; and direct communication with stakeholders (Howatson, 1990)

As identified in Table 18-2, other stakeholders have an interest in the corporation's treatment of the environment. This discussion has dealt with the predominant issues to illustrate the efforts necessary to consult with stakeholders.

Corporate Environmental Accountability

Many business enterprises are reporting on the effect of their operations on the environment and the initiatives undertaken to reduce adverse affects. The environment is a popular and desired topic in annual reports, giving enterprises and industry associations opportunities to advertize the actions they are taking to protect the environment. In November 1989, McDonald's placed full-page advertisements in major Canadian newspapers elaborating "Our Commitment to the Environment," and placed brochures on the topic in their restaurants.

Many enterprises have prepared environmental policy statements or codes. One such code is reproduced in Exhibit 18-5. The purpose of environmental codes is much the same as it is for codes of ethics: to increase awareness of the issue throughout the organization and to signal to other stakeholders that the enterprise is active in this area. Industry associations also develop codes such as that illustrated by the pulp and paper industry in Canada (Exhibit 18-6).

Governments have passed legislation such as the federal government's *Environmental Protection Act* and *Ontario's Environment Assessment Act* to protect the environment. It is not uncommon for the legislation to require an environmental audit be undertaken by enterprises or governments involved in environmentally sensitive projects. The U.S. Environmental Protection Agency defines such an audit as "any systematic documented, periodic, and objective review by a firm (or other regulated entity) of facility operations and practices related to meeting appropriate requirements."

Government legislation often stipulates that an environmental assessment document, or report, be submitted to the Department of the Environment for review, and approval. The report usually has to contain a description of the project, a list of reasons for the project, alternatives to the project, an outline of how the project and its alternatives will affect the environment directly or indirectly, an identification of the actions necessary to prevent those effects, and an evaluation of the advantages and disadvantages of the project to the environment and alternative ways to carry it out. The report is submitted for evaluation to an environmental assessment agency and is often followed by public hearings. Organizations are now familiar with the environmental process and incorporate it into their decision making. Enterprises also conduct audits and assessments even when not required by governments. Such audits are often of the whole organization and not restricted to particular projects or plants, and are designed to provide a "total picture" of the environmental circumstances of the enterprise.

Another form of accountability is the award programs administered by government agencies or private sector organizations. An example of the latter is "*The Financial Post* Environment Awards for Business," sponsored by the newspaper, The Royal Society of Canada, and Air Canada. The purpose of the awards is to identify, encourage and promote technology, design and management initiatives which have helped to protect and/or improve the environment. Exhibit 18-7 lists the award categories and recent winners.

Exhibit 18-5

Royal Bank Policy on the Environment

The Royal Bank of Canada believes that human welfare depends upon both sound economic growth and maintenance of a healthy environment, and recognizes that the two are inextricably interconnected. The Bank is therefore committed to managing its operations in such a way as to promote these twin aims. Our policies and business actions shall be so shaped as to promote environmental protection in ways which meet the needs of the present without compromising those of the future.

The Bank's policy is to:

• responsibly manage all aspects of its business to help ensure that recognized environmental standards and legal requirements are met;

• continues to give appropriate consideration to environment regulations and risk in its assessment of proposed loans and investments, and in management of its assets;

• so manage its internal operations as to promote environmental protection in all feasible ways, having due regard for associated benefits and costs;

• work with industry, government and public groups to help determine economic and environment priorities;

• provide support, through its program of corporate philanthropy, for selected non-profit groups doing sound and effective work in conservation and/or the environment;

• communicate with relevant stakeholder groups, in timely and candid fashion, on the environmental aspects of the Bank's policies and operations;

• encourage all employees, throughout the organization, to be conscious of environmental considerations and, in a pragmatic way, be protective of the environment and in their work.

SOURCE: Used by permission of the Royal Bank of Canada.

Exhibit 18-6

The Pulp and Paper Industry of Canada
ENVIRONMENTAL STATEMENT

The Pulp and Paper Industry of Canada shares with all Canadians important responsibilities to the environment in which we live and work. It supports the responsible stewardship of resources, including forests, recyclable materials, fish and the aquatic habitat, wildlife, air, land and water. Responsible stewardship makes possible sustainable economic development. In this spirit, the industry believes that a set of principles should govern its attitude and action in environmental matters. As endorsed by the member companies of the Canadian Pulp and Paper Association, these are as follows:

■ The companies commit themselves to excellence in sustained yield forestry and environmental management, and will conduct their business in a responsible manner designed to protect the environment and the health and safety of employees, customers, and the public.

■ The companies will assess, plan, construct, and operate facilities in compliance with all applicable regulations.

■ The companies will manage and protect forest resources under their stewardship for multiple use and sustained yield.

■ The companies, beyond or in the absence of regulatory requirements, will apply sound management practices to advance environmental protection and reduce environmental impact.

■ The companies will promote environmental awareness amongst employees and the public, and train employees in their environmental responsibilities.

■ The companies will report regularly to their Board of Directors on their environmental status and performance.

■ The industry will work with governments in the development of regulations and standards based on sound, economically achievable technologies, and the analysis of environmental impact.

■ The industry will continue to advance the frontiers of knowledge in environmental protection through the support of scientific research and, as appropriate, apply such knowledge at its facilities.

SOURCE: Canada Pulp and Paper Association, 1155 Metcalfe Street, Montreal, Quebec H3B 4T6.

EXHIBIT 18-7

The Financial Post Environment Awards for Business
Award Categories and 1992 Winners

1) THE POLLUTION ABATEMENT/CLEAN-UP AWARD for the development and/or adoption of technologies, processes and/or products which reduce the impact of industry on the environment.

    Winner: Blacks Photo Corp. Ltd. of Toronto and Technology Transfer Inc. of Edmonton for reformed non-toxic photo-finishing processes.

2) THE ENVIRONMENTAL MANAGEMENT AWARD for the integration of ecological considerations into overall corporate or management decisions.

    Winner: Canadian Pacific Hotels and Resorts of Toronto for its wide-ranging strategy to minimize the impact of its business on the environment.

3) THE GREEN MARKETING AWARD for honest and innovative promotion of ecologically responsible products and processes.

    Winner: Black & Decker Canada Inc. of Brockville, Ontario, for its program that encourages consumers to return small home appliances to dealers for recycling.

4) THE APPROPRIATE TECHNOLOGY AWARD for the development and/or transfer of ecologically sound technology adopted to the needs of developing countries.

    Winners: Electrolyser Corp. of Toronto for its photovoltaic hydrogen generator and storage system.

5) THE GREEN PRODUCT AWARD for products already on the market or prototype-tested, which have incorporated environmental considerations from the earliest stages of planning design.

    Winner: Envisoblock Surfacing Canada Inc. for using waste plastics recovered in blue box programs, used tires, and used asphalt to create blocks and paving stones.

SOURCE: The Environment, Special Report. (1992, October 26). *The Financial Post*, pp. S37 – S49.

In the 1990's, concern for the environment is high among Canadians, and business is being increasingly called upon to respond. This section has provided illustrations of corporate accountability for the environment.

The "Greening" of the Business Function

"Green" Finance

Financial management now includes consideration of environmental factors and will be discussed in relation to accounting, insurance, banking (lenders), and mutual funds.

Since 1991, accounting guidelines require companies to unequivocally state on their balance sheets the estimated liability for restoring capital assets to environmentally sound conditions. Such guidelines are particularly relevant to resource industries such as mining and petroleum. Where the economic lives of existing plants are shortened by tougher anti-pollution requirements, their remaining costs must be written off over a shorter period. Possible future contingent costs can also be mentioned as a note to the financial statements.

Accountants are also looking at the effect of environmental laws on future toxic materials storage and management or accident-prevention costs and whether current expenses should be increased to cover them. The development of accounting guidelines is ongoing, and will evolve as the profession and industry becomes more familiar with environmental risks and costs (Gunning, 1990). One of the challenges is accurately estimating the costs of pollution control and restoration costs in the future, and of the requirements of increasingly strict government requirements.

"Eco-insurance" products are now available in response to the liability associated with environmental problems. The types of insurance include: cleaning of site; third-part liability, which covers any pollution damage to others; errors and omissions for professional liability for engineers and consultants; damage caused to consumers by an insured's products; and property transfer, which covers government-ordered cleanup costs for newly acquired property when contamination was undetected (Mahood, 1992). There is belief that such insurance is needed because of various forms of environmental liability. But the costs are high, and a problem exists for the insurance industry—if an enterprise really needs insurance it is unlikely to get it, and if the enterprise can get it, it is likely that the coverage is not needed.

The banking industry has also been affected by the environmental issue. Bankers, or lenders, are accustomed to assessing credit-worthiness now with environmental regulation and legislation. Environmental assessments are necessary to determine the influence on financial performance. Some lenders actually require an environmental statement or audit prior to loan approval. The concern focuses on tougher environmental laws in some provinces that increase the liability of lenders. There is fear that lenders will assume direct liability for polluted property and be liable for clean-up expenses when such property is acquired from bankrupt organizations. Also, there is fear that the rights of secured creditors may rank behind environmental clean-up costs. The Canadian Imperial Bank of Commerce has created the position of general manager of environmental risk to assist in evaluating credit risk and to gain a better understanding of environmental consequences (Mahood, 1991).

Finally, investments are being screened for environmental pollution. Environmentally friendly stocks include petrochemical producers leveraged to methanol, waste disposal firms, packaging companies with recycling programs, oil producers with leverage to natural gas, and firms developing anti-pollution technologies. Environmentally unfriendly stocks are the pulp and paper makers, smokestack industries, base metal smelters, gold refiners, and plastic companies (McMurdy, 1989). "Green" mutual funds are also available, where portfolios are limited to socially responsible environmental companies. Examples of such funds are the Dynamic "Global Green" Fund and three funds managed by Clean Environment Mutual Funds—Canadian Equity, Balanced, and the Money Market Fund.

"Green" Marketing

Green seems to be the most popular colour with business today, since it expresses society's concern for the environment. Take, for example, the following headlines: "Going for the Green—Marketers Target Environment"; "Ignoring Green Revolution Means Disaster, Companies Warned"; "Marketers Must Plan for Green Future"; and "Greening the Profits." Green marketing involves selling environmentally friendly goods to consumers. As the headlines suggest, doing so may be necessary if enterprises are to survive, and doing so can provide a new opportunity to make money.

Dozens of friendly so-called "green" products are on the market: liquid soap products that offer plastic refill pouches to reduce packaging waste; coffee filters made without bleach, which can contain dioxin; recyclable or degradable trash bags; dishwasher detergent that is phosphate-free; and foam plates and cups without chlorofluorocarbons. Packaging is an obvious area where the three R's, reduce, reuse, and recycle can be practiced, and is getting considerable attention. There are now shopping guides available for environmentally sensitive consumers, *The Canadian Green Consumer Guide* (1990) and *The Ethical Shopper's Guide to Canadian Supermarket Products* (Helson et al, 1992).

The federal government has begun an "Environment Choice" program certifying products that are environmentally friendly, examples of which are re-refined oil, insulation material from recycled paper, and types of household and office products made from recycled plastic.

Green or environmentally friendly products and the whole green marketing approach, however, have been questioned. It is not clear whether or not "green marketing " is as friendly to the environment as it appears. Some of the debate is as follows:

1) Will the promotion of green products provide an opportunity for marketers to inflate prices?

2) Will products labelled "green" or " environmentally friendly" in advertising actually be so, or will they mislead consumers?

3) Are adequate methods of assessment available to evaluate the claims of particular products regarding their "greenness?"

4) Will the participation in the "Environment Choice" program benefit manufacturers more than consumers?

5) How long will the "environment phenomenon" last with business and
consumers?

With the economic downturn in the early 1990's, consumers because less
concerned about environmentally friendly products as they sought out bargains.
There has also been a decline in the percentage of new packaged goods promis-
ing to be environmentally friendly (Rusk, 1993). Thus business is performing a
careful balancing act as it attempts to interpret the mixed signals of consumer
desires.

"Green" Production

Business is trying to implement environmentally friendly processes and technologies into all aspects of the production function. Three areas of activity have
been briefly mentioned, pollution reduction, waste management and recycling,
and energy conservation.

All Canadians pollute the environment, and the volume of garbage is growing faster than the Canadian population. But despite the fact that pollution is so
widespread, there are still problems defining it. Some potential definitions are
(1) anything that degrades the quality of the environment, (2) anything that
detrimentally changes ecosystems, and (3) the deliberate discharge of particular
or effluent matter that is harmful to the natural environment and to people.

No matter how it is defined, pollution comes from many sources, including
aerosols, hydrocarbons, automobile exhaust, untreated sewage, and pesticides.
Even packaging is a form of pollution. Convenience goods usually packaged in
throwaway containers pollute. Often pollution is attributed to large business
enterprises that dump wastes into the water, air, or landfills. But consumers also
create pollution. Thus, business enterprises are concerned with reducing not
only their own pollution activities but also those of consumers.

Waste management is the handling and disposal of unwanted materials left
after industrial production or individual consumption. The traditional method of
getting rid of our garbage has been to bury it in landfills. These are easy to operate
and are relatively inexpensive. But the problem exists of finding locations for new
landfill sites: no one wants to live near a "dump." As a result, many governments
and businesses are developing methods to use or manage waste. The reduction of
waste is sought, but there is also emphasis on recycling, the retrieval and reuse of
suitable waste material such as paper, glass, metal, and plastics.

The diagram in Figure 18-1 serves as a basis for discussion of the involvement of business in recycling. Raw materials are used in the manufacture of
goods at the beginning of the production process. Today, R & D and design take

Figure 18-1 The Recycling Process

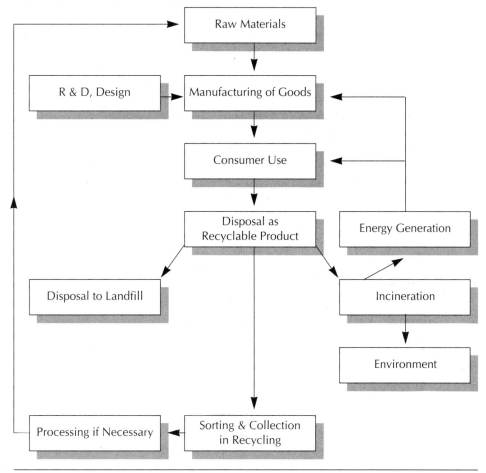

SOURCE: Adapted from a student assignment by Gary G. Bradshaw, Winter 1989. Memorial
University of Newfoundland.

the impact of particular materials on the environment into account. Waste from
the manufacturing process can be recycled as an input in the production of
another product.

Once a good has been used by the consumer, it can be disposed of as waste
in a landfill or it can become a recyclable product. As a recyclable product, two
alternative means of disposal exist: incineration or reuse. Incineration can be
used to generate energy, which in turn can be utilized by consumers or manufacturers, although the process discharges some pollution to the environment.

Reuse involves collecting and sorting items, and is often performed by business enterprises. New technology for the processing of recycled materials, and the availability of markets for recycled materials, are making recycling businesses more viable. But problems still exist. The public has been so enthusiastic about recycling materials that the capacity of recycling facilities has been overtaxed. Markets for recycled materials have not grown fast enough to keep pace with the collection of recyclable materials. Once processing of the materials has occurred, they are recycled as raw materials in the manufacturing process.

Canadians are great users and abusers of energy, and growth in energy consumption has been only recently levelling off. As consumption rises, additional sources of energy must be found, placing demands on the environment. Hydro sites and petroleum production areas must be established. Furthermore, preserving the environment adds costs to energy that consumers may not be aware of.

Business is taking many actions to conserve energy. Companies are reducing their consumption in producing and marketing goods and services as well as in the construction of energy-efficient buildings. Also, enterprises are introducing products that will enable consumers to conserve energy.

Public Policy and Regulation

There is extensive government involvement through public policy formulation and the regulation of all aspects of the natural environment. The federal and provincial governments have passed environmental legislation, and are considering further legislation. The federal government released its "Green Plan" in 1990 allocating $3 billion in new money for five years to create cleaner air, land and water, to encourage sustainable resources, to develop parks and wildlife areas, to protect the Arctic regions, and to reduce global warming, ozone depletion and acid rain. This section will not examine government initiatives in detail, but instead discusses the coordination of public and corporate policies on environment and identifies a range of policies that will impact on business.

The Policy Life Cycle

A variety of environmental issues exist that vary greatly in scope, sources, efforts, risk, and social and economic consequence. This variety suggests that specific solutions are appropriate for each issue. Winsemius and Guntram (1992) proposed a "policy life cycle" analysis for issues which consisted of four phases (as shown in Figure 18-2): recognition, formulation, implementation, and control. The authors suggest that different political attention is attached to a specific issue at any time.

The recognition phase is begun by researchers or environmentalists. Opinions usually differ greatly as to the nature and extent of the problem. The

Figure 18-2 Policy Life Cycle

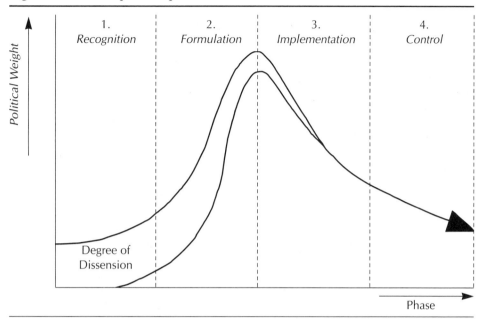

SOURCE: Pieter Winsemius and Ulrich Guntram. Responding to the environmental challenge. Reprinted from Business Horizons, March/April 1992, p. 14. Copyright © 1992 by the Foundation for the School of Business at Indiana University. Used with permission.

causes and effects may not be clear because factual knowledge is incomplete. Government agencies will seek a suitable policy to address the issue once it is decided that a problem exists. Phase 2 involves political discussion about the appropriate measure and distribution of costs. Media coverage is extensive. Solutions are sought by governments that tend to emphasize effectiveness rather than efficiency being reflected in legislation.

Implementation of policy in Phase 3 is often costly and has a major impact on the target groups involved—for example, industry, power generation, transportation, agriculture, or private households. In this phase, political and societal attention tends to wane and focus shifts toward operational management, with more emphasis on refining and streamlining regulation, that is, on efficiency. Lastly, in the final phase, the targeted improvement in environmental quality has been accomplished, and the issue is reduced to politically and technically acceptable levels. The problem is now considered controlled and regulations may be simplified or even abolished (Winsemius and Gruntram, 1992, pp. 14–15).

The authors assess the environmental "state of the art" in industrial countries as follows: Phase 1, recognition—recombinant DNA technology, indoor air pollution; Phase 2, formulation—greenhouse effect, soil protection; Phase 3, implementation—noise abatement, household waste, ozone depletion, acidification, chemical waste; and Phase 4, control—quality control, sewage, and animal plagues. This assignment varies among countries (1992, p. 15).

An important consideration is to recognize that the different stakeholders—government, environmental groups, managers, and consumers—require different skills in the various phases. In particular, business is involved in Phase 3, where operational tasks are necessary to comply with regulations, and when incidents may create adverse publicity for the company. Government policy makers are most involved in Phase 2 and environmentalists and researchers in Phase 1. It is important for managers to identify the specific environmental issue and where it is on the cycle. Then interaction should occur between the key stakeholder with business to learn about the issue in the recognition phase, to influence government in the formulation phase, and to manage the implementation phase.

This is a general view toward public policy and regulation in relation to environmental issues. The following sections briefly consider an array of possible government initiatives.

Policy and Regulation Initiatives

The following list contains initiatives that are not proposed or enforced by government legislation. They are policies or approaches that government might encourage business to undertake and which could be implemented with little government involvement. The list is not exhaustive, and is presented as an alternative to detailed descriptions of current government legislation.

Tax-Free Environmental Bonds   These are bonds issued to raise money for construction, renovation, or improvement of infrastructure necessary to ensure a healthy environment; for example, for sewage and water systems. The financial institutions could market such bonds at lower interest rates, as purchasers would not pay tax on the income received.

Environmental Flow-Through Shares   Investors would gain tax benefits by investing in a partnership that, in turn, invests in companies exceeding environmental standards. Companies would obtain capital at a discount and society would benefit from greater corporate responsibility (Cassils and Tatrallyay, 1988).

Environmental Venture-Capital Funds   Such funds would finance businesses contributing to improving environmental quality. Tax incentives would be granted to investors to improve potential returns.

Emergency Environmental Fund   The fund would be established by a one-time tax on corporate profits. The fund would be used to clean up environmental messes, and users of the fund would be charged with a liability appearing on their financial statements.

Pollution Permits or Credits   Permits or credits would be distributed to polluters which would allow them to discharge certain amounts of a compound based upon an overall pollution target for that region or industry. Demand for the credits would come from companies for which controlling pollution is expensive. Cleaner companies would have credits for sale to "polluters," and incentives would exist to protect the environment as allocated costs. Over time, the number of available credits would be reduced to achieve stricter standards and to encourage new pollution reduction technologies.

Traditional legislative controls are also available through, for example, packaging regulation, higher standards for pollution emissions, or mandatory recycling. There may, however, be a change in thinking on the part of government away from traditional types of regulatory controls and penalties toward the types of incentives already mentioned.

Government is an influential stakeholder in the management of the natural environment. Business enterprises must understand the status of specific regulatory issues so as to anticipate or influence government. In the future, there may be new government initiatives to induce business to respect the environment instead of reliance on the penalties and regulation of the past.

Public Opinion and Mixed Signals

It is not easy to interpret public opinion as illustrated by consumption patterns, concern for jobs, and the reluctance to pay for improvements.

Despite the polls that confirm the concern Canadians have for the environment, we still purchase environmentally unfriendly products. Canadians still lead the world in energy consumption and generate the most household garbage. A minority of consumers follow the advice in "green" shopping guides and, while "saving" the environment with one purchase decision, may violate it in another. Finally, it is not always clear what the "green" choice is. Most products have pros and cons on an environmental checklist.

Canadians express strong views about conserving forests, reducing pollution, and halting hydro electric projects. But many are seeking the jobs provided in logging or in the construction of dams. Consumer decisions to switch from a perceived environmentally unfriendly product to another often creates job loss. For example, jobs were reduced in the polystyrene packaging industry after adverse public reaction, even though the substitute packaging is not without its environmental problems and although the case against polystyrene had not been proved.

The final question is "who pays?" Public opinion polls consistently indicate that a majority of Canadians are concerned about the environment. But most actions to improve environmental quality cost money, and the issue becomes one of who will pay—in particular, government, business, or consumers.

Governments have assumed many of the costs of environmental cleanups, waste disposal, and recycling, and have financed such activities through taxation. The burden is spread equally through society if tax policies are fair. The problem with this is that neither business nor consumers fully appreciate the costs. Business has little incentive to change environmentally wasteful or damaging practices, and the individual taxpayer may not recognize either the problem or the cost.

Business could pay the costs directly; for example, they could be charged for product disposal. These costs would become a portion of the "costs of doing business" and would be reflected in prices charged for goods and services. The advantage is that costs to the environment would be recognized in pricing, and business enterprises would have an incentive to keep their environmental costs as low as possible in order to gain an advantage on competitors.

A final possibility is to charge consumers directly; for example, to charge for each bag of garbage or place a deposit on containers. This approach encourages consumers to reduce waste and to recycle materials, but it is unlikely to stimulate business to become efficient in the monitoring and controlling of costs associated with the environment. The need is for a combination of payments, but trends may be occurring to incorporate environmental costs directly into the prices of goods and services. Again mixed messages are being sent, with no one wishing to accept all the costs.

Public opinion may express concern for the environment, but this concern is not always reflected in consumption patterns, the desire for jobs at the expense of the environment, and the reluctance to pay. These factors leave business enterprises and managers in a state of environmental uncertainty.

THE ENVIRONMENTAL ISSUE: POTENTIAL OPPORTUNITIES AND THREATS

A review of this chapter will identify the challenges facing business as it responds to the environment. These challenges are both opportunities and threats.

The reputation of companies that make an effort to address the environmental issue are most likely enhanced, and they gain greater prominence in the marketplace. Customers are attracted, as might investors be after a positive investment screening for environmental matters. Costs of materials are reduced through recycling of materials, better control of pollution, energy conservation, and lower insurance. More competent staff might be attracted, and the enterprise becomes better integrated with the local community (Hutchinson, 1992, p. 55).

Business opportunities emerge by providing the technology or expertise to address the problem. Process redesign, material substitution, and reduction of pollution are areas where consultants can assist clients in addition to the provision of environmental audits. Environmental product manufacturers include those providing equipment for water pollution control, air pollution control, solid waste management, measuring instruments, chemicals for pollution control, and noise control. Examples of environmental services include waste handling, consultation services, assessment and control functions, laboratory services, and environmental research.

There are several threats for business enterprises if the environment is ignored. The corporate image deteriorates, and sales may suffer as customers prefer products and services less damaging to the environment. Investors become more difficult to attract as the enterprises cannot meet the criteria for environmental and ethical screening. Material and production costs may increase faster than for firms practicing reduction and recycling. The financial penalties are becoming higher and directors and managers are being held legally responsible for pollution. Insurance premiums are high for firms who do not reduce their pollution risk. Alienation may occur from the local community and failure to act may provoke stricter legislation and regulation (Hutchinson, 1990, p. 55).

Overall, the management of the natural environment is a challenge for managers. They must make the existing business effective while deciding on pollution reductions to be undertaken, how recycling and reuse of materials will occur, developing new business opportunities, and providing fulfilling work for employees. As an ideal, the enterprise should be guided toward an environmental and sustainable development strategy.

SUMMARY

The impact of business activities on the natural environment cannot be avoided. Several stakeholders are influenced by business's approach to the environment, and the enterprise is influenced by various stakeholders' interest in, or concern for, the environment. Simply stated, "it's a green world."

Corporations have taken a variety of approaches. There is no doubt that in society today an environmental ethic exists, often expressed as recycling, reusing, and reducing. The concept of sustainable development has also emerged, and has been translated into economic or business terms. In response to the presence of the environmental issue, business enterprises can form and implement four strategies regarding fixing problems, compliance with laws and regulations, comprehensive environmental management, or sustainable development. Canadian business enterprises are most likely following the first three strategies in some form. Ideally, enterprises should be working toward the fourth strategy, sustainable development.

In formulating and implementing the strategies identified, business enterprises are encountering a variety of considerations with which they must cope. Enterprises must be structured, organized, and staffed to respond, and appropriate stakeholders must be consulted. There are increasing demands for accountability, or the reporting of their progress in protecting and restoring the environment. All functions of a business enterprise are being impacted by the environmental issue, including finance, marketing, and production.

The government is a prominent stakeholder in the environmental issue through public policy and regulation. Public policies on the environment have a life cycle and it is important for business to recognize the phase in the cycle at which specific issues are located. Managers can in this way respond appropriately to not only government but also to environmental interest groups. In addition, governments are promoting a range of initiatives to encourage business to take action on the environment. These initiatives appear to move along the lines of marketplace incentives instead of penalties and stricter control.

Public opinion polls have found Canadians very concerned about the state of their environment. Yet business receives mixed signals from society. Consumption patterns are not always consistent with environmentally friendly goods or services. In some areas, jobs are preferred over the activities that will preserve the environment. Lastly, it is not clear who is going to pay for environmental protection, or how.

In general terms, business can address the environment in the following ways: (1) as a social obligation, where laws and regulations protecting the environment are obeyed; (2) as a social responsiveness, where actions are undertaken to meet society's demands; and (3) as a social responsibility, where specific endeavours are undertaken to reflect a sincerity to address the issue. Canadian business most likely institutes all three approaches, and still faces substantial challenges.

REFERENCES

Achieving Environmental Excellence: A Handbook for Canadian Business. (1990). Ottawa: Canadian Chamber of Commerce.

Block, Walter E. (1990). *Economics and the Environment.* Vancouver: The Fraser Institute.

Business Strategy for Sustainable Development: Leadership and Accountability for the '90's. (1992). Winnipeg, Manitoba: International Institute for Sustainable Development.

The Canadian Green Consumer Guide: How You Can Help. (1990). Toronto: McClelland and Stewart.

Cassils, J. Anthony and Geza P. Z. Tatrallyay. (1988, October 21). Let's give business an incentive it understands. *The Globe and Mail*, p. A7.

Drucker, Peter F. (1972, April 23). Saving the environmental crusade from saboteurs. *The Denver Post*, p. 30.

Gunning, Ken. (1990, October 15). Accounting standards go green. *Financial Times of Canada*, p. 38.

Helson, Joan, Kelly Green, David Nitkin, and Amy Stein. (1992). *The Ethical Shopper's Guide to Canadian Supermarket Products*. Toronto: Broadview Press.

Hooper, Todd L. and Bart T Docca. (1991, May/June). Environmental affairs: Now in the strategic agenda. T*he Journal of Business Strategy*, pp. 26–30.

Howartson, Allan C. (1990). *Toward Proactive Environmental Management: Lessons from Corporate Experience*. Ottawa: The Conference Board of Canada, Report 65 - 90.

Hutchinson, Colin. (1992). Environmental issues: The challenge for the chief executive. *Long Range Planning*, 25 (3), pp. 50–59.

Kesterton, Michael. (1991, January 24). The Green Planet. *The Globe and Mail*, p. A18.

Lush, Patricia (1990, April 3). Firms giving environmental bosses statute, if not clout. *The Globe and Mail*, pp. B1, B4.

Mahood, Casey. (1992, August 5). Environment right for green insurance. *The Globe and Mail*, p. B3.

Mahood, Casey. (1991, November 26). Green factor becomes part of banking life. *The Globe and Mail*, p. C3.

McMurdy, Deirdre. (1989, March 6). Smart investors eye pollution factors. *The Financial Post*, p. 27.

Rusk, James. (1993, February 12). Green loses sheen as shoppers try to stay out of red. *The Glob and Mail*, p. A1.

The World Commission on Environment and Development. (1987). *Our Common Future*. New York: Oxford University Press.

Winsemius, Pieter and Ulrich Guntram. (1992, March/April). Responding to the environmental challenge. *Business Horizons*, pp. 12–20.

RESPONDING TO THE MEDIA AND INTEREST GROUPS

INTRODUCTION

This chapter examines the role of two stakeholder groups, the media and interest groups. The use of the word "responding" in the title is meant to indicate a two-way relationship where managers must learn about these stakeholders, recognize their role in society, and develop mechanisms for interacting with them. Thus, the focus is not meant to be a one-way relationship but instead a proactive relationship in which managers understand and respect the roles of the two stakeholders.

RESPONDING TO THE MEDIA

Managers should realize that dealing with the media is a part of their responsibility and that the media is important in earning and keeping public trust and acceptance. Some managers see the media as intrusive, prying, and prejudicial, an unwelcome and necessary evil. But business needs to communicate with all stakeholders, and the media serves as a vehicle which reflects owner, employee, consumer, community, and other stakeholder expectations. The media is entitled to gather, digest, and regurgitate information on business as it does for any other institution in society, and media coverage of business activities can improve economic literacy and attitudes toward business.

This section explores the relationship between business and the media—newspapers, periodicals, television, and radio. The media is a stakeholder that can influence the views held by the public about business, and cannot be ignored. In turn, business has some influence over the media. Most media operations are owned by private sector enterprises, and advertising is a main source of revenue for them. It is claimed that business, through the media, has taken on improved respectability, and this has led to increased coverage, especially for international business and personal finance.

The Right to Know

Business is a major institution in society, and like any other major institution, people have an intrinsic curiosity about it. People have developed a belief that they have a right to know about things that affect them, and this has been reinforced by access to information law. Thus, over the years, veils of secrecy that sheltered many institutions and organizations have been removed, or at least lifted. People now want to take a closer look at business and are asking tougher, more pointed questions (Mindszenthy, 1987).

Many businesspersons now realize that they operate by some form of public consent, or that the legitimacy of business is dependent upon the public's knowledge of events and issues. The media is one forum through which information about business is provided. If that information is not forthcoming, the public has no firm ground on which to base its attitudes.

Coverage of Business

There are numerous newspapers and periodicals catering to business audiences, or those interested in business. Daily newspapers have some business coverage, even if an abbreviated stock market listing. *The Globe and Mail* (Toronto) has a "Report on Business" section daily, and *The Financial Post* offers daily coverage of finance and business. *The Financial Times of Canada* is a weekly business newspaper. *The Globe and Mail* and *The Financial Post* publish several business magazines each year. Other monthly magazines include *Inside Guide, En Route, Small Business Magazine*, and *Canadian Business*. There are also several regional business magazines, for example, *Atlantic Canada Business* and *Alberta Business*.

Television and radio also cover business topics. CBC-TV has a business program called *Venture* and Global TV has a regular business program called *Everybody's World*. The National Film Board (NFB) has an extensive listing of films on business topics, issues, and personalities. CBC-TV has shown NFB films such as *A Choice of Two*, a film about white collar crime and corporate in-fighting, and *The Formula Factor*, a film about the sale of baby formula in developing countries. CTV has also shown NFB films—for example, *Double or*

Nothing: The Rise and Fall of Robert Campeau. Not all the business coverage has been supportive or complimentary. Even business publications like *The Financial Post* and *Canadian Business* are questioning of business actions or attitudes.

Coverage of business has changed to one dominated by print to live television. However, even newspapers respond to events quickly, with lengthy analysis of major business-related events. This trend to instant news has also resulted in the instant expert opinion. If a company produces an unsafe product or pollutes a waterway, experts are available to offer their analysis or comment, although sometimes biased or peripheral.

A variety of media plays a significant role in the business enterprise system. The following topics will discuss the interaction between business and the media: problems arising from business-media interaction, issues of ownership, the changes in media attitude toward business, and things that business can do to improve its image.

Complaints About the Relationship

Businesspersons have complained about what they consider to be inappropriate coverage in the media. On the other hand, the media complains about attitudes held by most businesspersons about their reporting practices. Exhibit 19-1 summarizes complaints from both perspectives.

Exhibit 19-1

Business-Media Relations

Business Complaints About the Media

- Reporters are not sufficiently knowledgeable about business and economics and fail to do their homework.
- The media is only interested in "bad" news that can be sensationalized.
- The media is unable to place the information it is provided with in the correct context.
- The media has an inherent bias against business and is dominated by leftist journalists who neither support nor understand a market economy.
- Reporting on business is not only biased, but oversimplified and lacking in insight.
- Reporters do not respect "off-the-record" comments.

Media Complaints About Business

- Businesspersons confuse issues by waffling on details, by stonewalling, by attempting to hide negative information, or by lying.
- Businesspersons use the excuse that they are only accountable to shareholders, not the media.
- Businesspersons overreact to the process of reporting events and covering issues.

Some managers have attempted to manage the relationship to suit their purposes. Press releases are an example of this. The media is viewed as a tap that can be turned on or off depending on what managers think the stakeholders should know. The hostile attitude of business reflects the fear of the damage that can be done by a reporter to a manager's or a corporation's image. But the consequence of not responding to requests from the media is also dangerous. If the media is rebuffed, it will turn to more cooperative sources of information which may not be sympathetic to the business view. On their part, businesspersons and managers have threatened to cancel subscriptions when (or if) negative stories are carried. Advertising has been withdrawn by some businesses as retaliation for an editorial view or certain news coverage.

Another phenomenon influencing coverage, and in particular the publication of books, is "libel chill." This occurs when a business threatens legal action if a particular article or book is published. With this threat present, writers, editors, and publishers impose on themselves a form of self-censorship, holding back on potentially controversial stories. This has an impact on the freedom of speech and the public's right to know. There have been several recent instances of libel chill. The Reichmann family launched a lawsuit against *Toronto Life* magazine over a published profile of the family. Conrad Black has threatened legal action in some instances and obtained a public apology from McClelland & Stewart for offensive comments in *God's Dominion* (Graham, 1990). The most disturbing incident occurred in 1992 when Hees International Bancorp Inc., a Bronfman holding company, indicated in a letter to Macmillan Canada that it would consider legal action if a book about its complex financial transactions were published. Macmillan left the book unpublished without having read the manuscript.

The issue is one of balance. The media should not get away with irresponsible, inaccurate, or scandalous reporting, but neither should businesspersons be allowed to intimidate reporters and publishers. This discussion of the relationship between business and the media leads to a discussion of unfairness and biased reporting.

Unfairness and Bias

The issue of fairness in business reporting came to a head between 1978 and 1980. During this period, about 30 corporations and trade associations formed the Committee for Improved Business Reporting. It was assembled as a result of concern for a lack of balanced reporting in certain public affairs programs, in particular in the *Fifth Estate* and *Marketplace*. The manner in which business issues were often portrayed was not felt to be fair, and the Committee believed popular misconceptions about business were being promoted, leading to a public anti-business bias. The Committee was especially concerned with the CBC. It felt that business was treated more fairly in dailies, the business press, and private broadcasting. The Committee intervened at hearings for the renewal of the CBC's licences. It wanted the CBC to establish an independent board to hear complaints and investigate breaches of coverage policy.

The Fraser Institute was so concerned about bias in business and economic coverage that it established the National Media Archive in 1986. The Archive's computerized database of transcripts of national news and public affairs programming of CBC and CTV television have formed the basis of several studies of television news. These studies assess the kind of information the public receives on public policy issues, and issues of balance, fairness, and reporter's influence are scrutinized (*Annual Report 1992*, p. 7).

From coverage of federal civil servants and Canada Post strikes, the Institute's Archive concluded that the CBC gave similar attention to labour and employer in the strikes; labour was given balanced evaluations by the CBC and CTV; and employer actions were given negative attention (Mitjan, 1992, p. 28). More recently, the Institute has found that television in Canada gives more attention to bad economic news than it does to good news. Bias can occur in a number of ways: reporting bad news more often than good news; reporting selectively; and reporting stories that reflect the preferences of reporters rather than their audience. For example, between 1989 and 1992 CBC and CTV were twice as likely to report decreases in economic growth as they were to report increases, and rising inflation was reported more often than falling inflation. A solution to reducing bias is to privatize and deregulate the media (Palda, 1993, pp. 27–29).

A question arising from this discussion of fairness and bias in the media is whether or not it makes a difference. Corporations certainly think so.

Corporate Reputation and Media Exposure

Managers worry about the type and tone of information that appears in media and the influence this has on a company. The results of research in the relationship between media exposure and change in corporate reputation have been for the most part inconclusive. A recent study on the relationship between intensive media exposure and changes in corporate reputation concluded that media is a pervasive element in society and appears to be an important influence on the performance of modern companies (Wartick, 1992). Despite some positive findings, the author concluded that there remains much to be done before the relationship is fully understood.

Wartick defined media exposure as "the aggregated news reports relating to a specific company within a prescribed period," and for corporate response used the definition "the aggregation of a single stakeholder's perception of how well organizational responses are meeting the demands and expectations of many organizational stakeholders" (1992, p. 34). He based his study on Fortune's "Most Admired Corporations" and related the magnitude, direction, and total movement of change in corporate reputation with the amount, tone, and recency of media exposure. The tone of media exposure is a key factor associated with both the direction of the change in corporate reputation and the total movement of the change in corporate reputation. Recency is significantly associated with the magnitude of the changes in corporate reputation (1992, p. 43).

The study illustrates the complexity of the relationship between corporate reputation and media exposure, and how little is known about it. Companies appear to consider their reputation to be an important asset and are willing to defend it. An example is provided by the automobile industry, which is constantly examined by the media. In 1993, *Dateline NBC* failed to advise viewers that the scenes of a General Motors' truck bursting into flames was a trumped up demonstration and was forced by GM to issue a public apology. GM is now pursuing a much more aggressive response to criticisms of its products and is "lashing out at plaintiffs' lawyers, safety advocates, and the media" (Serwer, 1993). Whether or not this is the best tactic is questionable, but it illustrates that one corporation believes that excessive and possibly misleading exposure must be countered with action.

Ownership of the Media

Another dimension in the relationship between business and the media comes about because business enterprises own and operate media operations. The ownership of the broadcast media is concentrated in business enterprises such as Baton Broadcasting, CHUM Ltd., Moffat Communications, Rogers Communications, Selkirk Communications, and Tele-Metropole. The print media is dominated by: Thompson Newspapers Ltd., Southam Inc., the K.C. Irving Group, Power Corp., Torstar Corp., Toronto Sun Publishing, Quebecor, and Hollinger Inc.

Several issues emerge as a result of this ownership, including those surrounding: (1) the newspaper monopolies held in some cities by large corporations; (2) the interlocking ownership between print and broadcasting media; (3) the licensing process in broadcasting where some corporations are allegedly favoured over others; and (4) the operation of newspaper chains that are more concerned with financial performance than professional journalism.

The rationalization of newspaper operations in several cities in 1980 lead to the establishment of a Royal Commission on Newspapers. Some corporate owners were also accused of attempting to influence editorial policy, and the public became sensitive to the domination of media by a few enterprises. The stricter ownership controls recommended by the Commission were never implemented.

Private broadcasting media does compete with the government-owned Canadian Broadcasting Corporation (CBC). At times, the private owners allege that the CBC operates at an advantage, as it is subsidized by the taxpayers. On the other hand, government regulation of licensing limits the number and type of competitors for privately owned media operators. Most private broadcast firms are profitable because of this regulation. Broadcasting media are subject to Canadian content regulations which is considered burdensome, but these same enterprises are protected from takeover by firms from outside Canada, as foreign ownership of the media is discouraged by government policy.

The power associated with media ownership is one issue. A related issue is the centralization of the media. This involves the concern that there may be too few voices in the media. Newspapers are suffering declining readership, especially with some age groups, and some have failed. But, the availability of magazines has increased, as have alternatives available on television and radio. A problem with control arises when all media is concentrated in one or a few owners, this is not yet the case. However, although the independence of the media is an aspect of free privilege, this is countered by the professionalism of journalists and the management in the media.

There is increasing specialization and fragmentation in the media. Mindszenthy (1987) listed the following types of media: trade journals, specialized consumer publications; all-news networks; cable TV stations; and the dedicated religious, lifestyle, business, weather, and sports networks. In addition, there are household or free-distribution newspapers, call-in and call-out radio and TV programs, and interview programs.

Changes in Attitudes Toward Business

Business topics and issues appear to have a new respectability in the media in recent years. There is increased coverage of business news in newspapers, regional business magazines have been established, and television and radio have started programs on business. The new focus is evident at the CBC. Examples of this are a series developed from Peter Newman's book (1975) *The Canadian Establishment*, and dramas with business themes such as *Takeover*. CBC radio and television networks now have weekly business programs.

Overall, there appears to be a more favourable approach to business coverage now than in the 1960's and 1970's. It is not clear what has caused this change. It may reflect a general trend in society toward greater interest in and understanding of business issues. Most people who represent the media claim there is an increasing number of better educated, better prepared, and better equipped reporters and editors. This counters one of the complaints by business that reporters are uninformed and not knowledgeable of business. Reporters and editors now have more background material available to them through access to electronic data banks and indexes, government files, and business libraries.

Business Initiatives

Businesspersons have recognized that they can influence the media by improving their relations with reporters. In large corporations, public relations departments sometimes have a press relations officer who maintains contacts with the media. These departments, or hired consultants, also prepare executives for media appearances. The preparation includes such things as teaching business spokespersons how to answer aggressive questions, how to dress for television appearances, how to project a trustworthy and believable image, how to speak effectively, how to use body language, and how to maintain control of press conferences.

Chief executives are appearing more frequently in print and broadcasting media advertising promoting their corporations' products. The most widely known examples are from television and include David A. Nichol, formerly president of Loblaws Ltd.; Llewellyn S. Smith, President of E.D. Smith & Sons; and Tom Leon, President of Leon's Furniture Ltd. These appearances help to create the image that chief executives are much like anyone else, and that they are interested in their product and their purchasers.

In addition to improving the performance of business spokespersons in the media, an effort is being made to enhance the quality of written business coverage. Each year the National Business Writing Awards are given to recognize outstanding achievement by Canadian business and financial writers. The awards are jointly sponsored by the Toronto Press Club and The Royal Bank of Canada.

Business activities appear to be of increasing interest to the public. This seems to have lead to increasing coverage of business topics and issues by the media. Businesspersons have responded by complaining less about biased reporting and by preparing themselves better for interacting with media reporters.

Summary: Responding to the Media

Businesspersons must recognize that the media can be an influential stakeholder and that the media has a legitimate role in society. There should also be recognition that the media seldom sets the social agenda, but that corporations, governments, and other institutions in society do. Thus, the media as a stakeholder influences business, but business can also influence the media by carefully managing the relationship between itself and the media.

The media should be viewed with respect, and an understanding should be created between the media and business. Businesspersons should avoid constantly complaining about the media or attempting to upstage it. They must learn about the media's role in society as another aspect of their job and speak candidly and clearly. There is no reason to be adversarial, and the media should be helped to learn about the company and its products. The relationship should be viewed as ongoing and long term.

Managers must recognize that their actions are subject to greater scrutiny, and should voluntarily recognize this. There is always risk in dealing with the media, but managers can reduce this risk by being trained in media interview skills and by being prepared to respond to current issues confronting the corporation. On the other hand, managers should insist that their quotations are not taken out of context, that their points are reported accurately, and that there is fair and balanced reporting of their views. The media should be monitored on a regular basis through clipping and video monitoring services. Managers cannot afford to ignore the media if they wish to effectively manage the corporation in an environment where the public, that is, stakeholders, want to know what is occurring in business.

Media stakeholder relationships should be monitored, but so should the multitude of relationships that exist between the corporation and the interest groups that exist in society who have a stake in the activities and performance of the corporation.

RESPONDING TO INTEREST GROUPS

The definition of this stakeholder is problematic as different terminology can be used—for example, "public interest," "special interest," or just "interest." Such groups are usually discussed in the context of their influence on public policy formulation; thus the "public interest group" terminology. "Special interest group" is used to describe an association that seeks the advance of pecuniary interests of its members—for example, doctors or lawyers. Although both groups indirectly influence business, the focus of this section is on "interest" groups that interact with or influence business directly. Thus, the definition used in this section is that the "special group" stakeholder is any group which holds shared values or attitudes about issues relating to business and makes certain claims or demands of business to take actions that will be consistent with the group's attitudes. It should be noted that these groups are a part of the private sector, not a part of government, and are usually non-profit organizations supported by volunteer members and activists. "Interest groups" are further explained in the following sections.

Types of Groups and Issues

There are thousands of interest groups in Canada that express views on a multitude of issues. Some of the more common groups are formed to represent the following: multiculturalism, environment, aboriginal concerns, feminism, senior citizens, nuclear disarmament, and disability issues. The issues may include energy conservation, equality, education, northern living conditions, acid rain, endangered animals, animal rights, land use, and health. The list of groups and issues seems endless. Table 19-1 lists some examples merely to illustrate the specificity and variety of groups. Managers must monitor not only Canadian interest groups, but also those located elsewhere in the world. For example, European groups have protested against Canadian forestry industry practices.

Managers in business cannot possibly monitor all groups, but they should monitor, and perhaps even be in contact with, groups that are, or might be, influential in their industry or to their corporation. Thus, management of interest groups is one component of issues and stakeholder management discussed in Chapter 9. A later section in this chapter discusses how managers can cope specifically with interest groups.

Impact On Business

Interest groups affect business in two ways. They lobby for changes in government legislation or regulation that impacts on business; for example, by seeking stricter controls over smokestack pollution, as advocated by the Coalition on Acid Rain. Secondly, the groups lobby or attempt to influence corporations directly; for example, by meeting with corporate executives or organizing boycotts. Thus, remembering the definition of a stakeholder, it is important that managers not ignore these groups.

Table 19-1 Examples of Interest Groups and Their Issues

Industry	Name	Issues
Toy Manufacture	Canadians Concerned About Violence in Entertainment	Opposed to militarizing culture
Manufacturing/Resource	Canadian Coalition on Acid Rain	Opposed to smokestack pollution and advocating cleanup
Tobacco	Non-Smokers' Rights Association	Opposed to tobacco industry business practices
	Smokers Freedom Society	Promotion of the right to smoke
Alcohol	Mothers Against Drunk Drivers (MADD)	Lobbying for solutions to drunk driving
Pharmaceutical	ARKII & Lifeforce & others (Animal rights groups)	Opposed to mistreatment of animals in product testing
Nuclear	Food Irradiation Alert Group	Concerned with dangers to health of exposing food to gamma rays

These groups use a variety of approaches to influence business besides the lobbying of government and the corporation. Interest groups attempt to persuade or educate the public to hold particular beliefs about issues. Often this is achieved through the careful use of media. Representations are made at public hearings to publicize issues and influence changes in government policies. Some have research capability, either through their own paid staff or volunteer expertise. Sometimes groups will initiate legal action to draw attention to issues, although this approach is not common.

Some groups use feats of "daring activism" to make their views known. This might take the form of a roadblock or intervening with Japanese whalers, as Greenpeace has done. Violence, or threats of violence are resorted to at times. For example, a group opposed to nuclear weapons exploded a bomb outside of a Litton Systems plant in Toronto in 1982 in protest.

The imposition of economic sanctions or boycotts is another tactic. As this tactic is becoming more common, it is discussed in more detail.

Economic Boycotts

In the 19th century, Charles Boycott, an Irish land agent, refused to reduce rents. His tenants held the first boycott (Mittelstaedt, 1989). Table 19-3 lists more recent boycotts. Boycotts are usually associated with consumers and decisions of whether or not to purchase particular products. It is suggested in the 1990's that consumers are becoming ultra-conscientious, that is, sensitive to social and other issues (Milbank, 1991). Consumers are pressuring corporations to account for their actions by exercising consumer sovereignty, a fundamental component of capitalism. In this way, consumers are exerting social control over business, or making it socially responsible (Smith, 1990).

Managers should not be misled by considering boycotts as an expression of consumerism. Instead, they must understand the issue and the interest group promoting the boycott as they relate to particular products or corporations. In the short list provided in Table 19-2, the groups and issues are diverse. The groups identified should not be thought of as a general consumer advocacy organization such as the Consumers' Union or the Consumers' Association of Canada, but as sovereign bodies.

The challenge provided by boycotts becomes more complicated when it is recognized that groups are not always identifiable. Sometimes boycotts occur in the general population without a formal organization to promote them. These boycotts are motivated by attitudes in society, making it even more difficult for managers to respond. Boycotts are sometimes encouraged by publications such as the National Boycott News, which reports in all boycotts or guidebooks on "ethical shopping" or "socially responsible shopping." Rather than advocating a boycott, a "boycott" is suggested in some cases by directing consumers to purchase products from what are considered ethical or socially responsible corporations. Boycotts, whether sponsored by particular interest groups or encouraged by societal attitudes, must be monitored by management.

Dealing with Interest Groups

Coping with interest groups is not easy, but there are particular approaches that can be mentioned here. Public opinion polling is a possible venue when a corporation wishes to stay ahead of major turnabouts in public attitudes. Monitoring the polling results of others can be helpful—for example, *Macleans'* end of year poll, and polls conducted by business and trade associations. Sometimes corporations within an industry can sponsor research on the public's views of that industry. This has been done in the petroleum and financial services industries. Studies can be conducted into special-interest issues as the need arises. Consultants are available to undertake polling and research studies.

Table 19-2 Examples of Economic Boycotts

Firm/Industry	Group(s)	Issue
Celestial Seasonings, Boulder, Colorado	Gay Groups	Protest the State of Colorado's Amendment forbidding Colorado cities from designating gays an official minority group eligible for hiring quotas or set-aside contracts. Celestial's CEO did not oppose amendment strongly enough.
General Electric	Infact, group organized to boycott G.E. Voice of Women	The production of nuclear weapons.
Holiday Inns	American Family Association	Hotel offers adult movies.
Canada Safeway and Canadian Tire	Canadian Labour Congress	Industrial relations practices.

Managers must recognize the pressures on those who run non-profit interest groups. Some of these groups, in particular wildlife and environmental groups, have been criticized for using too high a proportion of donated funds on administrative costs. Business should not necessarily confront groups on this basis. Also, some groups have used campaigns to distort business positions and mislead the public, and business must be careful not to counter by resorting to the same tactics. Interest groups use a variety of techniques to enhance their positions, and business must be careful how it responds, as an inappropriate response might enhance the interest group's status.

Business can financially and otherwise support the operation of interest groups that are favourably disposed to business points of views. For example, in Table 19-1, the tobacco industry allegedly supports a "Smokers Freedom Society." This activity should only be engaged in with considerable caution.

Summary: Responding to Interest Groups

Interest groups are a component of society's pluralistic makeup. They address a variety of social, economic, technological, and political issues, and are made up of people wanting to change and improve society. In general, an interest group has expertise, experience, and a particular "stake" in the well-being of society, and thus has a contribution to make. Members of the interest group believe it is their right and duty to be an integral part of the democratic structures and processes.

Interest groups do influence governments, but they should also be viewed as a stakeholder that may directly influence the corporation. There are thousands of interest groups, from which managers must select those that will influence their corporation. Such groups impact business in a variety of ways, as groups use different tactics, including economic boycotts. Lastly, managers must learn how to manage relationships with these groups effectively, including influencing the group's views about business.

SUMMARY — PART III

Part III has identified and examined many of the challenges confronting business and managers in environments in which they are influenced by many stakeholders. In each of the chapters, challenges associated with some key stakeholders were discussed. The following summarizes the contents of this part by chapter.

Chapter 11   The owner stakeholder was discussed, with emphasis on how ownership patterns have shifted and the consequences for managers. Owners, even if widely dispersed cannot be taken for granted and are a stakeholder group that is, in some ways, more influential in the business system.

Chapter 12   Boards of Directors were examined, with focus on the changing roles that might, or should be, occurring in this aspect of corporate governance. There has been considerable discussion and research on reforming corporate governance. The future will indicate whether or not the recommended changes are implemented.

Chapter 13   The government has been a major stakeholder in the business system in the past and will continue to be so, but the nature and scope of its influence will change. Government is a good example of a stakeholder who influences business and also one who is influenced by business.

Chapter 14   Business has been involved in philanthropic activities for a hundred years. For this chapter, three types of philanthropy or corporate giving were discussed: donations, voluntarism, and sponsorship. The chapter also identified trends in this area and challenges to business.

Chapter 15   In every business enterprise, employees are a key stakeholder. Rather than discuss human resource management in general terms, the chapter focused on the changing workplace. The changes occurring at this time are more substantial than change since the Industrial Revolution. For managers, numerous ethical and socially responsible issues arise from these changes.

Chapter 16   Competitors are seldom forgotten by a business enterprise. But, there are different degrees of competition in the marketplace, and governments become involved to encourage competitive markets. The discussion of competitiveness highlighted the increased global nature of markets and the need for Canadian business to be able to compete internationally.

Chapter 17   It is argued that consumers may be a neglected stakeholder in the business system. Although fundamental to the business system, consumer sovereignty is often ignored or prevented. Business practices have been counter productive to this sovereignty, but government involvement in the business system has been particularly harmful to the enhancement of consumer sovereignty.

Chapter 18   The state of the natural environment is a worldwide concern or issue. Business's impact on the physical environment cannot be denied, but business enterprises are responding to the influence of various concerned stakeholders including owners, consumers, society at large, and environmental groups.

Chapter 19   Two particular stakeholders who can exert considerable influence, the media and interest groups, were outlined. Monitoring stakeholders and responding to their influence are aspects of a manager's job that cannot be ignored.

This part did not discuss all the stakeholders identified in Chapter 2, but it has examined several stakeholders in relationship to various issues that are prominent at this time. The discussion of the resulting challenges is placed in the context of the background on the Canadian business system provided in Part I and the concepts relating to corporate social responsibility, responsiveness, and performance outlined in Part II.

These challenges must be placed in the context of the business enterprise, which has a multitude of challenges. In order to appreciate this context, Chapter

20 discusses how the challenges identified in Part III are incorporated into the strategic management planning process of the corporation. The challenges discussed are also contemporary. There will be new and different challenges in the future, the topic of Chapter 21.

REFERENCES

Annual Report 1992. The Fraser Institute, Vancouver, B.C.

Graham, Ron. (1990). *God's Dominion.* Toronto: McClelland & Stewart.

Mindszenthy, Bart J. (1987, March). Issues and media relations. *Business Quarterly*, pp. 76–83.

Milbank, Dana. (1991, April 25). It's getting tougher to stay consumer-pure. *The Globe and Mail*, pp. A1, A6.

Miljan, Lydia. (1992, April). CBC pays equal attention to labour, employer in PSAC, Canada Post strikes. *Fraser Forum*, p. 28.

Mittelstaedt, Martin. (1989, November 30). Consumer activism sweeping the U.S. *The Globe and Mail*, pp. B1, B5.

Newan, Peter C. (1975). *The Canadian Establishment.* Toronto: McClelland and Stewart.

Palda, Filip. (1993, February). Bias in the media: Causes and consequences. *Fraser Forum*, pp. 27–29.

Serwer, Andrew Evan. (1993, May 31). GM gets tough with its critics. *Fortune*, pp. 90–97.

Smith, N. Craig. (1990). *Morality and the Market.* London: Routledge.

Wartick, Steven L. (1992). The relationship between intense media exposure and change in corporate reputation. *Business and Society* (Roosevelt University), 31 (1), pp. 3349.

PART **IV**

MANAGING FUTURE SOCIAL AND ETHICAL CHALLENGES

Chapter

20 – Strategic Management and the Social and Ethical Environment

21 – Influences on the Future Management of Stakeholders and Social and Ethical Challenges

The three parts of this book have provided a background on the Canadian business system, reviewed corporate social responsibility, responsiveness and performance, and examined some challenges in the business environment. Through this presentation of materials, a foundation has been provided upon which to analyze the social and ethical demands placed on Canadian business. Key concepts such as social responsibility, business ethics, stakeholder management, and corporate social performance were explained. Chapters 11 through 19 outlined a spectrum of issues relating to a variety of stakeholders. This final part is a brief look at the future.

Two chapters make up this part. Chapter 20 focuses on integrating social and ethical considerations into long-term planning, or strategic management. A final chapter speculates about the future and what social and ethical issues will confront the manager.

STRATEGIC MANAGEMENT AND THE SOCIAL AND ETHICAL ENVIRONMENT

INTRODUCTION

The focus of this book has been on the social and ethical perspectives of managing a business enterprise. But economic and legal perspectives have not been forgotten or ignored. They are fundamental to the successful operation of the business enterprise. Managers have the skills, tools, methodologies, and frameworks to cope with economic and legal perspectives of managing, although they do not always successfully apply them. Business enterprises do fail, and do violate laws and regulations. Nevertheless, as we move into the 21st century, social and ethical perspectives will not go away, and hence managers must learn to cope with social responsibility and business ethics.

This topic will be dealt with by outlining how social and ethical concerns might have been incorporated into long-term planning and by explaining a more comprehensive approach to integrating social and ethical concerns with strategic management.

DEFINITION OF STRATEGIC MANAGEMENT

In order to provide a context for the discussion, it is necessary to define and clarify the meaning of strategic management. It establishes an enterprise's mission and objectives, analyzes the environment and resource capabilities in order to formulate strategy, creates the organizational systems and processes needed to implement the strategy, and devises mechanisms for monitoring and reviewing the enterprise's performance. From this definition, eight components emerge. These are found in some form in all descriptions of a strategic management process, although different terminology may be used.

Establishment of a Mission   A mission is key. It identifies the enterprise's reason for being.

Assessment of the Environment   An enterprise must develop the capability to assess the external environment in which it operates and to understand when and how this environment influences it. The environmental factors considered include the structure of the industry, social trends, developments in technology, government policies, the behaviour of competition, and demographic changes.

Assessment of Enterprise Resources and Capabilities   Management evaluates the enterprise's internal resources to ascertain its ability to take advantage of opportunities in the environment and to overcome any threats. An audit is performed of resources—for example, an audit of financial, production, marketing, and human competencies. An assessment is also made of how well these resources integrate or interact with each other to determine resource capability.

Establishment of Objectives   The setting of objectives is critical to strategic management from the outset, since the mission statement is an objective stated in general terms. However, not all objectives can be established at the beginning of the process. After assessing the environment and enterprise resources, managers or strategists are in a position to set specific objectives and priorities, as they now have a better understanding of what the enterprise is likely to achieve.

Identification of Strategic Options   The next step is to identify the strategic options available to the enterprise. There are usually more than one, and they are described by terminology such as cost leadership, differentiation, internal growth, vertical integration, diversification, and strategic alliances.

Selection of a Strategy   From the strategic options, or alternatives through which the objectives can be achieved, one is selected as the most appropriate, given the circumstances of the enterprise.

Strategy Implementation   This component includes designing the enterprise's structure, allocating resources, developing information and decision processes, and managing human resources, including such areas as the reward system, approaches to leadership, and staffing. In other words, the enterprise must focus on "how" the strategy will be executed.

Monitoring and Review   Any planning process needs some form of control through monitoring and review to see whether or not it is accomplishing what was intended—that is, to confirm that the strategy is being followed and the objectives met.

APPROACHES TO VIEWING SOCIAL AND ETHICAL CONCERNS

Social and ethical concerns have to be dealt with in any business that wishes to remain in tune with society. This has not necessarily been the case in the past: a variety of views of corporate morality relating to planning have emerged, and are identified as the financial or stockholder view, managerial preferences view, the role of corporate culture, organizational values, and the stakeholder view.

The Financial or Stockholder View

The primacy of return to stockholders is emphasized in this view, and the corporation should act in the their interests. Managers are the loyal agents of stockholders and their efforts in the form of strategic management are therefore aimed at furthering stockholder interests. Freeman et al. state that "the issue of evaluating corporate strategies from the moral point of view and that of understanding the role of values, in general, in corporate strategy just never seems to arise" (1988, p. 833). The models used in strategic management with this view include portfolio theory, value-added, competitive rivalry, and transaction cost models. The financial view is considered to be too narrow in perspective to thoroughly incorporate social responsibility and ethical considerations into strategic management.

Managerial Preferences View

This view suggests that the corporation should act in an efficient manner consistent with the values of the senior managers or their agents. An example of this view is found in the Harvard Policy Model as outlined by Andrews (1971, 1980), which incorporates analyses of personal values of senior management and social responsibilities into the formulation and implementation of strategic management. The same view is incorporated into the teaching of strategy at the School of

Business Administration at the University of Western Ontario, where management preferences are examined as they relate to strategy selection and corporate performance (Fry and Killing, 1989, pp. 142–161).

A manager's biases affect whether or not the enterprise even practices strategic management, and if it does, the form it will take. A manager's, that is, strategist's, outlook shapes all the components in the strategic management process, including the business activity of the enterprise, the selection of a strategy, and the attitudes about social and ethical concerns.

The strategist's preferences are reflected through factors such as:

Values   Values are the basic assumptions about which ideals are considered desirable or worth striving for. These values are derived from personal experience including family backgrounds, religious training, and educational systems.

Beliefs   Beliefs are basic assumptions about the world in which an individual operates and how it works. Personal experience also plays a major role in determining beliefs. For example, experiences in the past led to particular beliefs about business practices, or how much the judgment and expertise of others is trusted. An individual also has beliefs about his or her own competencies or capabilities.

Basic Needs   All individuals to some degree have basic needs for achievement, power, security, and recognition. The drive to fulfil these needs influences the degree of success or failure of the strategist in pursuing particular strategies.

Situational   The circumstances in which a strategist operates also influences preferences—for example, the size of the enterprise, the hierarchical structure, the type of technology used, and the practices of the industry.

Groups   Strategists often must convince others, and in some cases strategic decisions are made by groups. The dynamics of group leadership and the interactions of group members influence the preferences for particular strategies.

The factors listed mold strategists' preferences, including the values they hold, their beliefs about society, the personal needs that motivate them, the circumstances of their workplace or industry, and the influence of peer groups. These factors shape the attitudes of strategists about risk, ethics, social issues, profits, and short- versus long-term planning either positively or negatively. They can create the force that drives the initiation and maintenance of strategic management process, or they may act as filters that prevent the identification of all viable strategic options, or even the social and ethical implications of corporate decisions. Although this view is broader than the financial view, it is still too narrow in scope and is unlikely to include diverse views from outside the corporation.

The Role of Corporate Culture

Corporate culture is the complex set of values, beliefs, assumptions, and symbols that define the way in which an organization conducts its business (Barney, 1986). Often this culture is not stated explicitly and instead is reflected in structures, behaviours, processes, rites and rituals, myths, traditions, symbols, language systems and metaphors, and value systems (the values generally held by employees of the organization). Well-run organizations have a distinctive culture that promotes the creation, implementation, and maintenance of successful strategies.

An organization's culture impacts on all strategic management components. The following are some examples of this:

Establishment of a mission   A mission might reflect the organization's culture in its wording. If the culture is changed, the mission statement is revised.

Assessment of the Environment   The prevailing culture influences how managers interpret the environment. Managers must always be sensitive to cultural impact when involved in any strategic analysis or assessment.

Assessment of Resources and Capabilities   Managers must accurately evaluate resources and judge how committed all employees are to the organization's culture.

Establishment of Objectives   Objectives must be established that are reasonable, considering the culture that exists.

Identification of Strategic Options   The range of options considered is influenced by cultural considerations such as the innovativeness of the organization and its employees, and how long the culture has operated in a positive manner.

Selection of a Strategy   Selection of a new strategy is influenced by the existence of a culture appropriate to implement a past strategy. If this culture is strong, it might limit choice to fewer options, at least in the short term until the culture can be altered.

Strategy Implementation   Culture is critical to the successful implementation of a strategy. For example: Are marketing, production, and financial policies consistent with the culture? Is the organization's structure consistent with the culture? Are resources allocated in a manner consistent with the culture? Can cultural rites, rituals, symbols, and so on be consistent with what has been done to implement the strategy?

Monitoring and Review   Strategists must make sure that the control and performance evaluation systems are consistent with the organization's culture. The type, timing, and criteria of evaluation must all be considered in relation to culture, as must the form of remedial actions taken.

Managing the culture of an organization is critical to the institutionalizing of the strategic management process. Sometimes a change in strategy necessitates a change in culture. Culture is a strength if it is consistent with the strategy, and can be driving force in implementation. But a culture inconsistent with strategy is a weakness and can result in failure.

Figure 20-1 is one conceptualization of organizational culture. The focus in such an analysis is internal and economic. The organizational systems influencing culture are labelled "internal," and most of the environmental influences are economic rather than social or ethical in nature. Insufficient emphasis is placed on social and ethical considerations when examining corporate culture. Freeman et al. state that cultural management is not sufficient to take care of the problems of the effectiveness and morality of strategy. That is simply the managerial view in a different guise. They claim that corporate culture is based on the inseparability of organizational and employee interests, and all are largely based on the premise that employees adopt corporate values determined by senior managers to be the "correct values" (1988, p. 833). In conclusion, corporate values do not appear to capture all the social and ethical concerns that should be addressed by the enterprise.

Organizational Values

Most business enterprises are concerned to some extent about ethical behaviour, integrity, employee health and safety, the environment, quality, and service. Such concerns are a part of corporate life in the 1990's. Some corporations have articulated their values in "values statements," also referred to as creeds and statements of philosophy (two examples are provided in Exhibit 20-1).

Value statements contain some description of the beliefs, principles, and basic assumptions about what is desirable or worth striving for in an enterprise. There is no uniformity in content or format. Kooten found that a value statement may contain any combination of components such as:

- the key interests to be satisfied and balanced; for example, the public or community interest, owners, employers and suppliers;

- an emphasis on quality and/or excellence in relation to product and service, employees, and technology;

- efficiency as indicated by low-cost, high-productivity, and value for money or investment;

- the atmosphere or climate of enterprise; for example, a good place to work, an emphasis on teamwork, managers' support of staff, and development of employees;

Figure 20-1 Analyzing Organizational Culture

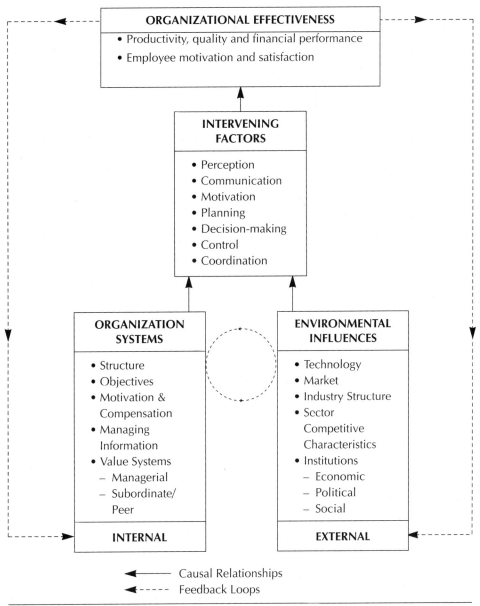

SOURCE: Reprinted from Long Range Planning, 26(2), Malcolm J. Morgan, "How Corporate Culture Drives Strategy," p. 112, copyright © 1993, with kind permission from Elsevier Science Ltd., The Boulevard, Langford Lane, Kidlington OX5 1GB, UK.

Exhibit 20-1

Examples of Values Statements

Corporate Values—Wascana Energy

The history of Wascana Energy has been characterized by change and progress. The values shared by the company's employees have enabled them to perform their daily tasks with a sense of trust and confidence. Respect, high ethical standards, teamwork and innovation have helped Wascana Energy achieve its corporate objectives. In 1992, a formal statement of values was adopted to serve as a guideline for positive change and to provide employees with a consistent framework to define relationships with fellow employees, partners, customers and the communities in which Wascana Energy is active.

Profitability—We conduct our business to ensure that Wascana Energy has the profits to continue to meet its obligations to its employees, investors, host communities, customers, suppliers and other stakeholders.

Integrity—We conduct our activities with integrity, displaying the highest ethical standards.

Teamwork—We encourage and place a high value on teamwork.

Confidence—We approach our work with confidence in our abilities, individually and collectively.

High Standards—We strive for high standards in technology, business and our personal lives.

Respect—We exercise care, attention, consideration and respect for our stakeholders and strive to earn the same in return.

Innovation—We promote creative and entrepreneurial skills to foster innovation in concepts, methods, opportunities and solutions.

Job Satisfaction—We approach work with enthusiasm, dedication and good humour and take enjoyment from our daily activities.

Source: Wascana Energy, Annual Report 1992

Values—Bank of Montreal

Our values are what each of our stakeholders can expect of us.

Our customers come first...

- They will be served at all times by friendly, caring, responsive and well trained employees. Our service will be characterized by fairness and respect, professionalism, integrity and ethical conduct.

Employee satisfaction leads to customer satisfaction . . .

The Bank is committed to attracting, developing and retaining the best people.

- Employees can expect us to demonstrate respect for the individual, to be a fair and equitable employer, and to provide the opportunity for a full and challenging career. We will offer competitive compensation and benefits programs, and will recognize and reward personal achievement as well as teamwork. And we will provide opportunities for continuous professional development through training and through mobility within the Bank.

- Pensioners are valued members of the Bank family. We will treat them not as individuals who used to work for the Bank, but rather as pensioned employees who continue as important members of our team.

The Bank, in turn, seeks from every employee:
- commitment to the Bank's principles and goals,
- a strong customer orientation, and
- a sensitivity to public concerns and actions which are at all times socially responsible.

We manage the Bank on behalf of our shareholders...
- Our first responsibility to them is to provide sound, responsible management and to keep them fully informed.
- We will be responsive to emerging threats and opportunities, and will invest—or divest—accordingly.
- We will maintain a prudent risk profit and a strong credit rating to protect shareholder investment.
- Shareholders can expect to see their investment steadily increase in value and achieve on an annual return that is competitive with other banks.

We do business only with the permission of the communities we serve...
Communities expect us to consistently demonstrate social responsibility as an employer and as a corporate citizen. This we achieve by serving the public interest, and the interests of consumers and local businesses in communities nationwide. We will encourage our employees to participate in community activities, and provide financial and other assistance to educational, cultural, health care and sports programs.

SOURCE: Bank of Montreal, Annual Report 1990

- the observance of codes of conduct to enhance integrity and to ensure fairness in all dealings (1989, 125).

By using value statements, managers are recognizing that individual and corporate actions are caused, in part, by the values that the individuals and the corporation have in common. Values need to be shared by everyone, at least to some degree, so that the values are reinforced and widely accepted. It is important that everyone in the corporation should be able to identify the shared values and describe their rationale.

The values the organization wishes to operate with the future are not necessarily the values implicit at the present. It is important to identify the organizational values desired, to compare them to individual values, and to ascertain how they can be reinforced. Value statements should be developed with the involvement, over time, of as many employees as possible. Although the production of a statement is the desired end result, the process used to accomplish that end is an important learning process.

What happens in practice is often quite different. The statements usually express the beliefs of the chief executive or top level management and little, if any, effort is made to communicate or explain the values. In other cases, value statements, creeds or philosophies are designed to improve the public image of the corporation and are only cited in advertisements, press releases, and newsletters. As a result, they are not taken seriously. A related problem is that no effort is made to instill the values throughout the corporation. In effect, the values are not shared and do not become a part of daily life, with the ideals expressed not reflected in reality, the meaning of the values being unclear, and employees and others not understanding the process.

Despite these problems, it is argued that management should be value-driven; that is, all plans, decisions, actions, and rewards are governed by a value focus. Thus, values have influence on organizational objectives, corporate plans, individual accountability, standards of performance, and reward systems (Ginsberg and Miller, 1992, p. 24). This type of thinking is necessary if values are to have an influence on corporate operations. Values must be identified, defined, prioritized, and then communicated throughout the enterprise, including corporate training programs and employee meetings. Whether or not the desired values are being practised should be measured within the organization and with customers or clients. In particular, current management practices must be monitored to ascertain the extent to which values are supported and incorporated into decision making which may necessitate a modification of leadership styles and management systems. Finally, values must be reinforced including through the reward system.

The Stakeholder View

Another approach to assessing corporate social and ethical concerns is through stakeholders, as discussed in Chapters 2 and 9. The approach can be narrow or wide.

Narrow Stakeholders View   According to Freeman et al. (1988), this view means that the corporation should act in the interests of a small number of stakeholders, including shareholders, competitors, customers, employees, and suppliers. This view extends consideration beyond that in the managerial and financial views, but is mostly internally focused and emphasizes stakeholders with a direct economic interest in the corporation.

Wide Stakeholders View   The corporation should act in the interests of as many stakeholders as possible (Freeman et al, 1988; Patrick and Wagley, 1992) but without sacrificing efficiency or long-term fiduciary obligations to stockholders. Thus, the additional stakeholders that should be considered include local communities, the media, interest groups, and religious organizations. This view means that corporate strategy is taking place within a network of interdependent choices made by many interested parties with agendas of their own. Viewing strategic managing this way ensures the consideration of values and ethics. Freeman et al. argue that if there is an understanding of the role values or morality plays in strategic management, then any theory of strategic management that is developed will be more coherent and powerful (1988, p. 821).

All approaches to viewing social and ethical concerns are used by managers, but two problems are associated with them: (1) an approach may not be sufficiently comprehensive to cover all the concerns; and (2) an approach may not be implemented completely or correctly by managers. The following section identifies how a corporation can incorporate social and ethical concerns into the planning process through the strategic management planning process.

THE INTEGRATION OF SOCIAL AND ETHICAL CONCERNS WITH STRATEGIC MANAGEMENT

The awareness of social and ethical issues and the responsibility and responsiveness involved has increased and led to a "corporate social policy" which should be integrated or meshed with corporate strategic management. The integration of strategy with social policy will be explained, discussing social and ethical concerns and polices as they relate to the eight components of strategic management.

Establishment of a Mission

The development of a mission statement is the first step in a strategic management process. It is an enduring statement that specifies in very broad, even philosophical terms, the organization's "reason for being" and what distinguishes it from similar organizations. Considerable diversity exists among organizations in the composition and uses of mission statements, variously called creed statements, statements of purpose, statements of beliefs, statements of business principles, or statements defining our business (David, 1989, p. 90).

The following list illustrates the reasons why an organization should develop a written mission statement.

1) To ensure unanimity of purpose within the organization.

2) To provide a basis, or standard, for allocating organizational resources.

3) To establish a general tone for organizational resources.

4) To serve as a focal point for individuals to identify with the organization's purpose and direction; and to deter those who cannot from participating further in the organization's activities.

5) To facilitate the translation of objectives into a work structure involving the assignment of tasks to responsible elements within the organization.

6) To specify organizational purposes and the translation of these purposes into objectives in such a way that cost, time, and performance parameters can be assessed and controlled (King and Cleland, 1979, p. 124).

A survey by Fred R. David identified the following as the main items included in the mission statements of business enterprises:

1) Who are the enterprise's customers?

2) What are the firm's major products or services?

3) Where does the firm compete?

4) What is the firm's basic technology?

5) What is the firm's commitment to economic objectives?

6) What are the basic beliefs, values, aspirations, and philosophical priorities of the firm?

7) What are the firm's strengths and competitive advantages?

8) What are the firms's public responsibilities and what image is desired?

9) What is the firm's attitude toward its employees? (David, 1989, p. 91)

The definition and the list of reasons for such statements clearly indicate the fundamental sense of purpose, direction, and priority given to the organization. The strategists most involved in mission development are the Board of Directors and top management. The mission statement becomes a critical document in communicating and influencing other strategists and the firm's employees.

An examination of the list reveals that there is little reference to social and ethical concerns; that is, social and ethical matters are not mentioned explicitly. This conclusion appears to be substantiated by a review of many corporate mission statements, some of which are shown in Exhibit 20-2. There is little mention of social and ethical concerns except for TransAlta Utilities' reference to the environment. To be fair, it should be pointed out that mission statements are usually accompanied with statements of values principles or philosophics and there is often explicit mention of social and ethical concerns in such statements.

Assessment of the Environment

An assessment of the environment should provide the organization with insights into social issues of importance. The issues of concern will vary by industry. For example, pharmaceutical manufacturers are very concerned by the treatment of animals in drug testing. For McDonald's restaurants, the environmental impact of the materials it uses to package its products may be of concern. Part II,

---

EXHIBIT 20-2

Examples of Mission Statements

- Bell Canada's mission is to be a world leader in helping communicate and manage information.
- The business mission of Atco Ltd. is to achieve an international reputation for excellence by providing products and services to the energy and resource industries and to invest principally in energy-related assets in North America.
- The mission of RBC Dominion Securities is to be the Canadian-based integrated investment dealer providing the highest quality advice, service, and products to clients on a global basis.
- To be the very best at what we do, through our commitment to quality (Reimer Express Lines Ltd.).
- To satisfy customers with competitive electric and thermal energy services in a safe, reliable, and environmentally responsible manner (TransAlta Utilities Corporation).
- The business mission of Investors Group is to satisfy clients in need of general and comprehensive financial planning. Through product development and a well-trained sales distribution organization investors will assist in implementing financial plans and providing effective ongoing service.

Chapters 7–10, explained approaches or methods that can be used by management to examine the environment for social and ethical issues.

It is easy for managers to omit social and ethical concerns when examining the environment using well-known approaches such as Porter's "competitive rivalry" model or the competitive forces approach (1980). This approach sees market structure as the primary determinant of firm and industry profitability. Firms are to choose markets with favourable structures and, if possible, alter market structure to their benefit by raising barriers to entry or mobility, differentiating their product, or otherwise attempting to gain a degree of power in the market. Miles (1993) evaluated this approach on two criteria: the matter of intentions versus results, and the trade-off between private gain versus public good. The first criterion is based on the assumption of the free market system that "if everyone selfishly pursues their own interests the welfare of the larger society will be maximized." Miles concedes that this may be partially true, but believes that many in society are still uncomfortable with a system designed around selfish intentions because results as well as intentions are a useful measure of the ethics of a firm's strategy (1993, p. 221).

The second criterion relates to the trade-off between private gain and public good and involves the distribution of wealth. Profit is a reward for hard work and risk taking, but there is concern that profits are sought and obtained at someone else's expense. Everyone wins if the firm earns a reasonable profit and at the same time provides something worthwhile to the market; that is, a good or service to consumers. Miles states that in practice this as not always the case, and thus comparing private gain, or profit, to the public good provides a useful measure of legitimacy on profit-making activity (1993, p. 221).

Miles concludes that the competitive forces approach prevents the proper functioning of markets, and the success of this approach rests on the ability to violate the intentions versus results ethical criterion. He claims that the second criterion is also challenged. Avoidance of competition allows higher prices, and the firm earns a higher profit without providing an equal return to society. Monopoly profits exist and harm the public good, as the distribution of wealth is artificially skewed (1993, p. 222).

This discussion has provided insight into one approach used in assessing a corporation's environment in the strategic management approach.

Assessment of Resources and Capabilities

An assessment of the corporation's resources and capabilities should provide some indication of what the corporation is doing to respond to social and ethical issues. Audits of resources and capabilities usually are based on assessments of marketing, production, research and development, finance, and human resource management with a "social/ethical" component seldom being explicitly stated or is a sub-component of the business functional areas. The entries under the "internal" organization system box in Figure 20-1 are an example. Value systems are listed, but appear to focus on the values of managers and employees and not explicitly upon the moral implications of various activities. Thus, there is an argument for a "social and ethical" assessment category which would determine resources and capabilities in this area.

Miles recently examined an approach to the assessment of resources and capability that is receiving considerable attention, "resource-based theory." Instead of focusing on factors in the external environment as the drivers of strategy, this theory examines the relationships between resources, competition, and profitability and defines business in terms of what it is capable of doing. This may offer a more durable basis for strategy. Resources are appraised, capabilities identified, the sources of competitive advantage established, and a strategy formulated (Grant, 1991; Amit and Shoemaker, 1993).

Miles concluded that the resource-based approach to profitability is preferable, as the corporation develops assets and capabilities to reduce cost, raise quality, or otherwise do or offer something its competitors cannot match. Thus self-interested behaviour should result in positive results for society by adding value to the corporation as well as society. This approach better satisfies both the intentions versus results and private versus public gains criteria (1993, p. 222).

Exhibit 20-3

Examples of Socially Oriented Corporate Objectives

- To conduct all operations in a manner which safeguards the environment (Cameo Corporation, an integrated uranium producer).
- To provide a workplace that protects and promotes the health and safety of all employees (Cameo Corporation).
- To act in a responsible and ethical manner, including concern for the environment and the community (Air Canada).
- To be a valued corporate citizen by participating in and sharing with the communities we serve. To always conduct our business with integrity and respect for all people (Fairweather).
- Our company will take a leadership role in the community (Newfoundland Power).

Establishment of Objectives

Objectives are the ends the corporation seeks to achieve through its existence and operations. Most corporations have more than one objective, and many have other than economic ones like profitability, rate of growth, and market share. Socially oriented objectives are often included by a corporation, and when this occurs it reflects the strategists' preferences, their personal values and beliefs, and the enterprise's culture. It indicates that the enterprise recognizes social issues and wants to do something about them. Exhibit 20-3 lists examples of socially oriented objectives.

It should be noted that economically oriented objectives are also based on values. As an extreme example, an objective to earn above-average profits might be based upon greed. Thus, an objective includes values, but they may not be consistent with social or ethical concerns.

Identification of Strategic Options

Awareness of social issues will influence the number of options to be considered. In some cases, it will limit the options. For example, the options available to forestry industry firms has been limited by society's awareness of environmental problems. On the other hand, concern for the environment has increased the options for some enterprises who are producing "green" products formerly not demanded by consumers.

Selection of a Strategy

The strategic decision relating to the solution of a strategy will be influenced by an awareness of the view to social policy established in the above components.

Strategy Implementation

This component is involved with actually putting social policies in place and making them work, and with establishing operational objectives throughout the organization to make sure implementation occurs. The policies are guides for helping operational managers carry out the macroview to social policy. Examples of policies would be: social response starts in the immediate area of the enterprise's operations prior to addressing more distant regions; social action concentrates in areas strategically related to the economic activities of the enterprise; for example, pharmaceutical companies might support hospital fundraising campaigns; and enterprises may limit their social actions to a particular area; for example, support of literacy programs or art museums. Operational objectives are a further specification of general objectives established at the macroview level. For example, a general objective would be to minimize dysfunctional economic impacts on communities in which corporate operations are terminated. An operational objective would be to donate $20 000 to a community industrial development organization to aid in attracting new industry to the community.

A review of the material covered in this book provides a long list of approaches managers can take to social and ethical issues, including some methodologies. Exhibit 20-4 is such a list. As can be seen, there is a whole range of options.

A discussion of implementation cannot avoid the mention of rewards in the process, especially those received by top management. They are paid well, even too well, according to some stakeholders. It could be argued that managers are paid to be socially responsible; that is, to see that their corporation is a satisfactory corporate social performer as well as a satisfactory economic one. One reason for high executive salaries is because executives are responsible for social and ethical matters relating to the corporation and they are expected to avoid moral, along with financial, risks. Lastly, executives are in positions to educate and influence others in the corporation to ensure satisfactory social and ethical performance. Executives should send messages that emphasize ethical business practices, and they should ensure that codes of ethics are developed, discussed, and enforced. Strategy implementation is orchestrated by top management, and the social and ethical aspects of this process are no different.

Monitoring and Review

Any evaluation of the strategic management process should include the monitoring and review of actions and initiatives undertaken to address social and ethical issues. Many of the approaches and methodologies listed in Exhibit 20-4 serve to monitor and review social and ethical behaviour and initiatives in the corporation, including ethics audits and ethics "checklists." Chapter 10 discusses corporate social performance and the role of social reporting and performance criteria.

Exhibit 20-4

List of Approaches and Methodologies Available to Managers in Addressing Social and Ethical Issues

The Stakeholder Concept: Chapter 2

Management Initiatives to Reinforce Ethical Behaviour: Chapter 8
       Statement of Values or Philosophy
       Codes of Ethics
       Ethics Training
       Ethics Audits
       Ethics Consultants
       Ethics Ombudsman (or Ethics Advocate)
       Ethics Committees (or Business Conduct Committees)
       Executive Speech Making
       Ethics "Checklists" of Questions or Guides

Issues Management: Chapter 9

Stakeholder Management: Chapter 9
       Stakeholder Management Capability
       Diagnostic Typology of Organizational Stakeholders
       Clarkson's Stakeholders Performance Profile

Influencing Government: Chapter 13
       Business Involvement in Politics
       Business Lobbying
       Corporate Public Affairs Departments

Corporate Philanthropy: Chapter 14
       The Charitable Investment Approach
       Strategic Giving

Strategies for the Environment and Sustainable Development: Chapter 18

Considerations in Managing the Environmental Issue: Chapter 18
       Organizational Structural Arrangements
       Stakeholder Consultation
       Corporate Environmental Accountability
       The "Greening" of the Business Function

Responding to the Media: Chapter 19

Responding to Interest Groups: Chapter 19

There are several reasons why it has become important for strategists to incorporate social policies into the strategic management process. Professional managers today realize that business legitimacy depends on enterprises being responsible for social issues. Secondly, there is still a threat that governments will increase regulation if business does not take some initiatives in the social area. Lastly, business enterprise success and continued existence are interrelated with how well it responds to social issues. Therefore, social issues, forces, trends, and concerns have an influence on the strategic management process. Hopefully, social and ethical concerns are considered throughout the strategic management process and not viewed by managers as an "add on" or something that has to be done in a token manner.

The integration of social and ethical concerns with the strategic management process in corporations has been discussed in the literature. The following section presents three views of this integration as it exists or as it should exist.

THREE VIEWS OF SOCIAL AND ETHICAL INTEGRATION

The three views presented vary in several ways. The macro and micro view of social policy imposes the social policy process on the commonly recognized model of strategic management, and is similar to the approach discussed in the previous section in that it describes how things should be. The second view emerges from an empirical study of the social responsibility initiatives of corporations. Hypotheses are developed from existing evidence and tested to ascertain the relationship between strategy and social responsibility. The third view argues that ethics should be at the centre of a consideration of corporate strategy in the modern corporation.

Macro and Micro Views of Social Policy in Corporate Strategy

A distinction between corporate policy levels was made by Carroll and Hoy (1984) in their discussion of integrating corporate social policy into the three phases of strategic management. The strategy formulation phases involved the establishment of social policy from a "macroview" perspective; that is, social policy as top management perceives social concerns or issues. Social policy is designed and articulated in the formulation stage, and this sets the tone and posture of the corporation. The overall corporate social policy is shaped by four factors:

- the company's competence and resources (what the corporation can do);
- the market opportunities (what the corporation may do);
- the personal values and aspirations of the management group (what the corporation wants to do);
- the acknowledged obligations to societal segments (what the corporation ought to do).

Figure 20-2 Corporate Strategy and the Social Policy Process

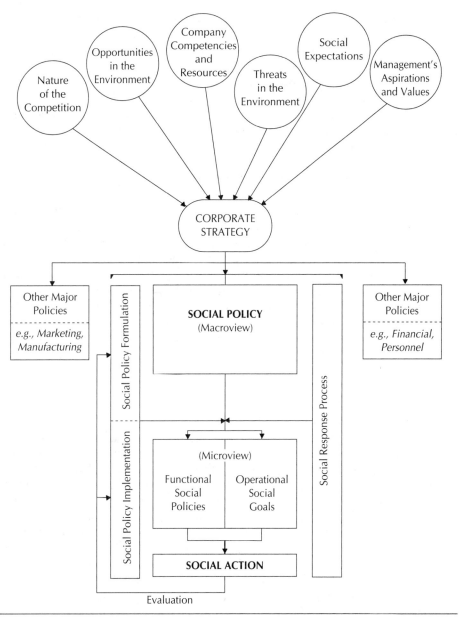

SOURCE: Archie Carroll and Frank Hoy. (1984). Integrating Corporate Social Performance into Strategic Management. *The Journal of Business Strategy,* 4(3), p. 54.

A microview of social policy is established at the functional level in the implementation phase of the strategic process. Specific policies are developed at this level that serve as vehicles or guides for helping operational managers carry out the macroview of social policy held by the corporation. A third phase of the strategic process is evaluation where corporate social policy is evaluated, reaffirmed, or changed.

Figure 20-2 illustrates how social policy becomes a part of the corporation's overall strategy. Social policy is developed by top management, as are other major corporate policies in view of the various factors in the environment (circles at top of the figure). The social response requires the setting of social policy at the macro level and the establishment of specific social policies and operational social goals at the functional level. The outcome is a social action that is evaluated with feedback to the social policy formulation and implementation phases.

The Carroll and Hoy model is one conceptualization of the integration of social policy and strategic management. The authors state that social responsibility meshes with, affects and helps determine overall corporate strategic choice and is a necessary part of the strategic management process. The reasons given for this integration are: professional managers recognize that business legitimacy depends on responsiveness to the full range of social responsibilities; the threat of increased government regulation encourages management initiatives; and the development of responsive corporate social policy makes social managerial sense, as social policy is intertwined with corporate economic performance and success (Carroll and Hoy, 1984).

Strategy and Social Responsibility

Some researchers have explained why some corporations pay more attention to social responsibility than others. The reasons given for greater attention are that poor social responsibility leads to poor profitability through costs associated with regulation; some corporations have benefited financially from the positive publicity from social projects; and there is a positive correlation between social responsibility and profits. Some argue that the corporate motive for social responsibility is merely to reduce costs or to increase profits, while others argue that the motives may be more complex than this and that social responsibility and profitability can be compatible. Kraft and Hage investigated the relationship between profits and social responsibility by formulating and testing the hypotheses listed in Exhibit 20-5. The hypotheses were based on previous research and evidence from the practices of corporations (1990, pp. 11–14).

The results are complex, but overall significant relationships were found for #2, 3, 4, 6, and 11. It was concluded that community service or social

---

Exhibit 20-5

Hypotheses About the Relationship Between Strategy and Social Responsibility

1. The greater the profitability of the firm within its industrial sector, the greater the emphasis on community service.
2. The greater the emphasis on the prestige of the firm within its industrial sector, the greater the emphasis on community service.
3. The larger the size of a firm within its industrial sector, the greater the emphasis on community service.
4. The greater the emphasis on assets growth of a firm within its industrial sector, the greater the emphasis on community service.
5. The greater the structural complexity of a firm within its industrial sector, the greater the emphasis on community service.
6. The greater the emphasis on product quality of a firm within its industrial sector, the greater the emphasis on community service.
7. The greater the technological complexity of a firm within its industrial sector, the greater the emphasis on community service.
8. The broader the product line of a firm within its industrial sector, the greater the emphasis on community service.
9. The greater the emphasis on price competition within an industrial sector, the less the emphasis on community service.
10. The greater the centralization of the decision-making structure of a firm within its industrial sector, the less the emphasis on community service.
11. The greater the emphasis on short-term profits of a firm within its industrial sector, the less the emphasis on community service.

SOURCE: Kenneth L. Kraft and Jerald Hage. (1990). Strategy social responsibility and implementation. *Journal of Business Ethics*, 9, pp. 11–19.

---

responsibility appeared to be compatible with profitability. Organizational size and profits may be the dominant characteristics in determining community service. Emphasis on community service depends on the availability of slack resources and the motivation; that is, on the values and goals of the strategists. Community service goals appear to be either desirable as direct outcomes (e.g., altruism) or as important in achieving other outcomes (e.g., increasing community service activities to improve the prestige) or to increase assets (1990, pp. 15–18).

The results are not a definitive indication of the relationship between a strategy to achieve profits and a corporation's community service or social responsibility. It does find some significance in the relationship in some circumstances, and serves to illustrate the complexity of the relationship.

Strategy and Ethics

According to Freeman and Gilbert (1988), a revolution in management theory has occurred on two fronts: (1) the discovery that organizations consist of human beings who have a complex set of values, leading to the adaption by managers of "values management" or "cultural management" techniques; and (2) the discovery that organizations do not exist in a vacuum by ignoring the impact on others in society. They explain these two discoveries as principles:

The Values Principle

Individual and organizational actions are caused in part by the values that individuals and organizations have.

The Interdependence Principle

Organizational success is due in part to the choices and actions of those groups that have a stake in the organization.

These principles are linked in that the first applies to those groups which the second says are important. The two fronts of the revolution in management are summed up by two axioms or assumptions:

First Axiom of Corporate Strategy

Corporate strategy must reflect an understanding of the values of organizational members and stakeholders.

The Second Axiom of Corporate Strategy

Corporate strategy must reflect an understanding of the ethical nature of strategic choice.

Freeman and Gilbert conclude that almost all questions of corporate strategy are questions of ethics, yet the role of ethics in strategic management has been ignored. Corporations should incorporate consideration of ethics into managerial decision making and summarize the real point of the revolution in management as "We must put ethics in its rightful place at the very centre of discussions about corporate strategy" (1988, pp. 6–8).

This section reviewed three views of how and why social and ethical concerns are integrated with strategic management. The first view indicated how this should be done, the second finds a relationship between social responsibility and profits (or the economic strategy of the corporation), and the third justifies the consideration of ethics as a critical ingredient of corporate strategy.

SUMMARY

It appears that insufficient attention has been placed on integrating social and ethical concerns and values into the planning processes in corporations, in particular, into strategic management. There is an incomplete understanding of why managers adapt certain strategies unless these concerns are incorporated.

Existing approaches to viewing social and ethical concerns have been inadequate. The financial or stockholder view is too narrow in its outlook, while the managerial preferences view tends to be too inward-looking. Corporate culture and organizational values incorporate some stakeholders outside the corporation, but instilling values throughout the corporation is seldom done. The wider stakeholder approach has the broader perspective, and if practised seriously would recognize and accommodate the social and ethical concerns of those individuals and groups who have some interest in the corporation.

The chapter discusses the eight components of strategic management and illustrates how social and ethical concerns are involved in each. All aspects of strategic management have social and ethical implications, thus making the process a satisfactory approach to integration.

Three views of social and ethical integration were outlined. The first reinforces the previous discussion by proposing a macro and micro view of social policy in corporate strategy. The second view evolves from a study of social responsibility and strategy in corporations. It provides a good reason for social and ethical concern, as it proves a relationship between strategy—that is, economic performance—and social responsibility. Lastly, it is argued that ethics are simply critical to strategy. Good ethics is a prerequisite for good strategic management, or stated another way, good ethics is just good business.

More corporations are sensitive to social responsibility and business ethics than ever before. But, more should integrate their treatment of social and ethical concerns more deliberately and in a more organized fashion. Integrating social responsibility and business ethics into strategic management is one viable approach to accomplishing this objective.

REFERENCES

Amit, Raphael, and Paul J.H. Shoemaker. (1993). Strategic assets and organizational rent. *Strategic Management Journal*, 14, pp. 33–46.

Andrews, K. (1971). *The Concept of Corporate Strategy*. Homewood: R. D. Irwin.

Andrews, K. (1980). *The Concept of Corporate Strategy*. (revised edition). Homewood: R. D. Irwin.

Carroll, Archie and Frank Hoy. (1984). Integrating corporate social performance into strategic management. *The Journal of Business Strategy*, 4(3), pp. 48–57.

David, Fred R. (1989). How companies define their mission. *Long Range Planning*, 27(1), pp. 90–97.

Freeman, R. Edward and Daniel R. Gilbert, Jr. (1988). *Corporate Strategy and the Search for Ethics*. Englewood Cliffs: Prentice-Hall.

Freeman, R. Edward, Daniel R. Gilbert, Jr., and Edwin Hartman. (1988). Values and the foundations of strategic management. *Journal of Business Ethics*, 7, pp. 821–834.

Fry, Joseph N. and J. Peter Killing. (1989). *Strategic Analysis and Action*. Scarborough, ON: Prentice-Hall Canada.

Ginsberg, Lee and Neil Millier. (1992, May/June). Value-Driven Management. *Business Horizons*, pp. 23–27.

Grant, Robert M. (1991, Spring). The resource-based theory of competitive advantage: Implications for strategy formulation. *California Management Review*, pp. 114–135.

King, W.R. and D.I. Cleland. (1979). *Strategic Planning and Policy*. New York: Van Nostrand Reinholt.

Kooten, Jack. (1989). *Strategic Management in Public and Nonprofit Organizations*. New York: Praeger.

Kraft, Kenneth R. and Jerald Hage. (1990). Strategy, social responsibility and implementation. *Journal of Business Ethics*, 9(1), pp. 11–19.

Miles, Grant. (1993). In search of ethical profits: Insights from strategic management. *Journal of Business Ethics*, 12(3), pp. 219–225.

Petrick, Joseph A. and Robert A. Wagley. (1992). Enhancing the responsible strategic management of organizations. *Journal of Management Development*, 11(4), pp. 57–72.

Porter, M. E. (1980). *Competitive Strategy*. New York: Free Press.

INFLUENCES ON THE FUTURE MANAGEMENT OF STAKEHOLDERS, AND SOCIAL AND ETHICAL CHALLENGES

INTRODUCTION

This chapter serves two purposes; to speculate on what will influence the recognition and handling of social and ethical issues in corporations in the future, and to provide conclusions.

It is never easy to anticipate the future, but some future influences on how corporations and managers will deal with social and ethical issues are presented. Nor is it easy to select which influences will prevail, as materials about the future point in many directions. In this chapter, four predominating influences have been selected in an attempt to give some appreciation of the future to come:

1) *Changing Management Approaches*   Numerous new, innovative management approaches are being introduced, or reintroduced, continually. This section

only identifies some of these developments by illustrating that the treatment of social and ethical issues is not prominent in any. It is not clear what this means for corporate social responsibility and performance in the future.

2) *Changing Stakeholder Influences* Chapter 2 identified stakeholders and Chapter 7 discussed how management can respond. In this chapter, the possible influence of various stakeholders is examined.

3) *Changing Circumstances of Managers* The first two influences have implications for managers, but managers are also confronted directly by an array of pressures relating to how they should manage. This section establishes the complexity of the circumstances confronting managers.

4) *Changing Economic and Business Environment* The fourth influence is a broader one involving the Canadian economy (as discussed in Chapter 1) and the business system in this country (as discussed in Chapters 3, 4, 5, and 6). Numerous views are expressed, and this section only samples some of the suggestions and recommendations being offered.

Figure 21-1 presents these influences in diagram form.

Figure 21-1 Influences on the Identification and Management of Social and Ethical Issues

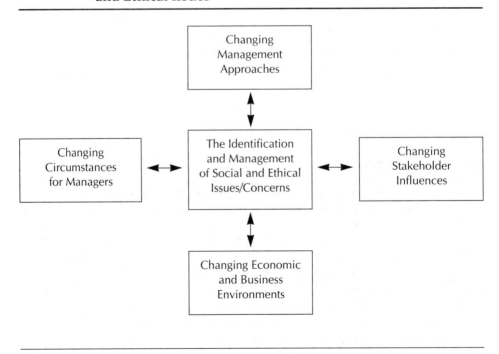

The word "changing" was used deliberately with these four influences. Ideas presented in this chapter are those based upon knowledge available at one point—they cannot possibly be accurate! However, these influences do summarize some dominating issues and trends.

CHANGING MANAGEMENT APPROACHES

There are always new approaches to managing emerging issues—sometimes referred to as fads or fashions. This section identifies some of the recent trends in management, and short descriptions are provided that are not intended to be comprehensive. References are given for readers wishing to follow up on these developments. There is little literature analyzing these approaches as they impact on social and ethical concerns. Thus, in the following discussion, questions are often posed instead of definitive statements being made.

The Horizontal Corporation

Corporations have been downsizing (becoming smaller) and delayering (fewer levels in the hierarchy) for some time. But there is also a trend to a nonvertical, or horizontal, corporation (Byrne, 1993). This type of corporation eliminates both hierarchy and functional or departmental boundaries. Top management executives occupy traditional support functions such as in finance and human resources. Everyone else in the corporation operates as a multi-disciplinary team whose performance might be measured by customer satisfaction instead of profits or shareholder value.

The social and ethical implications of downsizing and delayering have been discussed, especially as they relate to the employee stakeholders and managers. The horizontal corporation only exists in a few instances, and functional management will most likely remain, as most corporations will be hybrids between the traditional hierarchical and horizontal forms. There are implications for managers and employees, as career paths will be altered, and the goals of individuals will change. Little, if anything, is known of how the new structure will deal with social and ethical concerns confronting the corporation and its other stakeholders. Will these concerns be dealt with by the few executives remaining at the top? Or will the handling of such concerns be the responsibility of a team? If teams are involved, how will consensus be obtained about particular issues?

The Virtual Corporation

A virtual corporation (also referred to as a shamrock or network organization) is a temporary network of companies usually formed through joint ventures and strategic alliances that come together quickly to exploit some fast-changing opportunity or to complete some particular task. The organization doesn't exist as a traditional corporation except for a small group of managers to plan the corporation's activities and then "outsource" most tasks that are needed to operate. They seek others who can provide the best skills, or competencies, most efficiently, and at the best price. Another way to describe the approach is that everything the corporation does is subcontracted to others.

The virtual corporation is, in effect, a temporary network of independent companies who are suppliers, customers, and even competitors. Because each of the companies or partners is bringing a particular core competence, a "best of everything" organization is created. Joint ventures are involved that vary in type and ownership. The ventures may or may not be enduring relationships, as the managers of the virtual corporation are continually reassessing the performance of their suppliers or partners. It is unlikely that many, if any, pure virtual corporations exist, but many companies are involved in virtual corporation projects—that is, some aspects of these operations are conducted along the lines of a virtual corporation.

Technology plays a role in the creation and operation of such corporations. Electronic data integration (EDI) systems are often involved which handle dealings and transactions among the partners. There must be considerable trust among the partners with a requirement to play fair. In effect, a corporation may lose control over some of its operations in a virtual corporation arrangement; corporations become more reliant on others and there is a need for more trust, given the sense of co-existence involved.

It is not clear what the implications are for the management of social and ethical issues. The management of the "virtual corporation" may not encounter many issues, as most of its interactions would be with the supplier and creditor/lender stakeholders. It has few employees and little direct contact with the public or even the ultimate purchasers of its products or services. The negotiation, maintenance, and termination of the numerous contracts with its "outsource" corporations or its joint venture partners no doubt raises some issues. This is a whole new way of thinking about the corporation, and will require a new approach to considering social and ethical issues.

The Learning Organization

The learning organization is one that is highly flexible and adapts quickly to change, resulting in continual improvement. Employees are encouraged to look outside their own jobs and at the "big picture" to recognize that the world is made of various relationships. It is important to understand the interdependency of the various parts of the business in order to improve organizational processes.

Besides the holistic view, the approach involves direct feedback to participants, the absorption of externally generated information, the combination of discrete areas of knowledge to create new information, the questioning of assumptions, and learning from the history of their own organization and from others. Employees are constantly and deliberately learning and understanding new things, and the organization consciously develops systems to anticipate, create, modify, and disseminate the knowledge needed in the future.

Peter Senge (1990), the principle proponent of this approach, identifies five disciplines necessary to achieve the spirit of team work: systems thinking (examining how an individual's actions affect other parts of the organization); mental modelling (disregarding outdated or limiting assumptions); team learning (engaging in open-minded dialogue instead of adversarial debate so that groups will achieve more than individual effort); personal mastery (pursuing personal aspirations at work); and building shared vision (pooling personal aspirations into a vision for the organizations's future).

This approach is in favour now, but it is not clear whether or not it incorporates social and ethical concerns. It most likely addresses these concerns within the organization, but may not apply to such concerns external to the organization. However, if the organization is a "learning one," as Senge advocates, it would be logical that it would learn about social and ethical issues in the same manner as other issues confronting the organization.

Organizational Architecture

Organizational architecture provides managers with a metaphor comparing the architecture of buildings to that of organizations. The design of a building reflects the interaction of four key components: the purpose of building provides a design problem; the structural materials available define the opportunities and parameters for solving the design problems; a new design combined with innovative structural materials often leads to a new architectural style; and collateral technologies or innovations can shape the building's design.

While architects are confronted with fundamental questions about purpose, structural materials, style, and collateral technologies, senior managers are presented with a parallel set of questions. Business corporations are organized according to traditional bureaucratic models that are unable to respond quickly enough to continuous technological innovation, fast-changing markets, and globalization. The changing environment is redefining the fundamentals of corporate purpose, which must focus on quality, speed, and customer satisfaction. Corporations have new structural materials to reshape their organizations in order to achieve these new purposes; for example, new information technologies, advanced telecommunications, computer networks, and desktop video conferencing.

These new purposes and new structural materials are leading to new organizational styles. Examples of these styles include self-managed teams with responsibility for satisfying customer requirements, and the closer coupling of corporate units to customers and suppliers. Lastly, new collateral technologies are required, such as new methods for selecting, training, evaluating, and rewarding employees that will be consistent with the greater autonomy, responsibility, and continuous change inherent in the new designs.

There is a need for a "fit" among the architectural components, which must be performed by a manager as it is unlikely to occur automatically. The CEO must take the responsibility to make sure the fit occurs so that the integrity of the organization's design is ensured (Nadler et al, 1992).

Again, it is assumed that social and ethical concerns will be addressed in such an approach.

Core Competencies

Core competencies are what corporations do best and what differentiates one corporation from another. Management searches for sources of advantage which are achieved through its ability to consolidate corporate-wide technologies and production skills into "competencies." Core competencies are the result of collective learning in the corporation, especially in coordinating diverse production skills and in integrating multiple streams of technologies.

Corporations are thought of as having a portfolio of competencies instead of a portfolio of businesses. The tests to ascertain the existence of a core competence are: they provide a potential for access to a wide variety of markets; they make a significant contribution to the customers' perceived benefits of the end product; and they are difficult for competitors to imitate. Thinking of core competence as organizational capabilities has emerged recently. Capabilities are business processes that consistently provide the customer with superior value and extend beyond the usual recognized resource bases which employ a stagnant but available stock of resources. Also, capabilities are greater than core competencies which are usually attributable to various parts of the value chain. Capabilities differ in that they encompass the entire value chain (Prahalad and Hamel, 1990).

Core competencies and capabilities do not directly include social or ethical resources. They do involve vision, culture, driving forces, and incentives which touch on social and ethical issues. The core competencies and organizational capabilities are further examples of modern management concepts which do not appear to directly incorporate social and ethical concerns or issues.

Five examples of new approaches to management have been described. There are others: for example, total quality management, continuous improvement, time-based competition, and visioning. One conclusion is clear from this discussion: social and ethical issues or concerns are not prominent features. There is a possibility that managers may overlook social responsibility and business ethics as a result. It appears that the new approaches do not influence managers on social and ethical issues any more than do the traditional approaches.

CHANGING STAKEHOLDER INFLUENCE

The influence stakeholders (Chapter 2) have over the corporation and/or the influence the corporation has over stakeholders shifts over time. The changes are usually not dynamic but subtle and occurring gradually. Managers should monitor the corporation's environment to detect these shifts if they want to remain informed. The influence of other stakeholders stays much the same so it is important to distinguish among stakeholders.

The following is an overview to some of the changes in stakeholder influence that have occurred recently. Some of these changes have been identified and examined in this book, while others are a result of organizational changes within organization structures or management processes.

Shareholders The increasing number of institutional shareholders has led to some concentration of ownership. In addition, the role of these shareholders has changed from a relatively passive to a more proactive one. Institutional owners are increasingly challenging management and board decisions, and especially the interests of minority shareholders in takeovers or mergers. It appears that this more active role will continue.

Directors Directors may be more demanding of management now than previously. The failure of many companies in the early 1990's made directors more sensitive to their liability. Several lawsuits have been initiated against directors who had allegedly not performed their fiduciary duties with due care. During 1993, several boards ousted executives for a variety of reasons; for example, for weak financial performance. In addition, there appears to be a trend to the appointment of more independent and outside directors who are less willing to rubber stamp management decisions. It has been suggested that there is a power struggle between chief executives and boards with more accountability being demanded of management. The Berle and Means (1932) thesis that management controls widely held corporations may be weakening. Nevertheless, there is still an argument that chief executives possess power in the corporation (McKenna, 1993).

Employees Chapter 15 identified many challenges confronting managers as they deal with employees. But there is an interesting phenomenon occurring. Corporations are introducing programs on total quality management, empowerment, and working in teams, while at the same time restructuring, delayering, and downsizing. The latter activities create uncertainty and insecurity amongst employees, surely offsetting the benefits of the programs mentioned. In addition, the phenomenon leads to many social and ethical issues as employees are reassigned, retrained, and released.

Consumers   Many corporations claim that they have become more consumer-focused by seeking their input, providing better service, or offering superior products. Marketers claim that consumers are more demanding and discriminating. Whether or not consumers are more sovereign is questionable, as proof is difficult to obtain.

Suppliers   Suppliers are exerting greater influence as network organizations evolve, value chain analysis extends backward, and electronic data integration emerges. No doubt, suppliers are viewed as partners now more than in the past.

Competitors   More competitors have emerged with North American free trade and world-wide trade agreements. The increasing formation of small business enterprises has also increased competitive rivalry. As mentioned in Chapter 16, there is also evidence of collaborative arrangements, such as joint ventures. It is not clear whether increased competition will result in more socially and ethically sensitive corporations.

Joint Venture Participants   There is an increasing variety of joint venture organizations being formed. Social and ethical issues arise regarding the partnership relationships that are developed. Little is known of these issues, but they will be discussed more in the future.

Interest Groups   The influence of interest groups is unlikely to decrease in the future. More and more of these groups are being formed and focus on a variety of issues. Managers must continue to not only monitor the activities of such groups but to also interact with them and, where appropriate, influence their views.

Government   Governments will continue to influence the relationships between business and society. Many aspects of corporate activities will continue to be regulated, but there are several other changes. Demands for integrity in government may reduce the influence of corporate lobbyists. Governments will continue to downsize through various forms of privatization, providing opportunities for entrepreneurs. Government spending will be curtailed, most likely reducing the amounts of goods and services sold by corporations to government.

The changing nature of stakeholder influence cannot be ascertained for certain. The significant point is that business and managers must monitor such changes and alter their approaches, that is, how they interpret the influence of stakeholders or how they influence stakeholders. There will be increasing need for managers to master the challenges of stakeholder management including: resolving conflicting demands among stakeholders (for example, employees and shareholders versus environmentalists); striking a balance between public expectations and sound corporate planning; and communicating more effectively with stakeholders. Managers cannot sit in their offices and speculate on the interests of stakeholders but must be proactive in managing the relationships.

CHANGING MANAGERIAL CIRCUMSTANCES

It is always claimed that change is greater now than in the past. Whether or not this is true for managers today is debatable. What is known is that managers face substantial challenges as they oversee their organization. The following are some of the challenges presently being discussed in the media and management literature: corporations need to be more focused, even specialized, instead of conglomerates; vertical dis-integration is being promoted instead of integration; a continuous improvement philosophy is prevalent; value must be created for customers instead of solely for the shareholder; the geographic orientation is global; environmental issues are prominent; and approaches to management education and development are changing (Steingraber, 1990).

These, and other challenges, put pressures on managers and influence how they behave. This section deals with some of the challenges to illustrate how they influence managers. These are increasing competition; managing large-scale change; changing managerial skills and career expectations; increasing accountability; and changing management styles. A final section summarizes the changes occurring in corporations.

Increasing Competition

Chapter 16 dealt with the nature of competition facing Canadian business. It is agreed that corporations face increasing competition today, and that this competition is driven by many factors. Capital is mobile in today's world, where there used to be national barriers restricting flows. Investors are more likely to move their money to what they perceive as more attractive investments.

Customers, whether corporate or consumer, are more educated and thus more demanding. Excess productive capacity exists in many countries, especially for commodities like aluminum, newsprint, coffee and petroleum. Trade agreements have opened markets internationally—for example, the new GATT Agreement reduces trade barriers, as does NAFTA. Progress is even being made on reducing interprovincial trade barriers.

These challenges pressure managers and influence how they behave. In this book, behaviour relating to social and ethical issues is the main focus, yet little is known of the impact of increasing competitiveness.

Managing Large-scale Change

Despite all that is known about organizational change, managers are apparently hesitant and ill-prepared to implement change. Few are prepared despite anticipating the need. Given all the challenges, identified above, confronting managers that result in change, this is an unfortunate situation.

Many managers are not good at introducing change. They do not have the organizational structures available to accomplish it. For example, communication processes are insufficient, and planning committees or task forces are not properly mandated. They often underestimate what is involved in time, effort, and resources to bring about change, and usually fail to include the necessary changes to the corporate culture (Gibb-Clark, 1993). During their careers, managers most likely experienced stability and become competent at managing this stability. In the past, challenges occurred and were settled one at a time. The changes taking place now are more fundamental and complex.

A common response to the challenges confronting a corporation is to slash jobs. This may be a short-term solution to financial problems, and often does not address more fundamental problems of the way employees are hired, trained, rewarded, and punished, all of which may need changing. Another common criticism is the failure of managers to communicate information about necessary changes. It is agreed that there is a need to improve this type of communication in particular.

Thus, another type of pressure is placed on managers—that is, understanding, coping with, and communicating change. The challenges confronting a corporation often require large-scale change, change throughout the organization, and change fundamental to the way things have been done. Social and ethical issues occur throughout the change process, particularly relating to the human costs involved.

The Shift in Managerial Skills

Despite being educated and experienced in business, management, and economics, many managers are not prepared for or capable of obtaining the new managerial skills necessary to operate the corporation. For example, most managers' experience is based on inflationary times. The skills needed for operating a business during periods of inflation are quite different than those needed in disinflationary periods, a time when prices are not increasing as rapidly, or may be even declining. Skills are now needed to move costs down and to continually keep pushing them down while focusing on core businesses that create goods and services appealing to consumers so that premium prices can be charged.

Learning to manage on a global basis is also necessary. Business is conducted differently from country to country, and managers have to learn about customs, traditions, governments, and consumer preferences. Failure to provide a global vision for the corporation is a problem, but so is failure to implement such a plan by not learning about the country.

A third area is information technology. Managers do not need to be familiar with the technical features, but they must know what the technology is capable, and not capable, of doing. They must understand what information is important to management decision making and not let the availability of information immobilize them.

Finally, this book is about managing stakeholders and the social and ethical issues present in the relationship to the corporation. It is also important for managers to be competent in skills that can address stakeholders and the relevant issues.

Different Career Expectations

In the past, it was not uncommon for a manager to have spent his or her entire career with one corporation. There was a progression up the hierarchy through promotions with increasing salaries and responsibilities. This scenario will be less common in the future.

Managers are likely to work for several corporations, and may even be self-employed during their careers. Downsizing, and the resulting layoffs, has displaced many middle-aged managers who have been forced to seek other employment or establish some sort of business. Those managers that remain are less likely to receive promotions and raises in the differently structured organizations. Lateral moves are more likely and new ways will have to be found to motivate in such situations. Lateral moves may result in more responsibility but raises are likely to be based on performance and not seniority. Human resource policies will have to change to reflect the new working environment. Transfer to offshore locations will have to be made attractive and sabbatical leaves introduced so that managers can retool themselves with the necessary managerial skills. Corporations will have to be more flexible in allowing managers to decline transfers for personal reasons relating to dual careers. Overall, career planning will not be the same in the future for the manager or the corporation.

Managerial Accountability

Greater accountability is being imposed on managers from a variety of sources. This is through employee rating of managers; through customer demand for quality standards; through shareholders; and through establishing relationships between performance and salary.

In 1994, publicly traded corporations had to disclose the compensation received by top management. Prior to this, there was no requirement to disclose salaries, except if the corporation offered securities in the U.S. market. The disclosure of salaries is an issue on which pros and cons could be debated. However, now that disclosure is required, other issues have arisen. Shareholders are attempting to establish the relationship, if any, between compensation and corporate performance. It is not uncommon for executives to receive higher salaries while the corporation is laying off employees or when lower profits have occurred. Thus, the disclosure of salaries is making executives more accountable to shareholders.

Some corporations now have evaluation systems in operation where employees are allowed to rate the performance of executives. Examples are Levi Strauss, DuPont, United Parcel Service, and Hewlett-Packard. It is argued the employees are in a good position to identify performance. Furthermore, the highest managers in a corporation seldom receive feedback in a formal manner, and employees are one source of such feedback. This type of evaluation could be performed by using a consultant or through anonymous questionnaires. For the process to be effective, executives would have to respond or react in some way to the evaluation.

Some customers are being very demanding in terms of the quality of the goods and services purchased. Some are now requiring suppliers to obtain a quality assurance standard known as the International Standards Organization (ISO) 9000. The ISO is a non-governmental body formed in 1947 to develop worldwide standards to ensure product quality, compatibility, safety, and reliability. It is comprised of standards organizations from several industrialized nations, and includes the Standards Council of Canada. The ISO 9000 is a quality standard designed to meet several objectives: to ensure that the customer receives the product or service that is expected, to prevent errors in all operations, to prevent delivery delays, to reduce costs of operation, to increase productivity, to increase the reliability of the product or service, and to meet all quality assurance requirements specified by the customer. This outside measure of quality is another form of accountability being imposed on corporations and managers.

A final example involves corporate governance and the role of the board of directors. Chapter 12 examined this issue and outlined how shareholders are making directors and management more accountable.

Executive Style

Another aspect of accountability is the style of managerial behaviour exhibited by executives. "Tough" managers are hired during economic downturns to institute harsh measures. Their attitude is usually to "just do it" and "to do it now." Olive claims that often these managers are a menace to corporations. They disrupt relationships with customers, suppliers, employees, and most likely other stakeholders. He suggests that boards of directors are less likely to find it appropriate to hire such "autocrats" and "bullies" (Olive, 1993).

Business Week (April 1, 1991, pp. 52–60) discussed this problem in a cover story referring to it as the CEO disease, or egotism. The executive's style results in his or her losing touch with the corporation because of the attitudes held, including the belief that he or she can do no wrong. One indication of egotism is when the executive spends more time outside the corporation with directorships and otherwise trying to obtain personal recognition. Such executives surround themselves with "yes" persons, make all decisions usually without knowing details, attempt to get "one-up" on peers in other corporations, relish media attention, and hang on to the job too long. This behaviour often emerges from the pressures of the job, and the symptoms are often not noticed.

There are few restraints on CEOs. They have unlimited expense accounts, few, if any, appraisals are given, and their power to make decisions goes unchallenged. Such CEOs are often morale busters and do much to impede the corporation's ability to compete. Their reporting procedure is often not clear, and boards undemanding. Finally, they eliminate heirs apparent so that they can retain power.

The stakeholders that can prevent this "disease" are shareholders, through the Board of Directors. Some of the control mechanisms might be: imposing limits on perks; demanding that executives stay focused on the job (e.g., limiting outside directorships), not assuming that toughness must define leadership, and keeping communications open (Byrne, 1991).

Managers are human beings, and can assume this type of behaviour over time unless Boards of Directors monitor their activities and behaviour closely. The "tough" or "egotist" manager is unlikely to be sensitive to social and ethical issues.

The New Corporation

Another way to illustrate the changing circumstances confronting managers is to speculate about how the corporation will look in the future. There are many views held about this topic. Throughout this chapter, several suggestions have been made about what the corporation might do in the future. Table 21-1 compares what the present corporation looks like, with a most likely description of the corporation in the future according to 11 characteristics.

Topics omitted from Table 21-1 include social responsibility and business ethics. All the characteristics listed involve social and ethic issues as well as economic and legal ones. Again, the areas of social and ethical concerns is not explicitly addressed, and it is assumed that managers will be sensitive to them.

CHANGING ECONOMIC AND BUSINESS ENVIRONMENTS

Managers must monitor the economic and business environment and formulate a conclusion of future events. This task is made challenging by the multitude of views being expressed about this environment. To illustrate the diversity of views, this section will briefly describe some of the books published since 1990.

These books are usually critical of the economic or business system and provide some solution for the problems identified.

The books are listed according to the ideological spectrum developed in Chapter 4. The title of the book is provided by the author's name and occupation, if known. Refer to the references at the end of this chapter for complete bibliographic information. The likely ideological perspective is identified.

Madness and Ruin: Politics and the Economy in the Neoconservative Age

Mel Watkins, University of Toronto political economist (1993).

In a series of essays, Watkins expresses concern for the rebirth of neoconservatism. A theme uniting the essays is Watkins' critical view of neoconservatism, and in particular, its central pillar, the Free Trade Agreement. A left-of-centre view of economics is presented which claims that Canada is experiencing its most miserable economic times since the 1930's.

Ideological Perspective: Collectivism.

Table 21-1 The New Corporation

Characteristic	Current Description	Most Likely Future Description
Organizational Structure	Corporations are designed as hierarchies with many levels.	Horizontal organizations, or networks
Relationship to Other Organizations	Mostly self-sufficient, self-contained. Vertical integration model.	Interdependent with key stakeholders, e.g., suppliers, customers. De-integration model.
Worker Expectations	Security with career path based on promotions and transfers.	Personal growth within same job, or varied careers.
Leadership	Largely autocratic, lacking true participation by others.	Inspirational, based upon visions, values.
Nature of Work	By individuals and specialized.	By teams and multi-skilled.
Markets	Focused on domestic.	Increasing emphasis on global.
Competitive Advantage	Often based on cost.	Time and specialization.
Performance Focus	Profits and shareholders.	Customer satisfaction.
Resource Allocation	Primarily based on capital.	Increasingly based on information.
Governance	Board of Directors allegedly representing shareholders.	Other stakeholders involved.
Quality	Inspection and statistical techniques, cost-driven.	Quality built-in, no exceptions.

SOURCE: Adapted from Reinventing the corporation. (1992). *Business Week/Reinventing America*, pp. 62–63.

Take Back the Nation 2: Meeting the Threat of NAFTA

Maude Barlow, Chair, Council of Canadians, and Bruce Campbell, research fellow, the Canadian Centre for Policy Alternatives (1993).

This book is written expressly to criticize the North American Free Trade Agreement. Barlow and Campbell claim that the FTA and NAFTA threaten Canadian sovereignty and serve only the interests of American multinationals and those Canadians who believe in stripped-down American-style social benefits and taxation. They allege that the Conservative government and corporate interests conspired to dismantle Canada through public policies such as high interest rates and reduced UI payments. Ideological Perspective: Collectivism.

False God: How the Globalization Myth Has Impoverished Canada

James Laxer, political scientist, York Univ. (1993).

This book is concerned with the free trade agreements with the U.S. and Mexico. Laxer is very concerned with the impact of globalization on social justice in Canada, and that Canada itself may have aligned with a declining economic power (i.e., the U.S.). He dislikes the globalization promoted by American multinational corporations; for example, the idea of the borderless world with few barriers to impede the movement of goods, services, jobs, or capital. Canada risks losing its sovereignty to the American market-centred domestic economic policy based upon individualism. Ideological Perspective: Collectivism.

The New Bureaucracy: Waste and Folly in the Private Sector

Herschel Hardin, writer and lecturer (1991).

Hardin resents the fact that the private sector represents itself as being lean, mean, and efficient, when in his perception it is bloated, wasteful, unproductive, and greedy. The problem he sees is that the private sector has built up a huge and wasteful bureaucracy we are all suffering from, with resulting misallocations and distortions occurring in the economy. Hardin dislikes liberal capitalism, and he is determined to explode what he sees as the greatest myth of our time, that the private sector is necessarily more frugal and much more efficient than the public sector. Ideological Perspective: Collectivism and Monopoly Mentality.

The Wealthy Banker's Wife

Linda McQuaig, writer (1993).

McQuaig supports spending on social programs and argues that the universality of such programs is not only possible, but necessary, more humane, and very efficient. The economic performance of the country is not hindered by social spending. She considers the social programs in European countries as the model that Canada should emulate to avoid domination by the United States and its approach to social programs.

Ideological Perspective: Monopoly Mentality and Mixed Economy.

Making Canada Work: Competing in the Global Economy

John Crispo, economist, Univ. of Toronto (1993).

The author identifies all kinds of problems with the Canadian economy and suggests an array of solutions. The problems include media bias, lack of competitiveness, the education system, and the high cost of medicare. The solutions include short-term capital gains taxes, tax write-offs for training, a voucher system for health care, stock market reform, and an overhaul of education. Newly created government bodies would oversee the necessary changes; for example, an agency to assess competitiveness, and a super-agency to regulate costs and incomes.

Ideological Perspective: The Mixed Economy.

The Next Canadian Century: Building a Competitive Economy

David Crane, journalist (1992).

According to Crane, the problem with the economy is Canada's inability to respond to global competitiveness. He concludes that the economy is in very bad shape. His solution to the problem is an innovative economy driven by new ideas and knowledge, and by the potential of science and technology. Specific government programs, or programs which see government in partnership with the private sector, are advocated to address the problems. He stresses the cooperative partnership between business, labour and government—in other words, a interventionist approach to the problems of the economy and the business system.

Ideological Perspectives: The Mixed Economy and Corporatism.

Quebec Inc. and the Temptation of State Capitalism

Pierre Arbour, former mutual manager, Caisse de dépôt placement du Québec (1993).

Since the 1960's, the Quebec government has been involved in a form of economic planning to increase francophone control of the economy. He outlines the costs of well-intended government involvement in the economy. Taxpayers' and pensioners' funds were invested in projects with questionable viability, and tax shelters guided investors into risky investments where they lost money. Arbour claims that political pressure influences corporate decision making not always in the interest of investors. Even Quebec's interventionist policy of using Hydro-Quebec to subsidize energy-intensive industries by providing cheap electricity

has encountered problems. The economy was adversely affected when aluminum and magnesium prices fell and the U.S. slapped countervailing tariffs on subsidized magnesium.
Ideological Perspective: Corporatism.

Meditations On Business: Why Business As Usual Won't Work Any More

John Dalla Costa, President and CEO of Miller Myers, Bruce Dalla Costa Inc. (advertising agency) (1991).

The author states that business needs to reflect on what it is doing and to look for a new paradigm, as most of the presently used management structures and marketing techniques are no longer appropriate. For example, business lacks humanity and a sense of greater purpose, which is reflected in several ways: the treatment of the environment; the growing irrelevance of its stakeholders, in particular its lack of respect for employees; the dehumanizing vocabulary used; and the inappropriate mythology relating to growth, bigness, and the entrepreneur. Thus, there are fundamental problems with the Canadian business system that need to be addressed. Dalla Costa's solutions are varied. For example: the need for new business leadership; a call for a reduction in the imbalance of media power; a need to learn from history; and the search for new ideas and potentials through "opening to art: opening for change."
Ideological Perspective: The Managerial Approach.

Shifting Gears: Thriving in the New Economy

Nuala Beck, business consultant (1993).

Beck conducted a four-year study of corporate growth and concluded that a new economy was replacing the old one. The old economy was based on industries like automobiles and steel, or mass-manufacturing-type industries. They were material-intensive, and supported by petroleum as a source of energy. The new economy is based on technology, innovation, and information. Typical new economy industries will be based upon computers, communications, instrumentation, and health services. Whereas the old economy industries were based upon physical assets, the new economy industries are human-based with people being the main asset.
Ideological Perspective: The Managerial Approach.

Money Has No Country: Behind the Crisis in Canadian Business

Ann Shortell, journalist (1991).

Ann Shortell's critique of the business system focuses on the inadequacy of Canada's response to globalization and the country's need to develop new attitudes about foreign investment and to take competitiveness seriously. The problem is stated clearly: The country must respond to global competition and seek ways to get the most out of foreign investment. The author concludes that there is a need for a change in attitudes toward foreign investment and global trade. Besides the solution of calling for a challenge of old, nationalist ways of thinking, the author also wants specific solutions, such as changes in the investment strategies of pension funds, and the lobbying of government and business to increase and improve R & D initiation.

Ideological Perspectives: The Managerial Approach and Neoconservatism.

No Small Change: Succeeding in Canada's New Economy

Dian Cohen, journalist and consultant, and Guy Stanley, (1993).

The authors provide their interpretation of the "new economy" and the potential role of Canadians in it. They claim that Canadian governments, financial institutions, and the educational system prevent us from benefiting from the opportunities in such an economy. Change is prevented for several reasons, including the uselessness of national economic models and the failure of education systems. Globalization must be embraced, and mass-manufacturing industries are on the decline. For solutions, the authors rely on the private sector and a market system.

Ideological Perspective: Neoconservatism.

A Matter of Survival: Canada in the 21st Century

Diane Francis, journalist (1993).

Francis is concerned with problems created by Canada's increased debt and claims that Canadians must get out from under this burden before a financial crisis occurs. Some of the things Canada should do are: become a tax haven to attract U.S. capital, sell off Crown corporations to pay off debt, streamline government by reducing bureaucracies and the number of governments, and convince Canadians to be less dependent on government. Social programs should be reduced and overhauled, and the anti-entrepreneurial culture existing in Canada must be altered.

Ideological Perspective: Neoconservatism.

These brief comments barely capture the diversity of views on the problems existing in the Canadian economy and business system. The solutions range from government initiatives to total reliance on the private sector and the market system. Books are used to illustrate the diversity of views about the changing economic and business environment. But books are only one source of these views. Others include radio and television, executive speeches, seminars and conferences, newspapers and periodicals, management development courses, and government task forces, inquires, and commissions. There is no shortage of views, and the manager is challenged to monitor these views and integrate them into managerial decision making about the management of stakeholders and social and ethical issues.

THE IDENTIFICATION AND MANAGEMENT OF SOCIAL AND ETHICAL ISSUES/CONCERNS

Managers are responsible for identifying the overall environment in which the corporation operates. This book has taken the perspective that managers are still the key decision makers ascertaining how business considers and responds to social and ethical issues/concerns and how the corporation interrelates with stakeholders.

Managers must see the larger picture and perceive trends while also managing to ensure the corporation is innovative, achieves high levels of productivity and quality, and, of course, manages financial affairs appropriately. Some researchers are arguing that managers must rethink how they view the functions of the corporation (Mitroff et al, 1994). Six emerging functions are identified and are presented along with the core activities of each in Table 21-2. The emerging functions of significance for social responsibility and business ethics are issues management, environmentalism, and ethics.

Issues management is described in Chapter 9, and the core activities identified are very similar. Firstly, managers must track broad societal and industry trends in a deliberate and organized manner. After identifying issues, managers must determine which issues pose a threat or opportunity to their organization and the stakeholders associated with those issues. The influence of stakeholders on the corporation must be assessed relative to the influence of the corporations on the issues and stakeholders. Lastly, managers must discover the impact that the stakeholders and issues will have on the corporation's products, services, manufacturing processes, and reputation.

Environmentalism involves risk assessments of threats to the environment posed by the corporation's products and manufacturing processes. Managers must consider how they design products and examine the manufacturing processes used. Corporate-wide programs are necessary to coordinate activities relating to the environment. As described in Chapter 18, environmental programs must be overseen by senior management and have sufficient budgets.

The third emerging function of interest is ethics. The key business principles of an organization are examined in this function as they affect the health and safety of employees, value received by consumers, and the consequences on the general environment. An assessment in done of the corporation's contributions to society as discussed in Chapter 14. The corporation institutionalizes ethics in many ways—for example, through codes of conduct, as outlined in Chapter 8. Ethics is of concern to everyone in the corporation and is a component of its culture (Mitroff et al, 1994, pp. 13–14).

Table 21-2 Emerging Functions and Core Activities

Emerging Functions	Core Activities
Crisis Management (CM)	Assess the major crises, systems, stakeholders, and manufacturing processes that pose a threat to products, services, manufacturing processes, company reputation, employees, the environment, and communities.
	Design and implement plans, organization and manufacturing processes, procedures, products for the detection, prevention, containment, recovery, and learning from major crises.
Issues Management (IM)	Assess broad societal and industry trends and the power of associated stakeholders in shaping issues.
	Design and implement strategies to minimize organizational impact.
Total Quality Management (TQM)	Assess product defects and poor quality due to poor initial designs, raw materials, management, manufacturing processes, operators, shipping, and distribution systems.
	Design and implement products, manufacturing processes, manufacturing systems, and operator training that lead to continuous improvement in all phases of company operations.
Environmentalism (ENV)	Assess threats of products, services, and manufacturing processes to environment and communities.
	Design products, services, and manufacturing processes to benefit the environment/communities.
GLOBALISM	Assess products or services to compete in worldwide markets.
	Design products or services to compete in worldwide markets.
ETHICS	Assess ethical and moral attributes of the organization's behaviour, policies, decisions, and procedures.
	Design and implement communications, controls, codes, credos, and culture.

SOURCE: Ian I. Mitroff, Richard O. Mason, and Christine M. Pearson. (1994, May). Radical surgery: What will tomorrow's organizations look like? *The Academy of Management Executives*, 8(2), p. 12.

It is important to note that of the six emerging functions described in Table 21-2, three relate to social responsibility and business ethics. This is an indication of the significance of these manners in the management of the corporation in the future. This chapter emphasizes the importance of management consideration of social responsibility and business ethics, especially as there are changes occurring in management approaches, stakeholder influence, the circumstances of managers, and the economic and social environment.

SUMMARY

The identification of the influences on future management of stakeholders and social and ethical challenges serves as a concluding chapter to the book. Businesspersons, owners or managers, are impacted by four influences which in turn affect their attitudes toward social and ethical issues.

New management approaches are constantly being introduced to entrepreneurs and managers on the best or most effective approach to managing. Five such approaches were described, the horizontal corporation, the virtual corporation, the learning organization, organizational architecture, and core competences. Many more exist. The significant point to recognize is that none of these new approaches focus much on social or ethical issues.

The concept of stakeholders and their management is discussed throughout the book. The relationships between management and its stakeholders is not static and requires constant monitoring. Some stakeholders will be more influential in the future and managers must be sensitive to this. Conflicting demands will be made by stakeholders and managers must continuously balance these demands in their responses.

Managers also face changes in another dimension, the circumstances in which they work. Competition is increasing and managers must cope with profound large-scale change. The skills needed will change and managers must take initiatives to keep up-to-date. Managers will face different career circumstances, with fewer spending their whole careers with one corporation. The demands for accountability of business and managers are increasing, and abrasive and arrogant executive leadership styles are less likely to be appropriate. Lastly, the corporation, the principal institution of business, has altered, and will continue to do so.

The fourth influence relates to the changing economic and business environment. Several possibilities were presented: no one is sure of the environment in the future. Together, these four categories of influences will impact on how businesspersons manage and how they react or respond to stakeholders and social and ethical issues.

This book establishes the complexity of the relationship between business and society. Canadian business and society involves many stakeholders and numerous social and ethical challenges. The responses to these challenges are not simple, as the interaction is dynamic and what is socially responsible is not always easy to identify.

We have emphasized several things about the Canadian business system:

1) the importance of understanding Canadian capitalism, business ideology, the stakeholders involved, and the attitudes toward business;

2) the need to be aware of business's role in society and how business has incorporated social responsibility and ethics into its operations;

3) the many responses business has made to the social and ethical challenges in its environment; and

4) the perspective of the manager.

Social and ethical issues continuously confront managers. The material in this book prepares managers to respond in an appropriate manner so that the significant and challenging role of business in Canadian society will be maintained.

REFERENCES

Barlow, Maude and Bruce Campbell. (1993). *Take Back the Nation 2: Meeting the Threat of NAFTA.* Toronto: Key Porter Books.

Beck, Nuala. (1993). *Shifting Gears: Thriving in the New Economy.* Toronto: Harper Collins Publishers.

Berle, Adolph A. and Gardiner C. Means. (1932). *The Modern Corporation and Private Property.* New York: MacMillan.

Byrne, John A. (1993, December 20). The horizontal corporation. *Business Week,* pp. 76–81.

Byrne, John A. (1992). Paradigms for postmodern managers. *Business Week/Reinventing America,* pp. 62–63.

CEO Disease. (1991, April 1). *Business Week,* pp. 52–60.

Cohen, Dian and Guy Stanley. (1993). *No Small Change: Succeeding in Canada's New Economy.* Toronto: Macmillan.

Costa, John Dalla. (1991). *Meditations On Business: Why Business As Usual Won't Work Any More.* Scarborough, ON: Prentice-Hall Canada.

Crane, David. (1992). *The Next Canadian Century: Building a Competitive Economy.* Toronto: Stoddart Publishing.

Crispo, John. (1993). *Making Canada Work: Competing in the Global Economy.* Toronto: Random House.

Francis, Diane. (1993). *A Matter of Survival: Canada in the 21st Century.* Toronto: Key Porter Books.

Gibb-Clark, Margot. (1993, September 24). CEO's hesitancy costs jobs. *The Globe and Mail,* p. B5.

Hammer, Michael and James Champy. (1993). Reengineering the Corporation: *A Manifesto for Business Revolution*. New York: Harper Collins Publishers Inc.

Hardin, Herschel. (1991). *The New Bureaucracy: Waste and Folly in the Private Sector*. Toronto: McClelland and Stewart.

Laxer, James. (1993). *Fake God: How the Globalization Myth Has Impoverished Canada*. Toronto: Lester Publishers.

McKenna, Barrie. (1993, September 10). CEOs wield power. *The Globe and Mail*, pp. B1, B2.

McQuaig, Linda. (1993). *The Wealthy Banker's Wife*. Toronto: Penguin Books Canada.

Mitroff, Ian, Richard O. Mason, and Christine M. Pearson. (1994). Radical surgery: What will tomorrow's organizations look like? *Academy of Management Executive*, 8(2), pp. 11–21.

Nadler, David A., Marc J. Gerstein, and Robert B. Shaw (Eds.). (1992). *Organizational Architecture: Design for Changing Organizations*. San Francisco: Jossey-Bass.

Prahalad, C.K. and Gary Hamel. (1990, May-June). The core competence of the corporation. *Harvard Business Review*, pp. 79–91.

Olive, David. (1993, September). No more Mr. Tough Guy. *Report on Business Magazine*, pp. 11–2.

Senge, Peter. (1990). *The Fifth Discipline: The Art and Practice of the Leaning Organization*. New York: Doubleday & Co.

Shortell, Ann. (1991). *Money Has No Country: Behind the Crisis in Canadian Business*. Toronto: Macmillan.

Steingraber, Fred G. (1990, January-February). Managing in the 1990's. *Business Horizons*, pp. 50–61.

Watkins, Mel. (1993). *Madness and Ruin: Politics and the Economy in the Neoconservative Age*. Toronto: Between the Lines Press.

INDEX